ACKNOWLEDG

This book has been long in preparation, and it is my pleasure to acknowledge the debts incurred throughout its writing. First I would mention the many Italian archivists and librarians whose knowledge and advice have assisted my research in so many ways. It is impossible to name them all. I extend special thanks to the staff of the Archivio di Stato in Lucca, particularly to the director, Dr Giorgio Tori; his predecessor, Professor Vito Tirelli; Professor Antonio Romiti (now of the University of Udine); Dr Sergio Nelli; and Dr Laura Giambastiani. Individual thanks are due also to Don Giuseppe Ghilarducci of the Archivio Arcivescovile di Lucca, to Dr Mario Piloni of the Archivio Storico Comunale di Pietrasanta, and to Dr Giuseppina Lucignani of the Archivio Storico di Gallicano.

The writing was completed in Florence in the privileged environment of Villa I Tatti, with the assistance of a Fellowship from the Harvard University Center for Italian Renaissance Studies. The basic research was made possible by two Senior Researcher awards from the Human Sciences Research Council of South Africa and by two periods of long leave together with a series of research and microfilm grants from the University of the Witwatersrand, Johannesburg.

In Johannesburg I am very grateful to my colleagues Mr Graham Neame and Dr C. I. Hamilton for their thoughtful and provocative reading of my evolving manuscript. Neither would claim any specialist knowledge of fifteenth-century Italy, but their professional expertise and general historical insights not infrequently contributed to the clarification and reworking of my thoughts. Among colleagues of other disciplines mention is due to Professor Rita Wilson of the Italian Department for many discussions on matters Italian. The redrawing of my maps, charts, and diagrams has been the work of Mr P. J. Stickler, chief cartographer of the University of the Witwatersrand's Geography Department.

My periods of research in Lucca have been rendered both more pleasant and more profitable by the company and conversation of a number of distinguished students of Lucchese history: Professors Thomas Blomquist, Louis Green, Duane Osheim, and Christine Meek. I am particularly grateful to Professor Meek for her generosity in interrupting her own researches in Lucca to read and comment on an earlier version of this book. Needless to say, any errors or misconceptions that remain are entirely my own.

Finally I pay tribute to my wife, Susan Frances Bratchel, for her skill in transferring a family and household between Tuscany and the Transvaal over the past twenty years and for her forbearance of the times of my physical and mental absenteeism during the writing of this book. Her involvement at every stage of the research and writing is reflected throughout the present study.

CONTENTS

LIST OF FIGURES

LIST OF TABLES

ABBREVIATIONS USED IN FOOTNOTES

AAL	Archivio Arcivescovile, Lucca
AN	Archivio de' Notari (ASL)
Anz. Temp. Lib.	Anziani al Tempo della Libertà (ASL)
ASCP	Archivio Storico Comunale, Pietrasanta
ASF	Archivio di Stato, Firenze
ASG	Archivio Storico, Gallicano
ASL	Archivio di Stato, Lucca
AS Massa	Archivio di Stato, Massa
BSL	Biblioteca Statale, Lucca
LA	Libri Antichi (AAL)
MAP	Archivio Mediceo il Principato (ASF)
NAC	Notarile AnteCosimiano (ASF)
Rif.	Consiglio Generale, Riformagioni Pubbliche (ASL)
SB	Sentenze e bandi (ASL)

NOTE

For convenience, manuscript chronicles and genealogies are cited in the footnotes by author and short title, even when this differs slightly from the precise manuscript title as provided in the Bibliography. 'Baroni, Notizie genealogiche', refers to BSL MSS 1101–39, G. Vincenzo Baroni, Notizie genealogiche delle famiglie lucchesi. References to the two volumes of the *Regesti*, edited respectively by Fumi and Lazzareschi, are to document numbers rather than page numbers, unless otherwise stated.

In volumes which contain several sets of foliation, I have used modern pagination where this exists. Where there is neither pagination nor foliation, I have identified documents by date. Many volumes have been newly paginated or foliated in the period since I consulted them, and this process is continuing.

I

INTRODUCTION

On the night of 14/15 August 1430 Paolo Guinigi, lord of Lucca for thirty years, was seized in his palace by a group of patrician conspirators. 'Turning-point' and 'watershed' are terms long overworked by historians; but events in Lucca in the summer of 1430 were to prove of especially enduring significance. For more than a century the history of this small Tuscan city-state had been punctuated by periods of foreign domination, and by submission to a series of native lords and foreign conquerors. In the humiliating years following the death in 1328 of the Ghibelline *signore* Castruccio Castracani, Lucca had passed rapidly for money from one local Italian power to another. The ensuing period of Pisan rule from 1342 to 1369 brought greater stability, but, with whatever justification, has been recorded in Lucchese historiography as a time of unparalleled oppression. The reconstructed republic of 1370 survived only until the end of the century. Already by the early 1390s the Guinigi, an ancient and wealthy Lucchese family with extensive landed and mercantile interests, had emerged as the dominant political force; in October 1400 Guinigi rule was formally established with the election of Paolo as Captain and Defender of the city.[1] By contrast with the political and constitutional vicissitudes of the past, Lucca, after the overthrow of Paolo Guinigi, was to continue as an independent city-republic until the very end of the eighteenth century. The constitutional and administrative restoration of 1430, though periodically amended in detail, in essentials survived until 1799, when Lucca (like Venice two years before) capitulated before the French armies of the Revolution.

In April 1491 fra Giorgio Luti a Sienese of the Order of the Gesuati, walking with a friend, Girolamo Franciotti, in the garden of S. Girolamo of Lucca, swore his companion to secrecy, and then prophesied a chain of

[1] A summary of Lucchese history in the 14th cent. appears in C. E. Meek, *Lucca 1369–1400: Politics and Society in an Early Renaissance City-State* (Oxford, 1978), 1–16. For an assessment of the period of Pisan rule, see *idem*, *The Commune of Lucca under Pisan Rule, 1342–1369* (Cambridge, Mass., 1980).

dramatic events that were soon to trouble not only Lucca but the whole of Christendom.[2] Fra Giorgio foretold that, in Lucca, many towers would fall to the ground and the city would suffer many deprivations; and that, especially in Italy, God would soon punish the pride of lords and princes with the traditional scourges of war, famine, and plague. As supporting evidence fra Giorgio grafted a piece of rose bark upon a dry stake, claiming that, should his prophecy be true, the stake within eight days would bear roses. The blooms duly appeared; the following year Girolamo Franciotti, released from his vow of silence by his friend's death, recorded in writing everything that he had heard and seen.

In the fuller, or less carefully edited, versions of fra Giorgio's vision, it appears that its true emphasis lay not so much with impending disasters but rather on how Lucca, though small—like Bethlehem, and equally favoured—would emerge purified and strengthened to lead Crusades and to reform Christendom. These 'certe belle cose' were to find less tangible fulfilment than the misfortunes that were to herald them. In June 1495 a tower belonging to the di Poggio family, rising above that family's houses in the *contrada* of S. Lorenzo in Poggio, collapsed, killing several of the kinsmen.[3] The authorities responded to the disaster by ordering the destruction of dangerous towers that still dominated the late fifteenth-century urban skyline. Of more general significance, in the previous year Charles VIII of France invaded Italy in pursuit of the claims of the French crown to the throne of Naples. The first French invasion enabled Lucca to recover, temporarily, the lost territory of Pietrasanta, but the lasting achievements of the French expedition of 1494 were notably limited. Continued French ambitions in the peninsula, the Spanish response, and ultimate Spanish hegemony were essentially to transform the Italian political, social, and economic scene.

The years between the recovery of republican liberty in 1430 and the first French invasion of 1494 constitute a clearly defined chapter in the history of the Lucchese state. Yet if this period may boast a distinctive integrity, it has signally failed to attract the attention of local chroniclers and of more recent scholars. Within the rich, local Lucchese historical tradition of the sixteenth, seventeenth, and eighteenth centuries, the post-Guinigi era is typically traversed in few words and with evident

[2] C. Franciotti, *Historie delle miracolose imagini, e delle vite de' Santi, i corpi de' quali sono nella città di Lucca* (Lucca, 1613), 556; BSL MS 116, Notizie di Lucca, fo. 85^{v}; MS 939, Can: Gio: Lunardo Dalli, Cronache della città di Lucca, pp. 386–9; MS 2599, Antonio Iova, Annali Historici della città di Lucca, pp. 968–9.

[3] BSL MS 1128, G. Vincenzo Baroni, Notizie genealogiche delle famiglie lucchesi, fo. 44^{v}.

indifference. The fifteenth century receives sustained attention only in the late sixteenth-century chronicle of Salvator Dalli and in the later, longer compilation of canon Gio: Lunardo Dalli.[4] Writing of the latter, the historian of Lucchese letters Cesare Lucchesini found a reproduction of insignificant detail that offended the dignity of history:[5] modern historians might rather regret the quite extraordinary flair for factual error and analytical confusion displayed by both the Dalli. Other early writers preferred to follow the example, and often the text, of the sixteenth-century chronicler Giuseppe Civitali.[6] Accordingly the events of the Florentine wars before and after the overthrow of Paolo Guinigi are recorded in some detail, but after 1438 attention wanders to the affairs of popes and emperors and to the fortunes of neighbouring states.

Until comparatively recently, the precedent set by near-contemporary writers has been well observed by their successors. The principal modern narrative history of Lucca after Paolo Guinigi remains the two brief chapters devoted to the period 1430–94 by Girolamo Tommasi in his 'Sommario della storia di Lucca'.[7] Only in the last two decades has this picture been significantly modified, by a series of specific studies: notably the work on criminality in the *contado* by Antonella Casali, on the Lucchese Church by Giuseppe Benedetto, and on the vicariate of Massa by Franca Leverotti.[8] Such monographs have greatly facilitated the present study, but this wider history of fifteenth-century Lucca must be regarded as a pioneering undertaking carved very largely from the

[4] BSL MS 710, Salvator Dalli, Croniche della inclita città di Luccha e di altre città cavate da molti autori brevemente per me Salvator Dalli dell'anno 1583, 84 e 85; MS 939, Gio: Lunardo Dalli, Cronache.

[5] C. Lucchesini, *Della storia letteraria del ducato lucchese*, in *Memorie e documenti per servire all'istoria del ducato di Lucca*, ix–x (Lucca, 1825–31), x. 80: 'Scrisse una voluminosa storia di Lucca in sei tomi con semplicità di stile, dove molte sono le cose che non erano meritevoli d'essere ai posteri tramandate.'

[6] ASL Biblioteca (Manoscritti), 38, Giuseppe Civitali, Storia di Lucca scritta da Giuseppe Civitali e riordinata da Daniello De' Nobili, dall'origine di essa città sino al 1572, fos. 406^{v}–457^{v}.

[7] G. Tommasi, 'Sommario della storia di Lucca dal MIV al MDCC', *Archivio storico italiano*, 1st ser., x (1847), 311–47.

[8] A. Casali, 'L'amministrazione del Contado Lucchese nel '400: il Capitano del Contado', *Actum Luce*, vii (1978), 127–37; *idem*, 'Aspetti della criminalità nel contado lucchese intorno alla metà del 1400, secondo i registri del "Capitaneus Comitatus" ', *Annuario della Biblioteca Civica di Massa* (1981), 1–21; G. Benedetto, 'Potere dei chierici e potere dei laici nella Lucca del Quattrocento al tempo della signoria di Paolo Guinigi (1400–1430): Una simbiosi', *Annuario della Biblioteca Civica di Massa* (1984), 1–54; F. Leverotti, 'Ricerche sull'amministrazione della vicaria di Massa alla fine del xiv secolo', *Annuario della Biblioteca Civica di Massa* (1980), 99–173; *idem*, *Massa di lunigiana alla fine del trecento* (Pisa, 1982).

magnificent state archives of Lucca housed today in the Palazzo Guidiccioni.

If in Lucca, as elsewhere, the fifteenth century forms a temporal no man's land between medieval/early Renaissance and modern scholarship, this neglect can hardly be ascribed to a lack of source material. In the Riformagioni Pubbliche of the General Council of Lucca there is a full record of the proceedings of the Council, except for the latter half of 1431 and a few turbulent months in 1434, details of which can be largely recovered, for the former period at least, from other sources.[9] The correspondence of the ruling Anziani with Lucchese ambassadors and with foreign powers has been calendared in two published volumes edited respectively by Fumi and Lazzareschi.[10] Life in Lucca and within the Lucchese state can be reconstructed from the acts of a large number of civil and criminal courts and from Lucca's particularly rich notarial archives which appear largely extant for this period. The archival riches of Lucca itself, preserved in the Archivio di Stato, the Archivio Arcivescovile, and the Biblioteca Statale, are supplemented by the holdings of communal archives (notably those of Camaiore, Gallicano, and Pietrasanta) and by the wealth of material relating to Lucchese affairs to be found in the neighbouring state archives of Florence, Genoa, and Massa. The bulk of the evidence may well have encouraged historians to divert their energies to preceding ages. Only in the field of commercial activity is there reason to lament a paucity of source material: there has been an almost total disappearance of merchants' account books; the records of the *Gabella Maggiore*, without which it is impossible confidently to reconstruct Lucchese mercantile fortunes, have been lost for the whole of the post-Guinigi period; the records of the *corte de' mercanti* are very fragmentary before the late 1470s.

Whilst noting these important lacunae, there can be no doubt that the fertile yet relatively compact archival collections for this highly distinctive chapter in the history of the Lucchese state provide a very exciting medium for exploring a number of problems currently exercising the minds of Italian historians. The industrious compilations of seventeenth- and eighteenth-century Lucchese genealogists,[11] working mainly from

[9] Esp. Anz. Temp. Lib. 5: Minute di Riformagioni 1430–1443.

[10] L. Fumi (ed.), *R. Archivio di Stato in Lucca: Regesti*, iv, *Carteggio degli Anziani (dall'anno MCCCCXXX all'anno MCCCCLXXII)* (Lucca, 1907); E. Lazzareschi (ed.), *R. Archivio di Stato in Lucca: Regesti*, v, *Carteggio degli Anziani MCCCCLXXIII–MCCCCLXXXXII* (Pescia, 1943).

[11] Notably Giuseppe Vincenzo Baroni, esp. his Notizie genealogiche delle famiglie lucchesi, BSL MSS 1101–39.

notarial sources, greatly aid the study of the enduring role of the patrilineal lineage, marriage politics, and patrician family history. An unbroken series of political records offers opportunities for a structural analysis of changing patterns of office-holding. By comparison with the immediate past, the political history of the oligarchic republic after 1430 becomes less spectacularly eventful. But incidents such as the murder of the Anziano Pietro Cenami (1436) and the conspiracy of Tommaso Lupardi, the Guidiccioni/Arnolfini rivalry of 1456, and the treason of Michele Guerrucci (1460) can be utilized to tell us a great deal about party formation and urban and rural tensions in fifteenth-century Italy. The sustained rebellion against Lucca of the men of Pietrasanta, richly documented in the important local archives of Pietrasanta and from Florentine sources, provides the material for a significant contribution to the continuing debate on the relationship in Italy between the hegemonic city and its subject communities. Finally, fifteenth-century Lucca has been the setting for two recent studies that examine the concept of a 'return to the land' in late medieval Italy.[12]

In all these matters, Lucca, whose archives are not too vast for systematic study, nor too insignificant to be representative, nor yet dispersed by the accidents of foreign conquest, constitutes an especially precious case-study. But beyond its contribution to wider Italian historiography, a history of fifteenth-century Lucca is also important in its own right. On the one hand, it was precisely during this period that so many of the features of future Lucchese development were beginning to take shape. At the same time, this era that pre-dates the invasions, the Reformation, and the gradual closing of the Lucchese patriciate as a governing caste has a character and interest of its own which it is a prime aim of the present study to recover.

It was during the course of the fifteenth century that the Lucchese state established the territorial boundaries that, in essentials, it was to retain throughout the remaining centuries of independence. In 1430, with a Florentine army at the very gates of Lucca, the city commanded the loyalties of only a handful of fortified strongholds in the surrounding countryside to the south and west. Again in the wars after 1436 Lucca was able to exercise very little control beyond the city walls themselves. On this latter occasion, a number of individuals felt constrained to bring their

[12] S. Polica, 'An Attempted "Reconversion" of Wealth in XVth-Century Lucca: The Lands of Michele di Giovanni Guinigi', *Journal of European Economic History*, ix (1980), 655–707; M. E. Bratchel, 'The Return to the Land: Investment Opportunities and Commercial Decline in Late Medieval Italy', *Middeleeuse Studies* (1984), 22–47.

animals—including pigs and cows—into the city for protection, and found themselves accused of causing damage to grain and other crops planted on land belonging to ser Massino di Bartolomeo da Pietrasanta: interesting testimony to the continued existence of open land in that part of Lucca that had been demolished for the castle of Castruccio Castracani known as the Augusta, and used later for the fortress of Paolo Guinigi.[13] After these inauspicious beginnings, by the peace treaties at the end of the Florentine wars, most of her former territories were returned to Lucca. By the later fifteenth century Lucca again ruled over much of the area of the traditional Lucchese state: from Minucciano in the north to the area around Lucca in the south and stretching westward to the sea at Viareggio. But losses sustained during the fourteenth century and in the wars of the 1430s were never fully redressed. Barga and, more recently, Montecarlo had been acquired by the Florentines; Castelnuovo was ruled by the Este dukes of Modena; the Genoese ruled in Pietrasanta after 1436, this territory finally falling to the Florentines at the end of the century; and in Massa there was a local rising which gave control of that area to a branch of the family of the Marchesi Malaspina. If the Lucchese state was never again to attain the area of its greatest territorial expansion, achieved during the early fourteenth century under Castruccio Castracani, from the 1450s it is clearly legitimate to speak of relative stability and the consolidation of authority. The map of the Lucchese state executed in the later sixteenth century by Alessandro Resta[14] remains a useful visual guide to the territories of Lucca as they had evolved by the second half of the fifteenth century.

The fifteenth century also foreshadows Lucca's future place in Tuscany and within the wider Italian political scene. It is true that in a recent article Michele Luzzati has questioned the view that already by this period Lucca had renounced any autonomous political initiative, and in a spirit of renunciation sought passively to coexist with her more powerful neighbours.[15] Luzzati is no doubt right to suggest that later writers, influenced by the world around them, were over-inclined to regard

[13] SB 161, fos. 116^{v}–117^{r}, 156$^{r–v}$, 222^{v}, 237^{r}, 271^{r}–272^{r}; ASL Podestà di Lucca Inquisizioni, 5230; Rif. 15, pp. 284, 445.

[14] The *carta geografica* of Alessandro Resta, dated 1569, hangs in Lucca in the Archivio di Stato. The map, reproduced here as the frontispiece, excludes the two small, detached northern vicariates of Minucciano and Castiglione.

[15] M. Luzzati, 'Politica di salvaguardia dell'autonomia lucchese nella seconda metà del secolo xv', in *Egemonia fiorentina ed autonomie locali nella Toscana nord-occidentale del primo rinascimento: Vita, arte, cultura. Settimo convegno internazionale del Centro Italiano di Studi di storia e d'arte, Pistoia, 18–25 settembre 1975* (Pistoia, 1978), 543–82.

Florentine ambitions for a consolidated Tuscan state as a constant and manifest threat to Lucchese independence; equally, the image of the 'pacifico et populare Stato' presented in Marino Berengo's authoritative work[16] threatens to colour perceptions of Lucca at all times and in all circumstances. But Luzzati has certainly missed the very substantial body of evidence that shows the continuing covert intervention of the Florentines in Lucchese affairs; the threat posed, throughout the fifteenth century, to Lucchese territories and to Lucchese political stability; the intense awareness of Florentine activities on the part of the Lucchese authorities; and the frenetic efforts, except at times of impossible provocation, to mollify Florentine opinion. In a concluding reflection, Luzzati has stressed how, in the fifteenth century, Lucca was not yet constrained to bend to every prevailing wind[17]—and this is true. There is a good deal of material, beyond the evidence of the Colloqui used by Luzzati, to show the formation of pressure groups on issues of foreign policy within the Lucchese patriciate and how on occasion fifteenth-century Lucchese statesmen debated real foreign policy options. No one would wish to equate this state with the Lucca of the succeeding century, protected by Imperial forces and chastened by the example of Siena. To locate such differences is not to deny that Lucca was already fully aware of the precariousness of her position and was beginning to adopt a stance that was to be refined but not radically altered over the next hundred years.

In the area of constitutional development the formative, or reformative, role of the fifteenth century is less ambiguous. A great deal of recent scholarship has been directed at showing how little Italian political life was really changed by the coming of the Despots. In the case of Lucca, a much needed modern study of the rule of Paolo Guinigi would, no doubt, further illustrate this theme, and reveal the extent to which Guinigi protected traditional interests and operated through a thoroughly traditional nexus of interdependent and interrelated oligarchic interest groups. And yet the Guinigi period marks a break in a number of important Lucchese archival series and in the history of the institutions that produced them. Two councils, the Consiglio Generale del Comune and the Consiglio del Popolo, can be traced back to the early thirteenth

[16] M. Berengo, *Nobili e mercanti nella Lucca del Cinquecento* (Turin, 1965).

[17] Luzzati, 'Politica di salvaguardia', 580: 'La conclusione alla quale ho tentato di giungere è questa: nel '500 Lucca si limita a seguire il vento che tira, senza alcuna possibilità di far spostare questo vento né da una parte né dall'altra, riducendo tutta la sua politica all'accortezza di sapere quello che le capiterà domani; nel '400 invece Lucca è un po' più attiva, ha una certa autonomia di azione, si muove, cerca di pianificare qualche cosa.'

century; in the reformed statutes following the overthrow in 1316 of Uguccione della Faggiuola as *signore* of both Lucca and Pisa, a single Consiglio Generale del Popolo e del Comune made its appearance. The powers and functions of this General Council might be restricted by foreign overlords in the troubled decades that were to follow, but its history remains unbroken until suppressed for the entire thirty-year period of Paolo Guinigi's rule. If the highest authority in the state normally rested with the General Council, executive power in normal times from the middle of the thirteenth century rested with the college of Anziani. The power of the Anziani might vary, as did the means of their election, but, like that of the communal councils, the history of the Lucchese Anzianiate is interrupted only by the years 1400–30.

The old institutions of republican government were rapidly and faithfully restored after the revolution of mid-August 1430. Certainly during the early years it was found necessary to resort to a number of extraordinary expedients. The revolution itself was sanctioned by a general parliament, which elected a *balìa* of twelve men to organize the restoration of republican forms. In January 1431, against a background of continuing warfare, there was the appointment of a committee called the *Officiali di Guerra* (later the *Difensori della libertà*) with very extensive powers. But from the beginning, appointment to political office was based on the three *terzieri* of S. Martino, S. Paolino, and S. Salvatore, into which the city had been divided in 1370. The college of Anziani, headed by a Gonfaloniere di Giustizia, elected initially by the *balìa* of twelve, was restored immediately on 16 August 1430. The important Council of Thirty-Six was reconstituted on 30 August, and the General Council appears again from 11 October. By 1432 political life in Lucca had very largely returned to pre-Guinigi normality. Obviously political forms did not remain unchanged for the whole of the fifteenth century, far less for the remaining three and a half centuries of Lucchese liberty. The General Council was restored with 120 councillors in October 1430. This membership was reduced to ninety councillors in 1432, expanding again to the earlier figure by a reform of 25 May 1531. In the middle of the sixteenth century the 'legge martiniana' restricted the number of those eligible for election to the General Council, further restrictions being imposed during the early seventeenth century. Difficulties in filling vacancies in the General Council resulted in a series of changes in its structure and composition throughout the eighteenth century. After 1430, as in the past, emergencies might result in special powers being vested in a *balìa*; the fifteenth century saw the establishment of various commissions and committees for specific administrative purposes. But with due recognition of *ad hoc* arrangements and future changes, the Lucchese legislators of the 1430s, in trying to recapture much of the past, rebuilt the basic political structures that were to survive for as long as the republic itself.[18]

In other respects Lucca of the fifteenth century appears less as a prescription for the future, but displays rather the vestiges of her medieval past. The city remained encircled by the walls begun in 1198 and completed in 1265, though the fortifications were extended in the late fourteenth and early fifteenth centuries to embrace suburbs that had grown up to the north and east of the city. Within Lucca, a list dating as late as 1560 records and names forty towers built by noble Lucchese families and still standing:[19] references to individual towers in the fifteenth-century Lucchese records would seem to lend a great deal of support to those historians who have argued that towers disappeared from the Italian urban vista less because of communal legislation than because of time, decay, and changing architectural tastes.[20] Albeit decaying, the urban prospect was still largely that of the medieval city. But the physical remains of an earlier ethos no more recapture the essence of fifteenth-century Lucca than does the image of the post-Guinigi period as forging the Lucchese republic of future centuries. There is no difficulty in locating a series of collective preoccupations—none of them, of course, without antecedents or sequels—that give a special coherence to these decades in the history of the republic.

The backcloth is one of warfare, recurrent plague, and periodic shortages. The decade after 1430 was largely dominated by the personal and financial demands of the Florentine wars and by the consequent devastation, the threat to livestock, and the collapse of property prices in and around Lucca.[21] The potential impact of fifteenth-century warfare on

[18] Lucchese political structures are discussed in some detail in S. Bongi (ed.), *Inventario del Regio Archivio di Stato in Lucca*, 4 vols. (Lucca, 1872–88), i. 82 ff. For Lucca in the second half of the 14th cent., see Meek, *Lucca 1369–1400*, 1–16. The political reconstruction after 1430 is described by A. N. Cianelli, *Dissertazioni sopra la storia lucchese*, in *Memorie e documenti per servire all'istoria della città e stato di Lucca*, ii (Lucca, 1814), 151, 217.

[19] BSL MS 38, Ricordi Storici di Martino Bernardini, fo. 423^{r-v}.

[20] For the perilous tower of the Guidiccioni, see Rif. 18, p. 422. Recent discussions of Italian towers and tower societies include J. Heers, *Family Clans in the Middle Ages* (Amsterdam, 1977), 169–206; F. W. Kent, *Household and Lineage in Renaissance Florence: The Family Life of the Capponi, Ginori, and Rucellai* (Princeton, NJ, 1977), 3–17.

[21] Some of the most telling evidence of personal losses and hardships during the campaigns of the 1430s appears in the records of the court of the Podestà: e.g. ASL Podestà di Lucca, Curia Civile, 1177, fo. 73^{r-v}; 1308, fos. 70^{r}–76^{v}. Damages to ecclesiastical property are

civilian populations is well illustrated by episodes such as the sacking and burning of Collodi by the Florentines in August 1432.[22] The fiscal burden of defending Lucchese independence is chronicled in the series of *prestanze*, or forced loans, which occupy so much space in the Riformagioni of the General Council for this early period, and which disappear after the truce with Florence of 1438. The series of forced loans recommenced after 1477, and the whole of the fifteenth century was a period of sporadic and localized conflict. But clearly the military threat, the strained resources of the Lucchese state stretched to meet the external challenge, and the depredatory incursions of both allied and hostile armies did not remain the same ever-present reality of Lucchese life after the treaties of 1438–41. The plague, which together with war and famine had assailed Lucca in 1430, was not so easily consigned to memory.

In 1430 the plague had made it difficult to achieve a quorum in the college of Anziani or to convoke a full assembly of the General Council, and these problems were in part responsible for the *ad hoc* constitutional arrangements of the early 1430s. In the decades that were to follow, the renewed visitations of the plague, together with a fear of the spread of leprosy, resulted in numerous ordinances designed to check the spread of disease in the city of Lucca and its subject territories. Measures were taken to provide for the appointment of doctors of medicine in emergency situations, and for the isolation of the sick. There were attempts to limit the pernicious consequences which the flight of citizens from Lucca in plague years might hold for the security of the state, for the continued operation of political and administrative offices, and for the well-being of the Lucchese economy. During the two years before the French invasions the same kind of provisions continued to exercise the minds of Lucchese legislators, and these included the decision of 1492 to provide a house outside the city where those infected by the plague might be isolated from the rest of the community.

Some insight into the psychological impact of the plague can be gained from a civil case involving Giovanni Ottolini of Pugliano and Bartolomeo di Lorenzo de' Nobili di Albiano in the mountainous far-northern extremity of the Lucchese state. In this case it is explained how Bartolomeo, a great local lord, prevailed upon Giovanni's father, Ottolino, to take up residence in the house where Bartolomeo's wife, and later his

detailed in numerous notarial acts, notably AN 576(2) (ser Benedetto Guarguaglia), fo. 26^{v}, and in the Libri Antichi preserved in AAL.

22 ASL Biblioteca (Manoscritti), 38, Giuseppe Civitali, Storia di Lucca, fo. 423^{v}; Rif. 14, p. 266; 17, p. 85. See also the petition of the men of Coreglia: Rif. 17, p. 57.

servant and his mother, died of the plague. Bartolomeo himself hurried to the safety of his property in neighbouring Pugliano, whilst Ottolino complained to one witness, who for fear of the plague ('per amore del morbo') refused to stop and drink with him, that it was like being sent to prison, as the men of Albiano had threatened to cut him in pieces if he ever dared to venture outside Bartolomeo's house and the garden where he was to bury the other inmates. Exactly how long Ottolino remained in the house is uncertain, but it appears to have been customary, at least in this part of the territory, for the man hired to care for the sick to remain two months to ensure that he would not carry the sickness away with him.[23]

Throughout the fifteenth century the plague set the scene not only for countless personal traumas such as that endured by the men of Albiano, but also for a number of political acts of lasting significance: it was at a time of serious plague that the men of Minucciano rebelled against the Malaspina, in 1449, and restored themselves to obedience of the Lucchese republic. More generally, the plague, and to a lesser extent warfare, resulted in depopulation which was a constant cause of concern to the Lucchese authorities. In the 1450s and again in the 1480s and 1490s concessions were granted in efforts to encourage people to repopulate the city and its walled suburbs. In the countryside, depopulation and the hardships suffered during the wars were the two themes continually raised in attempts to reduce the tax burden and other local obligations. Certainly much of the rhetoric portraying a devastated and impoverished state is far from disinterested, and reliable demographic statistics are difficult to obtain. It seems clear that the city of Lucca itself was markedly smaller at the end of the fourteenth century than it had been in the years before the Black Death or than it was to become by the 1540s. The most convincing calculations available indicate that Lucca had a population of about 15,000 in 1331, which fell to about 10,000 by the 1380s, and rose to 18,821 by January 1540.[24] The population trends of the Lucchese state are distorted by changing political boundaries, but the overall pattern is not dissimilar. It appears likely that the Lucchese state, including both the Sei Miglia and the vicariates, supported a population of 40,000–45,000 at the beginning of the fifteenth century; that this population fell further by perhaps 10–20 per cent during the plague-ridden first three decades of the fifteenth century; and that the population of the Sei Miglia and the vicariates had

23 ASL Podestà di Casoli oltre Giogo, Atti Civili, 31, fos. 3^{r-v}, 9^{v}–10^{v}, 19^{r-v}, 25^{r-v}, 47^{r}–48^{v}.

24 Meek, *Lucca 1369–1400*, 21–6; Berengo, *Nobili e mercanti*, 280–1; BSL MS 38, Martino Bernardini, Ricordi Storici, fo. 424^{r}.

recovered to about 62,000 by the early 1540s.[25] At what point between 1430 and 1540 the population of the city and state of Lucca ceased to decline, or at best to stagnate, remains largely a matter of guesswork. Despite recurring disasters, and despite the continuing complaints of the city authorities, my own inclination would be to think in terms of a more favourable political and social environment in Lucca after 1438, even if a more spectacular demographic recovery probably did not take place until the early decades of the sixteenth century. In the countryside there are some indications of renewed pressure on land from the 1450s.[26] In general, Christine Meek's image of Lucca in 1369 as 'the contracted city' remains true; but the fifteenth century also contains the seeds of recovery as typified by the return of exiles and by the Indian summer enjoyed by the fifteenth-century Lucchese silk industry.

Notions of a reviving silk industry, of qualified economic recovery, of plague, and of temporal uncertainties come together in the long series of sumptuary laws enacted in Lucca throughout the fifteenth century. As soon as things returned to normal after the Florentine wars, a law was passed, in 1440, to curb lasciviousness in clothes and decoration.[27] Additions were still being made to these statutes in 1489, and in the intervening years attention was paid to excessive display at weddings and funerals in Lucca and the *contado* and at balls and evening parties.[28] In the

[25] Meek, *Lucca 1369–1400*, 25–6, estimated the inhabitants of the vicariates at 30,000, to which she added 9,000 to embrace the Sei Miglia. G. Pinto, *La Toscana nel tardo medio evo: Ambiente, economia rurale, società* (Florence, 1982), 71–3, has correctly noted that since the Sei Miglia occupied the most fertile and most densely populated part of the Lucchese state, the ratio of 30:9 between the vicariates and the Sei Miglia probably indicates that Meek, using the 1381 assessment for the militia, has underestimated the population of the Sei Miglia. According to Martino Bernardini, Ricordi Storici, the population of the vicariates in Jan. 1540 comprised 30,000 'bocche'. With the loss of some territory, including Pietrasanta, the Lucchese state was smaller in 1540 than it had been at the time of the census of 1383. Nevertheless, if Meek's calculation of a population of 30,000 in the vicariates in 1383 is correct, the population of the vicariates had increased by relatively little in the 150 years after the 1383 census. By contrast, the population of the Sei Miglia of 31,838, according to Berengo following ASL Colloqui, 7, fo. 114^{v} (rounded to 32,000 in Martino Bernardini, Ricordi Storici, fo. 424^{r}), would indicate a very substantial increase in the countryside immediately around Lucca if the late 14th cent. estimates are even vaguely accurate. I have not seen the forthcoming study of F. Leverotti, 'Popolazione, popolamento e insediamenti', in *La Toscana nel secolo xiv: caratteri di una civiltà regionale: 1° Convegno di studi, Firenze-San Miniato 1–5 ottobre 1986.*

[26] See Ch. 6. Writing of Tuscany as a whole, Pinto, *La Toscana*, 74, writes: 'Solo nell'ultimo terzo del XV secolo i segni della ripresa cominciarono a manifestarsi in modo univoco un po' in tutte le parti della regione.'

[27] Rif. 15, pp. 482–7.

[28] Rif. 20, pp. 25–6, 49–52; 21, pp. 325–6, 351–6, 579–80, 597–9; 22, pp. 264–5, 269–71.

very detailed legislation of March 1473, items of jewelry and dress were restricted by absolute prohibitions and by the specification of the number of silk dresses that a woman might possess. To prevent fraud, dresses were to be marked, and the particulars were recorded in a book kept in the court of the *officiale del fondaco*. Further restrictions were imposed as determined by age, sex, marital status, and membership of certain professions. Permitted attire varied for those resident in the city and for those of the countryside, with special provisions made for the wives of artisans living in the *contado*.[29] The intimate details of the statutes are not matched in the written records by a similar attention to the motivations behind the legislation: at best the Lucchese authorities spoke vaguely of growing pomp and display and of the great ills that flowed from this. No doubt competitive ostentation stirred the pervasive contemporary preoccupation with public order, whilst the highly influential Observant Franciscans of late quattrocento Lucca thundered from the pulpit against the evils of excessive splendour.[30] But more generally, the sumptuary legislation of fifteenth-century Lucca, with its roots in the late fourteenth century,[31] fits into a broader late medieval and European pattern which has been convincingly explained largely with reference to the psychological and material consequences of the plague epidemics which struck Europe in and after 1348.[32]

If concern with sumptuousness of dress is one highly revealing theme that permeates the legislative records of fifteenth-century Lucca, equal consternation was aroused by the prevalence of blasphemy, sodomy, and illegal gaming. In April 1435 the Gonfaloniere di Giustizia, ser Silvestro di Giovanni Corsini, spoke of the daily growth of the vices of blasphemy and sodomy, which he attributed to the late wars and the accompanying dislocation of the Lucchese state.[33] The following year, remedies were sought for the growing popularity of prohibited games of chance.[34] Clearly

[29] Rif. 20, pp. 49–52.

[30] ASL Biblioteca (Manoscritti), 65, Libro del Sommario delle Cronache della città di Lucca del Sig. Pietro Carelli Dottore, dal 1369 al 1499 inclusive. Con giunte posteriori, fo. 105r. There are various examples of preachers of the reformed Franciscan Order prodding the General Council into action on matters of public morality: e.g. Rif. 21, pp. 559, 561–2. The preambles to the sumptuary legislation often speak of ostentatious display as being displeasing to God, as well as being wasteful and without profit to the city and a source of corruption and unnecessary expense.

[31] Meek, *Lucca 1369–1400*, 32, 44–5.

[32] See esp. H. A. Miskimin, *The Economy of Early Renaissance Europe, 1300–1460* (Englewood Cliffs, NJ, 1969), 116–63.

[33] Rif. 14, p. 697.

[34] Rif. 15, pp. 79–80. Before the General Council the games of 'la diricta', 'la ritrosa', and 'al trenta' were specifically mentioned.

it would be naïve to see any of these problems as the peculiar product of the post-1430 situation. Paolo Guinigi had been particularly concerned about the incidence of sodomy, and the court records of the 1420s contain many prosecutions for male homosexuality.[35] At the same time a special office, the *Offizio sopra l'onesta*, was established in 1448 largely for the extirpation of sodomy,[36] and thereafter few issues reappear in the deliberations of the General Council with such unfailing regularity. Spates of prosecution followed upon acts of legislation, but it remains impossible to assess how far the evidence indicates heightened awareness and concern, and how far it is possible to speak with the legislators of an increasing practice. The prevalence of sodomy in fifteenth-century Italy has generally been attributed, like the fostering of public brothels, to pressures which resulted in patrician males marrying late or remaining unmarried.[37] The explanation appears less applicable to fifteenth-century Lucca than to contemporary Florence. The scions of the great Lucchese families were, no doubt, the prime concern of those who framed the anti-sodomy laws. But it should be added that many of those prosecuted were foreigners and marginals, and that the occasion for prosecution was often the rape of children.[38]

In all these matters, Lucca mirrors faithfully the findings of scholars working on neighbouring and contemporary societies. The plague was a scourge of very widespread occurrence: the Italian peninsula was stricken by major epidemics in 1400, 1422–5, 1436–9, 1447–51, 1477–9, and 1485–7. On 4 August 1457, following an earlier decision to prevent all foreigners from entering Lucchese territory whilst the plague was raging in Florence and elsewhere, a *Colloquio* granted special permission to Cosimo de' Medici that he might come to Lucca with his family to escape the plague.[39] Gregory XI (1370–8) spoke of sodomy (together with usury) as the sins that the Florentines commit; in the fifteenth century S. Bernardino of Siena was pronouncing Italy, shaped like a womb, to be the

[35] SB 150, *passim*; Rif. 14, p. 406; 16, p. 88.

[36] Rif. 16, p. 796.

[37] R. C. Trexler, *Public Life in Renaissance Florence* (New York, 1980), 378–9; D. Herlihy, 'The Tuscan Town in the Quattrocento: A Demographic Profile', 96; *idem*, 'Vieillir à Florence au Quattrocento', 1348, in *Cities and Society in Medieval Italy* (London, 1980) (no continuous pagination).

[38] SB 165, fos. 115^{r-v}, 421^{r-v}, 428^{r-v}; ASL Capitano o Bargello del contado, 55, 2nd foliation, fos. 27^{r}–30^{v}; Rif. 18, p. 154. In the wave of enthusiasm that accompanied the setting up of the special magistrature in 1448, a number of prominent men were arraigned: SB 165, fos. 51^{r}–70^{r}.

[39] ASL Colloqui, 1, p. 6.

mother of sodomy.[40] The preoccupation with dress was widely characteristic not only of Italy but of the whole of Europe at this time. In fifteenth-century Lucca, as in neighbouring states, there was an administrative reorganization, especially with regard to relations with the *contado*, and there was the same proliferation of special magistratures with specific judicial and administrative functions. In Lucca, as elsewhere, the late fifteenth century witnessed an assault upon the important Jewish community, and the founding of the Monte di Pietà.

Elsewhere Lucca appears less convincing as a replica in miniature of the fifteenth-century Italian city-republic. Manifestly Lucca was never a Renaissance centre after the model of Florence or Siena. It is true that in Matteo Civitali, born in 1436, Lucca possessed a sculptor in marble of the first rank, whose workshop established in late fifteenth-century Lucca a significant and original tradition of Renaissance sculpture, and whose work forms an important part of the visual impact of Lucca to this day.[41] The same era saw the mooting of plans to establish in Lucca a *Studio generale*. These plans were never brought to fruition, but the deliberations of the General Council continued frequently to include the granting of bursaries for local students to study at Bologna and other institutions.[42] Throughout the fifteenth century the General Council, fearing that the city's youth were growing up ignorant and illiterate, granted salaries and subsidies to entice schoolmasters to come to Lucca to teach grammar, rhetoric, moral philosophy, and arithmetic. In a dispute of delightful modernity, ser Pietro Bartolomeo Tucci, attending the school of magister Giovanni Bartolomeo of Brescia next to the church of SS. Giovanni and Reparata of Lucca, occupied the desk of another scholar, from which he refused to move. On being told to leave the school, ser Pietro informed the master that he had no right to expel him, as the school was common and public. The inevitable brawl followed, which ended when ser Pietro, 'contrary to all due reverence that he owed to the master and his fellow scholars', attacked them with a knife.[43] This, and other more successful

[40] There is a collection of pertinent remarks from S. Bernardino, and later from Savonarola, in Trexler, *Public Life in Renaissance Florence*, 40, 279, 350, 379–82, 470.

[41] S. Rudolph, 'Matteo Civitali', in *Dizionario biografico degli italiani*, xxvi (Rome, 1982); S. Bule, 'Matteo Civitali's Statues for the Cathedral of Genoa', in S. Bule, A. P. Darr, and F. Gioffredi (eds.), *Verrocchio and Late Quattrocento Italian Sculpture* (Florence, 1992), 205–15.

[42] There is an oral tradition in present-day Lucca that the city fathers never established a university because, in their wisdom, they understood that a student body would be a threat to public order, and that it was therefore in the interests of Lucca to send local youth away to cause trouble elsewhere.

[43] SB 171, fos. 75^{v}–76^{r}; AN 702 (ser Benedetto Franciotti), 27 July 1459, p. 233.

attempts by the Lucchese authorities to promote learning, hardly transforms Lucca into one of the capitals of the Italian Renaissance. The real priorities of the Lucchese state stand revealed in the decision taken by the General Council on 30 October 1447 that surplus revenues should be diverted first to the repair of the city walls, then to the maintenance of the ditches, and finally—should any remain—to the beautification of the public piazza.[44] The wisdom of Lucchese priorities is fully vindicated by the fact that the city in 1447 could look ahead to a further 350 years of political independence.

The selection of themes to capture the essence of the fifteenth-century Lucchese state has been, inevitably, a subjective exercise. Behind the exercise lies the conviction not only that fifteenth-century Lucca has been neglected, but that the neglect is unmerited. At one level the present study aims to explore through the Lucchese case-study a range of issues which are central to current Italian Renaissance scholarship. At another, the story is of a highly distinctive political entity striving to find and defend its place in the changing and largely hostile arena of an Italian politics dominated by the ambitions of a dwindling number of larger territorial states.

[44] Rif. 16, p. 749.

2

LUCCA 1430–1440: THE POLITICS OF RECONSTRUCTION

In November 1429 Niccolò Fortebraccio, encouraged by his Florentine employers and motivated by personal grievances, invaded Lucchese territory, and captured the fortresses of Ruota and Compito. The depredations of the *condottiere* were rapidly transformed into official warfare. Florence harboured resentment against the Lucca of Paolo Guinigi on a number of accounts. Guinigi had acted with discretion during the late wars, but was viewed in Florence as an ally of the Duke of Milan and an adherent of the *parte Ghibellina*; Paolo's son Ladislao had served the Duke at the head of 600 lances. In the councils of Florence messer Rinaldo degli Albizzi advocated the acquisition of Lucca as an easy and highly profitable venture. And in attacking Lucca, Florence was again able to pose as the champion of liberty, freeing that city from the rule of a tyrant. Consequently it was decided by a general council held in Florence on 14 December 1429 to make war against Lucca, and very soon the Florentine army under Niccolò Fortebraccio occupied the greater part of the Lucchese state and the plain around the city of Lucca itself. The scheme of the Florentine architect Filippo di ser Brunellesco to flood Lucca by diverting the waters of the River Serchio came to nothing when the Lucchese succeeded in turning the waters back upon the Florentine camp. But under continuing siege the lord of Lucca sent ambassadors to request military assistance from the Duke of Milan. Unofficial help arrived from Milan in the person of Francesco Sforza. Sforza entered Lucchese territory on 20 July 1430, and within a month a plot to overthrow Paolo Guinigi was arranged and successfully executed.[1]

The factual details of the *coup d'état* that took place in Lucca in mid-

[1] The military events of 1429–30 are generally familiar from the writings of Niccolò Machiavelli, *Istorie fiorentine*, ed. Plinio Carli, 2 vols. (Florence, 1927), i. 207–17. The period is well treated in published works, including Tommasi, 'Storia di Lucca', 302–6; A. Mazzarosa, *Storia di Lucca dalla sua origine fino al 1814*, 2 vols. (Lucca, 1833), i. 270–83. Most of the Lucchese chroniclers treat the events of these years in meticulous detail.

August 1430 have been fully recorded, and the accounts are largely mutually consistent and compatible. On 14 August Sforza invited Ladislao Guinigi, with his troops, to join him at Monte S. Quirico on the pretext of planning a new assault against the enemy. That night a group of armed Lucchese citizens, headed by Pietro Cenami, gathered in the vicinity of Guinigi's palace in Lucca. These men overpowered the palace guards, climbed the stairs to the chambers where Paolo Guinigi slept, and attempted to force an entry. Paolo was aroused by the commotion, and went to confront the conspirators, many of whom were now clamouring for his death. Fearful for his life, the *signore* addressed the crowd: 'You well know, my assembled citizens, that you have never received anything from me but good, and that I have never given injury to any one of you.'[2] The plea for clemency was taken up by Pietro Cenami, who argued that the shedding of blood would be contrary to their honour. Guinigi and his remaining sons were left in the custody of Pietro Cenami, whilst others left the palace to arouse the city with cries of 'Viva populo et libertà: Populo et libertà'. Outside the city, signals were sent to Francesco Sforza, who, on learning of the successful execution of the plot, detained Ladislao. In this way, 'without death or injury to anyone', Lucca recovered her liberty. Ladislao was imprisoned with his father, and within a few days Paolo Guinigi and his sons were despatched into the custody of the Duke of Milan.

If a narrative of events presents few problems, the motive forces behind these events remain obscure. Certainly there is no shortage of explanations proffered by Lucchese, Florentine, and Milanese sources; but the attempts at explanation are always in tension, and often contradictory. Within a few days of the revolution Lucca was writing to the Pope, to various foreign powers, and to the Lucchese communities in Venice and in northern Europe that Guinigi had been ousted by a spontaneous popular uprising, unplanned and unled.[3] In closer conformity with the evidence, Lucchese writers of the fifteenth and later centuries described a conspiracy entered into by a number of important and patriotic citizens who risked their lives to restore Lucca to its pristine liberty, and who took advantage of the presence of Francesco Sforza to achieve their aims.[4] A

[2] BSL MS 102, Compendio delle storie scritte da Alessandro Boccella ricavate da vari frammenti compendiate da Giuseppe Civitali, fo. 33^{v}: 'Cittadinanza mia voi sapete bene che da me mai non avete ricevuto che bene, et mai verso di un feci fallo.'

[3] Anz. Temp. Lib. 531, fos. 1^{r}–2^{r}; Fumi (ed.), *Regesti*, 1.

[4] This tradition is well expressed by BSL MS 2599, Antonio Iova, Annali Historici, pp. 849–52.

fifteenth-century Milanese chronicler, Giovan Pietro Cagnola, whilst retaining the notion of a Lucchese initiative, believed that the citizens were so dazzled by the presence of conte Francesco Sforza that they offered the government of their city to him.[5] Against such views, there is a strong historical tradition that the dynamic for change came less from within the walls of Lucca than from outside. When Paolo Guinigi turned for help to the Duke of Milan, he asked for the services of Sforza's rival, Niccolò Piccinino. There is abundant evidence that Guinigi was bitterly disappointed to receive Sforza rather than Piccinino, and this disappointment was translated into various acts of distrust and provocation. Francesco Sforza was offended by Guinigi's ill-concealed preference for Piccinino; he was received in Lucca with little respect; he appears to have believed, wrongly, that Paolo Guinigi was planning to sell Lucca to the Florentines; he had grievances over the delayed payment of sums owed to him; and the more ingenuous of the local chroniclers believed that he felt sympathy for the citizens of Lucca living under the yoke of tyranny. There is no doubt that Francesco Sforza was a leading actor in the events of August 1430. Where the disagreements appear are between those accounts that portray a jealous Sforza as the willing tool of patrician conspirators who bribed him to set Lucca free with promises of a settlement of the money due to him; those that see Sforza as the prime mover, calling leading citizens before him and exhorting them to join him in overthrowing the Guinigi regime; and those that view Sforza as the sole agent of the revolution, cajoling and bullying a very reluctant citizenry to assist him in the undertaking.[6] Other sources paint Francesco Sforza as

[5] 'Croniche Milanesi scritte da Giovan Pietro Cagnola, Giovanni Andrea Prato e Giovan Marco Burigozzo', *Archivio storico italiano*, 1st ser., iii (1842), 39: 'Paulo la vole vendere (Lucca) a Fiorentini; ma Luchesi, avedutosi, dimandano Francesco Sforcia, e pigliano Paulo et li lo danno ne le mane, e lo pregano che toglia il governo; ma lui lo rifiuta, e manda Paulo a Milano.'

[6] There are numerous minor variations and modifications of these themes. The idea of Lucchese citizens seeking an interview with Sforza and bribing him to help them recover their liberty is found, e.g., in BSL MS 47, an 18th-cent. collection of divers historical writings drawn from various histories and chronicles entitled Antichità di Lucca e sue famiglie con repertorio delle famiglie e notizie annuali dal 1368, fo. 296^{r}. The image of Sforza arousing the citizens to recover their liberty appears in BSL MS 38, Martino Bernardini, Ricordi Storici, fo. 272^{r}; in BSL MS 98, Croniche della città di Lucca composte per messer Bastiano Puccini e Sommario de' successi di Lucca di Gherardo Sergiusti, p. 189; and BSL MS 108, Historie di Lucca descritte da Nicolao Tucci e Cronache di Giovanni Saminiati, fo. 332^{r}. Bernardini, Sergiusti, and Tucci were all writing in the 16th cent.: Lucchesini, *Della storia letteraria*, i. 39–41, 183, 199–200. The Lucchese take on the guise of very unenthusiastic conspirators in ASL Biblioteca (Manoscritti), 38, Giuseppe Civitali, Storia di Lucca, fo. 403^{r-v}.

merely the executive of orders of the Duke of Milan, who had decided to dispense with Paolo Guinigi, whether because he had ambitions to lay hands on Guinigi's reputed wealth or because he had heard rumours of Guinigi's alleged dealings with the Florentines.[7] Yet others would attribute an instigating, as opposed to merely a co-ordinating role to Antonio Petrucci di *Checco rosso*, a Sienese who arrived in Lucca to help Paolo Guinigi and was soon busily engaged in providing channels of communication between Sforza, the Duke of Milan, and the leading Lucchese conspirators.[8]

The chronicle evidence does not lend itself to easy evaluation. Giuseppe Civitali, more thoughtful and with greater critical faculty than his near-contemporaries, drew much of his account from the work of Alessandro Boccella. Boccella served Ladislao Guinigi in the pay of the Duke of Milan. He was probably in Lucca during the events of August 1430; these he described in the fragments of his history which survive in the form of a transcribed, edited copy made by Civitali in 1549.[9] According to Boccella, Antonio Petrucci, who had been sent by Paolo Guinigi as one of his ambassadors to Milan, fanned the resentment of Francesco Sforza by relaying to him stories that Guinigi was displeased that the Duke had not sent him the services of Niccolò Piccinino. The plot to dispossess Guinigi stemmed from Sforza's jealousy of Piccinino. At the same time Petrucci

[7] ASL Biblioteca (Manoscritti), 38, Giuseppe Civitali, Storia di Lucca, fos. 402ᵛ–403ʳ, raises the thesis that instructions came from Milan, only to reject the argument. The minor 17th-cent. historian Martino Manfredi argued that Sforza wrote to the Duke of Milan to inform him that Guinigi was negotiating to sell Lucca to the Florentines, and thereupon received instructions from the Duke to depose him: BSL MS 121, Compendio istorico delle memorie di Lucca più degne di osservazione circa le mutazioni e alterazioni di stato o governo accadute in detta città dalla sua edificazione fino all'anno 1660 di Martino Manfredi, fo. 72ʳ. See also BSL MS 38, Martino Bernardini, Ricordi Storici, fo. 119ʳ; BSL MS 47, Antichità di Lucca, fos. 295ᵛ–296ʳ.

[8] For Antonio Petrucci, see E. Lazzareschi, 'Francesco Sforza e Paolo Guinigi: Contributo di documenti inediti', in *Miscellanea di studi storici in onore di Giovanni Sforza* (Turin, 1923), 405. The activities of Petrucci were emphasized by S. Ammirato, *Dell'istorie fiorentine* (Florence, 1600), 726–7. Ammirato's work is copied or paraphrased in many of the later Lucchese writings: e.g. BSL MS 91, Storie di Lucca, fos. 52ᵛ–53ʳ. See also BSL MS 62, Memorie diverse di Lucca, pp. 448–9 (which draws on Ammirato's history of Florence and Marco Antonio Sabellico's history of Venice). The above interpretations of the events of Aug. 1430 are not, of course, all mutually incompatible, and the same source can be quoted in support of more than one argument. Nor are the above sources intended as an exhaustive list of contributions preserved in the rich but, for the most part, highly derivative MS histories and historical notes of the BSL. I have tried rather to draw attention to some of the more trenchantly argued contributions to the debate.

[9] BSL MS 102. This is an 18th-cent. copy of Civitali's transcript. For the original copy, see BSL MS 893.

made contact with another Sienese resident in Lucca, fra Niccolò, a Dominican friar of S. Romano, who had great influence with many noble citizens. By means of fra Niccolò, Petrucci spread rumours in Lucca that Guinigi was planning to sell the city to the Florentines. Because of this information, a small number of leading citizens came together to plot the deposition of Paolo Guinigi, and these made contact with Francesco Sforza. The scheme to lure Ladislao Guinigi and his men out of Lucca appears to have been the inspiration of the citizen-conspirators, working in association with Antonio Petrucci. In Lucca the band of conspirators appointed a committee of six citizens to lead the revolution. Sforza was confident that he would be able to execute his part of the plan, but feared that in Lucca the citizens' spirit would fail them. In reality, under the valiant leadership of Pietro Cenami, the Lucchese participants showed themselves willing to risk their lives for the recovery of liberty; they captured Paolo Guinigi without faltering, and sent the signal to Sforza for the arrest of Ladislao. In essentials Civitali faithfully followed Boccella's account, though the later writer placed much greater stress on the reluctance of the citizens of Lucca to become involved in the machinations of Sforza and Antonio Petrucci. According to Civitali, the people of Lucca both loved and feared their lord, and it was only through the propaganda of the Florentine threat that Petrucci and fra Niccolò were able to persuade them to act.[10]

The deposition of Paolo Guinigi was not the result of a spontaneous uprising of the people of Lucca. Equally clearly, the people were not the passive and unwilling witnesses of events planned and executed entirely by outsiders. It is true that Guinigi's supporters were debilitated by the loss of Ladislao and his troops; but Paolo's capture was greeted with some show of enthusiasm and with no sign of resistance other than the short-lived refusal of the *castellano* of the citadel to hand over the keys. The events of 14/15 August 1430, dramatic enough in themselves, invite an explanation of why the citizens of Lucca were so ready to acquiesce in the expulsion of their lord. More important, the well-documented conspiracy which overthrew Paolo Guinigi provides a valuable opportunity to explore party formation and the ties that bound together a band of men embarking on a particularly dangerous political adventure.

The more general issue of the relationship between Paolo Guinigi and his subjects would require an analysis of the Guinigi period, which is clearly beyond the scope of the present study. Guinigi's reputation

[10] ASL Biblioteca (Manoscritti), 38, Giuseppe Civitali, Storia di Lucca, fos. 401^r–408^r.

remains controversial. For the late sixteenth-century chronicler Salvator Dalli, August 1430 represents, simply, a natural rising against the intolerable financial exactions and growing bloodthirstiness of the *signore*. Dalli's case is somewhat tarnished by his empirical evidence for Guinigi tyranny: the poisoning of Bartolomeo del Portico (who died in mysterious circumstances in Pietrasanta in 1434, long after Guinigi's own deposition and death in prison at Pavia); the execution of Tommaso Mercati, Arrigo (Andrea?) Mancini, and Nicolao Ridolfi (sentenced to death for the murder of Pietro Cenami in 1436); the death of ser Tommaso Lupardi (executed for treason by the restored republic in 1437); and the banishment of ser Cristoforo Turrettini and Stefano di Poggio (victims of the political crisis of 1434).[11] Others would be more inclined to attribute Guinigi's downfall to an excessive liberality and to a willingness to pardon and favour men proved to be disloyal to him. Two points emerge clearly. The first is the desolate condition of the city of Lucca in the summer of 1430. 'Here all manufacture had ceased, the fields were no longer cultivated, whether by day or by night no sound was heard in these streets other than the shrieks and tears of the abandoned and starving poor.'[12] Paolo Guinigi was the scapegoat for the sufferings of a city under siege. Second, there is the impact of Florentine propaganda. There is persistent, if somewhat intangible, evidence that the Florentines, unable to conquer Lucca by military means, disseminated false, forged letters with the aim of stirring up distrust between Guinigi and his subjects.[13] We have already seen how outsiders like Francesco Sforza and Antonio Petrucci may have been victims of this ploy. Events within Lucca seem, in part, to have been determined by the very widespread belief that Paolo Guinigi was intending to submit the city to Florentine servitude.

By common consent, Guinigi's capture was the work of six leading conspirators: Pietro Cenami, Tiero Gentili, Giovanni da Ghivizzano, Lorenzo Buonvisi, Nicolao Streghi, and Nicolao Neri. Constant repetition has enshrined these names in Lucchese hagiography, though it is not entirely clear whether these six initiated the plot or rather emerged as the

[11] BSL MS 710, Salvator Dalli, Croniche, fos. 132^{v}–134^{r}. The better-known chronicle of canon Gio: Lunardo Dalli has the misfortune to draw here on the earlier Dalli work. Gio: Lunardo adds to Guinigi's crimes the banishment of Giovanni da Ghivizzano to Perugia (1446): BSL MS 939, Gio: Lunardo Dalli, Cronache, p. 58.

[12] ASL Biblioteca (Manoscritti), 38, Giuseppe Civitali, Storia di Lucca, fos. 410^{v}–411^{r}: 'Qui non si lavorava di arte alcuna, li terreni non si coltivavano, non si sentiva il dì e la notte per queste strade altro che strida e lamenti di poveri affamati et abbandonati.'

[13] The pertinent material has been collected by Cianelli, *Dissertazioni sopra la storia lucchese*, 146–7.

chief actors from a larger and faceless group. The six met by night in the church of S. Frediano before the altar of S. Caterina, swore to be faithful to each other, and laid their plans.[14] The attack on the palace was led by Cenami, Gentili, and Giovanni da Ghivizzano, each accompanied by ten companions, 'all of Lucca and all being relatives and very close friends of these three good and perfect citizens'.[15] Buonvisi, Streghi, and Nicolao Neri appear to have been more fearful, and to have played a less visible role in the attack. The sixteenth-century chronicler Gherardo Sergiusti adds a seventh major conspirator in the person of Domenico Giovanni Gualanducci (Domenico di Giovanni), whom he places with Pietro Cenami at the very head of the undertaking.[16]

By any token the six 'capi e principali della congiura' constituted a very mixed body of men. The Cenami were a family whom Lucchese genealogists have attempted to trace back to the eleventh century, and were, less tendentiously, among the 'potentes et casastici' expelled from Lucca in 1308. Pietro's father, Giusfredo, had been a leading figure in the negotiations which brought Pisan rule to an end in 1368/9, and the family, economically and politically, was among the most powerful in Lucca of the late trecento.[17] The Gentili have been described as 'signori nobili di torre' as early as 1098. Again the uncertainties of Lucchese history before the early fourteenth century make it impossible to chart the family's early history with any confidence. But Baroni's notes seem to me convincingly to trace Tiero's line to a certain Michele del qd. Gentile Guasconi, who appears in numerous notarial acts in the second half of the thirteenth century, and whose descendants were very active as bankers and merchants by 1300.[18] The Streghi were without doubt a family of great distinction. The family has traditionally been associated with the lords of the Vallecchia, and Pina di Iacopo dello Strego was mother of Castruccio

[14] Canon Gio: Lunardo Dalli (who believed that these events took place in Aug. 1429) names 'the boldest and wisest of the conspirators' who met in great secrecy in the church of S. Frediano as Pietro Cenami, messer Giovanni da Ghivizzano, Lorenzo Buonvisi, Tiero Gentili, Iacopo Arnolfini, Nicolao Burlamacchi, Paolo Balbani, Lorenzo Trenta, ser Iacopo Turrettini, Carlo Buzzolini, messer Nicolao Manfredi, Forteguerra Totti, ser Domenico Arrighi, messer Iacopo Viviani, and messer Antonio Rossi (Petrucci) da Siena: BSL MS 939, p. 105. These names are plausible, but the unsubstantiated evidence of the Dalli chronicles is far too fragile a source from which to draw firm conclusions.

[15] BSL MS 102, Alessandro Boccella, Compendio delle storie, fo. 33^{v}: 'et certamente che tutti furon di Lucca Parenti e stretti amici di questi tre buoni e perfetti cittadini'.

[16] BSL MS 98, Gherardo Sergiusti, Sommario de' successi di Lucca, p. 189.

[17] S. Giancoli, 'Cenami', in *Dizionario biografico degli italiani*, xxiii (Rome, 1979); Meek, *Lucca 1369–1400*, 190, 192; Baroni, Notizie genealogiche, MS 1110, fos. 32^{r}–91^{r}.

[18] Baroni, Notizie genealogiche, MS 1113, fos. 314^{r}–329^{r}.

Castracani. Nicolao was not of the direct line of those Streghi who were very powerful in the countryside around Lucca and Pietrasanta in the first half of the fourteenth century, but appears to have been the descendant of a certain Averardo, for whom there are references from 1207.[19] Whether labelled as magnates or *popolani*, all three families were among the oldest and most distinguished members of the Lucchese oligarchy. The Buonvisi had risen to prominence within the ambit of urban politics much more recently. There are scattered references to the family throughout the fourteenth century, but little of substance is known of them before Lorenzo's father Neri occupied the office of Anziano for the first time in 1387.[20] If the Buonvisi were newcomers to the patrician oligarchy, the families of Giovanni da Ghivizzano and of Nicolao Neri had hardly arrived. Though there are references to men bearing the appellation 'da Ghivizzano' from the time of Castruccio, Giovanni di Piero Nossi da Ghivizzano, described as 'cordellarius', received Lucchese citizenship only by a grant of May 1409.[21] Nicolao di Lorenzo di Nicolao Neri was the son of a retail merchant of imported woollen cloth. There is a good deal of evidence for Nicolao Neri's impoverishment in and after 1430.[22]

The six families cannot be characterized as consistent opponents of Guinigi rule, either in the years preceding Paolo's seizure of power or in the thirty years after 1400. Rather, with the exception of the Cenami, the reverse is true. Pietro Cenami's father was a prominent member of the Forteguerra party in opposition to the Guinigi during the late fourteenth century, though, more frequently than most Forteguerra supporters, he continued to hold political office after the Guinigi victory of 1392.[23] Pietro himself was among the noble Lucchese citizens who accompanied Paolo Guinigi's daughter Ilaria to her marriage with Battista Campofregoso in 1420, and was sometimes used on commissions appointed by the Guinigi

[19] Baroni, Notizie genealogiche, MS 1133, fos. 168^r–171^v; MS 1134, fos. 246^r–262^v; V. Santini, *Commentarii Storici sulla Versilia centrale*, 6 vols. (Pisa, 1858–63), i. 88, 118, 139–49; v. 3–5. For a recent review of the relationship between the Streghi and the lords of Corvara and Vallecchia, see L. Green, *Castruccio Castracani: A Study on the Origins and Character of a Fourteenth-Century Italian Despotism* (Oxford, 1986), 48–9.

[20] Baroni, Notizie genealogiche, MS 1108, fos. 1^r–203^v; M. Luzzati, 'Lorenzo Buonvisi', in *Dizionario biografico degli italiani*, xv (Rome, 1972); M. E. Bratchel, 'Patrician Life in Fifteenth-Century Lucca: Lorenzo di Neri Buonvisi and his Peers', in *Conference Papers: Seventh Biennial Conference of the Medieval Society of Southern Africa* (1984), 33–56.

[21] Baroni, Notizie genealogiche, MS 1113, fos. 411^r–459^v; ASL Archivio Arnolfini, 18, no foliation, 'Albero di casa de Nozii da Ghivizzano oggi Ghivizzani'.

[22] Baroni, Notizie genealogiche, MS 1122, fos. 158^r–205^r; ASL Archivio Mansi, 493, Carte Nieri, no. 1, 'Famiglia Nieri, notizie genealogiche'; Rif. 14, p. 46.

[23] Meek, *Lucca 1369–1400*, 194–343.

regime.[24] But the Cenami had not been of the Guinigi faction, and there is no evidence that they received marked political favours after the establishment of the Guinigi lordship. By contrast, the Gentili, the Streghi, and the grandfather of Nicolao Neri had all been Guinigi supporters in the conflicts of the late fourteenth century.[25] Giovanni da Ghivizzano may have been related to that messer Tommaso da Ghivizzano described by Meek as 'one of the firmest adherents of the Guinigi party',[26] who was a member of the *balìa* appointed in July 1400 and one of the leading figures in the election of Paolo Guinigi as Captain and Defender of the People later that year.[27] Certainly Giovanni received Lucchese citizenship at the hands of Paolo Guinigi. The Buonvisi rose to prominence in the employment of the Guinigi; Lorenzo Buonvisi was married to Paolo's niece Antonia; and after 1407 Lorenzo was a member of the small ruling council of perhaps nine men chosen from among Paolo Guinigi's *parenti* and *amici*.[28] In later centuries, as the Buonvisi clan continued to flourish, Lucchese writers were much concerned to explain Lorenzo Buonvisi's betrayal of his benefactor. The admirable Lorenzo, claim the apologists, was so devoted to liberty and to the welfare of his *patria* that he forced himself to overcome even the natural bonds of blood, friendship, and gratitude.[29]

The individual grievances of the conspirators against Paolo Guinigi remain largely obscure. It can be posited that a man of Pietro Cenami's background and character resented his continued exclusion from the inner councils of government. The group as a whole were no doubt victims of

[24] G. Sercambi, *Le Chroniche Lucchesi*, ed. S. Bongi, 3 vols., *Fonti per la Storia d'Italia* (Rome, 1892), iii. 255; ASL Biblioteca (Manoscritti), 38, Giuseppe Civitali, Storia di Lucca, fo. 394^{v}.

[25] Meek, *Lucca 1369–1400*, 194–268, 366–8. Tiero Gentili was married to Elisabetta, daughter of Lazzaro di Nicolao Guinigi.

[26] Ibid. 338.

[27] According to the 'Albero di casa de Nozii da Ghivizzano oggi Ghivizzani' in ASL Archivio Arnolfini, 18, no foliation, Giovanni was the son of messer Tommaso's brother Piero. The genealogy is generally difficult to reconcile with Baroni's notes on the da Ghivizzano, Notizie genealogiche, BSL MS 1113, fos. 411^{r}–459^{v}. Messer Tommaso's sole brothers appear to have been ser Andrea and Giorgio, and these three brothers are always described as the sons of *ser* Nicolao di ser Azzolino da Ghivizzano. Giovanni was the son of Piero Nossi da Ghivizzano, and Baroni's efforts to link the various groups of men whom he finds bearing the name da Ghivizzano are entirely unconvincing. There is no doubt from Baroni's notes and from Meek, *Lucca 1369–1400*, 271, 332–43, that messer Tommaso and his close relatives were very active in Guinigi service.

[28] The evidence is collected in Bratchel, 'Patrician life', 34–6.

[29] BSL MS 99, Elogia insignium virorum lucensium Nicolao Tucci autore, fo. 80^{r}. Many of the early sources express suspicion of Lorenzo Buonvisi's motives, and stress his very lukewarm participation in the conspiracy.

the fiscal demands of the Florentine war. Lorenzo Buonvisi had joined Silvestro Trenta as ambassador to the Duke of Milan when Paolo Guinigi had requested the services of Niccolò Piccinino. Both men were the object of Guinigi's wrath when they returned not with Piccinino but with Sforza: 'You have disobeyed my instructions; I do not intend to pay a penny nor do I wish to have the men of conte Francesco inside of the walls, and I consider myself to have been very badly served by you.'[30] Silvestro Trenta retired to his house to sulk over the irate reception that he had received from his lord; Lorenzo Buonvisi may well have reacted to the criticism with more spirit. And Buonvisi may have been moved by more materialistic motives, whether because, as alleged, Guinigi went on to use his money to pay the soldiers, or because he had designs on Paolo Guinigi's jewels.[31] Personal motives here cannot be determined with any assurance; the structural composition of the party that formed around Pietro Cenami is highly revealing.

In the first instance the conspiracy shows the strength of neighbourhood bonds, in fifteenth-century Lucca as in other contemporary Italian societies. Plans were made and sealed by oaths, according to familiar fifteenth-century practice, in a church—that of S. Frediano. The chapel of S. Caterina, in which the conspirators met, housed the bones of the ancestors of Tiero Gentili; the present cappella Gentili in S. Frediano (della Speranza e del SS. Sacramento) was erected by the family in the mid-fifteenth century.[32] There are also early indications connecting the Cenami and the Streghi to the church of S. Frediano, though the Cenami chapel (S. Biagio) was endowed only in 1452.[33] By 1430 Lorenzo Buonvisi, who in an earlier will had asked to be buried in the tomb of his father in S. Romano, may have already been contemplating the building of an *avello* in

[30] BSL MS 102, Alessandro Boccella, Compendio delle storie, fo. 32^{r-v}: 'siete usciti di commissione, io non intendo aver pag^{to} un quattrino, ne voler dentro la gente del Conte Francesco, e mi tengo molto mal servito da voi'.

[31] ASL Biblioteca (Manoscritti), 38, Giuseppe Civitali, Storia di Lucca, fo. 402^{r}; S. Bongi, *Di Paolo Guinigi e delle sue ricchezze* (Lucca, 1871), 42 ff.; BSL MS 47, Antichità di Lucca, fo. 296^{r}; MS 71, Compendio delli successi più notabili della città e Rep. di Lucca di Paulo Minutoli, p. 60; MS 939, Gio: Lunardo Dalli, Cronache, pp. 108, 111.

[32] Baroni, Notizie genealogiche, MS 1113, fo. 315^{r} records that Pietro di Filippo Gentili, who died in 1400, was buried in S. Frediano: 'Hoc est sepulcrum dominorum domus filiorum Gentilis de Luca.' Two older Gentili sepulchres were in the chapel of S. Caterina: ibid.; and see also fo. 317^{v}; AN Originali Testamenti, 11 (ser Domenico Ciomucchi), fo. 65^{r}.

[33] The first reference to the Streghi is dated 1341, and relates to the alleged theft of 1,600 florins from the sacristy of S. Frediano: Baroni, Notizie genealogiche, MS 1133, fo. 171^{v}; MS 1134, fo. 249^{v}. In 1444 Alessandro del gia ser Giovanni di ser Masseo degli Streghi was acting as procurator for S. Frediano: Baroni, MS 1133, fo. 171^{v}. For the Cenami endowment of the chapel of S. Biagio, see Baroni, MS 1110, fo. 34^{r}.

S. Frediano, the church with which his family was soon to become very closely associated.[34] The towers of the Cenami, the Gentili, and the Streghi rose over the *contrada* of S. Frediano; those of the Gentili and the Streghi were still standing there in 1560.[35] Pietro Cenami, Nicolao Streghi, and Lorenzo Buonvisi in 1430 appear to have been close neighbours in the *contrade* of S. Frediano and of S. Giovanni capo di borgo.[36] Tiero Gentili lived a little to the south in the *contrada* of S. Pier Cigoli,[37] and Giovanni da Ghivizzano to the west in the *contrada* of S. Lucia verso Fillungo.[38] Of the six conspirators only Nicolao Neri was resident outside the *terziere* S. Salvatore: Neri lived in S. Paolino in the *contrada* of S. Masseo.[39] The strong neighbourhood links are illustrated in Figure 2.1.

For a generation, scholars have been stressing the importance of neighbourhood bonds in the highly fractured world of Italian urban politics. The neighbourhood facilitated, though never entirely circumscribed, economic interaction and social relationships—friendships, marriage partnerships, and political advancements.[40] Living in close physical proximity and attending the same church, fierce local loyalties had in earlier centuries forged the neighbourhood communities into armed camps. Samuel Kline Cohn has recently argued that in fifteenth-century Florence the patriciate was beginning to transcend the parochialism of the past, and that the leading Florentine families were coming to see themselves primarily as citizens of Florence rather than as members of a particular parish community.[41] The case for a developing Florentine

[34] Baroni, Notizie genealogiche, MS 1108, fos. 41^{r}, 49^{r-v}; AN 374 (ser Paolo Michele Federighi Bianchi da Massa), fos. 183^{r}–185^{r}.

[35] BSL MS 38, Martino Bernardini, Ricordi Storici, fo. 423^{r}; Baroni, Notizie genealogiche, MS 1110, fo. 33^{v}; MS 1134, fo. 258^{r}.

[36] The only problem relates to the Buonvisi. Lorenzo's father Neri appears in the *estimo* of 1399 as resident in the *terziere* of S. Salvatore in *prima ruga del Borgo*: Baroni, Notizie genealogiche, MS 1108, fo. 10^{v}. Lorenzo Buonvisi was assessed in May 1431 in *prima ruga del Borgo* (and Cenami and Streghi in the *contrada* of S. Giovanni capo di borgo): ASL Imprestiti, 21, fos. 25^{r}, 28^{r}. Until July 1432, however, Lorenzo Buonvisi appears regularly, in Rif. 14, as holding office for the *terziere* of S. Martino.

[37] e.g. AN 401(4) (ser Matteo di Giovanni de' Nobili), fo. 35^{v}; ASL Imprestiti, 21, fo. 30^{v}.

[38] e.g. AN 548(1) (ser Ciomeo Pieri), fo. 127^{v}. Giovanni was in fact assessed in 1431 in the *contrada* of S. Lucia verso archo: ASL Imprestiti, 21, fo. 35^{v}.

[39] There are continuous references to Nicolao Neri, his son, and their immediate forebears in S. Masseo from the 1390s and throughout the first half of the 15th cent. See, e.g., AN 259(1) (ser Simone Alberti), fo. 265^{v}.

[40] The literature is very large, but see esp. Kent, *Household and Lineage*, 124–7, 172–3; D. V. Kent and F. W. Kent, *Neighbours and Neighbourhood in Renaissance Florence: The District of the Red Lion in the Fifteenth Century* (New York, 1982), *passim*; and the more general survey in L. Martines, *Power and Imagination: City-States in Renaissance Italy* (New York, 1979), 34–41, 74–8.

[41] S. K. Cohn, *The Laboring Classes in Renaissance Florence* (New York, 1980), 43–63.

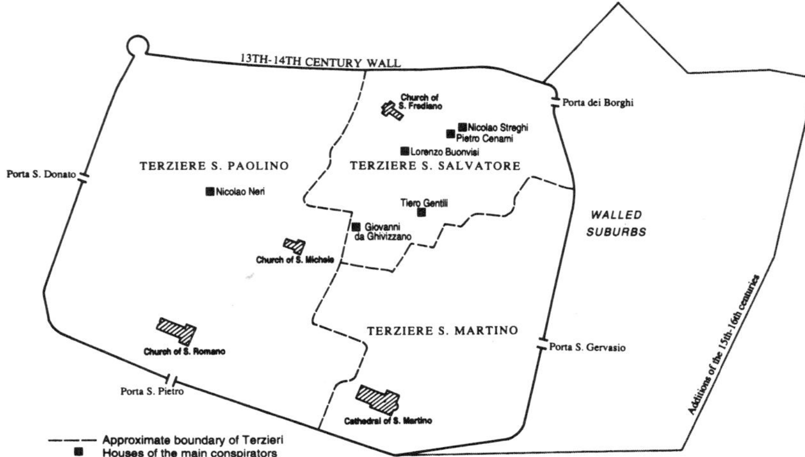

FIG. 2.1 Lucca in 1430: approximate location of the houses of the main conspirators in August 1430. *Source*: Based on G. Matraia, *Lucca nel '200* (Lucca, 1843); Meek, *Lucca 1369–1400*; I. Belli Barsali, *Lucca: Guida alla città* (Lucca, 1988); *Ordini che devono osservare li gonfalonieri delle contrade, Approuati dall'Eccellentissimo Consiglio Generale A 20. Luglio 1635* (Lucca, 1635).

self-identification is unproven;[42] in fifteenth-century Lucca the events of 1430, and later, indicate the continued vitality of local connections based on trust, familiarity, and good neighbourhood.

Neighbourhood bonds were reinforced by other associations. The fathers of Pietro Cenami, Tiero Gentili, and Lorenzo Buonvisi were all members of the important Lucchese community of merchants and exiles in late fourteenth-century Venice. The daughter of Giovanni da Ghivizzano was married to Lorenzo Buonvisi's brother Paolo.[43] The outsider Nicolao Neri, the only member of the band resident outside of the *terziere* of S. Salvatore, was left as an orphan aged 9 in April 1411 on the death of his father, Lorenzo. One of the guardians of the young Nicolao, appointed by his late father's will, was Alderigo di Matteo Vanni de' Martini, the long-time business partner of Lorenzo Buonvisi.[44] These

[42] See the thoughtful comments of R. F. E. Weissman, *Ritual Brotherhood in Renaissance Florence* (New York, 1982), 12.

[43] AN 385 (ser Massino di Bartolomeo da Pietrasanta), fos. 151^{v}–152^{v}.

[44] AN 259 (ser Simone Alberti), fos. 271^{r}–276^{v}; 290(2) (ser Domenico Lupardi), fo. 61^{r-v}; ASL Corte de' mercanti, Libro de' sensali (1423–4), 97, *passim*.

connections, which a full survey of the notarial protocolli for the late Guinigi period would no doubt extend, illuminate the nexus of personal and familial relationships that bound together the rather diverse group of men who so self-consciously pledged their lives at night before the altar of S. Caterina.

If the restoration of the republic was promoted by foreigners and executed by a narrow interrelated clique, it was consummated by acts of remarkable political unanimity. On 16 August there was a general assembly or *parlamento* of ninety-seven leading Lucchese citizens.[45] The means of convocation and selection are not entirely clear. Civitali says that the *primati* of Lucca, in order to provide for the setting up of the new regime, arranged a meeting of a *parlamento* of the heads of families.[46] What is clear is that the assembly was widely representative of the political nation. It contained members of most of the great families of early fifteenth-century Lucca, excluding the Guinigi clan. It included seventeen notaries, together with doctors of law and medicine. And to these were added a sprinkling of mercers, apothecaries, butchers, leather-workers, a dyer, and a weaver. This general assembly unanimously wished to maintain and protect the newly acquired freedom, and to this end elected a *balìa* of twelve men for two months with full powers to rule Lucca, to provide for the city's needs, and to appoint to offices.[47] In a series of acts that follow each other in rapid succession, the *balìa* of twelve, on the same day, 16 August, moved to restore the ancient constitution with the election of nine Anziani—three per *terziere*—and a Gonfaloniere di Giustizia. At the head of the new Anziani, the first to be appointed in thirty years, Pietro Cenami of the *terziere* of S. Salvatore was elected as Gonfaloniere di Giustizia. The three Anziani representing the *terziere* of S. Salvatore included Giovanni di Piero da Ghivizzano and Nicolao di ser Nicolao Streghi.[48]

[45] See Appendix.

[46] ASL Biblioteca (Manoscritti), 38, Giuseppe Civitali, Storia di Lucca, fo. 408^r. The official record in Rif. 14, pp. 21–2, speaks only of the meeting of a general assembly representing all the people and city of Lucca.

[47] Rif. 14, pp. 22–3. The members of the *balìa* were Bonagiunta del Fondo, Lorenzo del fu maestro Federigo Trenta, Nicolao del fu Gerardo Burlamacchi, Carlo del fu Bartolomeo Buzzolini, Stefano del fu Nicolao di Poggio, Forteguerra del fu Giovanni Totti, Pietro del fu Giusfredo Cenami, Paolo del fu Bartolomeo Balbani, d. Nicolao Manfredi, ser Domenico Arrighi, Domenico Giovanni speziale, and Piero Nucchelli.

[48] Ibid., p. 24. The fourth representative of S. Salvatore was Landuccio Bernardi. The *terziere* of S. Paolino was represented by Lorenzo Parpaglioni, ser Domenico Arrighi, and Domenico Giovanni speziale; that of S. Martino by Paolo Balbani, Antonio Tegrimi, and Gerardo Angiorelli.

The official records indicate an extraordinarily smooth transfer of power in Lucca in the summer of 1430. The main initial threat to the new government came from Francesco Sforza, whose intentions were suspect, and who was paid a large sum in money and merchandise to remove himself. In reality, the challenge to the restored republic was not merely an external one, and the next ten years were to be among the most turbulent in Lucca's history. Various plots to hand the city over to the Florentines were uncovered during the wars that continued until April 1433. These and later intrigues largely, though by no means exclusively, involved foreign officials and stipendiaries rather than Lucchese citizens. But in 1431 and again in 1433 members of the Guinigi family and their associates were accused of plotting to disturb the state of Lucca; on both occasions the charges resulted in imprisonment and exile. Tensions of these early years culminated in the political crisis of April and May 1434, which saw the banishment from Lucca of Stefano di Poggio and of the chancellor, ser Cristoforo Turrettini. Of all the intrigues and acts of political violence that marked the first decade of the restored republic, none reveals more clearly than the murder in 1436 of Pietro di Giusfredo Cenami the internal conflicts and rivalries that were rending Lucca at this time.

Pietro Cenami held the office of Gonfaloniere di Giustizia twice between 1430 and 1436, and was drawn as one of the Anziani for the two months May–June 1436. On the evening of Saturday 2 June 1436 there was a meeting in the house of Tommaso Mercati situated in the *contrada* of S. Lorenzo in Poggio. Those present were Lorenzo di Gerardo de' Cattani, Marco Antonio and Lazzaro di Francesco di Poggio, Giovanni di Gerardo Burlamacchi, the Anziano Andrea Arrighi called Del Mancino, and Tommaso Mercati himself. At the meeting it was agreed that the following day Lorenzo Cattani, Marco Antonio, and Lazzaro di Poggio would go to the palace of the Anziani, where they would meet Andrea del Mancino and together murder Pietro Cenami. Andrea del Mancino returned to the palace, and after lunch on Sunday 3 June discussed the plan with his fellow Anziano Nicolao Ridolfi, with whom he shared a room. On the same Sunday, before lunch, Lorenzo de' Cattani saw the weaver and Lucchese citizen Bartolomeo del fu Iacopo in the apothecary's shop of Andrea del Mancino, and drew him into the conspiracy. After dinner the assassins went to the palace, walking there in twos: first Lorenzo de' Cattani and Marco Antonio di Poggio, then Lazzaro di Poggio and Bartolomeo del fu Iacopo. Andrea del Mancino as Anziano gave permission for them to enter the palace, but the group immediately found themselves in the presence of Nicolao Ridolfi and the chancellor, ser Pietro

Torini. Andrea del Mancino and Nicolao Ridolfi both claimed for themselves the pleasanter duty of holding ser Pietro in conversation whilst the others passed on to effect the crime. In the event it was Ridolfi who remained behind with the chancellor, whilst the others continued to Cenami's chamber, which was the first room of the new palace. Here there was further hesitation. Bartolomeo del fu Iacopo decided that he had gone far enough; he refused to enter, and hurried out of the palace and back to his own house. Meanwhile Andrea del Mancino opened the door of Cenami's chamber with a key, and he and his companions rushed upon the sleeping Anziano. Bartolomeo del fu Iacopo, in his precipitous retreat, heard Pietro Cenami shouting 'Oy me, oy me' as the assassins fell upon him with their weapons and killed him with twenty-two blows. The murder accomplished, Andrea del Mancino retired to the room where he and Nicolao Ridolfi slept to inform Nicolao of what had happened. The others escaped, and together with Giovanni Burlamacchi and Tommaso Mercati rang the alarm in the hope of raising the city to arms in their favour. The hope was entirely vain; the conspirators appear to have won no popular support. Lazzaro and Marco Antonio di Poggio and Lorenzo Cattani fled to the safety of Pisan territory at Ripafratta. Andrea del Mancino, Nicolao Ridolfi, Tommaso Mercati, and Bartolomeo del fu Iacopo were executed. Giovanni Burlamacchi was also sentenced to death, but under pressure from his family this sentence was later commuted to one of perpetual banishment.[49]

The murder of Pietro Cenami was in part an isolated incident prompted by the unique status that Cenami had rapidly attained in the political life of the restored republic. By common consent Cenami was the leader of the patrician conspiracy against Paolo Guinigi; and his wisdom, discretion, and statesmanship during the events of August 1430 appear to have been panegyrized from a very early date. Pietro Cenami was a member of the extraordinary magistrature created to re-establish political order on 16 August 1430, and was the first Gonfaloniere di Giustizia of the new regime. In October 1430, when the period of office of the *balìa* of twelve came to an end, Cenami was elected to the new *balìa* (the *Balìa de' Riformatori*). In 1431 he was one of six citizens appointed with extensive powers to handle the war effort against Florence (the *Officiali di Guerra*—later called the *Difensori della libertà*), and in the year of his death he was

[49] The fullest record of the events of 2–3 June 1436 appears in the inquisitions made in the court of the *Podestà*: ASL Podestà di Lucca, Inquisizioni, 5229, no foliation. There is an accurate and very full account in F. Acton, *La morte di Pietro Cenami e la congiura di ser Tommaso Lupardi raccontate sui documenti dell'Archivio di Lucca* (Lucca, 1882), 17–28.

elected as one of the six *conservatori* of the republic of Lucca who were appointed with extraordinary powers on 2 January 1436 to guide Lucca through the international crisis which, it was anticipated, would follow the revolt of Genoa against Milanese rule. During the intervening years Cenami played a prominent political role as occasional ambassador for the republic, as a member of various *ad hoc* commissions, as one of the *impositori* selected to impose new taxes, and as one of the assessors of the forced loans imposed to further the war effort. In 1432 he had been one of the committee of three elected to raise money and handle the expenses relating to the forthcoming visit to Lucca of the Emperor Sigismund. The Lucchese political records conceal individual opinions and contributions to political debate, and consequently it is very difficult to isolate Cenami from the anonymous body of assentors and dissenters that constituted the ruling councils. But there are indications that he was a powerful and often controversial figure. In 1431, when the General Council voted 86:6 in favour of restoring to the noble clans of the Antelminelli and the Quartigiani the right to be elected to high political office, Cenami, it appears, led the opposing faction.[50] That Cenami's image and self-image as 'padre della patria' was promoting tensions is suggested by a rather obscure case in the court of the *Podestà* against the mason Nicolao Giovanni. In this inquisition it was alleged that in April 1436 Nicolao Giovanni met a widow named Biasina in the house of Nicolao Ridolfi, later to be numbered among Cenami's murderers. The course of the conversation between Nicolao Giovanni and Biasina is not entirely clear, but the former spoke of a plot to kill the leading men of the city whom he identified as Pietro Cenami, Giovanni da Ghivizzano, and maestro Antonio Arrighi. He referred to a plan to reform Lucca once these men had been removed, and hinted at a strong lord lurking in the background who would accomplish these things.[51]

Traditionally the murder of Pietro Cenami has been attributed to a personal quarrel. But the nature of this quarrel has never been fully explored. The vendetta concerned the marriage of the daughters of Bartolomeo del Portico. The del Portico were a very ancient family 'di grande nobilità' whose houses had been established in the *contrada* of S. Michele since at least the middle of the thirteenth century. The banker Andrea di Lemmo del Portico was resident in the 1390s in a house close to

[50] The official record in Rif. 14, pp. 173–4, preserves anonymity. But see ASL Biblioteca (Manoscritti), 65, Pietro Carelli, Sommario delle Cronache, fo. 78^{r}.

[51] ASL Podestà di Lucca, Inquisizioni, 5229, no foliation.

the church of S. Lorenzo in Poggio and touching the houses of the di Poggio family; and like the di Poggio, the del Portico were closely associated with the church of S. Romano. Andrea del Portico died in 1398, leaving a considerable fortune to his two sons and heirs, Guglielmo and Bartolomeo; and among the five guardians appointed by Andrea for his younger and minor son Bartolomeo were the names of both Nicolao del fu Ceccorino di Poggio and Stefano del fu Iacopo di Poggio.[52] The two brothers, Guglielmo and Bartolomeo, formed a company which went bankrupt in about 1415. The book of the creditors of Guglielmo and Bartolomeo del Portico, which covers the period 1416–18, shows *inter alia* the business and personal links that continued to bind the two men to the di Poggio. Their creditors included Stefano del fu Nicolao del fu Ceccorino di Poggio (for 2,830 florins of the total debts of 21,615 florins and 3 soldi), whilst among their debtors appear the heirs of Antonio and Paolo di Poggio. The two brothers and their families lived in a house in corte de' Overardi in *contrada* S. Michele which adjoined the houses or stables of Stefano di Poggio and his brother; and they possessed other property also in the corte de' Overardi that touched on one side the church of S. Lorenzo in Poggio and on another a small house belonging to Giovanni di Poggio and his brother. In the settlement that Guglielmo and Bartolomeo del Portico reached with their creditors, Guglielmo's procurator was Giovanni del fu Chello di Poggio.[53] The links between the two families were to continue into the sixteenth century. When the di Poggio family attempted to overthrow the state in 1522, a later Guglielmo and Antonio del Portico were numbered among the rebels.[54]

Despite the bankruptcy of 1415, Bartolomeo del Portico continued to prosper. He was assessed at the very considerable sum of 36 florins for the forced loan of 1431;[55] and between 1432 and 1434 Bartolomeo was buying enormous quantities of land in and around Lucca, particularly the lands of Paolo Guinigi in the territory of Pietrasanta, Camaiore, Massa, and surrounding areas which had been confiscated by the commune of Lucca and which were being sold by auction at this time.[56] Bartolomeo del

[52] Baroni, Notizie genealogiche, MS 1126, fos. 289ʳ–376ʳ.

[53] AN 371(3) (ser Paolo Michele Federighi Bianchi da Massa), fos. 2ʳ–26ᵛ. See also AN 370(1), fos. 121ʳ–125ᵛ.

[54] Berengo, *Nobili e mercanti*, 91.

[55] ASL Imprestiti, 21, fo. 36ʳ. The sum of 36 florins had been reduced from the larger one of 55 florins. Bartolomeo del Portico was assessed in 1431 in the *contrada* of S. Lucia verso Fillungo, the great house in corte de' Overardi having passed to the del Portico creditors of 1415.

[56] ASL Archivio Arnolfini, 2, fos. 1ʳ–27ʳ.

Portico's wealth was matched by his growing political influence. He was Gonfaloniere di Giustizia for the first time in November/December 1431; Anziano in November/December 1433; and during these years represented the republic in missions to Genoa, Siena, and Bologna. Bartolomeo was clearly flourishing during the early years of the restored republic, but this success ended dramatically in the political crisis that shook Lucca in the spring of 1434.

In July 1431 Stefano del fu Nicolao di Poggio was detained by the Duke of Milan, accused of having communicated with the enemy (presumably with the Florentines). At this time the Lucchese authorities displayed trust in their citizen, writing to the Duke that Stefano had held the keys of the city and suburbs at the time of the Florentine siege, and of his loyalty to the *patria*.[57] Three years later Stefano di Poggio, ser Cristoforo Turrettini, and messer Ceccardo da Massa were all arrested in Lucca. Stefano di Poggio and Ceccardo da Massa were despatched to imprisonment in Milan; ser Cristoforo Turrettini was detained in Genoa.[58] The political records for this period are entirely chaotic, partly, no doubt, because those banished included the keeper of the records—the chancellor ser Cristoforo Turrettini. Lucchese chroniclers speak of certain 'novelties' that were attempted in Lucca on 23 April 1434. Later, in letters addressed to the Lucchese authorities asking for clemency, ser Cristoforo confessed to personal ambition, which had caused him as chancellor to promote the election to office of men favourable to himself, whilst Stefano di Poggio admitted to ambitions of political pre-eminence.[59] Whatever the details, it seems clear that the machinations of April 1434 involved Bartolomeo del Portico. Bartolomeo became absent from council meetings, and was replaced in political offices at precisely this time. Some of the chroniclers include Bartolomeo del Portico as one of the guilty men. And writing at the end of the fifteenth century, the generally well-informed Nicolao Tegrimi referred to the execrable attachment to faction that resulted in the poisoning in Pietrasanta of Bartolomeo del Portico, Iacopo Arnolfini, and Tegrimo Tegrimi.[60] Whether Bartolomeo del Portico really did die of poison, it is impossible to adjudge. But he was

[57] Fumi (ed.), *Regesti*, 28, 101, 108, 137. Anz. Temp. Lib. 5, fo. 87^{r-v}.

[58] Fumi (ed.), *Regesti*, 671, 701, 713, 715, 743, (b) 13, 14.

[59] Rif. 14, pp. 750–2; Fumi (ed.), *Regesti*, (b) 13, 14. In recommending clemency, it was noted in the General Council that both men had committed far graver offences than those to which they referred in their letters.

[60] N. Tegrimi, *La vita di Castruccio Castracani de gl'Antelminelli Principe de Lucca, tradotta da Giusto Compagni da Volterra* (Lucca, 1556), 111.

taken ill in Pietrasanta, drew up his will there on 17 June 1434, and died very soon after.[61] In summary: although I have found no official record linking Bartolomeo del Portico with the plot of April 1434, there is strong circumstantial evidence that he was exiled from Lucca because of his participation or perceived participation in the plot. Although there is only the later testimony of Nicolao Tegrimi, it is possible that Bartolomeo del Portico was murdered on his way into exile. And there is stronger evidence that Bartolomeo's death was widely believed to have resulted from unnatural causes. Whilst all these events were taking place, Pietro Cenami headed the Lucchese state as Gonfaloniere di Giustizia for the months May/June 1434.

In his will, Bartolomeo del Portico asked to be buried, should he die in the district of Lucca, in the tomb or *avello* of his ancestors in the Dominican church of S. Romano. After various pious bequests, he instituted as his universal heirs (failing the future birth of any sons) his two infant daughters Nicoloxia and Margarita. And these two wealthy heiresses were entrusted to the guardianship of Bartolomeo's wife, Clara, the daughter of the late Forteguerra Totti; to Clara's mother, Nicoloxia, widow of Forteguerra Totti; and to the Lucchese merchant Lazzaro del fu Nese Franchi. Any two of these guardians were granted authority to act with or without the approval of the third; and in the succeeding months Nicoloxia and Lazzaro appear regularly in the notarial acts exercising this charge.[62] According to tradition, one of Bartolomeo del Portico's daughters had been promised in marriage to a member of the di Poggio family, perhaps to the young son of Stefano di Poggio.[63] On 30 March 1435, Nicoloxia and Lazzaro, as guardians of the infant del Portico daughters, assigned (*assignaverunt*) the two girls with their entire inheritance to the discreet and prudent man Pietro del fu Giusfredo de' Cenami, merchant of Lucca. Specifically, Pietro Cenami received Nicoloxia with all her property and rights on behalf of his son Francesco; and he received Margarita similarly on behalf of his nephew Rodolfo, son of Pietro's late brother Dino.[64] The totality of the girls' inheritance was taken as dowries on behalf of Francesco and Rodolfo Cenami, both of whom were still minors. The marriages were not, in fact, consummated

[61] AN Originali Testamenti, 11 (ser Domenico Ciomucchi), fos. 157^{r}–159^{v}.

[62] AN 429 (ser Domenico Arrighi (Ciomucchi)), fos. 10^{v}–12^{r}, 16^{r}–17^{r}, 36^{v}; 548(1) (ser Ciomeo Pieri), fo. 1^{r}; 580 (ser Francesco di ser Bartolomeo da Massa), fos. 70^{r}–71^{r}.

[63] See, e.g., the extraordinarily jumbled version of the story preserved in the miscellaneous collection of historical writings in BSL MS 47, Antichità di Lucca, fo. 157^{r-v}.

[64] AN 429 (ser Domenico Arrighi), fos. 37^{r}–38^{v}.

until 1448. The seizure of the entire inheritance as dowries was to cause problems. Just before the marriages took place, the earlier agreement was revoked, and the dowries were reduced to three-fifths of the total inheritance. The remaining two-fifths of the inheritance now passed into the unfettered possession of Nicoloxia and her sister Margarita. The settlement of 1447–8 was accompanied by the honouring of debts that the two girls, as heirs of Bartolomeo del Portico, owed to the sons and heirs of Stefano di Nicolao di Ceccorino di Poggio.[65] The story is a complicated one. What emerges clearly is that Pietro Cenami appropriated to himself the daughters and fortune of Bartolomeo del Portico, whose political exile and death occurred whilst Pietro was Gonfaloniere di Giustizia. Bartolomeo del Portico was closely attached to the di Poggio clan, and the verdict of the chroniclers that Pietro Cenami was murdered by Marco Antonio and Lazzaro di Francesco di Poggio because of a personal vendetta is entirely plausible.

The conflict with the di Poggio was paralleled by a quarrel with certain of the Ridolfi, who were also to be involved in Cenami's murder. Guaspare di Andrea Ridolfi had died in Genoa in 1427, leaving four infant sons: Andrea, Paolo, Matteo, and Giovanni. As guardians of his sons and heirs he appointed Paolo Guinigi, then lord of Lucca; Guaspare's widow, Maria; and Forteguerra Totti. Paolo Guinigi declined the office of guardian from the beginning, excusing himself because of the number of his own sons and the burden of government. By January 1431 two of the sons, Andrea and Giovanni, had died; Forteguerra Totti was also dead; and Maria was unable to act as guardian because of her remarriage. This situation was brought to the attention of the *Podestà* by Bartolomeo Ridolfi, who claimed to be next of kin of the late Guaspare, and on 9 January 1431 Bartolomeo was appointed guardian.[66] On 17 March 1431 the number of guardians was augmented by the inclusion of Nicolao di Antonio Ridolfi, and very soon there is evidence of friction between the two guardians Bartolomeo and Nicolao. By April 1432, Bartolomeo Ridolfi was insisting that a third guardian be added to make up the original complement. This move was made in the absence of Nicolao, but at Bartolomeo's insistence the name of a third guardian was advanced and accepted: Pietro del fu Giusfredo Cenami. Pietro Cenami opposed being appointed, like Paolo Guinigi before him, on the grounds of his burdensome public duties, but these objections were overruled, and Pietro

[65] AN 553 (ser Ciomeo Pieri), fos. 139^{v}–142^{v}, 207^{r}–211^{r}.
[66] AN 385 (ser Massino di Bartolomeo da Pietrasanta), fos. 124^{r}–125^{r}.

was formally appointed on 14 June 1432. From this date Bartolomeo Ridolfi and Pietro Cenami appear regularly in the notarial records acting on behalf of the minor sons of the late Guaspare Ridolfi. Nicolao Ridolfi, at least in the period immediately after June 1432, appears much less frequently in his capacity as guardian.[67] Not only does Pietro Cenami emerge as the candidate of Bartolomeo Ridolfi in some kind of personal tussle with Nicolao, but the way in which Cenami executed his duties towards Guaspare Ridolfi's young sons also seems to have aroused antagonisms. These sons held certain property in Lucca that had belonged to Guido da Pietrasanta, over which the commune of Lucca retained the option of repurchase. On 4 June 1434 Pietro Cenami advised that this property should be repurchased, and this was approved at the meeting of the General Council by ninety-four votes to eleven.[68] On this occasion Pietro Cenami's role as 'padre della patria' may well have been in conflict with his responsibilities as guardian. It is impossible to glean anything from the laconic official records, but there is certainly a tradition that this affair was resented by the Ridolfi.[69] Although the evidence is less compelling than in the case of the di Poggio, there is clear reason to believe that Nicolao Ridolfi also participated in the murder of Pietro Cenami because of private quarrels and in pursuit of a vendetta.

These private quarrels were transformed into events of political significance in part by the prominence of the men involved, but more so by the neighbourhood divisions and clientage networks of fifteenth-century Lucca. The di Poggio were a very ancient family, whose history can be traced, convincingly, from the twelfth century. They were very numerous—a fact which, in part, can be attributed to the prolific Porco di Poggio of the twelfth century. And by a veritable translocation of rural mentalities into an urban setting, they came to dominate that quarter of the city named after the family (il Poggio). Here were the houses of the family; the di Poggio tower, which was in a dilapidated condition by the late fifteenth century, and fell down, killing a number of the family, in 1495; the *loggia* built in or after 1378, where the di Poggio family could relax and play chess (*giocare a scacchi*); and the church of S. Lorenzo in Poggio, whose affairs were regulated by the di Poggio, and whose rector was elected by them. From at least the fourteenth century the family was

[67] Ibid., fos. 153^{v}–154^{v}, 198^{r}–201^{v}, 205^{r}, 207^{r}–212^{r}, 231^{v}, 233^{r}, 293^{v}–294^{r}; AN 429 (ser Domenico Arrighi), fos. 32^{r}–33^{r}; 463, fos. 68^{r}–73^{r}, 75^{r}–80^{v}.

[68] Rif. 14, pp. 388, 525.

[69] See, e.g., BSL MS 38, Martino Bernardini, Ricordi Storici, fo. 125^{v}.

organized as a *consorteria*, ruled by an elected consul who was assisted by two councillors. In a description of the residents of Lucca of 11 January 1371, it is said of the *contrada* of S. Lorenzo in Poggio: 'sono tutti di Poggio salvo 3.'[70] In 1390, when the consul summoned a meeting of all the *consorti*, twenty-two men obeyed the summons, of whom all but the son of the consul himself, the four sons of the late Chello di Lemmo di Poggio, and the brothers Tomasino and Nicolao di ser Franceschino bore different patronymics.[71] The di Poggio had a distinguished reputation for public violence, a reputation that finds ample confirmation in the court records.[72] When Pietro Cenami quarrelled with the di Poggio, he did not merely challenge specific individuals, but rather a powerful family clan with numerous dependants in the city and bands of supporters in the mountains. The geographical distribution of the people involved in the events of 2–3 June 1436 is indicated in Figure 2.2.

That the di Poggio should have attacked Pietro Cenami is less remarkable than the feeble and highly ineffective organization and execution of the plot. Marco Antonio and Lazzaro di Poggio were accompanied by Lorenzo di Gerardo de' Cattani, who was related to the di Poggio by marriage and who had acted as agent for Stefano di Poggio in the payment of the forced loan of 1431.[73] The conspiracy involved Tommaso Mercati, who was resident within the di Poggio labyrinth of S. Lorenzo in Poggio, and ensnared the weaver Bartolomeo del fu Iacopo, whose connection with the di Poggio seems clear if entirely unretrievable.[74] Stefano di Poggio himself, from the Milanese confinement which he was to endure for a further three years, appears to have had some hand in the business.[75] But in every respect the attack on Pietro Cenami was a much less serious threat to the Lucchese state than the better known di Poggio rising of 1522. In 1522, following the murder of the Gonfaloniere di Giustizia Girolamo Vellutelli, the di Poggio fortified themselves in their houses around piazza S. Lorenzo, and received armed support from their

[70] Ibid., fo. 346^{v}.

[71] Baroni, Notizie genealogiche, MS 1128, fos. 1^{r}–183^{v}; M. E. Bratchel, 'The *Consorteria* in 15th-Century Tuscany: In Pursuit of a Historical Definition', *Unisa Medieval Studies*, i (1983), 19–24; BSL MS 62, Memorie diverse di Lucca, pp. 378–9.

[72] See, e.g., SB 161, fo. 217^{r-v}.

[73] BSL MS 116, Notizie di Lucca, fo. 56^{v}; ASL Imprestiti, 21, fo. 5^{r}.

[74] For the Mercati, see Baroni, Notizie genealogiche, MS 1120, fos. 219^{r}–224^{r}. Bartolomeo del fu Iacopo is a very obscure figure. He and his brother Antonio, if I have correctly identified him, appear briefly in the court of merchants of 1432 as residents in the *contrada* of S. Giustina: ASL Corte de' mercanti, Cause civili, 150, fo. 45^{r}.

[75] Rif. 15, pp. 66–7, 399.

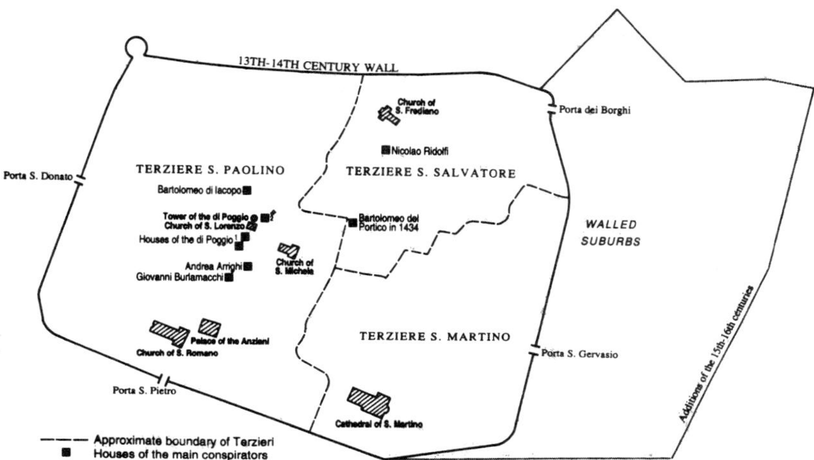

FIG. 2.2 The murder of Pietro Cenami (1436): approximate location of the houses of the main conspirators in June 1436. [1]Including Lorenzo Cattani who lived in the house of Stefano di Poggio with Marco Antonio and Lazzaro di Poggio, and also including the house of Tommaso Mercati. [2]Traditional place of residence of the del Portico. *Note*: In Feb. 1431 the *contrade* of S. Bartolomeo del Gallo and SS. Giovanni and Reparata were taken from the *terziere* of S. Paolino and added to S. Martino: Rif. 14, pp. 115, 117.

possessions in the mountains.[76] In 1436 it is difficult to imagine any other outcome than the swift flight into exile of the two young di Poggio brothers and their companion, Lorenzo Cattani. The contrast may in part be explained by the forced absence of Stefano di Poggio, an experienced figure who had been a member of Paolo Guinigi's council from at least 1419. This, together with the developmental cycle of Italian households, may have conspired to ensure that in the critical months of 1436 the di Poggio in Lucca were over-represented by young men of impetuous nature and little foresight. But both Paolo and Taddeo di Poggio were also in Lucca at this time, neither of whom was implicated in the plot. The events of June 1436 are more easy to understand if generated by immediate outside pressures than as a product of the reasoned deliberations of the di Poggio clan.

There is a long-standing tradition that the murder of Pietro Cenami was occasioned by differences within the Lucchese oligarchy over foreign

[76] Berengo, *Nobili e mercanti*, 83–107.

policy, and that the Florentines themselves were in some way responsible for his death. The seventeenth-century writer Antonio Iova reproduced the details of a debate which he claimed took place in a *Colloquio* summoned by Pietro Cenami whilst he was Gonfaloniere di Giustizia, in May 1434. According to this account, the Duke of Milan was pressing Lucca to renew the war with Florence. A peace party within the *Colloquio*, headed by Giusfredo Cenami, argued for the preservation of peace with Florence, claiming that the war would be an unjust one, and that God would so judge it. Giovanni, the brother of Stefano di Nicolao di Poggio, then arose to refute Cenami's arguments. Di Poggio spoke of the great faith with which Filippo Maria Visconti of Milan had always defended Lucca, and he urged the assembly to place obligation before self-interest. Di Poggio spoke with such eloquence that he won his case. But, according to Antonio Iova, this debate produced great antagonism between the factions, and lay at the roots of the outburst of June 1436.[77]

In reality, the story of the *Colloquio*, if dated to May 1434, makes no sense. Renewed hostilities with Florentine forces did not begin until late in 1436. No mention of the *Colloquio* survives in the official records. It might have taken place, as suggested by the sixteenth-century historian Nicolao Tucci, in the period following Pietro Cenami's murder.[78] This later date would sit more comfortably with the course of events, and would help to explain the bitterness of the debate between representatives of the Cenami and the di Poggio families. But if the *Colloquio* took place after 3 June 1436, it is no longer possible to attribute Cenami's murder to a festering debate aggravated by the devastation of renewed warfare. The story told by canon Gio: Lunardo Dalli is a very different one. According to Dalli, the Florentines remained constant in their ambition to conquer Lucca, but recognized that the greatest obstacle in their path was the 'sagacità' of Pietro Cenami. Taking advantage of the ancient 'inimicizia' between Cenami and the di Poggio family, the Florentines arranged to have Cenami murdered in the hope of capturing Lucca during the ensuing conflict. Unfortunately for Dalli's credibility, he conflates the murder of Cenami with the later conspiracy of ser Tommaso Lupardi. The greater part of Dalli's account in fact relates to the negotiations of ser Tommaso Lupardi with the Venetians and Florentines.[79] An understandable distrust

[77] BSL MS 2599, Antonio Iova, Annali Historici, pp. 887–97.

[78] BSL MS 108, Nicolao Tucci, Historie di Lucca, fos. 340v–341r. See also MS 26, Alessandro Spada, Storia di Lucca, fos. 96r–98v.

[79] BSL MS 939, Gio: Lunardo Dalli, Cronache, pp. 165–7. It may be noted that in Dalli's chronicle ser Tommaso Lupardi was executed in 1429 by Paolo Guinigi: ibid., p. 101. See also BSL MS 710, Salvator Dalli, Croniche, fo. 144r.

of Dalli has encouraged modern historians to dismiss all notions of Florentine involvement.[80] They may have been wrong to do so.

In the Archivio di Stato in Florence there is a letter to Cosimo de' Medici from Giovanni di messer Iacopo de' Viviani dated 26 November 1437.[81] Iacopo del fu Giovanni de' Viviani was a doctor of law much favoured by Paolo Guinigi during the early years of his reign. In 1407 Viviani committed unspecified great crimes against Guinigi, for which he was banished. He was pardoned and allowed to return to Lucca in 1410. By 1429 Viviani had so far recovered Guinigi's favour that he was sent as ambassador to Florence in a vain bid to avert war. Again Viviani betrayed his master: according to some accounts, it was Viviani who encouraged Florence to attack Lucca in order to restore that city to liberty.[82] Messer Iacopo de' Viviani's life remained turbulent after the restoration of the republic. In November 1432 messer Iacopo was accused of leaving Lucca with his wife, children, and servants whilst Florence and Lucca were at war and settling in the city of Florence despite his promise to the Anziani of Lucca that he would not remain in Florentine territory. Further, he was accused of conspiring with the Florentines and of writing letters with the intention of causing scandal and discord in Lucca.[83] As a result, messer Iacopo was sentenced to death, and his sons were exiled. In March 1449, after messer Iacopo's death, his son Giovanni pleaded successfully for permission to return to 'sua dolcissima patria'.[84] It is with this Giovanni di messer Iacopo de' Viviani that we are presently concerned. In the letter that Giovanni de' Viviani wrote to Cosimo de' Medici he made mention of the young exiled members of the di Poggio family (*questi giovani di Poggio*): clearly a reference to Marco Antonio and Lazzaro di Francesco di Poggio. Viviani spoke of their desperate state and of how they were likely to die of hunger. He requested Cosimo not to abandon them, and asked that they be sent 100 florins to enable them to live. The evidence, of course, is not conclusive. If the young di Poggio brothers received largess

[80] Acton, *La morte di Pietro Cenami*, 30–2. Luzzati, 'Pietro Cenami', in *Dizionario biografico degli italiani*, xxiii (Rome, 1979), 502, speaks only of the 'vendetta privata'.

[81] MAP, xi. 143.

[82] Baroni, Notizie genealogiche, MS 1139, fos. 225^r–248^r; ASL Biblioteca (Manoscritti), 38, Giuseppe Civitali, Storia di Lucca, fos. 389^r, 391^v; Machiavelli, *Istorie fiorentine*, i. 209.

[83] SB 160, fos. 127^r–128^r. This volume is in a very mutilated condition, and I am most grateful to Dr Giorgio Tori of the Archivio di Stato in Lucca for making special arrangements to enable me to consult it.

[84] Rif. 17, pp. 97–8. Giovanni's newly discovered affection for Lucca was short-lived. By Oct. 1452 he was again writing to the Medici of his 'ingrata patria', pledging his support to the Medici, and requesting a Florentine wife of good family for his only son: MAP, xvii. 96.

from Cosimo de' Medici, this may have been because, as important Lucchese exiles, they were potentially useful to Florence, rather than as a reward for the murder of Pietro Cenami. If the young di Poggio sought refuge immediately after Cenami's murder in Florentine territory, they had little alternative, given the political geography of fifteenth-century Italy. But the cumulative evidence for Florentine complicity is rather stronger than has sometimes been claimed.

Florentine involvement would not be difficult to explain. Throughout the 1430s the General Council of Lucca responded to the threat posed by private citizens communicating with foreign princes with decrees that the Anziani must be informed of all letters to and from foreign lords and captains.[85] Despite such measures, there can be no doubt that the Florentines remained well informed on divisions within Lucchese political life. In the same letter in which he advised Cosimo de' Medici to succour the di Poggio exiles, Giovanni de' Viviani begged Cosimo not to show favour to a nephew of messer Ceccardo da Massa. Messer Ceccardo, then 'fortunately' banished from Lucca, was described by Giovanni de' Viviani as a notorious Ghibelline, an enemy of Florence, and a great friend of the Duke of Milan. At this time of war, Viviani was hoping to receive information from inside Lucca.[86] And in time of peace, a series of rather obscure letters to Cosimo de' Medici indicates that the Florentines were following with great interest the misfortunes of Stefano di Poggio after 1434.[87] All the evidence suggests that the Florentines were well aware of the divisions within Lucchese society during the first decade of liberty as typified by the debate in the mysterious *Colloquio* of 1434/6, and by the veritable flourishing—in times both of peace and of war—of the political labels 'Guelph' and 'Ghibelline'. They were also fully cognizant of the peculiar stature of Pietro Cenami in the political life of the restored republic. Cenami was rather more than a private citizen. He wrote to the Medici in authoritative terms on behalf of Lucca, and the Medici turned to him with requests to influence judicial decisions in their favour in a spirit entirely reminiscent of correspondence directed to the Medici themselves.[88] It would be wrong to portray Pietro Cenami as an inflexible enemy of Florence, and the Florentines probably did not regard him as such. Indeed, it was the di Poggio clan that for centuries cherished a Ghibelline self-identity. These political labels were brandished in debate,

[85] Rif. 15, p. 360. See also Anz. Temp. Lib. 5, fo. 65^{v}.

[86] MAP, xi. 143.

[87] MAP, xii. 70, 78, 101.

[88] MAP, xii. 60, 78, 101. See also ibid. 100, 108.

but retained little real content in a world where the prime concern of the state was survival, and where individual family allegiances to outside powers changed with bewildering rapidity according to transient interests. Pietro Cenami did not assume the mantle of one of the notorious Lucchese Ghibellines who appear from time to time in the Florentine records. But there was every reason for the Florentines to anticipate that the removal of so prominent a figure would result in factional strife that might be turned to their advantage, particularly if the imminent renewal of hostilities was already anticipated.[89] The course of parallel conspiracies throughout the fifteenth century suggests that it is highly unlikely that the di Poggio brothers would have acted without consulting the Medici or their agents. Whether we should speak less of consultation than of Florentine encouragement and initiative it is impossible to determine.

In other cases the evidence of Florentine involvement is unambiguous. During the first Florentine war, the Florentines made a number of attempts to conquer Lucca by suborning Lucca's foreign-born defenders. The most familiar episodes of this type are the corruption of Giovan Matteo da Bologna, who offered to admit the Florentines by way of porta de' Borghi in 1430, and the bribing of the constable of Torrione di S. Giorgio in 1432.[90] In these cases the motives for treachery were chiefly mercenary. The best insight into such motives is offered by the examination by commissioners of ser Piero Paolo da Arezzo in January/February 1431.[91] According to the accusations made against him, in December 1430 ser Piero began to complain to a companion of his poverty, of the miserable pay that he was receiving from Lucca, and of his great desire to recover Florentine favour so as to be able to return home. Prompted by these ambitions and grievances, ser Piero spoke first with a certain Paolo da S. Vittoria whom—ser Piero then being *officialis custodie lucane civitatis*—he bribed with an offer of the post of notary to his office. Later he turned to a Florentine prisoner of war, Mazo da Arezzo, for whose custody he was responsible. In a series of conversations (most of which seem to have taken place in bed), ser Piero asked each man in turn to offer his services to the Florentine *condottiere* Niccolò Fortebraccio. The evidence hints at a larger body of unpaid foreigners within Lucca who might assist in handing the city over to the Florentine army.

[89] For a possible earlier Florentine-inspired attempt on the life of Pietro Cenami, see BSL MS 38, Martino Bernardini, Ricordi Storici, fo. 120^{r}.

[90] Rif. 14, pp. 46–7; BSL MS 26, Alessandro Spada, Storia di Lucca, fos. 94^{r}–95^{r}; MS 91, Storie di Lucca, fo. 57^{r}; MS 2599, Antonio Iova, Annali Historici, pp. 861–2, 874–5.

[91] SB 159, fos. 163^{r-v}, 182^{r}; Rif. 14, p. 115.

At time of war there is nothing surprising in the fact that some of Lucca's foreign-born stipendaries, particularly those exiled from their homes within the Florentine state, should offer to betray Lucca for monetary rewards and Florentine favour. More remarkable is the case of Nicolao del fu Lazzaro de' Guinigi.[92] According to the evidence presented against him, Nicolao Guinigi plotted in his own house in December 1430 with Agamennone, son of Nicolao Ruffo, Count of Cotrone and Marquis of Catanzaro.[93] Agamennone was another of the Florentine mercenaries captured and detained in Lucca at the end of 1430. At this meeting Nicolao Guinigi informed Agamennone that, for substantial financial or other rewards, he could become a very good and valuable friend of Florence during the present wars. Agamennone responded that he was very certain that Florence would be delighted to have such a friend in Lucca, and wanted to know what Nicolao would do in return for his money. Nicolao replied that he would reveal secrets, that he would use his large following in the city and state of Lucca in the interests of Florence, and that he would preserve the Garfagnana in its loyalty to Florence. Pressed further by Agamennone, Guinigi also promised to join his supporters to the Florentine mercenaries detained in Lucca in order to stir up a great commotion with shouts of 'Viva il popolo', whereby the palace might be attacked and the Anziani arrested. Nicolao Guinigi then arranged for a safe conduct for Agamennone Ruffo from the Lucchese captain Niccolò Piccinino, so that these plans could be communicated to the Florentines. Nicolao Guinigi also proposed to speak personally with the Florentines, under cover of a business trip to Siena, and meanwhile offered himself as surety that Agamennone would return from Florentine territory within the appointed time. Agamennone's mission was not particularly successful: he was able to speak only with the Florentine captain, the Count of Urbino. Agamennone returned to Lucca under the terms of his safe conduct, and throughout January 1431 there is the extraordinary spectacle of the two men parading through the streets of Lucca discussing the weak points in the city's defences and planning the best way to admit men to the city and to escape from it. To all these things Nicolao Guinigi allegedly confessed. He was fined 1,200 florins, under pain of execution, and exiled to Milan.

There are obvious problems in using the hostile court proceedings to

[92] SB 159, fos. 166^{r}–167^{v}, 178^{r}–179^{r}. The desperate financial position in which Nicolao di Lazzaro Guinigi found himself in 1430/1 is revealed in ASL Curia del Fondaco, 535, fo. 4^{r}.

[93] For Nicolao Ruffo of Calabria (Marquis of Cotrone and Count of Catanzaro), see Archivio di Stato, Catanzaro, Fondo Diplomatico (Pergamene), 8 May 1406.

obtain a balanced view of Nicolao Guinigi's intentions. But it appears that even in a situation of war Guinigi was prepared to turn to the Florentines to advance his own interests. This is particularly significant in view of the long-standing attachment of the Guinigi family to the Milanese cause. It is true that Milan had had a hand in the downfall of Paolo Guinigi, but in the following decades Milan—and Niccolò Piccinino—continued to champion Guinigi interests. Again, the impression is irresistible that any attachment to outside forces was more likely to be determined by considerations of immediate advantage than by firm principles or permanent loyalties. Individual citizens were accused of being Guelphs, and therefore predisposed to hand Lucca over to the Florentines.[94] But any ideological association of Guelphism with republican liberty was clearly inappropriate in Lucca where the chief threat to republican liberty came from Florence. There was clearly a pro-Milanese party in Lucca, but gratitude to the Duke of Milan was tempered, in time of peace, by the desire to avoid actions that might provoke military retribution from Florence. Against this background the Guinigi plot of 1431, like the tangled relationship of the di Poggio with the Florentines throughout the 1430s, should be seen primarily as the self-serving manœuvres of ambitious and aggrieved men.

Throughout the 1430s the only Florentine plot that may have involved wider visions is that of ser Tommaso Lupardi in 1437.[95] The war with Florence that caused the deposition of Paolo Guinigi ended in 1433. Hostilities were renewed in 1436. At the insistence of Niccolò Piccinino, for the better prosecution of the war effort, a *balìa* of eight was appointed in November 1436 with full powers to treat with Piccinino for the defence of the liberty of Lucca. This *balìa* included ser Tommaso Lupardi.[96] In March 1437 ser Tommaso summoned to his house in the *contrada* of S. Cristoforo his friend the cloth-shearer Bartolomeo del fu Antonio Chelli, whom he asked to journey to Venice to seek an audience with the Doge. Bartolomeo was to ask the Doge to accept Lucca into his network of alliances, and if this proposal was favourably received, the Doge should send an agent to Castelnuovo di Garfagnana, whence he was to enter into negotiations with ser Tommaso Lupardi. In Venice, Bartolomeo was

[94] See, e.g., the accusations against the apothecary and Lucchese citizen Rustico del fu Antonio in ASL Podestà di Lucca, Inquisizioni, 5229, no foliation.

[95] Acton, *La morte di Pietro Cenami*, 45–69; SB 161, fos. 118^r–121^v.

[96] Rif. 15, pp. 102–3, 105–6. The other members of the *balìa* were maestro Antonio Arrighi, Lorenzo Buonvisi, Nicolao de' Burlamacchi, Tiero Gentili, Nicolao Streghi, Battista de' Arnolfini, and Giusfredo de' Cenami.

successful in gaining admission to the Doge, Francesco Foscari, who professed interest, but who insisted that the consent of Venice's Florentine allies must first be obtained. Communications with Florence caused delays, but the Florentines agreed enthusiastically to the proposals, and Bartolomeo Chelli began his return to Lucca. Meanwhile in Lucca, ser Tommaso tried unsuccessfully to raise a band of mercenaries, with whose support he hoped to force the Florentine alliance upon Lucca, and then entered into negotiations with conte Francesco Sforza, Captain of the League. In these negotiations ser Tommaso detailed plans to admit Sforza into the city. The plot was uncovered, by means of the inevitable informer. Bartolomeo Chelli was arrested on his return to Lucca, and was interrogated under torture, and ser Tommaso Lupardi was executed on 6 May 1437 for crimes against both the liberty of Lucca and the Duke of Milan.

There are highly revealing parallels between the pro-Florentine Lupardi conspiracy of 1437 and the mysterious whisperings that took place at the house of Nicolao Ridolfi in April 1436. The earlier event involved a plan to kill the *condottiere* Moretto da S. Nazario;[97] ser Tommaso Lupardi was very concerned to circumvent Moretto because of his known loyalty to the Duke of Milan. The earlier event involved a plan to kill Pietro Cenami, Giovanni da Ghivizzano, and maestro Antonio Arrighi. Pietro Cenami was murdered in June 1436. In March/April 1437 ser Tommaso Lupardi determined that if maestro Antonio Arrighi and Giovanni da Ghivizzano were not killed in the fighting when Sforza's troops entered Lucca, they (together with Azzo di Dino and Michele di Giovanni de' Guinigi) should immediately be despatched as prisoners to Florence or to some other suitable place.[98] In both cases it is impossible to determine whether Ghivizzano, Arrighi, and Cenami (during his lifetime) were the prime target of the conspirators because they were regarded as important obstacles to Florentine interests, because of their position of peculiar political pre-eminence within the Lucchese state, or because of purely personal animosities.

As always, the Lucchese court records are much more informative as a

[97] ASL Podestà di Lucca, Inquisizioni, 5229, no foliation.

[98] SB 161, fo. 120v. In order to clarify the chronology, it should be noted that the events of Apr. 1436 were brought to trial on 1 June 1436, two days before Pietro Cenami's murder. Sentence was passed on 12 June, and was witnessed by ser Tommaso Lupardi. Hostilities with Florence, delayed until the end of the year, were presaged by the invasion of Lucchese territory near Viareggio by the Florentine *condottiere* Nicolao da Pisa, noted in a letter from Lucca to the lords of Florence dated 26 June 1436: Fumi (ed.), *Regesti*, 790.

meticulous record of the course of events than as a guide to motivation. Ser Tommaso's insistence in his instructions to Bartolomeo Chelli that Lucca's entry into the League should not be prejudicial to Lucchese liberty seems to be in conflict with his later willingness to admit Sforza's troops, with the dire consequences for Lucca of sack and pillage that would inevitably have followed.[99] Ser Tommaso Lupardi's true intentions are now unrecoverable. In the judicial proceedings it was alleged that his interest lay in making himself lord of Lucca, like Paolo Guinigi before him. Ser Tommaso was certainly well connected. He was the son of a prominent notary, ser Domenico, and the husband of Maddalena Arnolfini. His brothers were married to Antonia and Gianella, the daughters of Michele di Lazzaro Guinigi.[100] Whether he enjoyed sufficient support to dream of lordship is not at all clear. Francesco Acton, in his account of the conspiracy published in 1882, explored the possibility that ser Tommaso was moved by a broader political vision: that he saw Lucca's future to lie with the three great Italian republics of Genoa, Florence, and Venice; that he was distressed by the devastation caused by the mercenary troops sent by Milan to the defence of Lucca; and that he was disillusioned by the uncertain and self-interested support coming from the Duke of Milan. There is little hard evidence for these propositions. If true, they would distinguish the Lupardi conspiracy from the unalloyed expediency that characterized other appeals by Lucchese factions to Florence in the troubled decade 1430–40.

The true dynamics behind the series of conflict situations that dominated Lucchese political life in the 1430s remain shadowy, as befits the succession of clandestine acts with which this chapter has been concerned. Whatever the details, there can be no doubt that conflict was generated within the relatively small political oligarchy that directed Lucchese affairs. Quarrels were of an intensely personal nature, centred on individual rivalries, the control of heiresses, and the private abuse of power. These quarrels were made more dangerous by the proximity of Florence, to which aggrieved parties could turn—whether for financial rewards, in pursuit of political ambitions, or in search of a less tangible

[99] SB 161, fo. 120v: 'E queste cose accadendo verosimilmente la città di Lucca poteva esser sottoposta al sacco, e sottomessa al perpetuo giogo dei Fiorentini, vi sarebbe seguita strage di uomini e di donne, e queste ultime sarebbero soggetto di violenze e di ratti.'

[100] I am grateful to Professor Meek for discussions of the marriage relationships between the sons of ser Domenico Lupardi and the daughters of Michele di Lazzaro Guinigi. For Antonia di Michele as wife of messer Filippo del fu ser Domenico Lupardi, see AN 405(4) (ser Matteo di Giovanni de' Nobili), fo. 11r.

dream of Lucca's real interests in the jungle of fifteenth-century Italian politics. Popularist elements are entirely lacking from this picture, except in such guises as the unfortunate Bartolomeo del fu Iacopo, who was bullied by the di Poggio to accompany them in their adventure against Pietro Cenami. This impression of popular passivity can be confirmed from the totality of evidence extant for Lucca in the first decade after the recovery of liberty. The crowd, in revenge for Florentine acts against Lucca, attacked Florentines resident in Lucca, and despoiled their property in May 1431. Such acts of popular loyalty were restrained by the Lucchese authorities,[101] but there is further evidence of popular anti-Florentine sentiment after 1436.[102] Machiavelli tells of fears in May 1437, during the harsh Florentine siege of Lucca, that the crowd might prove fickle ('Solo temevono i mobili animi della plebe') and look to their own safety rather than to the defence of liberty. The people were called into the piazza, and a rousing patriotic speech delivered by a leading citizen was sufficient to inspire the *plebe* to pledge their lives in defence of the city.[103] Elsewhere, although leading citizens periodically aspired 'to stir up a tumult', the majority of Lucca's inhabitants were mere spectators of the political dramas of the 1430s. Acts of violence within the urban setting recorded in the criminal court proceedings provide no evidence of serious social tensions. Boys threw stones at each other; women clawed each other's faces in domestic arguments; prostitutes were frequently involved in urban brawls. Officials of the commune, particularly officials of the courts executing their duties, were regular victims of attack. The paid foreign defenders of the city fought each other; and, generally, a large number of crimes of violence involved the floating population of foreigners. Young patrician bucks and their retinues stuck out their tongues and bit each other in ritual encounters. But a full reading of the criminal court proceedings for the period 1430–40 reveals remarkably little conflict that, even optimistically, can be described as inter-class.[104] Only in the succession of Guinigi plots is there some evidence, not of popular movements, but of wider popularist support. The Guinigi plots as a whole can be considered most conveniently in the next chapter.

To explain the essentially élitist nature of Lucchese political strife

[101] Anz. Temp. Lib. 5, fo. 51^{r-v}; BSL MS 26, Alessandro Spada, Storia di Lucca, fo. 95^{r}; MS 108, Nicolao Tucci, Historie di Lucca, fo. 336^{v}.

[102] Rif. 15, p. 317; SB 159, fos. 222^{v}, 247^{r}; ASL Podestà di Lucca, Inquisizioni, 5229, no foliation.

[103] Machiavelli, *Istorie fiorentine*, ii. 18–21.

[104] SB 159–61.

would be to anticipate the structural analysis of fifteenth-century Lucchese politics that will be attempted in Chapter 4. Here it would be appropriate to draw attention first to the sustained paternalistic concern of urban government throughout the difficult war years to avoid popular discontent by ensuring adequate food supplies and controlling grain prices.[105] Political office was open to all Lucchese citizens of legitimate birth who met the relevant age requirements, regardless of occupation or wealth. Eligibility for office was not determined, as in Florence, by scrutiny councils or guild membership. And election was direct rather than by lot. As will be seen, the potential eligibility of all Lucchese citizens for the highest office did not result in practice in the election of a particularly broadly based form of government. But the absence of statutory restrictions removed a source of group discontent clearly to be found elsewhere. Finally, in Lucca, as elsewhere in fifteenth-century Italy, residential arrangements, clientage, and familial bonds conspired to place great emphasis on 'vertical' rather than 'horizontal' social alignments. The Cenami or the di Poggio acted on the political stage surrounded by their *parenti* and *amici*. This subject has, of course, become highly polemicized. It is self-evident that to demonstrate the existence of vertical social divisions does not, and cannot, preclude the coexistence in the same society, place, time, or individual of horizontal or 'class' animosities.[106] For the present it suffices to note that clientage support for the patrician conspirators of the 1430s was itself markedly circumscribed, and that there is no evidence at all that any of these movements were inspired by—or embraced—serious social or 'class' cleavage.

[105] Rif. 14–15, *passim*.

[106] See the sensible remarks of K. Wrightson, 'The Social Order of Early Modern England', in L. Bonfield, R. Smith, and K. Wrightson (eds.), *The World We Have Gained: Histories of Population and Social Structure* (Oxford, 1986), 177–202.

3

LUCCA 1440–1494: AN UNQUIET STABILITY

Writing at the end of the fifteenth century, Nicolao Tegrimi compared the factional strife and civic discord of the period 1300–1440 with the peace and harmony that had marked the succeeding fifty years. From 1440 the citizens of Lucca were united in one spirit, one will: now all men were princes, no one was lord; all were servers, no one served.[1] It is certainly true that the period after 1440 can be characterized as a time of external peace. Peace was made with Florence in April 1438, and was renewed for fifty years in 1441. In the 1450s there was conflict in the Garfagnana with the forces of Borso d'Este, lord of Ferrara; 1477 saw skirmishes with the Genoese around Pietrasanta; in 1479 the Florentines again attacked Lucchese territory, and relations with Florence were often tense thereafter. But generally the peace established in 1441 was to endure. The constitutional dispensation that had survived the challenges of the 1430s was also to endure. But it would be somewhat sanguine to describe the domestic politics of Lucca after 1440 as harmonious, tranquil, or fraternal.

Underlying tensions are indicated by the repeatedly expressed concern of the General Council regarding citizens prowling the streets at night without lights. The di Poggio reappear with one of that clan's characteristic acts of improvident violence when, in 1461, Nicolao di Poggio murdered ser Giovanni di Antonio del Camarlingho, *officiale di Porta S. Pietro*, whilst ser Giovanni was performing his official duties. A price was placed on di Poggio's head: 200 ducats dead, 400 ducats if taken alive. The most spectacular evidence of endemic public violence was to come in July 1482 when the General Council adopted extraordinary measures to deal with the threat posed to the city by the scandalous lives and activities of certain individuals.[2] It was there decided that every member of the Council should write down from one to four names of those

[1] Tegrimi, *La vita di Castruccio Castracani*, 106–12.
[2] Rif. 21, pp. 371–4.

whom he knew in his conscience to be malefactors and whom it would be expedient to separate from the body (*consortio*) of good citizens. The names were to be arranged alphabetically by the chancellors, and those of the four people who appeared most often in the lists were to be presented before the Council. The Council was to vote, without hearing any pleas of self-defence from those accused; and if three-quarters of the General Council voted against the individuals named most often in the lists, they were to be banished from the city and territory of Lucca for a period of three years. Those condemned were to leave the city on the same day, and the territory by the morrow. They were not to return during the period of their exile under pain of death, though provisions were made for the exiles to appear and defend themselves should legal proceedings be instituted against them. In terms of this resourceful ordinance four men were duly banished from the city: Lorenzo di Guido, *caseario* (despite six votes in his favour); Mariano di Guglielmo, called del Priore (despite eleven votes in his favour); Piero di Sandro Ciampanti (despite nine votes to the contrary); and Andrea di Biagio Mei (despite the efforts of eighteen dissenters).

In the troubled history of Lucca during the half-century after 1440, two unifying themes stand out from a long and chaotic succession of plots and assaults. First, throughout the 1440s, and perhaps later, members of the Guinigi family engaged in a number of conspiracies to overthrow the restored republic and to re-establish Guinigi rule. During the middle years of the century, political challenges to the republic almost invariably involved Guinigi intrigues. The history of the Guinigi family is richly documented, as is the progress of the various schemes of Paolo Guinigi's son Ladislao to recover the family's lost power. Consequently, the history of the Guinigi conspiracies presents special opportunities to explore further problems of party formation and popular support raised in the previous chapter. Secondly, the later fifteenth century saw continued foreign involvement in the domestic politics of Lucca. Every major conspiracy involved correspondence with, and usually encouragement from, Lucca's neighbours. That Florence should have fostered internal dissension in the 1430s is hardly surprising, since for much of that earlier period Lucca and Florence were at war. After 1440 Lucca was ostensibly at peace with her neighbours. The latter period thus offers the opportunity to explore the aspirations of foreign powers and the contacts of leading Lucchese citizens with foreign powers, not in times of overt conflict, but in the more normal environment pertaining after the peace of 1438.

In September 1440 news reached Lucca that Ladislao and Stefano, sons of the late Paolo Guinigi, had been released from prison and were living in Gavi under the protection of Battista da Campofregoso.[3] Paolo and his sons had been handed over to the custody of the Duke of Milan following the *coup d'état* of August 1430. Other members of the Guinigi family had remained in Lucca, where, throughout the 1430s, their loyalty to the restored republic was considered suspect. In the winter of 1430/1 Nicolao di Lazzaro de' Guinigi had plotted with Florentine agents;[4] in 1433 six other members of the Guinigi family were exiled for allegedly scheming to destroy the liberty of the city.[5] Whatever the real threat posed to Lucca by Guinigi ambitions in the 1430s, the release of Ladislao and Stefano di Paolo was greeted with dismay. At a meeting of the General Council on 5 September 1440 it was decreed that no son of the late Paolo Guinigi might at any time enter the city or territory of Lucca, under pain of death; and that no Lucchese citizen or anyone living within the Lucchese state might correspond with the sons of the late Paolo without licence from the Anziani, under pain of a fine of 500 ducats. Any communications from the sons of Paolo Guinigi should be reported to the Anziani as soon as possible. The fears engendered by the release of Ladislao and Stefano soon proved to be well founded.

By the summer of 1442 Ladislao's headquarters at Gavi were the scene of a major conspiracy to restore Lucca to Guinigi rule. In early August Ladislao despatched Nicolao di Lazzaro Guinigi to Pavia, where he was to make contact with a Lucchese citizen by the name of Nicolao Antonio Cencio. Nicolao Antonio was brought back to Gavi, and, meeting Ladislao in the piazza, was drawn into a neighbouring church. There, standing before one of the altars, Ladislao Guinigi discussed his plans to recover the lordship of Lucca. From this and subsequent meetings it emerged that Nicolao Antonio was designated to organize support for Ladislao in Lucca among fifteen unnamed citizens believed to be sympathetic to the cause of a Guinigi restoration. A list of prominent opponents was compiled: messer Nicolao Manfredi, Battista Arnolfini, Lorenzo Buonvisi, Nicolao Burlamacchi, the sons of the late Pietro Cenami, Giovanni da Ghivizzano, and

[3] Rif. 15, pp. 508–9. In 1420 Paolo Guinigi had married his daughter Ilaria to Battista da Campofregoso, brother of messer Tommaso, Doge of Genoa. For Gavi at this time, see C. de Simoni (ed.), *Documenti ed estratti di documenti per la storia di Gavi* (Alessandria, 1896), 127–9.

[4] See above, pp. 44–5.

[5] Rif. 14, pp. 445–6, 450. The Guinigi banished in Dec. 1433 were Michele di Giovanni, Azzo di Dino, Francesco di Giovanni, Nicolao di Dino, Girolamo di Giovanni di Michele, and Filippo di Giovanni di Lazzaro di Nicolao.

Pietro Guinigi. These enemies were to be murdered and their property destroyed.[6]

The plot was uncovered, and the series of inquisitions then conducted by the *Podestà* of Lucca provide some vivid insights into the unofficial court established at Gavi by Ladislao and Stefano in the early 1440s. The parties frequently resorted to the church on the piazza as the appropriate locus for matters of great secrecy and import; they came together regularly at table, an event clearly symbolic of unity. The inner group included Nicolao di Lazzaro Guinigi, an active agent moving backwards and forwards on Guinigi business between Milan, Pavia, and Gavi. Another leading figure was Carlo Masi da Silico,[7] formerly resident in Camaiore, who was entrusted with arousing support in the Garfagnana, and who clearly harboured intense if unspecified private grievances against members of the ruling oligarchy in Lucca. Among Carlo's companions was a certain Paolo da Sutri, whilst ser Iacopo da Siena appears to have been attached to Nicolao Guinigi. Behind this group lay powerful Genoese forces. Ladislao Guinigi was absent in Genoa during part of the conspiracy; Baldassare Spinola and his entourage were dinner guests of the Guinigi at Gavi. The sons of Battista da Campofregoso, under whose protection the Guinigi lived, offered Ladislao 200 archers from Gavi and a further 200 from Genoa if he could show that he enjoyed the loyalty of his friends within the walls of Lucca and the support of the *contadini*.

As late as October 1442 the Lucchese authorities continued to fear that Ladislao would penetrate Lucchese territory.[8] In fact, the plotting of that year seems to have borne little fruit. But late in October 1443 Ladislao journeyed south to Sarzana, in territory then held by messer Spinetta Fregoso.[9] Here, with the assistance of the prior, frate Dionisio, Ladislao Guinigi took up secret residence in a cell in the Dominican friary of Sarzana, where he was to remain until Christmas. Ladislao was closeted in Sarzana together with Nicolao da Bologna, a servant of long standing, and Borso di maestro Giovanni da Firenze, who was in the pay of messer

[6] ASL Cause Delegate, 3, pp. 3–6, 11–28, 33–42.

[7] For Carlo Masi da Silico, see also ASL Archivio Diplomatico: Pergamene (Serviti), 4 Oct. 1437; ASG MS 5, Libro delle Compositioni et Gratie concesse dall'Eccellentissima Repubblica di Lucca al Castello et Huomini di Gallicano et sua Vicaria fino nell'anno 1450, fos. 1^r–5^r.

[8] Fumi (ed.), *Regesti*, 849.

[9] Sarzana had formed part of the larger Lucchese state of the early 14th cent., but had been lost to the Visconti of Milan in 1369. For the later history of Sarzana, see E. Branchi, *Storia della Lunigiana feudale*, 3 vols. (Bologna, 1971), repr. of Pistoia edn. of 1897–8, i. 229; ii. 60; iii. 758–72.

Spinetta Fregoso. These two men were sent on several occasions to Lucca, where plans were laid for the capturing of the city and its restoration to Guinigi rule. Within Lucca the principal conspirators were named as Azzo di Dino Guinigi and Orlando di Silvestro da Piastra. Also involved in the plot were a large number of Pisan exiles living in Lucca, headed by the very wealthy Battista Maggiolini, who offered to subvent Ladislao with an amount of 12,000 ducats. With this promise and with an offer of military assistance from the Pisan Guido dalla Coppa, *Podestà* of Valditaro, the conspirators corrupted Ghirardino, one of the German soldiers responsible for the custody of the city's defences. The Pisan community inside and outside of Lucca was organized to give assistance to the forces of Ladislao and of Guido dalla Coppa. And, as in 1442, the capture of the city was to presage the murder of a number of leading citizens. The plot miscarried because of the inevitable informer. Nicolao Grasso, a relative of Battista Maggiolini, revealed details to the authorities. Some of the local conspirators were executed; others were banished. Azzo Guinigi and Orlando da Piastra fled from the Lucchese state, and found refuge at Castelnuovo.[10]

These abortive efforts did not discourage Ladislao. Within months he was discussing new schemes with Antonio Anguilla and with the priest Iacopo Pieroni, both of Lucca. On various occasions during 1447 these two met together in Genoa with the Lucchese citizen Gerardo di Stefano Spada to plan the means whereby Ladislao Guinigi might assume the lordship of Lucca. As with past attempts, details of the plot reach us largely in the form of a meticulously recorded discussion of the best way by which Ladislao's forces might be admitted into the city. Ladislao himself was absent from Genoa, in Naples, when Gerardo Spada's support was first solicited; but the conspirators were encouraged in Genoa by Ladislao's two sons, Bartolomeo and Filippo. Spada then travelled to Savona in connection with his own business, and on his return to Genoa was presented to Ladislao. During this audience Gerardo Spada was asked to go to Lucca, to gauge support there for the Guinigi cause. On arriving in Lucca, he went to the house of the medical doctor Giovanni di Iacopo da Firenze, who showed himself a willing accomplice. The plot was revealed to the Lucchese authorities before Gerardo was able to speak to others in whom Ladislao had placed trust: Ruberto Angiorelli and Orso del fornaio. The events of 1447 follow a familiar pattern. Guinigi efforts to recapture

[10] Fumi (ed.), *Regesti*, 905; Rif. 16, pp. 403–4; BSL MS 47, Antichità di Lucca, fos. 298^{v}–299^{r}.

Lucca rested on the promised support of the Fregosi of Genoa and on the anticipated support of Guinigi friends within Lucca. The threat to Lucchese liberty was revealed by an informer: the priest Iacopo Pierini, who had accompanied Gerardo Spada on his mission from Genoa to Lucca. For his part in the conspiracy, Giovanni di Iacopo da Firenze was exiled to Ancona, together with his son Iacopo. Gerardo Spada was banished 200 miles from Lucca.[11]

The year 1447 saw the last recorded attempt by Ladislao Guinigi to recover his political inheritance.[12] Some Lucchese chroniclers viewed Ladislao as the real force behind the *coup d'état* attempted by Michele Guerrucci in 1460.[13] The Guerrucci affair raises many problems, as will appear later in the chapter; but the view of Michele Guerrucci as the agent of the Guinigi is clearly mistaken. At the same time, the legacy of the Guinigi was to trouble Lucca long after the conspiracies of the early 1430s and the adventures of Ladislao of the 1440s. Following the events of August 1430, those children of Paolo and of Ladislao Guinigi who were still minors were held in the custody and at the expense of Lucca.[14] They were released in 1436, and sent to Milan at the request of the Duke. Despite promises that Pippa, the daughter of Paolo Guinigi, would not be married to any powerful man who might threaten Lucchese interests, Pippa by 1442 was the wife of Tommaso Ravaschieri, a relative of the Campofregosi Doge of Genoa.[15] Ravaschieri claimed his wife's dowry-rights and inheritance, a claim resisted by Lucca partly because the property of Paolo Guinigi had been confiscated in 1431[16] and partly because the Lucchese authorities had enjoyed no success in recovering large sums of money allegedly deposited by the late lord of Lucca with Venetian banks.[17] Ravaschieri was dead by 1447, but Pippa continued to pursue her rights.[18] And the situation was made more complicated by the fact that the Genoese had seized possession of Pietrasanta from Lucca in

[11] Rif. 16, pp. 747–8, 755, 760, 770–5, 786, 789; 17, pp. 58, 85, 132–3, 158.

[12] According to Vincenzo Santini, Ladislao in 1457 used traditional Guinigi support in Pietrasanta in an abortive attempt to return to power in Lucca: Santini, *Versilia centrale*, ii. 99.

[13] See, e.g., BSL MS 108, Nicolao Tucci, Historie di Lucca, fos. 348^{v}–349^{r}. Others name Ladislao's sons as the figures behind the 1460 plot: BSL MS 47, Antichità di Lucca, fos. 182^{r}–183^{r}. Some sources see Ladislao behind the attempt on Camaiore in 1457: Mazzarosa, *Storia di Lucca*, ii. 21.

[14] Rif. 14, pp. 423, 425, 758.

[15] Fumi (ed.), *Regesti*, 809, 836, 852.

[16] SB 160, fo. 107^{r-v}.

[17] Fumi (ed.), *Regesti*, 844.

[18] Ibid. 1043, 1351.

1436.[19] A settlement of sorts was reached in the 1460s, but the whole affair was finally terminated only in 1501.[20] In 1501 Pippa came to Lucca, as heir, to demand the dowries of Ilaria del Carretto, second wife of Paolo Guinigi; of Piacentina, his third wife; of Iacopa di Ugolino Trinci, fourth wife and Pippa's own mother; and of Maria da Camerino, wife of the late Ladislao. Though denying her claims, Lucca at last offered a monetary settlement that Pippa, with the consent of her son Paolo and of her grandson Costantio, was able to accept.

The threat posed by exiled members of the Guinigi family clearly owed a great deal to external support. Paolo Guinigi's daughter Ilaria had married Battista da Campofregoso, and thereafter Guinigi ambitions were promoted by the powerful Fregosi family in Genoa and in the Lunigiana. The *condottiere* Niccolò Piccinino had been much favoured by Paolo Guinigi. In the Duke of Milan's service, Piccinino was despatched periodically to Lucca during the Florentine wars of the 1430s. In Lucca, Piccinino proved a pressing advocate of Guinigi interests. In 1433 and again in 1436 it was Piccinino who worked to obtain the release from Lucca of Paolo's daughter Pippa.[21] It was because of Piccinino's intercession that Azzo and Nicolao di Dino, Filippo di Giovanni di Lazzaro, and Michele, Francesco, and Girolamo di Giovanni Guinigi, exiles of 1433, were permitted to return to Lucca in the summer of the following year.[22] And it was Niccolò Piccinino who intervened to save Nicolao di Lazzaro Guinigi when in 1436 he returned to the Lucchese state, contrary to the terms of his banishment. Indeed, Nicolao di Lazzaro had returned to Lucca in the military service of Piccinino.[23] Behind both Piccinino and the Genoese lurked the Duke of Milan, employer of the former and sometime overlord of the latter. The continuing relationship between Milan and the Guinigi is ambiguous, but the Lucchese authorities expressed fears on several occasions that the Duke of Milan was being insufficiently vigilant in his custody of the Guinigi in exile.[24]

Guinigi sympathizers within Lucca are less easy to identify. The Lucchese court records conspire, in the public interest, to conceal the

[19] Ibid. 852, 1123, 1163; ASCP, A3, Civile—Frammenti filze giusdicenti (1378–1493) (1448), fos. 8^r–9^r.

[20] Fumi (ed.), *Regesti*, 1470, 1484; BSL MS 91, Storie di Lucca, fos. 79^v–81^r.

[21] Fumi (ed.), *Regesti*, 465, 809.

[22] Rif. 14, pp. 527–8. For a selective genealogy of the Guinigi, see Table 3.1.

[23] Rif. 15, pp. 103–4.

[24] According to later Lucchese sources, Ladislao's military talents were utilized by Milan even during the period of his detention in the 1430s. See, e.g., BSL MS 2599, Antonio Iova, Annali Historici, p. 874.

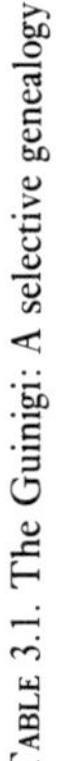

TABLE 3.1. The Guinigi: A selective genealogy

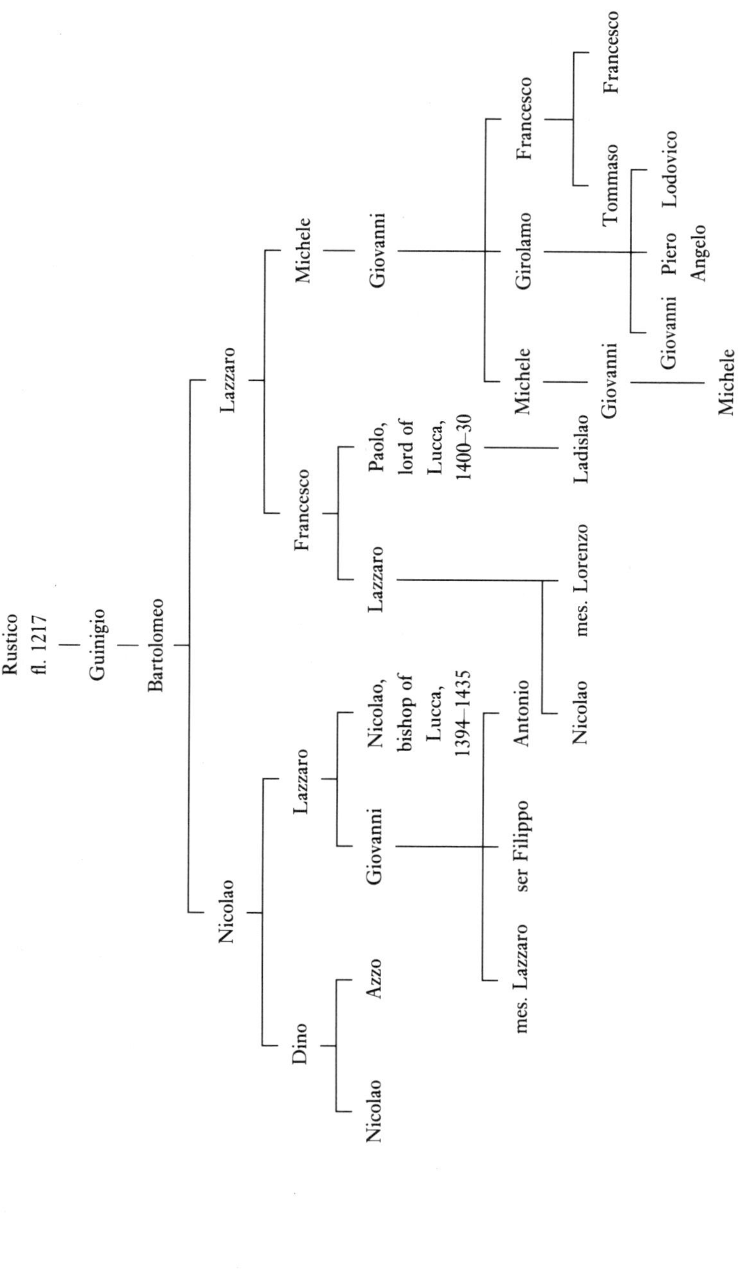

- Rustico fl. 1217
  - Guinigio
    - Bartolomeo
      - Nicolao
        - Dino
          - Nicolao
          - Azzo
        - Lazzaro
          - Giovanni
            - mes. Lazzaro
            - ser Filippo
            - Antonio
          - Nicolao, bishop of Lucca, 1394–1435
      - Lazzaro
        - Francesco
          - Lazzaro
            - Nicolao
            - mes. Lorenzo
          - Paolo, lord of Lucca, 1400–30
            - Ladislao
        - Michele
          - Giovanni
            - Michele
              - Giovanni
                - Michele
            - Girolamo
              - Giovanni
              - Piero
              - Angelo
              - Lodovico
            - Francesco
              - Tommaso
              - Francesco

names of men who might have been implicated in the succession of Guinigi plots. This, together with the cautious treatment of offenders, has caused later writers to emphasize the large and powerful following of the Guinigi in Lucca.[25] The caution, no doubt, was in part engendered by a respect for the Guinigi's foreign protectors. But Ladislao himself was confident that he enjoyed significant support within Lucca, and particularly within the Lucchese state. Despite deliberate reticence, the court and political records reveal a good deal about the nature of this support and about politico-personal grievances in Lucca after 1430.

Support for Ladislao might most obviously have been expected from within the ranks of the Guinigi family itself. Berengo, writing of sixteenth-century Lucca, claimed that the great Lucchese families still 'appear as monolithic blocks, not fractured but rendered even stronger by the multitude of their men and by the internal web of family relationships'.[26] It is true that Randolph Starn has argued that, by the fifteenth century, 'blanket condemnations of entire families' were becoming an increasingly rare reminder of the ethos of an earlier age when the communes sought to assert themselves against the great family clans by whom they were ruled and with whom the commune itself coexisted.[27] Yet, as late as 1522, Lucca revenged itself not only on certain delinquent members of the di Poggio family, but also on the dei Poggi as a whole, decreeing 'that this family of the di Poggio is in all generations pronounced to be transgressors and criminals, thirsting after the blood of their fellow citizens'.[28] In the case of the Guinigi after 1430, the restored republic cautiously moved only against specific individuals: initially against Paolo and his descendants, later against men suspected of subversive acts. But clearly the whole Guinigi clan was viewed with very considerable mistrust. The events of 1433 represent a broad offensive against adult male members of the Guinigi family. Apart from Pietro di Nicolao Guinigi (Anziano in March/April 1438, and regularly thereafter), no member of the Guinigi family was to hold office as Anziano until Girolamo di Giovanni in the 1450s and his brother Michele after 1460. Pietro di Nicolao was a member

[25] See, e.g., BSL MS 939, Gio: Lunardo Dalli, Cronache, p. 191, where Dalli argues that it was expedient not to pursue Guinigi supporters in Lucca, because they were 'persone da convenirsi potenti, e di gran seguito'.

[26] Berengo, *Nobili e mercanti*, 32: 'si presentano come blocchi compatti, non incrinati ma resi anzi piú forti dalla moltitudine dei loro uomini e dal viluppo interno delle parentele'.

[27] R. Starn, *Contrary Commonwealth: The Theme of Exile in Medieval and Renaissance Italy* (Berkeley, Calif., 1982), 112.

[28] Berengo, *Nobili e mercanti*, 98: 'quod hec familia Podia est hereditaria in delictis et facinoribus comittendis, sanguinem civium anhelando'.

of a very distant branch of the family, for whom a common ancestor must be sought as far back as Rustico (fl. 1217). Pietro was one of the notorious enemies who were to be eliminated when the sons of Paolo succeeded in recovering their inheritance.[29]

It is not clear with what justification suspicion continued to attach to all bearers of the Guinigi name (Pietro excluded). In his Libro di ricordi, Girolamo di Giovanni Guinigi noted how in 1433 he, his brothers, and other kinsmen were unjustly banished. But the good citizens of Lucca quickly realized that the sentence was unmerited, and they were permitted to return. Girolamo was anxious to add that this note was not made to inflame past passions; rather, he had pardoned all offences against him in view of the great benefits that he had received on being readmitted to the number of Lucchese citizens.[30] Girolamo's brother Michele engaged in a long dispute with the commune over part of the Guinigi palace in *contrada* SS. Simone e Giuda once held in common by the sons of Lazzaro di Bartolomeo Guinigi and confiscated by the commune as the property of Paolo.[31] Despite an occasionally stormy relationship with the commune, there remains no evidence that Michele or Girolamo worked for the restoration of Guinigi rule. Indeed, they were soon forging alliances with the families that had directed the revolution of 1430. Girolamo in 1443 married Pippa, the daughter of Lorenzo Buonvisi; his brother Francesco married Caterina, the daughter of the murdered Pietro di Giusfredo Cenami; his sister Pippa married Piero di Giovanni da Ghivizzano; and his sister Margarita married messer Nicolao di messer Manfredo.[32] Nicolao di Lazzaro Guinigi, it is true, was exiled for plotting against the Lucchese state. But Nicolao's later career in the service of Ladislao Guinigi was a product rather than the cause of his banishment. Of the Guinigi remaining in Lucca after 1430, only Azzo di Dino was unambiguously implicated in an attempt to restore Lucca to Guinigi rule.

The Libri di ricordanze compiled by Michele and Girolamo di Giovanni Guinigi provide abundant evidence of tensions and bitter

[29] ASL Cause Delegate, 3, p. 12.

[30] ASL Archivio Guinigi, 29, Libro di ricordi e note di contratti di Girolamo quondam Giovanni quondam Michele Guinigi, fatto e cominciato nel 1468, segnato AA—anzi in sua origine era segnato B—dell'archivio di nostra casa Guinigi, fo. 2^r.

[31] ASL Podestà di Lucca, Curia Civile, 1306, fos. 155^r–156^r; 1309, fos. 21^r–28^v, 63^v–70^v; Anz. Temp. Lib. 674, Appelli, no foliation, case beginning 28 Aug. 1458; Rif. 18, pp. 119–20, 391–2, 403; Archivio Guinigi, 151, Memorie e note di Michele q. di Giovanni q. Michele q. di Lazari Guinigi, principiate l'anno 1447, fos. 49^r, 51^r–54^r.

[32] ASL Archivio Guinigi, 29, Girolamo Guinigi, Libro di ricordi, fo. 3^v; 151, Michele Guinigi, Memorie e note, fo. 61^v.

disputes within the family. Girolamo's notes are dominated by a lengthy denouncement of the interested, dishonest administration of their father's inheritance by Michele as guardian for his younger brothers, whom Girolamo accused of wishing to appropriate and usurp their rights. Michele alone was the son of Giovanni Guinigi's first marriage, and to Girolamo's complaints about the administration of the inheritance was joined a more general protest against Michele's neglect and inconsiderate treatment of the children of the second marriage.[33] The dispute dragged on, and a settlement was only finally reached with Michele's young heirs after Michele's death in July 1461. The Memorie of Michele di Giovanni Guinigi chronicle the disputes that arose when he and his brothers took advantage of the financial and, later, political difficulties of Azzo and Nicolao di Dino Guinigi in order to acquire the inheritance of Dino's branch.[34] Yet these and other sources also reveal that acrimonious disputes over inheritance were entirely compatible with a very strong sense of identification with, and loyalty to, the *famiglia agnatizia patrilineare*.[35] All the *consorti* of the *casa* Guinigi identified with each other as patrons, protectors, and defenders of the altar of SS. Giovanni and Biagio in the cathedral of S. Martino.[36] Girolamo di Giovanni Guinigi did not allow his brother's double-dealing to deter him from assuming the guardianship of Michele's minor sons, nor did it temper the fears for the well-being of the Guinigi house occasioned by the death of one of Michele's sons and the serious illness of another.[37] Girolamo expressed outrage at the actions of Iacopo di Giovanni da Ghivizzano who named his two daughters as his heirs, thus disinheriting his nearest male kinsmen.[38] Girolamo's brother Michele was deeply concerned to trace the antiquity and record the history of the Guinigi family for the comfort and encouragement of his

[33] ASL Archivio Guinigi, 29, Girolamo Guinigi, Libro di ricordi, fos. 2^v, 3^v–7^v, 15^v; AN 385 (ser Massino di Bartolomeo da Pietrasanta), fos. 116^r–123^v; 771(3) (ser Giovanni Roffia), fos. 72^r–78^v.

[34] ASL Archivio Guinigi, 29, Girolamo Guinigi, Libro di ricordi, fos. 47^v–48^v; 151, Michele Guinigi, Memorie e note, fos. 44^v, 47^r, 48^r, 50^r, 55^{r-v}; Podestà di Lucca, Curia Civile, 1309, fo. 28^r; AN 555 (ser Ciomeo Pieri), fos. 198^r–203^v.

[35] For a recent discussion of this theme, see V. Tirelli, 'I "libri di ricordanze" a Lucca', in *La Famiglia e la vita quotidiana in Europa dal '400 al '600: Fonti e problemi: Atti del convegno internazionale Milano 1–4 dicembre 1983* (Rome, 1986), 123–65.

[36] ASL Archivio Guinigi, 151, Michele Guinigi, Memorie e note, fo. 48^v.

[37] On 27 Aug. 1473, on receiving news of the death of Francesco di Michele Guinigi, Girolamo wrote: 'E va male per la casa nostra': ASL Archivio Guinigi, 29, Girolamo Guinigi, Libro di ricordi, fo. 22^r. News that his other nephew Giovanni had made a will prompted Girolamo to write: 'Dio ci dia gratia che viva, che troppo pochi siamo' (ibid., fo. 23^v). Both comments are recorded by Tirelli, '"Libri di ricordanze"', 134.

[38] ASL Archivio Guinigi, 29, Girolamo Guinigi, Libro di ricordi, fos. 56^v–57^r.

descendants.[39] These efforts fully embraced the distant line of Pietro di Nicolao, the feared obstacle to the restoration of a Guinigi *signoria*.[40] Indeed, it was to Pietro in 1433 that Michele sent his minor brother Girolamo, to serve his commercial apprenticeship in Genoa.[41]

There is, I think, nothing mysterious about the way in which the patrician Lucchese family acted as both a centre of political loyalty and a unit of political action. Following the murder of Pietro Cenami in 1436, Nicolao Burlamacchi—to whom no suspicion attached—used his very considerable political influence to save the life of his brother Giovanni.[42] In the three decades after 1430 there are many examples of the Guinigi family in Lucca providing succour for members of the family in political disgrace. Nicolao di Lazzaro di Francesco Guinigi in November 1436 sold to Azzo di Dino his share of the family palace, but with arrangements made should his banishment from Lucca be lifted.[43] Azzo himself, much to the distress of the commune, was appointed *visconte* with temporal jurisdiction over the Iura and the lands of the bishopric in the Garfagnana by Nicolao Guinigi, bishop of Lucca in 1433.[44] Azzo's political crimes did not prevent him from reappearing in the 1450s at the baptism and confirmation of the children of Michele and Girolamo di Giovanni Guinigi.[45] Michele's Memorie show a continued lively interest in the affairs of the exiled descendants of Paolo in Genoa.[46] These signs of solidarity fully justify the distrust in which the family long continued to be

[39] 'La quale memoria faccio acio che vi sia incitamento e conforto al bene fare, vedendo et intendendo la nobilta del sangue vostro': ASL Archivio Guinigi, 151, Michele Guinigi, Memorie e note, fo. 60^{v}. See also fo. 42^{v}.

[40] Ibid., fo. 60^{v}. For Pietro Guinigi as perceived obstacle to Ladislao's ambitions, see nn. 6 and 29 above.

[41] Girolamo notes how on 8 July 1433 he left Lucca with Pietro quondam Nicolao Guinigi, and went with him to Genoa 'per garzone': ASL Archivio Guinigi, 29, Girolamo Guinigi, Libro di ricordi, fo. 2^{r}. In Feb. 1454, 'since common ownership often results in discord', Azzo Guinigi and the sons of Giovanni Guinigi agreed upon the division of property that they held in Saltocchio, and this settlement, enacted in the bishop's palace, was witnessed by Pietro di Nicolao: AN 555 (ser Ciomeo Pieri), fo. 201^{v}.

[42] Rif. 15, pp. 54, 58, 62, 65, 355–6.

[43] AN 548 (ser Ciomeo Pieri), fo. 123^{r-v}. In 1439, Nicolao assigned all his property and rights to Michele di Giovanni Guinigi, by the hand of a Milanese notary: ASL Archivio Guinigi, 151, Michele Guinigi, Memorie e note, fo. 46^{v}.

[44] Azzo was appointed by an instrument dated 6 Oct. 1433; the appointment was revoked, under pressure from the commune, on 31 Dec. 1433(4): LA 87, fos. 71^{r}, 75^{v}; Fumi (ed.), *Regesti*, 488.

[45] ASL Archivio Guinigi, 29, Girolamo Guinigi, Libro di ricordi, fo. 9^{r}; 151, Michele Guinigi, Memorie e note, fo. 50^{v}; Biblioteca (Manoscritti), 65, Pietro Carelli, Sommario delle Cronache, fo. 102^{v}.

[46] ASL Archivio Guinigi, 151, Michele Guinigi, Memorie e note, fo. 61^{v}.

held. Individuals were implicated in the succession of Guinigi plots. But a concern for the honour and prosperity of the lineage did not of necessity dictate a mindless support for the schemes of Guinigi exiles. In the sixteenth century, the writings of Gerardo Burlamacchi worked to distance his family from the mistakes and conspiracy of his cousin Francesco.[47] In 1436 members of the di Poggio family succeeded in retaining high political office despite the foolish actions of the young di Poggio murderers of Pietro Cenami.[48] Michele di Giovanni Guinigi was quite capable of denouncing the tyranny of Paolo when protecting his own and his family's interests.[49] All the evidence suggests that most of the Guinigi who remained in Lucca were soon anxious to identify with the new regime. This evidence is not a sign of weakening family cohesion; rather, it points to a more acute perception of where the family's best interests lay.

Ladislao, in the 1440s, received less ambiguous support from a small group of Lucchese exiles who saw in the Guinigi the instrument of their own restoration. Best documented of these is Carlo Masi da Silico, dreaming of the opportunity to re-enter Lucca and to repay those, apparently including many leading citizens of the restored republic, who had wronged him. Ladislao's entourage also attracted wanderers like Nicolao Antonio Cencio, absent from Lucca since the fall of the Guinigi, who was clearly impoverished, and for whom a Guinigi victory might be expected to bring lucrative rewards.[50] A few years later the priest Iacopo Pieroni articulated more candidly his personal ambitions. He anticipated appointment as chaplain to the new lord of Lucca. Pieroni's great friend, Antonio Anguilla, was resident in Genoa against his will and yearned for the day when he would be able to return home.[51] Much more interesting than the fantasies of *banniti* is that body of support that Ladislao Guinigi claimed to enjoy within Lucca from citizens and foreigners alike and from among the inhabitants of the *contado*.

[47] Tirelli, '"Libri di ricordanze"', 129–31.

[48] Taddeo di Poggio was one of the Anziani at the time of Pietro Cenami's murder. Paolo di Poggio attended the meeting of the General Council immediately following Cenami's death as *surrogato* for Lorenzo Cattani, one of Cenami's murderers: Rif. 15, p. 54.

[49] ASL Podestà di Lucca, Curia Civile, 1309, fos. 69^{v}–70^{r}.

[50] For both Carlo Masi and Nicolao Antonio Cencio, see ASL Cause Delegate, 3, pp. 3–6, 11–28, 33–42. Nicolao may have been a brother of 'Ciuccius', son of Antonio Michele, called Cencio, a Lucchese citizen detained in the summer of 1431 for certain unspecified crimes and excesses: Anz. Temp. Lib. 5, fo. 59^{v}.

[51] Rif. 16, pp. 770–1. See esp. Iacopo's 'Io saro suo [Ladislao's] cappellano et daromi buon tempo'; and Antonio's 'Io staro bene quando noi saremo in lucha et non gittera piu spuola perche ora non vi posso stare'.

The records abound in allusions to citizens implicated in the Guinigi conspiracies whose identity, in the public interest, was to be kept secret. Ladislao himself, in 1442, spoke of fifteen citizens of Lucca in whom he placed trust. Whilst it is impossible to recover a full list of actual or potential Guinigi supporters, a few names elude the conspiracy of silence. Orso del fornaio was listed as a likely sympathizer in both 1442 and 1447. Ladislao was not entirely convinced of Orso's loyalty, and regretted the death of Giovanni del fornaio who, Ladislao claimed in 1447, had always been his man.[52] Orlando di Silvestro da Piastra was exiled for his part in the Guinigi plot of 1443; Gerardo di Stefano Spada suffered a similar fate in 1447.[53] Spada, in 1447, reminded Ladislao of the support within the walls that he was likely to receive from Ruberto Angiorelli. And indeed in July of the following year Angiorelli was imprisoned and then banished from Lucca.[54] Later in 1448 we find Ruberto Angiorelli resident outside Lucchese jurisdiction in Pietrasanta,[55] though he had returned to Lucchese territory by the 1460s.[56] Whatever his political allegiance, it appears, however, that Ruberto Angiorelli should be classified as a victim of the more vigorous Lucchese offensive against sodomy, rather than as a martyr to the cause of a Guinigi restoration. In March 1448 a new council was established to provide a remedy for the sodomy said to be prevalent in the city.[57] One of the men to appear before this commission was Angiorelli, who was accused of having sexual relations with a number of boys in the stables of his house and elsewhere.[58] It was as a result of this, rather than because of his Guinigi connections, that Angiorelli was sentenced in 1448 to perpetual banishment from the city and territory of Lucca, a sentence that later, in 1451/2, was commuted to a fine.

Many of those who attached themselves to Ladislao's cause, both within Lucca and in exile, came from distinguished Lucchese families. The Anguilla had been proscribed as 'potentes et casastici' in 1308; members of

52 ASL Cause Delegate, 3, p. 19; Rif. 16, pp. 770–1.

53 Fumi (ed.), *Regesti*, 905; Rif. 16, pp. 403–4, 770–1, 774; BSL MS 47, Antichità di Lucca, fos. 298v–299r.

54 Rif. 17, pp. 29, 42, 45.

55 ASCP, A3, Civile—Frammenti filze giusdicenti 1378–1493 (S. Giorgio 1448), no foliation. This file is much mutilated, and is difficult to read in a communal archive without the facility of an ultraviolet lamp.

56 AN 704 (ser Benedetto Franciotti), p. 226; 706, p. 207. See also BSL MS 38, Martino Bernardini, Ricordi Storici, fo. 217r. Angiorelli was married to Zabetta, aunt of Girolamo di Giovanni Guinigi: ASL Archivio Guinigi, 29, Girolamo Guinigi, Libro di ricordi, fo. 18r.

57 Rif. 16, p. 796.

58 SB 165, fos. 57r–58r, 66r–67v.

the Angiorelli and the Spada families had held the office of Anziano periodically since the middle of the fourteenth century.[59] As in the case of the earlier conspiracies of the 1430s, the geographical cohesion of Ladislao Guinigi's potential supporters in the 1440s is immediately apparent. Orlando da Piastra was drawn as Anziano for the Guinigi *terziere* of S. Martino in 1435, 1437, 1439, and 1442; Ruberto Angiorelli for the same *terziere* in 1439, 1441, 1444, 1447, and 1449 (on the last occasion being surrogated as absent). Within the *terziere* of S. Martino the Anguilla lived in the *contrada* of SS. Giovanni e Reparata, the Angiorelli in the *contrada* of S. Maria in via, and the Fornari probably in the *contrada* of S. Quirico (see Figure 3.1). Of the men and families of Lucca implicated in the

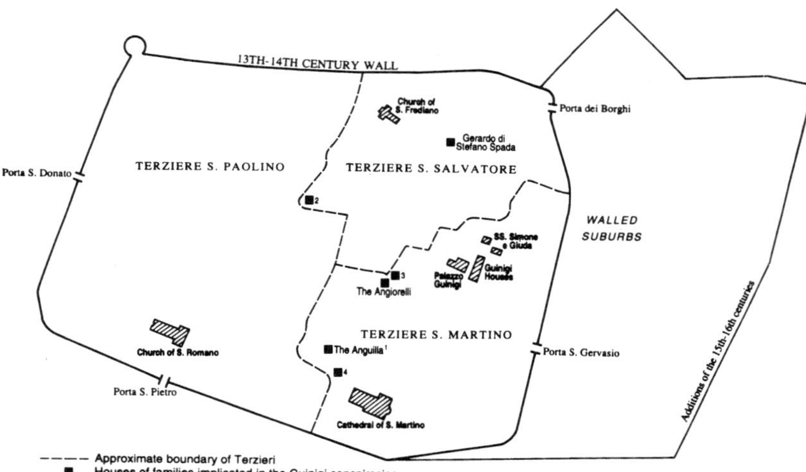

FIG. 3.1 Supporters of a Guinigi restoration within Lucca in the 1440s: approximate location of the houses of the families implicated in the Guinigi conspiracies. [1]The house of Francesco Anguilla, *pittore*, Anziano for the *terziere* of S. Martino in 1434. [2]The houses of Battista Maggiolini, Nicolao Grasso, and other members of the Pisan community resident in Lucca. [3]Probable location of the house of Giovanni and Orso del fornaio. [4]Probable location of the house of Orlando di Silvestro da Piastra.

[59] Meek, *Lucca 1369–1400*, 190, 233.

Guinigi plots of the 1440s, only the Spada, resident in S. Salvatore in *prima ruga del Borgo*, were established outside the *terziere* of S. Martino.

In other respects, the legacy of the Guinigi *signoria* gave a more distinctive character to the party of Ladislao in post-Guinigi Lucca. Ruberto Angiorelli had fought under Ladislao during the last years of Guinigi rule, and from Ladislao passed into the service of Carmagnola. It was as Ladislao's late 'uomo d'arme' that Angiorelli's loyalty was anticipated in 1447.[60] Orlando di Silvestro da Piastra was another who had devoted himself 'sempre alle armi'.[61] Orlando had been wounded in 1433 whilst serving the republic in the vicariate of Coreglia.[62] But his past too, in all probability, should be traced back to the youthful military career of Paolo Guinigi's eldest son. These professional soldiers, with their long-standing personal bonds to Ladislao Guinigi, were supplemented by, and overlap with, members of families that formed the old Guinigi party as forged in late fourteenth-century Lucca. Such were the Angiorelli, as were the Spada. Vincenzo Spada had married Tommasina, the sister of Paolo Guinigi. In appealing for the support of Gerardo Spada, a young man recently emancipated by the death of his father, Ladislao exploited the traditional loyalty that the house of Spada had always shown towards the Guinigi.[63]

A further distinctive feature of the Guinigi plots of the 1440s was the prominent role played in these conspiracies by foreigners permanently resident in Lucca or her territory. In 1444 Battista Maggiolini promised Ladislao that all the Pisans living in Lucca and the *contado* could be won over to support the Guinigi cause. A significant number of Pisans did in fact become involved in the plot to seize the city.[64] In 1447, one of the leading conspirators was a Florentine medical doctor long resident in Lucca in chiasso Barletti in the *contrada* of S. Lucia verso Fillungo or of S. Cristoforo: Giovanni di m. Iacopo de' Risaliti. Ladislao was particularly interested in gaining the support of dott. Giovanni and his son Iacopo as a means of establishing peace with the Florentines once he had seized control of the city.[65] There would appear to be two sets of interrelated

[60] Fumi (ed.), *Regesti*, 333; Rif. 16, p. 771. For one of the relatively rare references to Ruberto Angiorelli in Lucca in the 1430s, see SB 161, fo. 248^{r-v}.

[61] Fumi (ed.), *Regesti*, 868.

[62] SB 159, fo. 258^{r-v}.

[63] Rif. 16, p. 770.

[64] Besides Maggiolini, others involved included Piero di Carbone, a German tailor named Ghirardino who had long lived in Pisa, a Pisan *contadino* named Simone, a shoemaker named Bargellino, Girolamo da Cascina, Nanni di Bindo Lelli, Guido dalla Coppa, and Nicolao Grasso, Maggiolini's cousin and the eventual informer: Fumi (ed.), *Regesti*, 889, 905.

[65] Rif. 16, p. 771.

grievances involved here. First, the Florentine wars had undoubtedly imposed great burdens on foreigners living in Lucca, as upon all the inhabitants of the Lucchese state. In 1432 the Emperor Sigismund had ordered that Pisans living in Lucca should not be too hard pressed for forced loans.[66] Nevertheless, Maggiolini himself was to complain in August 1438 of being too burdened by *prestanze.* Unless he and his brother Pietro were freed from outstanding amounts, Battista Maggiolini threatened to depart permanently from Lucca with his entire family.[67] Secondly, a cursory survey of the Guinigi period suggests to me that Paolo Guinigi, as lord of Lucca, was markedly predisposed to welcome and to honour foreigners, including Pisan refugees following Florence's acquisition of that city in 1406. Battista Maggiolini was granted Lucchese citizenship by Paolo Guinigi following his arrival from Pisa in 1421.[68] At an individual and personal level these newcomers formed business associations with Guinigi supporters such as the Angiorelli;[69] and more generally they may have anticipated greater favours and rewards at the hands of a prince than from that body of citizens that came to rule Lucca following the events of 1430. For the Guinigi period, any conclusions must be tentative in the absence of a much needed modern study. For the later period, it must be conceded that the records of the General Council after 1430 show a continued preoccupation with the need to attract to Lucca and to reward learned, skilled, and useful foreigners. It is difficult to prove that foreigners were unfairly burdened with forced loans. A man like Maggiolini enjoyed high office and important appointments in the service of the restored republic; and the Lucchese authorities in both 1444 and 1447 were aggrieved that betrayal should come from foreigners upon whom so many bounties had been bestowed. But leading members of the Pisan and Florentine communities in Lucca did favour the return of Ladislao, and this fact can probably be explained by both the hardships of the 1430s and the more inward-looking vision of oligarchic republican rule.

The latter point receives convincing support if we turn from the affairs of the city to the loyalties of the *contado.* As early as 1430, Nicolao di

[66] ASL Biblioteca (Manoscritti), 65, Pietro Carelli, Sommario delle Cronache, fo. 80v.

[67] Rif. 15, pp. 270–1. See also p. 272.

[68] ASL Biblioteca (Manoscritti), 125, B. Baroni, Famiglie Lucchesi, p. 312. There is a general image of the Pisan conspirators of 1444 as refugees from Florentine rule: BSL MS 47, Antichità di Lucca, fo. 298v; Fumi (ed.), *Regesti*, 896.

[69] Gerardo Angiorelli 'ebbe compagnia all'arte della seta', with Giovanni Maggiolini and later with his heirs: Rif. 16, p. 485.

Lazzaro Guinigi was boasting of his great following in the countryside and of his ability to hold the Garfagnana against the entire world.[70] In the 1440s Ladislao Guinigi spoke confidently of the support that he was likely to receive from the Guelphs and Ghibellines of the Garfagnana and from *contadini* generally.[71] Out of this amorphous body of alleged support, one man, Giovanni di Matteo da Agnino emerges to speak for himself—through the prism of the criminal proceedings. And the motives attributed to Giovanni di Matteo are of the highest interest. Assuring Ladislao's agent that not only he and his brother but the whole population of the *castello* of Castiglione would rise to support a Guinigi restoration, Giovanni di Matteo expressed what he claimed as a common antagonism to 'questi cittadini' (the present rulers of Lucca), who treated the inhabitants of the *contado* like dogs. 'At the time of the Guinigi *signoria* we had one lord; now everyone wishes to lord it over us.'[72] A detailed analysis of the relationship between Lucca and her subject territories is reserved for Chapter 7. For the present, suffice it to note that the advantages of republican rule were less apparent to the majority of Italians who lived in the countryside and in subject communities than they were to the propagandists of fifteenth-century Florence. Apologists for Italian despotism have always written of the greater equity and equality of opportunity resulting from a common subjection to a common lord as compared with the interested and exploitative rule of a hegemonic city. The voice of Giovanni di Matteo would seem to indicate that this view was firmly rooted in contemporary, popular perceptions.

Nor was popular support for a Guinigi restoration limited to the countryside. Within Lucca, one man who greatly desired the return of Ladislao was the tailor Andrea Leonardi.[73] As always, the criminal proceedings are more concerned to portray the course of events than to explore the motivation of Guinigi sympathizers. Of Andrea we are told only that he was moved by a 'diabolical spirit'. Beyond this, the chief interest that surrounds the person of Andrea Leonardi relates to a series of spells worked by him. Andrea invited Ladislao's emissary into a room in his house, and, taking a crucifix suspended from a thread, recited a paternoster, an Ave Maria, and certain incantations. If Ladislao would return to the lordship of Lucca, the cross was to revolve twelve times—which it duly did. By similar means Andrea determined the future course

[70] SB 159, fo. 166ᵛ.

[71] ASL Cause Delegate, 3, pp. 13–15, 17, 38.

[72] Ibid., p. 18: 'Al tempo del segnore avevamo uno S. hora tucti ce volgliono segnorigiare.'

[73] Ibid., pp. 20–2, 25–8.

of action to be taken by Ladislao's agent, Nicolao Antonio Cencio, and by Nicolao di Lazzaro Guinigi. Of more mundane matters we know nothing. But if Andrea Leonardi was in any sense representative, the Guinigi cause may have enjoyed significant support from artisans within the city, as well as the documented support of *contadini* and foreigners. Earlier it was argued that there is little evidence of popular involvement in the political crises of post-1430 Lucca.[74] Here there appears to be an exception. And the programme of popularist forces within the Lucchese state in the 1440s was not a broadening of the base of government, but a return to the allegedly more even-handed rule of Paolo Guinigi.

A similar message emerges from the mysterious affair of Michele Guerrucci in 1460. For this reason, and because Guerrucci's conspiracy has often been described (mistakenly) as the last great effort of Ladislao Guinigi to recover his father's inheritance, it is appropriate to consider the events of 1460 here. The basic details of the Guerrucci plot seem clear enough. According to Nicolao Pinitesi, the Guerrucci family fled from Lucca in about 1312. From the 1340s there are frequent references to members of the family living in Venice, as Giovanni and his son Michele continued to do in the years following the overthrow of Paolo Guinigi.[75] Michele di Giovanni Guerrucci returned to Lucca in 1458, and by July of that year his brother Piero in Venice was expressing his joy that Michele had determined to remain in Lucca.[76] By 1459 Michele Guerrucci was a member of the General Council for the *terziere* of S. Paolino; he was drawn as Anziano for the months of September and October 1460. In the months before he held the office of Anziano, Guerrucci was plotting against the republic.

According to the later confession of Michele Guerrucci, the initiative came from his friend messer Antonio Bertini da Gallicano, who in May or June of 1460 expressed to him his discontent with the direction of affairs in Lucca and declared that a new Paolo Guinigi was needed to set matters right. Guerrucci showed himself sympathetic to his friend's views, and messer Antonio went on to denounce the wolves and traitors who presently held sway, particularly messer Gregorio Arrighi. At first messer Antonio had sought the new Guinigi in the person of Andrea del Portico, a nephew of the Bartolomeo who had suffered disgrace in 1434. Andrea

[74] See above, pp. 48–9.

[75] Baroni, Notizie genealogiche, MS 1114, fos. 486^{r}–492^{r}. A great deal of information relating to the history of the Guerrucci in Venice in the first half of the 15th cent. is contained in ASL Cause Delegate, 2.

[76] ASL Cause Delegate, 2, fasc. iii, pp. 439–40.

disappointed expectations. He had powerful friends, but failed to show the spirit necessary to rally them to his cause.[77] These confidences encouraged Michele Guerrucci to boast of his own resources and of his close connections with 'a man of standing in the world, who I believe would do anything for me',[78] later identified as Cosimo de' Medici himself.[79] Guerrucci's words assured messer Antonio da Gallicano that Guerrucci was 'vnomo da bene e riccho', and he immediately offered to make Michele Guerrucci *signore di lucha*. Michele was to achieve lordship of the city by means of his friendship with Cosimo; with the aid of Stefano di Antonio di Nellini, who was described as 'capo di parte', a man with great *parentado* in the Garfagnana, who had two or three hundred men at his command;[80] with the aid, similarly, of a friend of Michele himself who commanded 150 horse;[81] and by means of the resources of the Guerrucci bank in Venice. The plot was facilitated by the presence of Michele Guerrucci inside of the palace as Anziano in September 1460, and the preceding months were characterized by the journeying of the leading conspirators between Lucca, Florence, Siena, and Venice and by great bustling within the Lucchese state. The conspiracy did not progress as smoothly as had been optimistically hoped by the participants. Stefano di Antonio di Nellini now felt that he had placed himself in too great a danger, and informed messer Antonio Bertini that he had determined to report the matter to messer Domenico Bertini, brother of Antonio. In this way the plot was revealed. Messer Antonio fled; Guerrucci and Nellini were apprehended and executed.[82]

Lucchese historians have rightly stressed that official accounts of the Guerrucci plot contain much that is obscure and implausible. At the beginning of November 1460 Michele Guerrucci pleaded guilty to the charges against him, and he was subsequently sentenced to death. On 12 November a very large *Colloquio* of 106 citizens decided that Michele's

[77] Ibid., fasc. iv, pp. 745, 749, 753, 769, 773.

[78] 'una persona del mondo che credo faria (fare) per me ogni cosa': ibid., pp. 753, 773.

[79] Ibid., p. 769.

[80] Ibid., p. 755.

[81] 'Ma io ho uno mio compare il quale ha cavalli centocinquanta et e capo di la terra spezata': ibid., p. 754. This 'compare' is the same Sante who is named elsewhere in the proceedings: collate ibid. 760 and 765. He may be identified as Sante di Gavardo di q. ser Filippo da Giustinopoli, *armigero* in the 1450s of the Doge of Venice: ASL Archivio Diplomatico: Pergamene (Archivio di Stato), 15 June 1451.

[82] The fullest record of the Guerrucci plot appears in ASL Cause Delegate, 2, fasc. iv, pp. 731–77. See also Colloqui, 1, pp. 64, 67–71; Rif. 18, pp. 342–5, 411–12, 423, 501–2, 504–5; Podestà di Lucca, Inquisizioni, 5270, fos. 108^r–112^r.

petition for clemency should be referred to the General Council.[83] On 1 December the General Council approved amendments to the statutes dealing with offenders against the pacific and popular state. These amendments provided for the more expeditious handling of treason trials; and to make appeals more difficult, it was decreed that the Anziani and Gonfaloniere di Giustizia should present appeals to the General Council only once these had gained the support of a three-quarters majority in the Council of Thirty-Six. The following day Michele Guerrucci 'con lacrime et dolente cuore' petitioned the Council of Thirty-Six, acknowledging his demerits and humbly begging for mercy in an emotional plea of great originality and pathos.[84] The Council of Thirty-Six were so moved that they approved the submission of Michele's supplication to the General Council by fifty-one votes to four. On 4 December it was argued in the General Council that mercy should be shown to Guerrucci out of respect for those princes who had written asking that his life be spared, to satisfy Michele's relatives in the city of Venice, and out of pity for the supplicant himself. It was agreed by the General Council that the death penalty should be commuted to a fine of 10,000 ducats, half to be paid by the end of the present month of December, the other half by the end of January 1461. Meanwhile Michele was to be detained in prison, and the original sentence was to be executed if payment was not forthcoming within four days of the due date.[85] In the event, Michele Guerrucci failed to raise the money, and was executed following a very mysterious *Colloquio* held on 5 January 1461, the members of which were bound in perpetuity by oath of silence.[86]

The summary execution of the sentence against Michele Guerrucci, together with the great secrecy surrounding his death, would seem to suggest an uncharacteristic enthusiasm for the letter of the law. In the past, men with powerful backing had been treated with much more circumspection. Indeed, Guerrucci's death was to have serious international repercussions for the republic. Francesco Sforza was so incensed by Lucca's failure to honour the promise received in Milan to the effect that Guerrucci's life would be spared that Martino Cenami and Paolo Trenta, ambassadors with the Duke, were constrained to pay 3,000 ducats to recover 'the state of pristine friendship' existing between the two states.[87]

83 ASL Colloqui, 1, p. 64.
84 Ibid., pp. 65–6; Rif. 18, pp. 342–3.
85 Rif. 18, pp. 344–5.
86 ASL Colloqui, 1, p. 70.
87 ASL Cause Delegate, 2, fasc. iv, pp. 733–6; Rif. 18, pp. 411–12, 423.

Lucca might speak of the need to administer justice, but what considerations truly moved the *Colloquio* of January 1461 to reverse the generous inclinations of the earlier councils and to risk offending Lucca's powerful foreign protectors? There must be a strong presumption that Guerrucci possessed too much dangerous knowledge to be allowed to live. Puzzling over the affair, Lucchese chroniclers asked how a man unable to raise, albeit quickly, a fine of 5,000 ducats could ever have aspired to the lordship of the city, and how a man so recently returned to Lucca could have won sufficient backing even to plan such a venture.[88] The Guerrucci conspiracy contains so many suspicious features that there has been a tendency to see Guerrucci as an agent for Ladislao Guinigi or his sons. I have found no evidence that the events of 1460 masked a new attempt to restore Guinigi lordship. But it is clear Michele Guerrucci appealed to very much the same substratum of discontent and raised very much the same kind of forces as had the Guinigi in earlier decades.

Guerrucci, like the Guinigi, received much of his local support from *contadini*. It might be more accurate to say that Guerrucci was discovered, encouraged, and used by malcontents in the *contado*. Later chroniclers record that during his term as Anziano, Guerrucci's room in the palace was always full of *contadini*, and that it was this that first aroused the suspicion of the authorities.[89] Prominent among the conspirators was Antonio di Giovanni Bertini da Gallicano, canon of the cathedral and prior of Tassignano. Antonio's brother Domenico had acted within the General Council as spokesman for Gallicano interests, specifically intervening on behalf of the discontented of Gallicano in June 1459.[90] Antonio's own grievances appear deeply rooted in the turbulent domestic politics of Gallicano in the 1450s. Gallicano had rebelled against the Estensi, returning to Lucchese rule in 1451. By 1460 Antonio Bertini felt that he had received insufficient recognition for his risks and sacrifices at the time of Gallicano's recovery. His general discontent was focused on the person of messer Gregorio Arrighi, a powerful citizen who had 'undone' Antonio in ways never clarified. The other conspirator in 1460 to emerge with some concrete identity was Stefano di Antonio di Nellini, a menacing figure capable of raising substantial armed support in the vicariate of Coreglia and throughout the Garfagnana. Stefano had served Paolo and Ladislao

[88] BSL MS 47, Antichità di Lucca, fo. 182^{r-v}; MS 108, Nicolao Tucci, Historie di Lucca, fos. 348^{v}–349^{v}.

[89] BSL MS 710, Salvator Dalli, Croniche, fo. 151^{r}; BSL MS 939, Gio: Lunardo Dalli, Cronache, p. 259.

[90] Rif. 18, p. 218.

Guinigi during the Florentine wars that terminated the Guinigi *signoria*,[91] and in 1460 seems to have been influenced both by financial considerations and by a general ground swell of discontent within the Lucchese state. As in the case of the earlier Guinigi conspiracies, the court records of 1460 point to a plethora of intensely personal grievances, animosities, and ambitions, enforced by a popular antipathy to the hegemonic city-republic and its alleged failure to provide justice within the wider state. As before, there was much talk in 1460 of citizen-wolves and of the more equitable character of princely rule.

Michele Guerrucci was not approached at random by factions forming in Gallicano and Coreglia. Whilst still in Venice, he and his brother Piero inherited a house in Lucca in the *contrada* of S. Maria Corteorlandini, touching the property of Andrea del Portico. Del Portico was to be the first hope of the conspirators of 1460. In a contract of 1455, which foreshadows a later, more ominous linking of names, this house was sold by Guerrucci's procurators to Domenico Bertini.[92] But whilst, here and elsewhere, some personal bonds can be uncovered to unite the leading actors of 1460, it is very difficult to see Michele Guerrucci in Lucca as the head of a coherent group of *parenti* and *amici*. Guerrucci's extensive extant correspondence,[93] both before and after his return from Venice, reveals ties of business and friendship with many of the great families of Lucca. This may explain the sympathy displayed towards Michele in the councils following his arrest; there is no sign that his political ambitions enjoyed active patrician support. The problems of the Guerrucci conspiracy are in part resolved by seeing Michele Guerrucci neither as prime mover nor yet as a mere agent of the Guinigi, but rather as a useful figurehead for people like Bertini and Nellini. Guerrucci, as a representative of ancient nobility and of more recently acquired wealth, attracted the attention of dissidents from the subject communities. There are obvious burlesque ingredients, and the affair attained a certain gravity only because of Guerrucci's offer to mobilize the support of external powers.

From the time of Michele Guerrucci's arrest, the Anziani determined that he should be denied writing materials and any opportunity to converse with unauthorized persons.[94] Guerrucci's hastily arranged execution would appear to consummate this determination. The Guerrucci correspondence reveals both personal friendships and legal

91 Rif. 14, pp. 712–13.
92 Baroni, Notizie genealogiche, MS 1105, fo. 386^v; MS 1114, fo. 488^r.
93 ASL Cause Delegate, 2, *passim*.
94 Anz. Temp. Lib. 6, 23 Oct. 1460.

disputes with individual and prominent Lucchese citizens; but there is nothing in the letters to suggest that the frenetic emphasis on secrecy was occasioned—as it had been following earlier conspiracies—by a desire to accommodate potential allies of the conspirators within the city. The abiding concern of Lucca in the winter of 1460 seems rather to have focused on the possible international repercussions of the Guerrucci affair. Appeals to spare Guerrucci's life were made by unnamed *principes*,[95] whose number clearly included Francesco Sforza of Milan. Guerrucci himself anticipated support from Cosimo de' Medici in Florence and from Sante di Gavardo in Venice.

It is difficult to assess the true extent of Guerrucci's external support. Cosimo's name appears only in a version of the court record that patently was not destined for public revelation.[96] According to the court record, Cosimo succeeded in distancing himself from the actual plot, and Michele Guerrucci lied to his fellow conspirators in claiming Cosimo's support as an accomplished fact.[97] Any links with the Medici's Milanese ally remain entirely obscure.[98] Our vision is distorted by the court procedures in which the defendants were anxious to ameliorate their position, and in which the interrogators apparently sought comforting answers. Certain points do emerge clearly, however, from the court records. All the conspirators firmly believed that Florentine aid could be invoked to overthrow the restored Lucchese republic. Indeed, it was considered inevitable that Florence would use this opportunity to attempt to subjugate Lucca. The conspirators claimed that they were alert to this danger, and that they worked to avoid it.[99] It also seems clear that, in proffering friendship, Cosimo de' Medici spoke disparagingly of Lucca to Guerrucci. When Michele Guerrucci first returned from Venice, Cosimo offered him a house in Florence, forecasting to Guerrucci that he would not long be able

95 Rif. 18, p. 344.

96 Cf. ASL Podestà di Lucca, Inquisizioni, 5270, fos. 108^r–112^r; Cause Delegate, 2, fasc. iv, pp. 745–8, 749–52, 753–61, 769–72, 765–8, 773–7.

97 ASL Cause Delegate, 2, fasc. iv, p. 771.

98 Milanese support for the Medici during Cosimo's last years is discussed in N. Rubinstein, *The Government of Florence under the Medici (1434 to 1494)* (Oxford, 1966), 128–35. See also V. Ilardi, 'The Italian League, Francesco Sforza, and Charles VII (1454–1461)' and 'The Banker-Statesman and the Condottiere-Prince: Cosimo de' Medici and Francesco Sforza, 1450–1464', in *Studies in Italian Renaissance Diplomatic History*, Variorum Reprints (London, 1986), no continuous pagination. Perhaps through the Guerrucci bank, Michele's brother Piero seems independently to have possessed some influence with Francesco Sforza. See B. Beverini, *Annalium ab origine lucensis urbis*, 4 vols. (Lucca, 1829–32), iii. 432.

99 ASL Cause Delegate, 2, fasc. iv, pp. 754, 770.

to endure life in Lucca and speaking 'many things to the abuse of this city'.[100] Cosimo's interest was allegedly a legacy of the love that he had felt for Michele's father.[101] Like the Guinigi, Guerrucci posed a credible threat largely because of powerful friends beyond Lucca's borders. This ingredient explains the passion for secrecy that continues to obscure the whole affair.

From 1438, and for most of the period thereafter, Lucca was at peace with her neighbours. Nevertheless, the machinations of neighbouring powers lay behind every major conspiracy that disturbed Lucca in the later fifteenth century. This external dimension remained the most obvious thread running through a series of unrelated and disparate challenges to the constitutional restoration of 1430. The relations of private Lucchese citizens with Milan was one source of danger. In March 1439 Tiero Gentili wrote two letters from Lucca to the Duke of Milan at Pavia. These fell into the hands of the Florentines, and revealed a correspondence with Milan that was deemed damaging to the new Florentine allies. Gentili was passing on information concerning Florentine problems and intentions to the Duke, whilst distancing himself from current policies pursued by Lucca. Gentili's indiscretions led to exile for himself; Battista Arnolfini and ser Iacopo da Siena appear also to have been implicated in the same affair.[102] The latter soon reappears in Gavi among the conspirators in the entourage of Ladislao Guinigi.[103] Gentili was freed from his sentence of banishment in October 1443,[104] but within three years was party to secret negotiations conducted in Milan by Iacopo di Giovanni da Ghivizzano, which were again viewed in Lucca as being 'in preiudicio della nostra libertà'. In this later affair Iacopo da Ghivizzano wrote from Milan in May 1446 to his father Giovanni, then in Lucca and holding office both in the General Council and in the Council of Thirty-Six. The basic tenor of this correspondence was that the territory of Pietrasanta might be restored to Lucchese rule if Lucca broke her league with the Florentines and allied herself with the Duke of Milan. The

[100] Ibid., pp. 754, 769: 'molte cose a vituperatione di questa città'.

[101] 'Gia havuto amicitia con vostro padre e havendo amato lui debbo ancho amar voi e in ongni cosa che io possa per voi m'offero a vostri piaceri e per ongni vostro acconcio e comodo e exaltatione vi offero tanto quanto io possa': ibid., p. 754. In the version on p. 769 Cosimo speaks of his obligations to Guerrucci's father.

[102] The texts of the letters and their subsequent history are detailed in SB 161, fos. 226^{r}–227^{v}; ASL Podestà di Lucca, Inquisizioni, 5232, fos. 18^{r}–19^{v}. See also Rif. 15, pp. 488–9.

[103] ASL Cause Delegate, 3, p. 12.

[104] Rif. 16, p. 346.

Ghivizzano, both father and son, were to suffer exile for this indiscretion.[105]

Both of the above cases involved private Lucchese citizens treating of matters that did not concern them, and in both cases the Lucchese authorities feared the international repercussions of their actions. But there is also a sense of a Milanese party within Lucca—centred on Gentili, da Ghivizzano, and perhaps on Pietro Accettanti[106]—which posed a real threat to Lucchese internal political stability. Certainly the General Council feared that the case against Gentili would rupture 'peace and unity between citizens', and believed that a force of 300 *cerne* was required within the city when dealing with Giovanni da Ghivizzano.[107] Chronicle tradition holds that there was a new plot among Lucchese citizens to submit the city to Milanese rule during the ducal visit of 1471.[108] I have been unable to locate this conspiracy in the contemporary records, which may suggest confusion with the Guerrucci affair of ten years earlier or may reflect (as claimed) a desperate need for secrecy to avoid embarrassment during the festivities of the Duke's visit.

Florence, rather than Milan, has traditionally appeared as the more assiduous promoter of sedition within Lucca. In 1454 'a wolf disguised in priest's clothing', a hermit living to the south of Lucca in a cell at Pozzuolo, was discovered plotting the capture of Lucca by certain Florentines through the occupation of porta di borgho. In the seventeenth-century Iova manuscript this cell at Pozzuolo was described as still to be seen, and called *il Romitorio*.[109] The most dangerous of the later Florentine plots occurred in 1490, and centred on Nese Franchi and Andrea Mei. The prime mover behind the Franchi/Mei conspiracy was Francesco Gambini (Francesco Frachasino), citizen of Florence, *fattore* of Lorenzo de' Medici, and vicar of Ripafratta. By August 1489 Gambini was

[105] Ibid., pp. 576–8, 583–4, 607, 778; Fumi (ed.), *Regesti*, 952, 954.

[106] By March 1447 Lucca was again making use of the good offices of Tiero Gentili in dealings with Milan. A few months later, however, we find Tiero imprisoned in Milan, together with Pietro Accettanti: Fumi (ed.), *Regesti*, 978, 987, 1049, (b) 74, 95.

[107] Rif. 15, p. 488; BSL MS 38, Martino Bernardini, Ricordi Storici, fo. 134^{r-v}. Tegrimi, *La vita di Castruccio Castracani*, 111–12, sees Giovanni da Ghivizzano, exiled to Perugia, as the last victim of 'la discordia, e la esecrabile affezzione delle parti' that characterized Lucca from the early 14th to the mid-15th cent., here describing the abased and banished man as 'di grandissima autorità'.

[108] BSL MS 47, Antichità di Lucca, fos. 182^{r}–183^{r}. There is a detailed description of the visit of the Duke and Duchess of Milan to Lucca in BSL MS 2599, Antonio Iova, Annali Historici, pp. 944–5.

[109] ASL Biblioteca (Manoscritti), 38, Giuseppe Civitali, Storia di Lucca, fo. 437^{v}; BSL MS 2599, Antonio Iova, Annali Historici, pp. 931–2.

holding out favours to a Florentine exile, Giovan Maria di Bartolomeo della Filattiera, a courier perhaps already in the service of the commune of Lucca. Giovan Maria was to report to the Florentines on conditions in Lucca and on the defences of the city. By early 1490, either through Giovan Maria or directly, Francesco Gambini had made contact with two Lucchese citizens, Andrea di Biagio Mei and Nese di Lazzaro Franchi, and with Matteo di Giovanni da San Macario, who was then serving as *lanternarius* upon the walls of the city. The plan was for Andrea Mei and ten armed companions disguised as workmen ('vestiti a modo di lavoratori') to seize porta S. Pietro; the city was then to be taken by men sent by Gambini and handed over to the Florentines. The detailed plans for the conquest of Lucca came to naught when Giovan Maria was arrested in Lucca for some trivial, unrelated offence. Believing the conspiracy to have been uncovered, he revealed all to the authorities. The conspirators within Lucca were executed, and on 1 June a great procession of clergy and people gave thanks to God for the discovery of the plot and the delivery of the city.[110]

Examples of conspiracies fomented from outside are significantly augmented if we move beyond the politics of the metropolis. In 1443 the Genoese pledged their support to Pietrasanta for the recovery of Montignoso;[111] in 1476 the men of Pietrasanta were attempting to recover that territory on behalf of Genoa through the subornation of its guardians.[112] The lord of Ferrara was fully involved in 1451 when the men of Cerageto planned to withdraw from Lucchese obedience and place themselves under the Este.[113] All the above conspiracies, together with the Guinigi and Guerrucci plots discussed earlier, show without any doubt the continuing involvement of surrounding states. Before 1438 there is no difficulty in explaining why Florence in particular encouraged fifth columnists within the walls of Lucca. It was merely a dimension of the war effort. The hopes and ambitions of external powers in the decades

[110] ASL Cause Delegate, 4, ii, pp. 17–35; Archivio Guinigi, 29, Girolamo Guinigi, Libro di ricordi, fos. 38^{v}–39^{r}; Biblioteca (Manoscritti), 38, Giuseppe Civitali, Storia di Lucca, fo. 452^{r-v}; Baroni, Notizie genealogiche, MS 1120, fos. 57^{v}–58^{r}. Baroni notes how 'a di p^{o} giugno 1490 si fece una processione, alla quale andò tutto il clero, tutti i conventi, e tutte le compagnie de Battuti, e i MM Signori e piu di 8^{m} persone fra uomini e donne'. For attempts to distance Lorenzo de' Medici from this plot, see M. Luzzati, 'Benedetto Buonvisi', in *Dizionario biografico degli italiani*, xv (Rome, 1973).

[111] ASCP, I 2, Atti dei Genovesi (1433–1482), reg. I. 2, fos. 55^{v}–56^{r}.

[112] ASL Cause Delegate, 4, i, pp. 3–12; Capitano del Popolo, 36, fos. 57^{r}–66^{r}; Biblioteca (Manoscritti), 38, Giuseppe Civitali, Storia di Lucca, fo. 445^{r-v}; G. Sforza, *Memorie storiche di Montignoso* (Lucca, 1867), 44–5.

[113] Rif. 17, pp. 484, 512, 614–15, 700, 733, 750–1; Capitano del Contado, 52, fos. 3^{r}–8^{r}.

after 1440 require a rather more careful analysis. And the period as a whole serves to further our understanding of the motives of those Lucchese citizens who turned to foreign princes to accomplish their domestic plans.

There is a danger of exaggerating the peace and security obtained for Lucca by the peace with Florence of 28 April 1438, by the fifty-year league with Florence of March 1441, or, indeed, by the general Peace of Lodi of 1454. Throughout the fifteenth century Lucca remained deeply committed to recovering territories lost during the wars. These territories included Pietrasanta, lost to the Genoese in 1436 and conquered by the Florentines in 1484. Florence retained Montecarlo and Motrone, despite concerted efforts by Lucca from 1443 onwards to recover these lands.[114] Ferrara seized large areas of the Garfagnana in 1430, which she retained after the peace. Far from returning conquered territory Leonello d'Este also acquired Camporgiano in 1446, when negotiations there between Lucca and Florence for the restoration of Camporgiano led to a popular revolt. Aggression from Ferrara in the Garfagnana remained a major preoccupation of Lucca throughout the 1450s.[115] To the west, the people of Massa handed themselves over to the Malaspina in 1442.[116] All these conquests led to tension between Lucca and her immediate neighbours, and these tensions were exacerbated by endemic conflict in the localities between adjoining, feuding communities. Border disputes between Pietrasanta and Camaiore developed into open conflict and war with Genoa in 1477.[117] The 1480s and 1490s were marked by continuing conflict between the men of Gallicano and those of Barga,[118] and between the men of Montignoso and those of Massa,[119] though in these latter instances the dangers of a wider conflagration were avoided through negotiations.

[114] According to M. Bianco Bianchi of Camaiore, writing early in the 16th cent., at the time of the restoration of Camaiore to Lucca, in 1442, the Florentine captain, Andrea dalla Stufa, laboured to persuade the men of Camaiore to remain with Florence: ASL Biblioteca (Manoscritti), 26, Historie della terra di Camaiore e suoi contorni e altre guerre descritto da M. Bianco Bianchi da Camaiore, Dottore in medicina l'anno 1528, no foliation.

[115] See, e.g., ASL Colloqui, 1, pp. 3–4. Material on Camporgiano is conveniently collected in BSL MS 91, Storie di Lucca, fos. 98^{r}, 99^{v}–100^{v}, 102^{r-v}. See also Fumi (ed.), *Regesti*, 919.

[116] AS Massa, Pergamene, 349/374, 8 Dec. 1442.

[117] ASCP, I 2, Atti dei Genovesi (1433–1482), fos. 63^{r}–65^{r}; ASF Signori—Legazioni e Commissarie, 19, fos. 142^{r}–147^{r}; ASL Biblioteca (Manoscritti), 30, Pellegrino di Bartolomeo Pellegrini da Camaiore, Memorie, fo. 1^{v}; Santini, *Versilia centrale*, ii. 102–5.

[118] ASG MS 13, fo. 179^{v}. Similar disputes involved the men of Vallico and those of Molazane: ibid., fos. 138^{r}, 179^{v}, 182^{r}, 193^{r}.

[119] AS Massa, Archivio dei Malaspina di Fosdinovo Marchesi di Massa, 1, nos. 38, 40; 2, nos. 3–4.

Tension was generated, then, through failure to recover lost lands and through traditional disputes over confines between village communities. These tensions were increased by a clash of forces on the wider Italian stage, in which Lucca herself was not of necessity directly involved. Trouble between states was promoted by the movements of unemployed *condottieri* like Iacopo di Niccolò Piccinino.[120] Non-belligerents, like Lucca after 1438, suffered the devastation caused by the passing armies of their warring neighbours. One of the most touching references to the contemporary scourge of troop movements comes not from Lucchese sources but from Pietrasanta. On 12 June 1449 the General Council of Pietrasanta voted a gift to the magnificent captain Giovanni da Tollentino then passing through their territory, begging him not to linger and asking him to do as little damage as possible whilst he was there.[121] It was damage done to the Lucchese state in the war between Florence and Siena in 1478 that led to the reviling of the Florentine ambassador by the common people in the streets of Lucca. Such insults led in turn to an open attack by the Florentines upon Lucchese territory, resulting in the capture of Balbano, Quiesa, and Bozzano and the taking of many Lucchese prisoners.[122]

Against this background it is hardly surprising that distrust should flourish. In May 1467 the Gonfaloniere and Secretaries of Lucca felt obliged to write to Piero di Cosimo de' Medici to explain the sending to Milan of an ambassador, Bartolomeo Arnolfini. The previous year, at the instigation of Stefano ser Federighi, a Lucchese citizen resident in Savoy, the Duke of Savoy had granted reprisals against the property of Lucchese merchants. The affair was to trouble Lucca for the next quarter of a century. In 1467 the Lucchese authorities were anxious that Florence should not misinterpret Arnolfini's embassy on the Ser Federighi problem, and hastened to reassure the Medici that the ambassador would not treat of any matters prejudicial to the existing friendship between the two cities.[123] In 1485, Iova records that Florence sent a permanent

[120] For Piccinino see L. Banchi, 'La guerra de' Senesi col conte di Pitigliano 1454–1455', *Archivio storico italiano*, 4th ser., iii (1879), 184–97; *idem*, 'Il Piccinino nello stato di Siena e la lega italica (1455–1456)', *Archivio storico italiano*, 4th ser., iv (1879), 44–58, 225–45.

[121] ASCP Libro di Consigli (1449), fo. 17ᵛ.

[122] ASL Biblioteca (Manoscritti), 38, Giuseppe Civitali, Storia di Lucca, fos. 445ᵛ–446ʳ; Machiavelli, *Istorie fiorentine*, 187–8. Writing of Piero di Gino di Neri Capponi's reception in Lucca, Machiavelli recorded: 'il quale fu da loro con tanto sospetto ricevuto, per l'odio che quella città tiene con il popolo di Firenze, nato da le antiche ingiurie e dal continuo timore, che portò molte volte pericolo di non vi essere popolarmente morto: tanto che questa sua andata dette cagione a nuovi sdegni, piú tosto che a nuova unione'.

[123] MAP, xiv. 141.

ambassador to Lucca to spy and to ensure that no help was sent by Lucca to the Genoese enemy.[124] One result of this general climate of suspicion and distrust was to promote competition between foreign states in their dealings with Lucchese dissidents. In 1452 a plot was hatched to give the *rocca* of Castiglione to the Florentines. When, on this occasion, Florence proved a reluctant ally to the traitors, one of them, Giovanni Dinelli, countered with a threat to hand the *rocca* over to Ferrara.[125] Such rivalries must be borne in mind in attempting to explain the response of external powers to appeals for help from political factions within the Lucchese state.

In this turbulent environment, outside intervention was facilitated by the strong links often forged between private Lucchese citizens and neighbouring powers. This emerges most clearly in the case of exiled communities. The most familiar example is the Guinigi settlement at Gavi, who mobilized their powerful Campofregosi connections in a vain bid for restoration to the *patria*. But the problem was more pervasive—and more elusive. Pietrasanta after 1436 seems to have become a positive haven for refugees from Lucchese (and indeed Florentine) justice.[126] *Banniti* from Lucca might also find a convenient refuge in the lands of the Este of Ferrara.[127] No doubt the majority of these people were politically harmless, but in Lucca in 1444 the General Council was sufficiently concerned about the threat to the liberty of the people and commune of Lucca posed by rebels (both citizens and foreigners) to establish a special council of six men with authority to act against *exteros* and *forenses*.[128] Giovanni di Iacopo Viviani, in Pisa in the 1450s, spitting out venom against his *ingrata patria* and seeking the protection and patronage of the Medici, was clearly a danger.[129] And for their part the Florentines were intensely worried in 1477 by the presence of their rebel, Iacopo di Nicolao da Ciecina, called Morellino, of the *contado* of Pistoia, in the service of Lucca.[130]

More remarkable is the lively correspondence conducted by private Lucchese citizens with foreign lords, particularly with the Medici.

[124] BSL MS 2599, Antonio Iova, Annali Historici, p. 961.

[125] SB 165, fos. 613^{r}–614^{v}; ASL Capitano del Contado, 52, no foliation.

[126] For notable examples, see NAC, N 115 (ser Nicolao di Coluccio di Pellegrino da Pietrasanta, 1409–68), fos. 132^{r-v}, 163^{v}–164^{r}.

[127] ASG MS 13, fo. 95^{r}.

[128] Rif. 16, pp. 376–7.

[129] MAP, xvii. 96. In this particular letter to Piero di Cosimo, Viviani sought to marry his son to the daughter of a faithful supporter of the Medici party.

[130] ASF Le carte strozziane—serie prima, CCCLII, fo. 250^{r-v}.

Decrees were issued in Lucca against private individuals entering into correspondence with foreign princes, and special efforts were made to prevent the doings of the General Council from being revealed to the outside world.[131] These efforts seem to have enjoyed little success. The most substantial body of evidence in this regard is to be found in the collection Archivio Mediceo avanti il principato preserved in the Archivio di Stato di Firenze. Unfortunately for present purposes, the Medici correspondence is often difficult to use. Time and again, letters consist of an exchange of salutations, important and substantive matters being explicitly entrusted verbally to the messenger. In letters from Lucchese officials to the Medici it is often impossible to determine whether the writer appears in his private or his official capacity. But some letters clearly indicate a highly suspect relationship between leading Lucchese citizens and the *de facto* rulers of Florence. The case of Giovanni Sbarra *eques lucensis* Gonfaloniere di Giustizia, writing to the Medici in May 1459, in the middle of his term of office, for a loan of 150 ducats, would appear unambiguously personal and compromising.[132]

Initial links may often have been forged through business connections. Meo di Biagio was a *cuoiaio*, appearing in the records from the 1420s as a dealer in Spanish leather.[133] His son Biagio Mei was communicating regularly in the mid-1450s with the Medici agent Giovanni Macinghi, in dealings which included transactions in hides.[134] By the late 1460s Biagio Mei and his son Meo were writing to Piero de' Medici—and later to Giuliano di Piero (their 'benefactor' and 'protector')—to ask favours for themselves or for 'uno caro nostro amicho'.[135] In 1477 appeal was made to the Medici to intervene to make peace in the bitter dispute between the Tegrimi family and Biagio Mei, in this instance the appeal coming not from Biagio Mei but from the Tegrimi.[136] It was with these antecedents that the son of Biagio, Andrea, turned to the factor of the Medici in the plot of 1490.

Lucchese citizens had many legitimate reasons to correspond with the Medici. Many of the letters are of a purely business nature. These and other personal contacts rendered appropriate the expressions of congratu-

[131] Rif. 15, p. 130; Biblioteca (Manoscritti), 65, Pietro Carelli, Sommario delle Cronache, fo. 108ʳ.

[132] MAP, i. 254. Cf. MAP, x. 518.

[133] NAC, N 116(1) (ser Nicolao di Coluccio di Pellegrino da Pietrasanta), 17 July 1426.

[134] MAP, ix. 217, 220.

[135] MAP, v. 797, 799; xiv. 144.

[136] MAP, v. 859–61.

lations and condolences from Lucca that mark the fortunes of the Medici family. In 1492 there was a succession of letters from private Lucchese citizens recording grief at the death of Lorenzo.[137] The di Poggio family of Lucca held land adjoining that of the communes of Pescia and Buggiano, and turned to the Medici to resolve disputes over pasturage and jurisdiction.[138] Lucchese citizens sought employment in those offices reserved for foreigners in the Florentine state (as elsewhere). And there are a number of appeals for help and favour from Lucchese citizens pursuing lawsuits before courts in Florentine territory, particularly in Pisa.[139] Too much should not be made of the fulsome, fawning tone of many of the letters addressed to the Medici. The petitioners were often less than the humble, tearful, obedient sons that they professed themselves to be. But that the continual quest for, and receipt of, favours promoted ties of obligation, even of clientage, can hardly be denied.

The process operated both ways. The Medici requested, and expected, favourable consideration for their own clients in Lucca.[140] More brutally, Alphonso, Duke of Calabria, attempted to pervert the course of Lucchese justice in a capital crime by putting pressure on two Anziani of the college of November/December 1479. At their instigation, the *advocato fischale*, messer Gregorio Ciampanti, 'homo ignorantissimo et pazzo', induced two witnesses to commit perjury. The matter was quietly terminated to avoid giving offence to the Duke, then present in Siena with a large army.[141] External involvement in matters political must be seen against a general background of external pressures and interventions in many areas of Lucchese life.

The leagues and diplomatic tensions, the personal associations and correspondence, all provide the essential framework within which to explore the contribution of neighbouring states to political upheavals in Lucca. Florence constituted the most obvious threat. Here Luzzati was surely right in insisting that later fifteenth-century Florence was not implacably pursuing a policy of aggrandizement aimed at incorporating Lucca.[142] Yet the vision of a wider Tuscan state is not as anachronistic as Luzzati has claimed. In 1440 messer Nicolao Manfredi was writing of a

[137] MAP, xv. 76, 95. For official condolences, see xv. 46.

[138] MAP, vi. 229; xiv. 75.

[139] MAP, ix. 72, 92; xiv. 65; xvii. 614.

[140] See, e.g., MAP, vi. 576.

[141] ASL Biblioteca (Manoscritti), 65, Pietro Carelli, Sommario delle Cronache, fo. 123^r; Rif. 21, pp. 95–6; BSL MS 939, Gio: Lunardo Dalli, Cronache, pp. 327–8.

[142] Luzzati, 'Politica di salvaguardia', 543–57.

common belief, particularly in Siena, that Florence aimed to rule all of Tuscany.[143] In fact, there is little sign of a consistent Florentine policy sustained throughout the period as a whole. In the diplomatic relations between Lucca and Florence there were moments of true cordiality, especially when the Medici were visiting the mineral waters of Corsena.[144] In 1452, when offered the *rocca* of Castiglione, a certain Florentine citizen (presumably Cosimo de' Medici) rebuffed the overtures of the conspirators on the grounds that 'the Lucchese are our good friends and allies'.[145] At the same time Luzzati's portrayal of Florence in the later fifteenth century as an essentially benign neighbour is obviously mistaken. The seriousness of the sporadic Florentine threat is clearly revealed by the present chapter. The point is reinforced by correspondence between Florence and Milan which was discovered by Vincent Ilardi. These letters show that in 1463/4 Cosimo de' Medici aimed at securing a common border between Florence and Milan by means of the Florentine acquisition of Pietrasanta and Lucca, and that he hoped for Milanese support in the conquest of Lucca.[146] All indicators suggest that Florence and other Italian powers were moved by very immediate and inconstant considerations in their treatment of Lucca. They might respond to the importunities of clients within the walls if advantages were likely to accrue. They might be moved to accommodate their Lucchese ally; or they might be provoked to unfriendly acts by Lucca's temporizing policies in the face of competing and more powerful neighbours.

The history of Lucca between 1440 and 1494 shows not only the need for vigilance towards neighbouring states, but that individual citizens remained prepared to invoke external support for their domestic ambitions. Again, attachments were often formed through business interests. In the years before his disgrace Giovanni da Ghivizzano appears regularly as a representative of Milanese interests in Lucca. Tiero Gentili and Giovanni da Ghivizzano, both leading participants in the Milan-supported *coup* of 1430, both had connections with Pietrasanta (including business interests) that long pre-dated their involvement in the surreptitious negotiations for the recovery of Pietrasanta in Milan in

[143] MAP, xi. 418.

[144] MAP, xvi. 97; BSL MS 2599, Antonio Iova, Annali Historici, pp. 937–8.

[145] SB 165, fos. 613^{r}–614^{v}; ASL Capitano del Contado, 52, no foliation: 'li Luchesi sono boni nostri amici e collegati'.

[146] Ilardi, 'Banker-Statesman and Condottiere-Prince', 23. The reference is to Paris, Bibliothèque Nationale, Fonds Italien, MS 1590, fos. 51^{r}–52^{v}, 63^{r-v}. I am grateful to my colleague Dr C. I. Hamilton for obtaining for me a photocopy of the relevant pages.

1446.[147] Whether because of material interests or because of perceptions of Lucca's best interests, there was clearly some cleavage within Lucca over issues of foreign policy. This appears most forcefully in the mysterious *Colloquio* of the mid-1430s.[148] Luzzati has noted how in the crisis of 1478–9 opinion was divided in Lucca on whether the city should remain loyal to Florence or whether Lucca should abandon Florence and take advantage of the coming of the King of Naples to recover lost territory.[149]

If such cleavages existed, the origins of political disturbance in Lucca after 1440, as before, must be traced to grievances of an intensely personal nature. No better example can be adduced than the Mei/Franchi plot of 1490. The co-ordinator of the plot, Giovan Maria di Bartolomeo della Filattiera, was a Florentine exile tempted by prospects of remission.[150] His accomplice, Matteo di Giovanni da San Macario, was lured by a promise of favourable treatment in a lawsuit then pending before the court of the *Podestà* of Ripafratta.[151] Of the principals, Andrea Mei came from a family from Uzzano in Valdinievole (formerly Lucchese territory, held by Florence), which established itself in Lucca only at the very end of the fourteenth century.[152] In the fifteenth century the family had something of a reputation for public violence;[153] Meo di Biagio Mei died in 1473 from a blow to the head received in a quarrel with the Tegrimi and the Guidiccioni.[154] Andrea di Biagio himself was banished from Lucca in 1482 as a notorious malefactor.[155] According to testimony at his trial in 1490, Andrea Mei recognized that he should not have plotted with the Florentines 'for love of the people', but insisted that he had just cause in the matter 'because of the many injuries that he had received in the city of Lucca from many citizens'.[156] Nese di Lazzaro Franchi himself was no stranger to trouble. He was imprisoned in the Sasso in August 1474 for his part in the reprisals launched from Savoy against Lucchese property by

[147] Rif. 14, pp. 682–3; 15, pp. 244–8; ASCP Libro di Consigli (1431), fo. 10^{r-v}; NAC, N 116(2) (ser Nicolao di Coluccio di Pellegrino da Pietrasanta), fos. 66^{r}–67^{r}. Note also the effusive letter of 12 Dec. 1438 from Giovanni da Ghivizzano to Cosimo de' Medici: MAP, xi. 193.

[148] See above, pp. 40, 42.

[149] Luzzati, 'Politica di salvaguardia', 554–7.

[150] ASL Cause Delegate, 4, ii, pp. 27–8.

[151] Ibid., p. 32.

[152] Baroni, Notizie genealogiche, MS 1120, fos. 48^{r}–95^{v}.

[153] SB 165, fos. 441^{r}–442^{r}; Anz. Temp. Lib. 674, 27 Oct. 1457.

[154] ASL Archivio Guinigi, 29, Girolamo Guinigi, Libro di ricordi, fo. 22^{r}. It was this matter that led to calls for Medici mediation between the Mei and the Tegrimi in 1477.

[155] Rif. 21, pp. 371–4.

[156] ASL Cause Delegate, 4, ii, pp. 22, 29.

Stefano ser Federighi and Francesco Cagnoli.[157] Stefano ser Federighi claimed to be a creditor of Nicolao ser Federighi; Lucchese trade routes were severely threatened by the reprisals, and both ser Federighi and Cagnoli had been declared rebels and enemies of the *patria*.[158] Nese Franchi had been released from prison, apparently in 1481 at the behest of the Duke of Ferrara.[159] But grievances lingered. At his trial in 1490 it was claimed that Franchi decided to join Andrea Mei because of his earlier treatment and out of a desire for revenge.[160] We might add that Nese Franchi was married to the daughter of ser Eustachio Mei, Andrea's uncle, and that Andrea's brother Meo was married to a daughter of Giovanni Cagnoli.[161]

In the political history of Lucca the years after 1440 were less spectacularly eventful than was the first decade of restored republican liberty. Reflecting on the past two centuries, Nicolao Tegrimi was no doubt right to compare the political stability of his own age with the history of Lucca prior to 1440. But the stability was relative, and sometimes appeared fragile. The more overt challenges have been explored in the present chapter: less tangibly, the records of the General Council of Lucca show a continuing preoccupation with public order and with the danger of faction. The threat was perceived to come from the Guinigi, from outside, and from the clash of rival families. The most explicit portrayal of the Lucchese authorities as governed by a need to humour foreign princes and inclined to conceal the political indiscretions of their own citizens in order to preserve the peace appears in the late and thoroughly unreliable Dalli chronicle.[162] But the power of local factions emerges clearly enough in the quarrel between the Guidiccioni and the Arnolfini in 1458. Such was the following of these two families in Lucca, and such the danger that they would divide the *popolo* between them, that the General Council agreed that the case should be remitted to Rome, that

[157] Nese Franchi, already in 1460, was in dispute with Paolo di Nicolao ser Federighi: AN 704 (ser Benedetto Franciotti), p. 26. His imprisonment in 1474 may be related to the capture of Giovanni de Fornai alias Giovanni Francioso: ASL Biblioteca (Manoscritti), 65, Pietro Carelli, Sommario delle Cronache, fo. 118ʳ. For Franchi's imprisonment, see ASL Archivio Guinigi, 29, Girolamo Guinigi, Libro di ricordi, fo. 24ʳ; Rif. 20, pp. 79–80, 229–30.

[158] These reprisals figure very prominently in Lucchese sources after 1466. For the origin of the affair, see ASL Archivio Diplomatico: Pergamene (Tarpea), 3 May 1459, 27 May, 26 Aug. 1460; Pergamene (Archivio di Stato), 21 Apr. 1460; AN 597 (ser Luviso di Antonio Buonaccorsi), fos. 51ʳ–53ʳ.

[159] BSL MS 38, Martino Bernardini, Ricordi Storici, fo. 222ᵛ.

[160] ASL Cause Delegate, 4, ii, pp. 24–5.

[161] Baroni, Notizie genealogiche, MS 1105, fo. 389ᵛ; MS 1120, fo. 49ʳ.

[162] BSL MS 939, Gio: Lunardo Dalli, Cronache, pp. 88–402.

Piero de' Guidiccioni and Bartolomeo de' Arnolfini should themselves go to Rome within twenty days under pain of 1,000 florins each and banishment from the city and district of Lucca, and that the matter should be settled in Rome by Cardinal Calandrini (Cardinal of Bologna) and the Cardinal of Zamessa.[163] There was a similar alarm in May 1487 when it came to the notice of the Anziani that Federigo di Cristoforo Trenta and Bernardino de' Bernardi had come to arms with many of their followers in a dispute over possessions in the commune of S. Gemignano. Again, the fear in Lucca was that conflict between these armed bands would escalate and put the city in danger.[164] Then, as in the 1430s, 'una sollevazione di popolo' (never realized) was a fear inextricably associated with aristocratic faction fighting. The next chapter seeks to explain the essential success of the restoration settlement of 1430, a success witnessed by its endurance and characterized by popular passivity and by the dismal—often comic—failure of periodic aristocratic plots against the *pacifico et populare Stato.*

[163] Rif. 18, pp. 104–6; AN 597 (ser Luviso di Antonio Buonaccorsi), fos. 111^{v}, 263^{r-v}, 299^{r-v}, 314^{r-v}; BSL MS 108, Nicolao Tucci, Historie di Lucca, fo. 348^{r}; MS 2599, Antonio Iova, Annali Historici, p. 934.

[164] Rif. 22, pp. 30–1.

4

LUCCA 1430–1494: THE STRUCTURE OF POLITICS

The political settlement of 1430 was to survive the ambitions of individual citizens. The conspiracies themselves, for the greater part, are worthy of study less for their significance as serious challenges to the constituted order than for the insights that they provide into the contemporary political mentality. The republican constitution of Lucca, like that of Venice, was to endure (modified in constitutional detail) until swept away by external forces in the wake of the French Revolution. Historians and political commentators over centuries, albeit with diminishing conviction, have sought the secret of Venice's political stability within the tortuous constitutional arrangements of that maritime republic. Lucca's own stability, if not explained by images of the perfect constitution, must at least be explained against a background of the constitutional settlement of 1430. The settlement, and its subsequent amendments, are familiar through the work of Cianelli;[1] the working of that settlement, particularly as reflected in patterns of political participation and office-holding, have received much less attention.[2] Both statutory provision and constitutional practice will be explored in the present chapter.

In normal times, ordinary executive authority in Lucca rested with the college of nine Anziani, headed by a Gonfaloniere di Giustizia. In March 1370, following the end of Pisan rule, the Imperial representative had named the current Anziani (and their successors) as Imperial vicars. These events took place in the closing years of the reign of the Emperor Charles IV, following whose death Imperial authority in Italy became even more insubstantial than before. In fifteenth-century Florence, in

[1] Cianelli, *Dissertazioni sopra la storia lucchese*, *passim*.

[2] But see the recent contribution of S. Polica, 'Le famiglie del ceto dirigente lucchese dalla caduta di Paolo Guinigi alla fine del Quattrocento', in *I ceti dirigenti nella Toscana del Quattrocento: Comitato di studi sulla storia dei ceti dirigenti in Toscana: Atti del V e VI Convegno: Firenze 10–11 dicembre 1982; 2–3 dicembre 1983* (Florence, 1987), 353–84.

particular, the thought of Bartolus of Sassoferrato and Baldus de Ubaldis was forged into a belief in the city-republic as a truly sovereign community.[3] Writing of the Lucca of the restored Anzianate, Antonio Cianelli was inclined to question the authenticity of evidence that the people of Lucca swore an oath of fidelity and obtained confirmation of the privileges of Charles IV during the visit of the Emperor Sigismund in the summer of 1432.[4] The fact remains that after the thirty years of Guinigi rule Lucca again came to be ruled by its ancient magistrature, a magistrature that received its theoretical sanction from a designation of Imperial powers. As in the pre-Guinigi period, the Anziani and Gonfaloniere di Giustizia held office for a period of two months. The college again consisted of three Anziani representing each of the three *terzieri* into which Lucca was divided: S. Paolino, S. Salvatore, and S. Martino. The office of Gonfaloniere di Giustizia rotated between the *terzieri*.

The first college of Anziani, which held office until the end of October 1430, was elected on 16 August by a *balìa* of twelve. The *balìa* itself had been elected shortly before by the general parliament of leading Lucchese citizens that had been called immediately on the deposition of Paolo Guinigi.[5] The Anziani for November and December 1430 were named by the current Anziani together with the *balìa de' Riformatori*, the latter being the successors of the *balìa* of twelve, having been elected in October by the Anziani and by the outgoing *balìa* of twelve.[6] The Anziani for January and February 1431 were chosen in the same way.[7] Thereafter there was a return to a more regular and more traditional electoral procedure. An electoral assembly was re-established in February 1431, consisting of the Anziani presently in office together with eighteen *invitati* (six per *terziere*) and the Council of Thirty-Six. The *invitati* were named by the Anziani, as were the *surrogati* who filled the places of absent members of the Council of Thirty-Six.[8] The composition of the Council of Thirty-Six will be

[3] G. Guidi, *Il governo della città-repubblica di Firenze del primo Quattrocento*, 3 vols. (Florence, 1981), i. 25–49; B. Guenée, *States and Rulers in Later Medieval Europe* (London, 1985), 11–14; J. Canning, *The Political Thought of Baldus de Ubaldis* (Cambridge, 1987), esp. 93–158.

[4] Cianelli, *Dissertazioni sopra la storia lucchese*, 165–6. The evidence essentially consists of a letter written to Bruges on 14 July 1432 by Bartolomeo Martini and reproduced by Can. Gio: Lunardo Dalli, Cronache, BSL MS 939, p. 148.

[5] Rif. 14, pp. 21–4.

[6] Ibid., pp. 42–3, 51.

[7] Ibid., p. 71.

[8] Ibid., pp. 117–19.

discussed below.[9] It suffices for the present to note that for much of our period the Council of Thirty-Six was elected by the Anziani currently in office and by twelve men chosen by the Anziani from the ranks of the outgoing Council of Thirty-Six. The electoral assembly thus constituted made a *tasca* of Anziani to fill office for the forthcoming year, and also named a number of supernumeraries to take the place of those who might die or for other legitimate reasons be unable to take office. Each man nominated for office was voted on secretly, one by one. According to the constitution of 1372, the *tasca* was to be made for a two-year period. But it was decided in 1431 to make a *tasca* for only one year in view of the very unsettled conditions of war and plague then afflicting Lucca.[10] The next *tasca* of 7 February 1432 was made for two years, and the *tasca* was renewed regularly every two years after 1432.[11] Following the renewal of the *tasca*, those elected as Anziani were divided into colleges. This work was done by nine *Assortitori*, of whom three were members of the current college of Anziani and six were members of the Council of Thirty-Six. These *Assortitori* were chosen by the Anziani, joined after 1474 by the Council of Thirty-Six.[12] The *Assortitori* were also responsible for choosing from among those elected the men most suited to fill the office of Gonfaloniere di Giustizia. Once divided into colleges, the lists of names were then locked in a chest. Each new college was drawn from the chest in the presence of the Council of Thirty-Six eight days before its members were due to take office.

In many ways, eligibility for the highest political office was much more open in fifteenth-century Lucca than in other Italian city-republics. The essential qualification was Lucchese citizenship; few additional restrictions were imposed. Anziani had to be at least 22 years old and of legitimate birth. They had to be citizens in good standing and to have borne the 'onera realia et personalia' expected of citizens. Some individuals and some families were excluded from office for past misdemeanours. In earlier centuries such exclusions were extensive; after 1430 a few families like the Antelminelli and the Quartigiani[13] for whom the issue remained relevant were restored to honours. Individuals were periodically excluded because they had invoked 'benefit of clergy' for

[9] See below, pp. 124–6.

[10] Rif. 14, pp. 112–13.

[11] Ibid., pp. 213–15, 488–90.

[12] Rif. 20, pp. 171–2.

[13] Rif. 14, pp. 113–14. In May 1439 the house and *agnatione* delli Obizi were restored, the Obizi being *banniti* for distant political crimes: Rif. 15, pp. 369–70.

reasons of personal advantage in the pursuit of private lawsuits; these were regularly readmitted to honours after a transparent display of contrition.[14] Other restrictions stipulated the time period within which a man might return to office, and limited the number of family members that might fill office in successive colleges. Finally, doctors of law and of medicine were excluded from the Anzianate. This last provision excluded from the executive body men of considerable political importance. In other respects there are few substantive qualifications to be made to the idea that the Anzianate was open to all adult male citizens.[15]

In practice, Lucchese electoral procedures ensured that the office of Anziano was dominated by a relatively small, self-perpetuating oligarchy. It is symbolically significant that the college of Anziani in November/December 1494, at the very end of the period covered by this book, was headed by the Gonfaloniere di Giustizia Benedetto Buonvisi, and included the Anziano Nicolao di Francesco Cenami, the son and grandson respectively of the two leading conspirators of August 1430. Indeed, some measure of the continuity and stability of Lucchese political life can be gauged by tracing the careers of the six 'capi e principali della congiura' and their immediate families. The results are set out in Table 4.1. The statistics include the *surrogati* appointed to take the place of men unable to assume office; they also include men drawn but unable to take office for a variety of reasons. Pietro Cenami's brother Dino, for example, was already dead when he was drawn as Anziano for May/June 1435. Table 4.1 does not pursue political careers beyond 1494. Benedetto and Paolo di Lorenzo Buonvisi continued to be regularly elected as Gonfaloniere/Anziano into the sixteenth century, together taking office forty-two times in forty-eight years.

Table 4.1 shows that Nicolao Neri, 'the poor conspirator', never occupied the office of Anziano; he was already dead by May 1431. Nicolao's son Lorenzo is also absent from the lists, though Nicolao's brother Tommaso was elected at irregular intervals up to 1450. The careers of both Tiero Gentili and Giovanni da Ghivizzano were truncated by political disgrace, followed rapidly by death.[16] But over the period as a whole the six conspirators, their brothers, and their immediate descen-

[14] Examples are quite numerous. See, e.g., the case of Michele di Giovanni Guinigi in 1459: Rif. 18, pp. 213–14.

[15] Eligibility in 1430 was determined by the provisions of the statutes of 1372. Changes thereafter are of minor importance. See ASL Statuti del comune di Lucca, 13, i–ix.

[16] For the secret negotiations of both Gentili and da Ghivizzano with the Duke of Milan, see Ch. 3.

TABLE 4.1. Anziani, 1430–94: the conspirators of August 1430

Conspirator	GONF.	ANZ.	PERIOD	Brothers	GONF.	ANZ.	PERIOD	Total GONF.	Total ANZ.
Lorenzo Buonvisi	8	8	1431–60						
Sons: Antonio	0	5	1452–65						
Benedetto	2	8	1475–94						
Paolo	2	10	1468–93					12	31
Pietro Cenami	2	1	1430–6	Dino Cenami	0	1	1435		
Sons: Francesco	5	15	1450–93	Marco Cenami	0	0			
Giusfredo	7	18	1435–83	Sons: Guglielmo di Marco	0	2	1446–8		
Martino	4	8	1460–85	Rodolfo di Dino	0	17	1452–94		
Grandsons: Francesco di Martino	0	1	1492	Grandson:					
Nicolao di Francesco	0	4	1489–94	Girolamo di Rodolfo	0	4	1487–92	18	71
Tiero Gentili	0	3	1430–6						
Sons: Filippo	0	17	1459–91						
Manfredo	0	2	1476–80					0	22
Giovanni da Ghivizzano	3	5	1430–47						
Sons: Agostino	0	6	1450–63						
Iacopo	0	25	1439–92						
Piero	0	19	1438–76						
Grandsons: Nicodemo di Piero	0	5	1482–91						
Paolo di Piero	0	9	1472–91					3	69
Nicolao Neri	0	0		Tommaso Neri	0	6	1433–50	0	6
Nicolao Streghi	3	4	1430–43						
Son: Nicolao Filippo	0	10	1448–68					3	14
								36	213

dants were to be drawn no less than 249 times: thirty-six as Gonfalonieri di Giustizia and 213 as Anziani.

There are great difficulties in determining precisely how many men were drawn as Anziani in the period 1430–94.[17] In the 1430s, for example, it is not always possible to distinguish confidently between Landuccio di Giovanni, Landuccio di Iacopo, and Landuccio di Stefano Bernardi. Special problems are presented by the men drawn for the *terziere* of S. Paolino between 1438 and 1491 under the various designations: Antonio Diodati, Antonio di M. Nicolao da Coreglia, Antonio di M. Nicolao, and Antonio di M. Nicolao Diodati.[18] One might easily have failed to recognize Antonio Iacopuccii as the same man as Antonio Ruffini.[19] And I remain uncertain whether messer Nicolao di Francesco Iacobi Cittadella should be distinguished from Nicolao di Francesco Iacobi.[20] For the Anzianate, as for all other offices discussed in the present chapter, I have compiled biographies—sometimes very extensive biographies—of all office-holders. These biographies have helped me to avoid the numerous errors that would have resulted from a mere counting of names. Some ambiguities remain, and consequently some possibility of mistaken identity in a small number of cases.

According to my calculations, 546 individuals were drawn as members of the college of Anziani during the period 1430–94. The figure includes men like Giovanni Guerrucci who never actually took office because he was absent from Lucca, resident in Venice. The figure also includes men like the notary ser Massino di Bartolomeo Masini da Pietrasanta who only ever held office as a *surrogato*. Of these 546 individuals, 138, or 25 per cent of the total, were chosen on at least one occasion to head the college as Gonfaloniere di Giustizia. Again, the figure includes both *surrogati* and

[17] The basic source is Rif. 14–23. This has been supplemented where necessary by Anz. Temp. Lib. 5: Minute di Riformagioni. I have checked names against those conveniently provided by Pietro Carelli, Sommario delle Cronache, ASL Biblioteca (Manoscritti), 65, and against the printed lists published by Fumi (ed.), *Regesti*, pp. xiii–xliv, and by Lazzareschi (ed.), *Regesti*, pp. xxiii–xlii. The Fumi volume in particular contains various errors of transcription.

[18] Lucchese writers have tended to locate two distinct individuals here: Antonio da Coreglia and Antonio Diodati. See, e.g., BSL MS 2599, Antonio Iova, Annali Historici, pp. 937, 948. I believe this to be correct, and that we are dealing with Antonio di M. Nicolao di M. Michele Diodati da Coreglia and with Antonio, son of Diodato Nicolao, *cordellario* of Lucca.

[19] For clarification, see ASL Corte de' mercanti, Cause civili (1430), 150, fos. 63^{v}–65^{v}; AN 702 (ser Benedetto Franciotti), pp. 271–2.

[20] The Cittadella family was formerly called Iacobi, but I am inclined to see the second individual as the son of Francesco di Iacopo, *pannario* of S. Masseo.

those surrogated. Including *surrogati*, the office of Gonfaloniere/Anziano was filled 4,049 times between 1430 and 1494, each Anziano on average being drawn for office 7.4 times. The office of Gonfaloniere di Giustizia itself was filled 406 times during this period, giving each Gonfaloniere an average of 2.9 elections to the head of government.

A more detailed analysis is attempted in Figure 4.1. Ninety-eight men—or 18 per cent of the total—were elected on one occasion only. This figure includes a number of men whose sole appearance in the college was in the office of Gonfaloniere di Giustizia. Three hundred and fourteen men—or 57 per cent of the total—took residence in the palace, or were at least drawn, for five or more terms of office. Of these, 173 (32 per cent) were elected ten times or more; eighty-seven (16 per cent) were elected fifteen times or more; and a remarkable twenty-seven individuals (5 per cent of the total) were drawn for office on twenty or more occasions. These figures are greatly influenced by biological and chronological factors. In the 1430s the single appearance of a number of Anziani must be explained by the fact that the Anzianate was abolished for thirty years under Paolo Guinigi. They were old men at the time of the restoration; and they died shortly before or shortly after being called to office. More arbitrarily, a man like Bernardino di d. Cristoforo Bernardi appears only once in our lists merely because his first election as Anziano took place in 1494, in the very last months of our survey. At the other extreme, the more spectacularly lengthy careers of a small number of Anziani is as much a testimony to the tenacity of their hold on life through decades of plague and war as it is evidence of their political pre-eminence. In Figure 4.1 the men drawn for the office of Gonfaloniere di Giustizia (including *surrogati*) are extracted from the overall totals and given special attention. It will be seen that seventy-nine men (or 57 per cent of the total) were drawn for this office on only one or two occasions during their careers. A small élite of eleven men were elected and re-elected as Gonfaloniere di Giustizia seven, eight, and even nine times.[21]

There are particular problems in attempting to analyse the social composition of the fifteenth-century Anzianate in terms of the status and occupation of its members. A man bearing the designation 'mercer' might be a merchant; but he might be little more than a street pedlar. It is not uncommon for the same man to be variously described as 'citizen and merchant of Lucca', 'merciaio', 'pannaro', and 'lanaro'. Occupations are

[21] The consistent inclusion in the above survey of both *surrogati* and those surrogated distorts the number of office-holders, but is useful in identifying the number of men deemed suitable to occupy the governing magistracy.

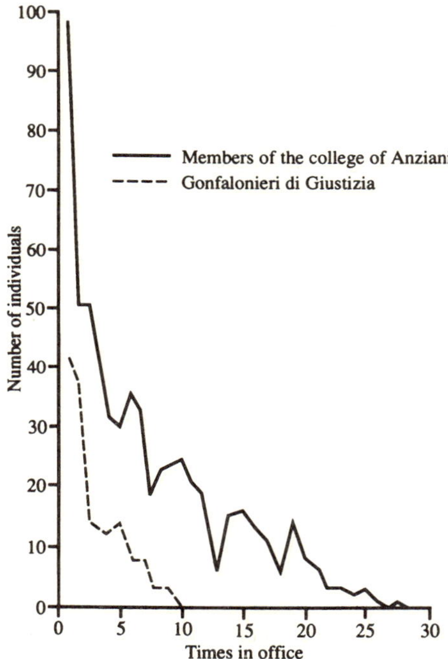

FIG. 4.1 Anziani, 1430–94: the incidence of office-holding.

seldom given in the lists of men elected to office, and have had to be gleaned from a wide range of miscellaneous sources. Sometimes identification must rest on the implications of family or business connections. No uncertainty can disguise the fact that the great majority of Anziani belonged to that mixed but essentially homogeneous group of men labelled 'citizen and merchant' in the Lucchese records. They were likely to belong to a small number of old patrician families; some, like Nicolao Domaschi and Iacopo Buiamonti, appear rather as the factors of the great companies.[22] They were engaged in the manufacture of silk cloth and in exchange transactions. They were likely to have substantial landed investments and to be involved in a wide range of business undertakings, including wool and minerals. Some, like Antonio di Lorenzo Buonvisi,

[22] The Domaschi were a prominent family by the second half of the fourteenth century, and the energy of Lucchese genealogists has traced the Buiamonti back to 1133: BSL MS 2598, Antonio Iova, Annali Historici, p. 352.

pursued administrative careers in the wider Italian arena.[23] Others became noted for their military prowess.[24]

It will be seen in Table 4.2 that 386 of the men drawn for the office of Anziano between 1430 and 1494 must be classified as merchants in the sense defined above. To these should probably be added a further twenty-one more obscure individuals. In the same category is the uncategorizable Domenico di Giovanni Bertini, humanist and *scrittore apostolico*.[25] Approximately three-quarters of all men drawn as Anziani in the years 1430–94 can confidently be identified as bankers and landowners engaged, with varying degrees of commitment, in *grand commerce*. Sixty-nine were notaries. Some notaries were members of the leading families of fifteenth-century Lucca, notably including the Antelminelli, the Gigli, and the Mansi. But as in all Mediterranean, Roman-law societies the notariate remained an attractive avenue of self-advancement for new men.[26] Somewhat less numerous were a group of men involved primarily in the retail trade: seven mercers, imperfectly distinguishable from two retail merchants of imported cloth (*pannari*); sixteen merchants engaged in the wholesale and retail trade in spices, dyes, and drugs (*speziali*); and a corn-dealer (*biadaiolo*). Then we might note a very mixed and statistically insignificant group: an artist (*pittore*), Francesco di Andrea Anguilla, some of whose work has survived;[27] a designer (of silk cloths); two goldsmiths (*orafi*); and the organist at the local cathedral. Next are a few individuals tied to the production, processing, and retailing of food and drink: one or two vintners (*vinattieri*); three butchers (*macellari*); and a dealer in dairy products (*caseario*). Finally there are a small number of artisans engaged in leather and cloth production: a hosier (*caligaio*), a shearer of cloth (*cimatore*), a leather-worker (*cuoiaio*), a spinner (*filatore*), three or four weavers (*testori*), and nine or ten dyers (*tintori*). Thirteen Anziani cannot

[23] For Antonio Buonvisi, see Michele Luzzati's entry in the *Dizionario biografico degli italiani*, xv (Rome, 1972), 302; Archivio di Stato, Napoli, MS Inventario: Sommario partium, 'Pandetta del repertorio, 1468–1580', fo. 21. The document to which the latter refers (Sommaria Licterarum Partium Antico, 19, fos. 70r–71v) appears to have been destroyed during the last war.

[24] Examples include Ruberto Angiorelli and Cristoforo Turchi; the latter was captain of the galley provided by Lucca for Pope Pius II's projected crusade against the Turks in 1464.

[25] Baroni, Notizie genealogiche, MS 1105, fos. 380r–445v; S. Paoli Puccetti, *Di Messer Domenico Bertini da Gallicano (1417–1506)* (Pescia, 1936); D. Corsi, 'Domenico Bertini', in *Dizionario biografico degli italiani*, ix (Rome, 1967), 535–8.

[26] A. Romiti and G. Tori (eds.), *Statuti e matricole del collegio dei giudici e notai della città di Lucca 1434, 1483, 1541* (Rome, 1978), 15–16; R. Abbondanza (ed.), *Il notariato a Perugia* (Rome, 1973), pp. xxxvi–xxxviii; I. Origo, *The Merchant of Prato: Francesco di Marco Datini* (London, 1957).

[27] I. Belli Barsali, 'Francesco Anguilla', in *Dizionario biografico degli italiani*, iii (Rome, 1961), 299.

TABLE 4.2. Anziani, 1430–94: composition of the college

Designation*	Confirmed	Probable	Total
Mercante	386	21	407
Scrittore apostolico	1	0	1
Notaio	69	0	69
Merciaio	7	0	7
Pannaro	2	0	2
Speziale	14	2	16
Biadaiolo	1	0	1
Pittore	1	0	1
Disegnatore	1	0	1
Orafo	2	0	2
Organista	1	0	1
Vinattiere	1	1	2
Macellaro/beccaio	3	0	3
Caseario	1	0	1
Caligaio/calzolaio	1	0	1
Cimatore	1	0	1
Cuoiaio	1	0	1
Ferrovecchio	1	0	1
Filatore	1	0	1
Testore	3	1	4
Tintore	9	1	10
Unidentified	13	—	13
			546

* I have retained Italian terms, since some are not easily replaced by a single English word.

be identified with any confidence. Mostly they appear in the lists on only one occasion. Many of them look to me like mercers, small merchants, and business agents.

Table 4.2 obscures certain distinctions and changes over time. Ten of the men drawn to head the college as Gonfaloniere di Giustizia were notaries;[28] two (Iacopo di Antonio Ruffini and Antonio di Bartolomeo ser Federighi) were dyers, of whom Ruffini appears only as a *surrogato*. Only three of the notaries (Antonio Morovelli, Cristoforo Turrettini, and

[28] Ser Francesco di Gabriello Antelminelli, ser Domenico Arrighi, ser Silvestro Corsini, ser Agnello di Fondora, ser Nicolao Gigli, ser Bartolomeo Guarguaglia, ser Antonio Morovelli, ser Michele Giovanni Pieri, ser Domenico Totti, and ser Cristoforo Turrettini.

Nicolao Gigli) held the highest office more than twice. Of those chosen as Gonfaloniere, 91 per cent were merchants; all of those regularly re-elected came from leading, established patrician families. Considering the college as a whole, 51 per cent of non-merchants (50 per cent if we include the thirteen unidentified individuals) were first elected in the 1430s. The figure rises to 70 per cent if we exclude notaries, *speziali*, and dyers. A man once elected might be re-elected, but the majority of artisans and small retail merchants achieved entry to the college of Anziani in the years immediately after 1430. Prominent butchers of later generations are absent from the lists; absent too are weavers as wealthy as Bartolomeo di Giovanni alias del Massaio, and his sons, though these might have the material resources to embroil members of the Lucchese patriciate in a nexus of debts.[29] Membership of the college of Anziani was not as open as it appears to have been in the previous century.[30] At the same time it was not as rigidly exclusive as it was to become in the cinquecento.[31] The artisans and small traders might slowly cease to be elected; but fifteenth-century Lucca continued to be characterized by a limited degree of social mobility. Silk merchants like Nicolao Lucchesini (drawn as Anziano six times between 1452 and 1464) were removed by just a generation from silk weavers and silk spinners.[32]

It is clear that for many men election to the college of Anziani was little less than a birthright. It is not easy to determine at what age young Lucchese patricians might expect first to be elected as Anziano. I have identified the birth dates of only twenty Anziani with reasonable precision. In this small sample the average age of first election was 31 years; fourteen men (70 per cent of the total) were 30 years old or less at the time of their first election. These figures may or may not be representative, but there is a lot of impressionistic evidence that many of the scions of Lucca's leading houses were in their mid to late twenties when they first entered the college. One way to establish the implicit criteria for office is to take those men whose first election as Anziani was delayed well into their adult years and examine how they differ from the rest.

[29] AN 702 (ser Benedetto Franciotti), p. 127; 703, pp. 310–21. See also 700(3), 1 Aug. 1457; 700(4), 2 Apr. 1455; 702, p. 161.

[30] This statement rests on impressions given by BSL MS 62, Memorie diverse di Lucca, pp. 211 ff.

[31] Berengo, *Nobili e mercanti*, 235–45.

[32] BSL MS 142, Racconto del principio e del progresso della famiglia Lucchesini, pp. 1–78.

Excluding men elected in the early 1430s, immediately after the restoration of the Anzianate, I have located 101 individuals who were active in Lucchese economic and political life a significant number of years before their first election as Anziani.[33] Seven of these were artisans: three dyers, two weavers, a cloth-shearer, and a goldsmith. Two were mercers, and two were *speziali*. No less than twenty-three were notaries, all of whom were active at least ten years before their first election to the college. The notaries constitute 66 per cent of all notaries elected to the college after the 1430s. Of these notaries, thirteen appear in the college more than twenty years after they first began to redact instruments. Ser Luviso di Antonio Buonaccorsi appears forty-seven years, and ser Francesco Pini a remarkable fifty years, from the date of their earliest protocolli.[34] High office was not the natural prerogative of everyone; clearly artisans and notaries needed first to accumulate experience and build up trust.

For those of more favoured birth, delay was more likely to be occasioned by the demands of the dynamic economic life of the fifteenth-century republic. The commercial apprenticeship of Lorenzo Cagnoli in Paris, of Martino Cenami in Bruges, and of Paolo Miliani in London demonstrably retarded political careers.[35] Pietro Guerci and Marco Guidiccioni were both *garzoni* in Venice thirteen years and more before they were drawn as Anziani.[36] Many young men were still absent from Lucca (and had to be surrogated) when first drawn as Anziani; many of course were never to return. Others, it is true, like Pietro Dati and Giovanni Guinigi, returned home from their early travels in good time to enter the college at the first possible opportunity.[37] In the case of individuals, financial difficulties of the type suffered by Nicolao Alberti and impoverishment, the lot of Michele Testa, might help to explain their late and brief appearances.[38] But standards were flexible, and neither bankruptcy nor the terms of the statutes excluded 'the good citizen' Paolo Balbani from office in August

[33] The defining qualities of this group are necessarily imprecise. Except when overruled by other indicators I have looked for men who held lower political office at least seven years before first election as Anziani or who were independently active professionally or economically ten years before entering the college.

[34] For dating the careers of notaries I have primarily used the data in E. Lazzareschi (ed.), *L'Archivio dei notari della repubblica lucchese* (Siena, 1916), 18–38.

[35] For Cagnoli, see ASL Imprestiti, 21, fo. 40^{v}; AN 700(4) (ser Benedetto Franciotti), 4 Nov. 1456. For Cenami, see ASL Corte de' mercanti, Libro de' sensali, 98, fo. 13^{r}; Corte de' mercanti, Cause civili, 152, fo. 30^{r}. For Miliani, see Imprestiti, 21, fo. 50^{v}; Corte de' mercanti, Cause civili, 151, fos. 142^{r}–147^{v}, 163^{r}–164^{v}.

[36] ASL Corte de' mercanti, Cause civili, 151, fo. 117^{v}.

[37] ASL Podestà di Lucca, Curia Civile, 1306, fos. 35^{r}–37^{v}, 91^{r}–93^{r}; Archivio Guinigi, MS 29, Girolamo Guinigi, Libro di ricordi, fos. 16^{r}, 20^{r}, 22^{r}.

[38] For Alberti, see SB 165, fo. 384^{r}; ASL Corte de' mercanti, Cause civili, 151, fos. 36^{r}, 38^{r},

1430.[39] The new citizen Antonio di Domenico da Montefegatesi crept into the Anzianate (as a *surrogato*) only late in life,[40] though second-generation members of new families, like Nicolao da Noceta or Domenico da Sandonnino,[41] might face no such obstacles. Some men had first to overcome the sins of their fathers. Ser Giovanni Turchi and all his sons were placed *in bannum* in 1422, from which his son Cristoforo was released only in 1438.[42] Girolamo and Michele di Giovanni Guinigi took a long time to re-establish their family politically in the post-Guinigi era.[43] Lunardo Ridolfi, son of one of Cenami's murderers, may have been freed from ban and exile in 1440, but it was nearly another forty years before he was to succeed his executed father as Anziano.[44]

Within the ranks of the ruling oligarchy, youthful indiscretion might be viewed with some toleration. Bartolomeo Angiorelli's sexual liaison with the slave of Angelo Bambacari (without her master's permission) might invoke a fine, but it in no way delayed Angiorelli's political prospects.[45] Several Anziani prefaced their entry into the college with street fights with other youths.[46] Shortly before assuming the highest office, Bernardino Bernardi and Federigo Trenta engaged in a traditional *imbroglio* between their rival families;[47] and Nicolao di Poggio was fined for the common offence of going abroad armed at night.[48] Others were less fortunate. Nicolao Totti's early career of violence may have been a factor in persuading the college of electors to await growing maturity.[49] Some

39^{v}; 152, fos. 4^{r}, 6^{v}, 24^{v}; AN 702 (ser Benedetto Franciotti), p. 65; 703, pp. 563–8; 704, pp. 42–3. For Testa, see ASL Imprestiti, 21, fo. 25^{r}; Rif. 16, p. 64.

39 Rif. 14, pp. 117–18.

40 For the granting of citizenship to Antonio da Montefegatesi, servant of Cardinal Aquileyensis, see Rif. 16, pp. 106–7.

41 Nicolao's father, d. Pietro, was secretary to Pope Nicholas V. Pietro, with his father and brothers, had been granted citizenship in 1445: Rif. 16, p. 518. Domenico was the nephew and adopted son of Bartolomeo di Andrea di Ugolino da Sandonnino. His father, uncle, and grandfather received citizenship in 1438: Rif. 15, pp. 285–6.

42 Rif. 15, pp. 272–3.

43 Polica, 'Famiglie del ceto dirigente lucchese', 377.

44 Rif. 15, pp. 491–2; 16, p. 217.

45 SB 171, fo. 79^{r}. Giorgio Franciotti was found not guilty of a similar offence: SB 161, fos. 309^{r}–310^{r}.

46 For Nicolao Gratta, see Anz. Temp. Lib.: Appelli agli Anziani, 674, unfoliated, 27 Oct. 1457. For Cristoforo Trenta, see SB 161, fo. 116^{r-v}. In 1432 Lorenzo Fanucci, *caligaio*, attacked ser Giovanni Arrighi in a shop in the *contrada* of S. Sensio: SB 159, fos. 224^{r}–225^{v}, 244^{r-v}.

47 Rif. 22, pp. 30–2.

48 Rif. 16, pp. 544–5. The offence also involved Francesco di Stefano di Poggio—elected Anziano shortly before and shortly afterwards—and his brother Pietro.

49 SB 159, fos. 218^{r}–219^{r}; Rif. 15, p. 273; 16, pp. 159–60. A Nicolao di Totto il Totti, but described as a butcher, was involved in a fracas in Lucca in the late 1430s: SB 159, fo. 176^{r-v}.

misdemeanours were clearly more threatening to the social fabric. In 1440 Francesco Pini refused to put away his concubine following his marriage to a daughter of the powerful Totti family. This, together with an earlier incident when Pini left his post on the walls of Lucca to fetch a glass of water for his mother, may well have contributed to a general reputation for unreliability that delayed Pini's first election as Anziano to advanced old age.[50] Though found not guilty, an accusation of theft against Antonio Narducci seems to have counted against him.[51] A number of young patricians, punished in 1474 by a *balìa* of twenty-four appointed to contain disorder, all appear as Anziani a little later than might have been anticipated for their rank.[52] It is impossible to determine whether Bartolomeo di Antonio Chelli's late arrival in the palace of the Anziani is attributable to his early involvement in the plot of ser Tommaso Lupardi[53] or to his lowly occupation as cropper of cloth.

Once elected, an Anziano was likely to be re-elected at roughly two-year intervals for the rest of his life. Ninety-two men were already dead when last drawn for office; at least nine others died during their two-month tenure of office. These figures are themselves an implicit testimony to the regular tempo of re-election. One hundred and forty-four men held office in the 1490s.[54] At least three of these died before 1494; the careers of many of the others extended far beyond the limits of the present study. Of the remaining 301 Anziani, forty-eight men can be shown without doubt to have died within three years—some within a few weeks—of their last period of office. Since this figure rests on entirely incidental references taken from a wide range of legal, notarial, and political sources, the true number would undoubtedly be very much greater. At least ten former Anziani left Lucca permanently to pursue commercial activities elsewhere in Italy or beyond the Alps. Of these, Lorenzo Mariani, with his newly acquired Genoese citizenship, was to continue to render most valuable

An early propensity to violence may have retarded others. For Giovanni Boccella, see ibid., fos. 222^{v}, 247^{r-v}. For ser Iacopo Ciampanti, see ibid., fos. 200^{r}–201^{r}. For Guaspare Micheli, see SB 161, fo. 12^{r-v}. Damiano Sabulini: Rif. 15, p. 396. Ser Pietro Tucci: SB 171, fos. 75^{v}–76^{r}; AN 702 (ser Benedetto Franciotti), 27 July 1459, p. 233.

50 Anz. Temp. Lib. 5, fo. 72^{r-v}; Rif. 15, pp. 457–8.

51 His brother Ambrosio, similarly accused in 1432, never became a member of the college of Anziani: SB 159, fos. 219^{r}–220^{r}.

52 ASL Biblioteca (Manoscritti), 65, Pietro Carelli, Sommario delle Cronache, fo. 118^{v}.

53 SB 161, fos. 118^{r}–121^{v}. For the Lupardi plot, see Ch. 2.

54 I have excluded Giovanni Battista Dati, ser Gerardo Nicolai, Paolo Parpaglioni, and Pietro di Poggio, who were among the ninety-two men already dead when last drawn for office.

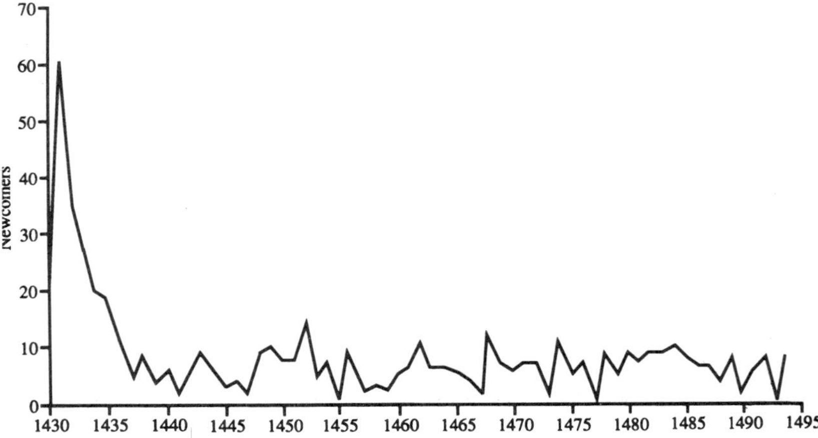

FIG. 4.2 Anziani, 1430–94: number of new Anziani per annum.

services to the republic.[55] At least two men left Lucca permanently to pursue administrative careers elsewhere in the peninsula. Guglielmo di Marco Cenami joined the Church and became prior of S. Frediano.[56] Newcomers to the college of Anziani, as shown in Figure 4.2, did little more than replenish the ranks of those who had died or were absent. After the 1430s an average of six new Anziani made their appearance every year among the sixty men who held office. There appears to be a clear correlation—most noticeably after 1450 and throughout the 1480s—between high mortality from plague and the number of new faces in the palace of the Anziani.

Of course not all Anziani were returned regularly until death. Excluding a few old men who (whether by their will or that of others) faded from the scene during their last years, I have found fifty-four men who simply ceased to be re-elected. Thirty men (including two of the above fifty-four) faced periods of absence of eight years or more between successive terms in office. Some of these latter lacunae are explained by periods of residence out of Lucca in the commercial colonies, a few by

[55] ASL Imprestiti, 21, fo. 21^{v}; Rif. 15, p. 265; 16, p. 270; NAC, N 116 (ser Nicolao di Coluccio di Pellegrino da Pietrasanta, 1435–39), 26 Nov. 1438.

[56] ASL Archivio Arnolfini, 2, fos. 52^{r}–54^{r}, 88^{r}–89^{v}, 164^{r}–166^{v}; BSL MS 415, Notizie antiche del monastero e chiesa di S. Frediano, fos. 49^{r}, 54^{r}, 63^{r}; S. Giancoli, 'Cenami', in *Dizionario biografico degli italiani*, xxiii (Rome, 1979), 496.

spells of exile. Others, like Antonio Streghi, who was absent from the palace for a remarkable forty-one years between 1439 and 1480, were clearly found unsuitable for reasons not easily recoverable. In individual cases we are allowed some insights into contemporary visions of unsuitability. Notaries generally had a bad reputation for ignorance, corruption, and immorality. Ser Iacopo da Fiano quickly disappeared from office once he had been convicted for falsifying the records of the *Gabella Maggiore* to the prejudice of the city's revenues.[57] Private acts of dishonesty might be treated with more understanding. Garzone Garzoni's conviction for stealing pears from a kinsman's garden had no implications for his political prospects.[58] And—more surprisingly—Cristoforo Ricciardi's theft of account books from the house of Nicolao Alberti resulted in a ban but no visible interruption to his regular re-election to the palace of government.[59] The insults given by Stefano Alberti to a leading citizen and the occasional acts of violence by Tommaso Neri (brother of Nicolao) may have been factors in the interrupted and eventually curtailed careers of both men.[60] But Antonio Buonvisi was soon able to rehabilitate himself after wounding the physician Michele da Coreglia.[61] And Nicolao di Iacopo Nuccii was back in office a year after his serious assault on Antonio Narducci.[62]

Two points should be stressed. First, twenty-four of those whose careers ended prematurely (44 per cent of the total) were artisans, notaries, *speziali*, or retail traders. Others were at best of lesser families. In Figure 4.3 I have traced the number of men elected to the Anzianate per quinquennium. It will be noted that (apart from the years of high mortality of the early 1450s) the corpus of citizens from whom Anziani were drawn was slightly larger immediately after 1430 than it was to become later in the century. It has been noted that artisans and retail merchants had a diminishing chance of being elected as the century progressed. The failure of some individuals to achieve re-election reflects this marginal tightening of the oligarchy. Secondly, at least ten of those who disappeared prematurely were guilty of political or quasi-political

[57] ASL Podestà di Lucca, Inquisizioni, 5257, fos. 17^{r}–19^{v}; AAL Cause civili della Curia (ser Ciomeo Pieri, 1453), fos. 5^{r} ff.

[58] SB 202, fo. 354^{r-v}.

[59] SB 165, fo. 384^{r}.

[60] SB 159, fos. 313^{r}–314^{r}; 161, fos. 228^{r-v}, 317^{r-v}. See also ASL Podestà di Lucca, Inquisizioni, 5229, no foliation, case beginning 1 June 1436.

[61] M. Luzzati, 'Benedetto Buonvisi', in *Dizionario biografico degli italiani*, xv (Rome, 1972), 302.

[62] SB 165, fos. 354^{v}–355^{v}, 357^{r}.

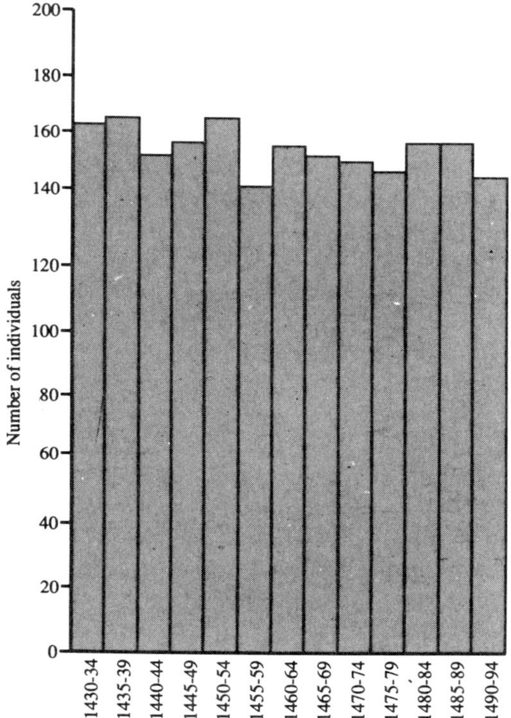

FIG. 4.3 Anziani, 1430–94: election to the college per quinquennium.

crimes. Many of these men have already been treated in some detail in Chapters 2 and 3. Some disappeared because of flight and exile. Others, like Pietro Accettanti or ser Massino di Bartolomeo Masini da Pietrasanta, returned, but never again held high office.

Significantly, political disgrace had no impact beyond the circle of those immediately involved. To this the fortunes of the Burlamacchi family provide compelling testimony. In the 1430s the arrest and exile of Giovanni Burlamacchi for his part in Pietro Cenami's murder in no way prejudiced his brothers Michele (elected Gonfaloniere five times, Anziano thrice) or Nicolao (elected four times Gonfaloniere and five times Anziano). In the 1470s the bankruptcy of Adriano Burlamacchi, with its serious political implications of reprisals from Milan,[63] did not interrupt

[63] ASL Archivio Guinigi, MS 29, Girolamo Guinigi, Libro di ricordi, fo. 25^{v}; Lazzareschi (ed.), *Regesti*, 115, 123–7, 129, 165, 167, 169–71, 176.

the regular re-election of his brothers Giovanni and Pietro. The di Poggio family weathered both the events of 1436 and the later murder by Nicolao di Poggio of the *officiale di Porta S. Pietro*, ser Giovanni del Camarlingho.[64] Sons were normally embraced in the sentences imposed on their fathers. But time and again these sons were readmitted to favour at the earliest possible opportunity. Giovanni Burlamacchi's son Girolamo was being elected Anziano from 1464; and, more tardily, Lunardo di Nicolao Ridolfi from 1478. Even the delinquents themselves (especially those of impeccable pedigree) were not shunned for ever. Iacopo da Ghivizzano was back in office by 1452; Stefano di Nicolao di Poggio was drawn again—posthumously as Gonfaloniere—in 1442; Stefano's ally ser Cristoforo Turrettini had already returned to the palace late in the previous year. The tolerance, and the disinclination to pursue a vendetta, are important. It is a theme to which we shall return.

The targeting of the individual for retribution does not diminish the importance of the Lucchese family as a political unit. In a frequently quoted phrase Marino Berengo, said: 'The key to the dynamics of office-holding is held by the [agnate] family rather than by [cognate] relatives.'[65] Of course, in the sixteenth century political eligibility itself came to be defined in terms of genealogy. But Lucchese statutes had long assumed the 'casata' as the entity with which constitution-makers had to work. The college of Anziani could not contain two members of the same family; each family was limited to one Gonfaloniere every two years. Four months had to elapse between the holding of office by brothers or by father and son. The links might be very distant, but the sense of common identity remained unimpaired. The last common male ancestor of those eighteen members of the di Poggio family who held the office of Anziano between 1430 and 1494 is lost in the mists of antiquity.[66] And there was significant intermarriage between the various branches of that family. But the di Poggio were organized under a consul, and met periodically to settle matters relating to the family and to administer property held jointly by the family.[67] In 1446 Francesco di Stefano di Nicolao di Poggio was unable to take his place as *surrogato* because Paolo di Stefano di Iacopo di Poggio was already a member of the college.[68] The *agnatione* might span not only

[64] ASL Biblioteca (Manoscritti), 65, Pietro Carelli, Sommario delle Cronache, fo. 107^{v}.

[65] Berengo, *Nobili e mercanti*, 32: 'Non tanto la parentela quanto la famiglia costituisce dunque la chiave nell'organismo delle cariche.'

[66] Baroni has made various contradictory and unsuccessful attempts at linkage: Notizie genealogiche, MS 1128, fos. 5^{r}–183^{r}.

[67] Bratchel, 'The *Consorteria* in 15th-Century Tuscany', 13–33.

[68] Rif. 16, pp. 632–5.

very distant branches of a family, but also a great variety of persons. At the beginning of the century the silk spinner Guido di Santuccio de' Martini claimed his right to be buried in S. Frediano in the sepulchre of the *consorteria* de' Martini, one of the most ancient noble houses of the city.[69]

For the most part the great Anziani-producing families of fifteenth-century Lucca displayed great social uniformity. And it must be remarked that most members even of families of unquestioned antiquity were able to trace themselves back to a single late fourteenth-century root. All Arnolfini Anziani were direct descendants of Giannino Arnolfini and of his two sons Nicolao and Arrigo. The Burlamacchi, resident for centuries in the parish of S. Alessandro maggiore, were all descended from Gerardo di Pietro, himself the family's first Gonfaloniere in 1387.[70] The Cenami, whose origins have been enthusiastically traced back to the early eleventh century, were all descendants of Guisfredo, who died *c.*1413 and whose five sons lived together in the family palace in *contrada* S. Frediano. This palace continued to be held undivided by the grandchildren after 1436.[71] It was common for brothers to continue to live together, though more extended arrangements invariably caused tensions. And the Cenami ménage broke up with characteristic bitterness *c.*1460.[72] Vito Tirelli has well captured the strange coexistence in Lucca of intense family feeling with the bickerings and petty jealousies of day-to-day life.[73] The latter is amply displayed among the patrician families that dominated the college of Anziani in the frequent squabbles over inheritance and by such incidents as the resentful protest of Vincenzo Spada at the little expenses he had incurred in supporting his 14-year-old orphaned brother.[74] The inclination to disinherit sons was, I believe, a peculiarity of the Bertini family.[75]

Just as there are problems in identifying the number of individuals who held the office of Anziano, so too there are problems in calculating the number of families. The counting of names is not enough. There was an interesting dispute over the fact that people bearing the derivation 'da Ghivizzano' were claiming the right to bear the arms issued to the heirs of

[69] ASL Archivio Diplomatico: Pergamene (Opera S. Croce, 1037), 11 Mar. 1406.

[70] M. Luzzati, 'Burlamacchi', in *Dizionario biografico degli italiani*, xv (Rome, 1972), 433.

[71] ASL Archivio Arnolfini, 2, fo. 66^{r}.

[72] Ibid., fos. 122^{r}–123^{v}, 138^{r-v}, 164^{r}–166^{v}, 167^{r-v}.

[73] Tirelli, '"Libri di ricordanze"'.

[74] ASL Podestà di Lucca, Curia Civile, 1309, fos. 32^{r}–33^{r}.

[75] The Anziano Domenico Bertini was disinherited by his father: Baroni, Notizie genealogiche, MS 1105, fo. 380^{v}. The Anziano Pierantonio Bertini was left only what was due to him according to the statutes.

Piero di Giovanni di Piero Nossi da Ghivizzano in 1469 by the Emperor Frederick III.[76] There would seem to be no compelling reason to link the descendants of Piero di Ciomeo da Ghivizzano with the family later associated with that name. Baroni collects together many men called Neri.[77] But there is only the most fragile hint of a link between the line of Gabrielle Neri *speziale* and that of Nicolao Neri *pannaro*.[78] And there is no doubt that the Streghi stem from two quite distinct roots: those from Barga and those who came to claim descent from the *signori* di Vallecchia.[79] There is the ever present danger of such confusions as di Michele with dei Micheli. Conversely, one might have missed the fact that ser Francesco Gabbrielli, Iacopo di Filippo Mugia, and Balduccio Parghia should all additionally be labelled degli Antelminelli.[80] It is impossible to determine how many Anziani called da Massa may meaningfully be placed in the great Cattani clan. Again, therefore, it must be conceded that calculations are tentative and fallible. It appears that 202 different families fed the college of Anziani between 1430 and 1494, but the figure may be as high as 207.

Of the 202 families, only sixty-two provided the college with its leadership as Gonfaloniere di Giustizia. This merely confirms impressions that the office of Gonfaloniere tended to become the special preserve of a small number of leading families. Between 96 and 101 families (48–9 per cent of the total) contributed just one man to the Anzianate; twenty-two to twenty-five of these were represented by one man elected just once. The correlate of this is that membership of the college was overwhelmingly drawn from relatively few families. In Table 4.3 I have set out the twenty-five most represented families. These twenty-five families (12 per cent of the total) were drawn for office no less than 1,936 times (48 per cent of the total number of places). The figure includes both *surrogati* and those surrogated. The top five families, representing 2.5 per cent of all families participating in the college, held nearly 18 per cent of all places.

Individual families were associated with particular *terzieri*: the di Poggio with S. Paolino, the Trenta with S. Salvatore, the Guinigi with S.

[76] Baroni, Notizie genealogiche, MS 1113, fos. 429^{v}, 447^{r}.

[77] Baroni, Notizie genealogiche, MS 1122, fos. 158^{r}–205^{r}.

[78] Bartolomeo di Gabrielle was procurator of Lorenzo di Nicolao Neri during his infirmity in Nov. 1454: ASL Corte de' mercanti, Cause civili, 151, fo. 96^{v}. The procuratorship is of course of no special significance, but the circumstances of Lorenzo's incapacity may suggest a closer relationship.

[79] Baroni, Notizie genealogiche, MS 1133, fos. 168^{r}, 262^{r-v}.

[80] Half a century earlier, there are references to a certain Giovanni Parghia degli Antelminelli. For Balduccio himself, see Belli Barsali, *Lucca*, 188.

TABLE 4.3. Anziani, 1430–94: membership by family

Family name	Number of individuals	Gonfaloniere di Giustizia	Anziano	Total
Trenta	22	27	145	172
Poggio	18	30	135	165
Totti*	18	19	139	158
Martini*	10	9	116	125
Bernardi	14	15	85	100
Gigli	9	15	78	93
Cenami	10	18	71	89
Rapondi	8	3	81	84
Arrighi*	10	9	74	83
Ser Federighi	8	8	70	78
Ghivizzano	6	3	69	72
Portico	7	10	60	70
Arnolfini	8	11	58	69
Balbani	5	13	49	62
Guinigi	5	9	48	57
Burlamacchi	6	9	42	51
Guidiccioni	7	13	38	51
Nocchi*	6	0	51	51
Tegrimi	5	10	38	48
Turrettini	4	9	37	46
Bernardini	8	14	31	45
Fondora	5	2	42	44
Buonvisi	4	12	31	43
Parpaglioni	4	6	34	40
Ser Giusti	5	0	40	40
				1936

* The families whose names are asterisked have for various reasons given me pause. Baroni considers the Arrighi to be a single family. But, as with the Totti, there are problems about attributing a common identity. I have deducted ser Marco Martini from the Martini. Ser Marco is, I believe, the man severally referred to as ser Marco di Martino, ser Marco Vannelli, ser Marco Martini da Lammari, ser Marco Martini Vannelli, and ser Marco di Vannello Martini. It is possible that the family of dyers called Nocchi should be distinguished from the notaries of the same name.

Martino. It is true that members of most of the larger clans were, during the course of the century, elected for two or even all three *terzieri*. Of the 202 families, sixty-eight (including eighteen of the twenty-five most represented families) represented more than one *terziere* during the course of the century; twenty-three families produced Anziani for all three *terzieri*. The statistics conceal the fact that in many cases, as with the da Ghivizzano, Gigli, or di Poggio, only one or two isolated individuals appear briefly for a different *terziere* from that of other members of the family. Looking at individuals, of the 546 men who were elected as Anziani between 1430 and 1494, fifty-five were elected for two different *terzieri* during the course of their careers; a further eleven men represented all three *terzieri* at one time or another. These figures fully support the strong territorial base of Lucchese familial politics suggested in earlier chapters. They also show that the simpler electoral procedures in Lucca meant that it was not as politically suicidal as in Florence to operate outside that base.[81] A change of *terziere* might be an illusion, a product merely of boundary changes.[82] Changes of *terziere* show some residential mobility, particularly but not exclusively among newer families. And changes of *terzieri* often seem to reflect a desire for closer association with business or political allies. Lorenzo Buonvisi (certainly) and Domenico di Giovanni (probably) were deeply involved in the revolution of 1430. Both men rapidly start to appear for the *terziere* of S. Salvatore together with the other conspirators of August 1430. Gerardo Cattani and his son Lorenzo were both assessed in 1431 in via Nuova in S. Salvatore.[83] Lorenzo was an ally of the di Poggio, and was centrally involved in their murder of Pietro Cenami. From 1431 Lorenzo was elected as Anziano for the di Poggio *terziere* of S. Paolino; his father continued to appear for S. Salvatore. When Cello Martini, between 1438 and 1440, changed from S. Martino to S. Salvatore, he was simply moving to the *terziere* of his leading business partner.[84]

Individuals and families were tied together by neighbourhood and business associations. They were tied together most firmly by marriage. For contemporary Florence a great deal of work has been done on the political consequences of marriages contracted between that city's great

[81] Kent, *Household and Lineage*, 171–85.

[82] For some a change from S. Paolino to S. Martino simply reflects the transfer of the *contrada* of SS. Giovanni e Reparata to the *terziere* of S. Martino.

[83] ASL Imprestiti, 21, fo. 29^{v}.

[84] From the late 1430s Cello Martini became increasingly involved in the silk companies of his father's former partner, Lorenzo Buonvisi. Cello married Buonvisi's daughter Caterina.

patrician families.[85] For Lucca the kind of evidence upon which such studies have been based is unquestionably less plentiful. But for Lucca too some traces have survived of marriage negotiations and of the role of the marriage-broker.[86] For the Anziani-producing families of fifteenth-century Lucca daughters were, of course, a mixed asset. On the one hand, a plenitude of nubile daughters was the most frequent preface to complaints of pressing financial difficulties. Such was the excuse of Giovanni Gigli (Anziano or Gonfaloniere twenty-two times between 1431 and 1475) when he protested himself a pauper and begged for five years in which to satisfy his creditors.[87] On the other hand, the betrothal of daughters was a well-tested mechanism for forging alliances, both economic and political, and for extending a family's influence. A word of caution remains apposite. We deal not merely with the passive instruments of inter-family politics or with the pawns of statistical historical analysis. Sentiment might intervene, and with unpredictable results. Slaves appear as mistresses as frequently in Lucca as in other late medieval Italian communities.[88] When Pietro Bernardi (Anziano or Gonfaloniere nine times between 1431 and 1449) chose to marry his slave, he initiated a family conflict with poignant consequences for the parties most immediately involved.[89] We have already noted how Francesco Pini's attachment to his concubine went beyond what was seemly when in 1440 he refused to receive his new wife.[90]

Most men were more conformist. Giusfredo Cenami was not dissuaded from a match with the Burlamacchi family by the fact that Caterina di Michele Burlamacchi was the niece of one of his father's murderers. Indeed, the marriage may represent a conscious act of conciliation between the two families. The importance of marriage as a tool of family politics ensured not only that the college of Anziani comprised the scions

[85] The pertinent literature is very considerable. Special attention might be drawn to M. M. Bullard, 'Marriage Politics and the Family in Florence: The Strozzi–Medici Alliance of 1508', *American Historical Review*, lxxxiv (1979), 668–87.

[86] Baroni, Notizie genealogiche, MS 1121, p. 440; ASL Archivio Guinigi, MS 29, Girolamo Guinigi, Libro di ricordi, fo. 57^v; AN 702 (ser Benedetto Franciotti), pp. 217–18.

[87] ASL Podestà di Lucca, Curia Civile, 1306, fos. 48^r, 69^r–74^v.

[88] See, e.g., AN 548 (ser Ciomeo Pieri), fo. 11^{r-v}. Besides the obvious role of female slaves within the household, the Lucchese criminal records make frequent reference to the damage likely to be caused to the master when Lucchese citizens resorted to slaves who were the property of another.

[89] ASL Podestà di Lucca, Curia Civile, 1309, fos. 40^v–50^r, 89^r–90^r, 192^r–199^r; AN 700(2) (ser Benedetto Franciotti), 21 July 1454, 2 July 1455; 700(4), 11 July 1454; 702, p. 111 (20 Jan. 1459).

[90] See above, p. 99.

of relatively few families, but that those families were inextricably bound together by marriage contracts. Paolino di Bartolomeo Bernardini married off six of his eight daughters, despite the fact that he also had five sons for whom to provide. Bernardini's daughter Giovanna married Cristoforo Bernardi, a doctor of law and thus excluded by statute from the Anzianate; his remaining five sons-in-law were all drawn periodically for the office of Anziano. The details are set out in Table 4.4. Paolino Bernardini was drawn for the college of Anziani on eleven occasions; his five eligible sons-in-law between them were drawn as Anziani sixty-two times prior to 1494. The seven families united by the marriages of Paolino Bernardini's daughters were drawn for office a total of 544 times between 1430 and 1494. These families account for 13.4 per cent of all places, 20.7 per cent of all places with regard to the office of Gonfaloniere di Giustizia. These calculations include both *surrogati* and those surrogated. Paolino Bernardini is not an isolated or atypical example. Giusfredo Cenami (perhaps because he had no sons) married off all six of his daughters. Three of his sons-in-law were Anziani prior to 1494; members of the families thus united were drawn as Anziani a total of 403 times between 1430 and 1494. Iacopo Galganetti, although he had two sons, arranged marriages for five of his daughters. Four of his sons-in-law were Anziani prior to 1494; these families accounted for 240 places in the period under consideration.

The above evidence raises certain questions in the context of the general historiography of fifteenth- and sixteenth-century Italy. In recent decades a number of regional studies have indicated that Italian patrician families were consciously limiting the marriage of daughters (and indeed of sons) as a strategy for the preservation of family wealth.[91] The concomitant increase in the number of daughters placed in nunneries is hardly illustrated by the anecdotal examples cited above. Only Chiara of the seven surviving daughters of Paolino Bernardini entered a nunnery—that of S. Michelotto. I lack the wealth of data that would be required to prove that this represents the norm, and things had clearly changed by the sixteenth century.[92] My impression for fifteenth-century Lucca is that fathers from all ranks of society were anxious to find husbands for as many daughters as possible. The impression stems both from individual examples and from the ambitions of fathers as expressed in wills, court

[91] See, e.g., R. B. Litchfield, 'Demographic Characteristics of Florentine Patrician Families, Sixteenth to Nineteenth Centuries', *Journal of Economic History*, xxix (1969), 191–205; J. C. Davis, *A Venetian Family and its Fortune (1500–1900)* (Philadelphia, 1975).

[92] Berengo, *Nobili e mercanti*, 50, 365–6.

TABLE 4.4. Anziani, 1430–94: marriage politics: the example of Paolino Bernardini

	Gonfaloniere di Giustizia	Anziano	Total		Gonfaloniere di Giustizia	Anziano	Total
Paolino Bernardini	5	6	11	The Bernardini	14	31	45
Sons-in-law:							
Cristoforo Bernardi (m. Giovanna)	0	0	0	The Bernardi	15	85	100
Pietro Burlamacchi (m. Angela)	0	6	6	The Burlamacchi	9	42	51
Giovanni di Poggio (m. Maddelena)	5	18	23	The di Poggio	30	135	165
Piero Rapondi (m. Appolonia)	0	26	26	The Rapondi	3	81	84
Francesco Sandei (m. Caterina)	0	1	1	The Sandei	5	16	21
Paolo ser Federighi (m. Elisabetta)	0	6	6	The Ser Federighi	8	70	78
Total	10	63	73		84	460	544

records, notarial acts, and a wide range of other miscellaneous source material. I would add that in practice patrician fathers dying without male issue showed a very marked propensity to name their daughters as heirs, however much this might be condemned by the advocates of the agnatic descent group.[93] Whether or not enjoying the status of heiress, it would seem undeniable that in the fifteenth century an abundant supply of young patrician girls was entering the local marriage market. We are left with the impression of a vast network of marriage alliances enfolding the vast majority of men from among whom, in practice, Anziani were elected.

One final point is suggested by the marriages of Paolino Bernardini's daughters. Paolino Bernardini was regularly elected as Anziano or Gonfaloniere di Giustizia for the *terziere* of S. Martino until his death *c.*1450. Four of his daughters married into families that produced Anziani for the *terziere* of S. Salvatore, two into families associated with the *terziere* of S. Paolino. In Figure 4.4 I have attempted to locate Paolino Bernardini and his six sons-in-law in urban space. The geographical spread is clearly indicated: from the Bernardini in *contrada* S. Benedetto to the Sandei in S. Pier Cigoli to the Burlamacchi resident for centuries in the parish of S. Alessandro maggiore. In order to explore how far the Bernardini may be regarded as typical, I have examined the marriages of all the daughters of Anziani (1430–94) for which I have reliable data. I have information relating to the daughters of ninety-six Anziani (18 per cent of the total). The sample involves 151 daughters and 161 marriages (since some of the data concern second marriages). The sample rests on incidental references, and embraces a wide variety of individuals, though it inevitably favours members of the leading families. Ninety-four of the above marriages (58 per cent) were contracted with men who themselves were to be elected as Anziani prior to 1494.[94] In only thirty-six cases (38 per cent of the sample) did the *terziere* represented, or primarily represented, by the son-in-law correspond with the *terziere* associated with the father-in-law. The sample can be extended. Whilst themselves never Anziani, fifty-one of the husbands were drawn from families regularly represented in the college. A further eight can be attributed to a *terziere* on the basis of holding an office other than that of Anziano. Of this enlarged sample of 153 marriages (95 per cent of the total), ninety-five (62

[93] Tirelli, '"Libri di ricordanze"', 158.

[94] The percentage is of no particular significance. Some husbands were ineligible for the office of Anziano as doctors of law or medicine; some were absent from Lucca; many were the victims of the chronological limits of the present study, beginning their careers only after 1494.

FIG. 4.4 Anziani, 1430–94: marriages of the daughters of Paolino Bernardini. [1]At this time, the houses of the Rapondi and of the Ser Federighi were centred around the Braccio Baioli, which I have been unable to locate with any confidence. They appear to have lived to the east of the church of S. Salvatore.

per cent) were contracted with families associated with a different *terziere* from that represented by the bride' s father. A similar pattern emerges if we turn from the daughters to the wives of Anziani. I have identified the wives of 154 Anziani (28 per cent of the total). The sample includes 172 wives, since it includes a number of second wives. The families of fourteen of these wives cannot be linked to a specific *terziere*, because they were non-Lucchese, or because they disappear from the records before the restoration of the Anzianate in 1430, or, in the case of Pietro Bernardi, because he married his slave. In only sixty-three of the remaining 158 marriages (slightly less than 40 per cent) is there a correlation between the *terzieri* of the contracting parties. Of course the use of *terzieri* is only a very crude guide to the geographical location of families. The above statistics are distorted by the fact that some husbands—for example, Cello Martini or Giovanni Garzoni—quickly changed to represent the same *terziere* as their new fathers-in-law. But with all the manifest imperfections of these calculations, it is abundantly clear that marriage politics bound together leading families from all parts of the city into a cohesive and intricately interrelated ruling group.

These findings may, at first sight, appear to contradict the stress on neighbourhood solidarities of earlier chapters. But this is not so. In previous chapters we treated of the specially intense relationships engendered by perilous political undertakings. In such circumstances lives and fortunes tended to be entrusted to a limited circle of agnatic kinsmen, clients, and near neighbours. In utilizing the political assets possessed in their daughters, Lucchese patricians might well seek to forge links to best advantage as and where opportunities arose. Even so, the bare statistics serve to conceal the regularity of intermarriage between and within certain families. And mention has already been made of the capacity of leading citizens to draw their sons-in-law into a new geographical orbit.

The composition of the college of Anziani between 1430 and 1494 offers useful insights into eligibility for high political office and into membership of Lucca's political élite. At the same time, many who were politically active, and even predominant, never resided in the palace of the Anziani. For a more comprehensive view of political participation in fifteenth-century Lucca, it is necessary to turn to the General Council: the Consiglio Generale. If ordinary executive authority rested in the college of Anziani, supreme deliberative authority and legislative power were exercised by the General Council.[95] Like the Anziani, the General Council disappeared during the thirty years of Guinigi rule. As with the Anziani, the essential qualification for membership of the General Council was Lucchese citizenship: the few additional statutory limitations related to matters such as age and to the prohibition against a single individual holding office in two consecutive years. As with the Anziani, too, the theoretical openness of the Lucchese political system was significantly qualified by electoral procedures.

The first General Council of the restored republic was elected on 11 October 1430 by that same *balìa* of twelve that, two months earlier, had been responsible for the reconstituted Anzianate.[96] The General Council was elected for a period of one year, and consisted of 120 members, forty representatives of each *terziere*. To this Council, together with the college of Anziani, was given full, free, and absolute authority and jurisdiction over Lucca and its territories. On 24 September 1431, at a meeting of the General Council, the current Anziani together with the *balìa* of six *Difensori della libertà* were given authority to elect four men per *terziere* from the Council of Thirty-Six. Altogether, and including the twelve

[95] The General Council is discussed by Bongi, *Inventario*, i. 132–6. For a more recent history, see A. Romiti (ed.), *Riformagioni della Repubblica di Lucca (1369–1400): Volume primo (Marzo 1369–Agosto 1370 e aggiunte)* (Rome, 1980), pp. xxi–xxviii.

[96] Rif. 14, pp. 39–41.

representatives of the Council of Thirty-Six, they were to proceed to the election of thirty to forty men per *terziere* to form the new General Council, whose authority was to commence on 12 October 1431 and to last for one year. It was at this time that the General Council was reduced to ninety members, thirty per *terziere*.[97] On 12 October 1432 the next General Council was elected in the same way, and was to hold office until the middle of March 1434.[98] Thereafter each successive General Council was to hold office for a period of one year, beginning on 15 March. And from 1434 each successive General Council was elected by the college of Anziani then in office together with twelve members of the Council of Thirty-Six (four per *terziere*) who themselves were elected by the college of Anziani.[99]

It is particularly difficult to calculate the number of men who were elected to the General Council between 1430 and 1494. More than in the case of the Anziani, individual members of the General Council are identified by a patronymic; so more members of the General Council have eluded attempts at compiling biographical data. In the General Council, therefore, there are very real opportunities for uniting separate individuals under a single name or for listing one councillor under several titles. According to my calculations, 955 individuals were elected to the General Council between 1430 and 1494. The office was filled 5,789 times over the period as a whole, each councillor being elected to office an average of 6.1 times. These figures may be compared with the 546 men drawn for the office of Anziano, each Anziano on average being drawn for office 7.4 times. For the Anzianate a minimum of 120 individuals (plus *surrogati*) were required to replenish that office over a two-year period; the General Council drew on a corpus of 180 individuals over the same two-year cycle. The number of men elected to the General Council is somewhat greater than might have been anticipated from a comparison of the relative recruitment requirements of the two bodies. It is clear that membership of the General Council was more open than that of the Anzianate, despite the fact that—directly or indirectly—election to the General Council was largely controlled by the college of Anziani.

A small number of Anziani were never elected as members of the General Council. It is difficult to attribute much significance to these anomalies, which are largely explained by premature deaths. More to the

97 Anz. Temp. Lib. 5, fos. 68^{v}–71^{v}.

98 Rif. 14, pp. 284–5.

99 Ibid., pp. 507–8.

point, 510 members of the General Council (53.4 per cent of the total) also held office as Anziani. The pre-eminence of sometime-Anziani in the General Council becomes more apparent if we calculate the number of times that these men were elected as councillors. The 510 sometime-Anziani were elected to the General Council no fewer than 4,440 times between 1430 and 1494. Though constituting little more than half of the men elected to the latter office, men who had also been drawn as Anziani filled 76.5 per cent of the available places in the General Council. Each sometime-Anziano was elected as councillor on average 8.7 times. They were regularly re-elected every two years; and it is common to find two brothers yearly succeeding each other in the General Council over a very considerable period. By contrast, every non-Anziano on average was elected to the Council only three times during the course of his career. But it is with this new ingredient in the political life of the fifteenth-century republic that we now concern ourselves.

Table 4.5 details the composition of the General Council between 1430 and 1494, with special attention to members who have not already been considered under the Anzianate. Three points deserve attention. First, the table shows the importance within the General Council of the *dottori*. Their numbers were not particularly large: forty-seven men altogether between 1430 and 1494 if we include sixteen individuals who should almost certainly be identified as doctors of law or medicine. But they were returned to the Council time and again, each on average being returned 7.1 times (or 5.7 times if we include the necessarily more obscure 'probables'). Secondly, more than 100 of the non-Anziani can confidently be identified as merchants. Unlike the sometime-Anziani, these merchants were likely to make only a fleeting appearance in the Council, each on average being elected no more than twice. Thirdly, the table clearly indicates that the General Council was open to a significant number of artisans and retailers of basic foodstuffs. At least 100 members of the General Council may be described thus, with weavers prominent amongst them.

Doctors of law and medicine had been excluded from the Anzianate since 1392.[100] The exclusion, which was common to other Italian republics,[101] was prompted by a fear that the silver-tongued lawyers would gain undue prominence over other citizens. Yet the exclusion remains curious, and hardly curtailed their political importance. The lawyers in particular were often members of Lucca's leading families: the Arnolfini,

[100] Berengo, *Nobili e mercanti*, 53.

[101] Guidi, *Il governo della città-repubblica di Firenze*, writes of a similar suspicion of lawyers in contemporary Florence.

Table 4.5. General Council, 1430–94: composition of the Council

	Confirmed	Probable	Total	Number of times in office	Average number of times elected per individual	Percentage of office-holders
Holders of the office of Anziano	510	0	510	4440	8.7	76.5
Mercante	102	15	117	255	2.2	4.4
Dottore di legge	21	0	21	152	7.2	2.6
Dottore di medicina	10	0	10	69	6.9	1.2
Dottore di legge/di medicina	0	16	16	45	2.8	0.8
Notaio	42	0	42	144	3.4	2.5
Merciaio	12	0	12	30	2.5	0.5
Lanaro/Pannaro*	19	2	21	77	3.7	1.3
Speziale	24	1	25	68	2.7	1.2
Pittore	1	0	1	1	1.0	0.0
Disegnatore	1	0	1	1	1.0	0.0
Orafo	2	0	2	6	3.0	0.1
Sensale	1	0	1	1	1.0	0.0
Vinattiere	2	0	2	3	1.5	0.1
Macellaro/Beccaio	11	1	12	42	3.5	0.7
Caseario	3	0	3	11	3.7	0.2

Forniere	2	0	2	8	4.0	0.1
Mugnaio	1	0	1	2	2.0	0.0
Artigiano	0	4	4	9	2.3	0.2
Caligaio/Calzolaio	6	1	7	10	1.4	0.2
Cerdone	4	0	4	16	4.0	0.3
Cimatore	1	0	1	1	1.0	0.0
Cocitore	2	0	2	11	5.5	0.2
Cuoiaio	7	0	7	25	3.6	0.4
Custode dell'orologia	1	0	1	4	4.0	0.1
Fabbro	2	0	2	6	3.0	0.1
Filatore	9	0	9	26	2.9	0.4
Legnaiuolo	2	0	2	2	1.0	0.0
Muratore	2	0	2	6	3.0	0.1
Pacterio	3	0	3	11	3.7	0.2
Sarto	1	0	1	2	2.0	0.0
Sellaio	1	0	1	7	7.0	0.1
Testore	29	2	31	115	3.7	2.0
Tintore	3	0	3	6	2.0	0.1
Unidentified	76		76	177	2.3	3.1
Total	913	42	955	5789		99.7

* All the individuals concerned are described at different times both as *lanari* and as *pannari*.

the Arrighi, the Bernardi, the Boccella, the Bocci, the Cattani of Massa, the Garzoni, the Martini, the di Poggio, the Rapondi, the Tegrimi, the Totti, and the Turrettini. Their brothers were Anziani, and their wives were often the daughters of Anziani. Even a man like Gregorio di ser Iacopo Ciampanti, described as 'homo ignorantissimo et pazzo',[102] was regularly re-elected to the General Council. The standing of the doctors of medicine was admittedly more ambiguous. They were excluded less because of respect for their oratorical skills than because of a fear that they might spread disease.[103] Although the *dottori* provided a significant proportion of the non-Anziani in the General Council, a purely statistical approach to office-holding tends to obscure their true importance, and especially that of the lawyers. Not only do we find these men frequently re-elected to the Council, but it was they who were accustomed to lead the debate there. The Lucchese authorities themselves were well aware of their usefulness to the republic. As Berengo has shown for the sixteenth century, the lawyers figured prominently in diplomatic missions, and it was to them that much of the work of commissions was entrusted. By 1444 Nicolao Manfredi—doctor of law, brother-in-law of Girolamo Guinigi, and an active member of the General Council from 1431 until his death in June 1452—had moved to Genoa. When he showed interest in returning to Lucca, the General Council decided that he was too useful a man to remain absent. To encourage Manfredi's return, the General Council voted 69 to 19 to offer him a pension of 10 florins per month until the end of June.[104] The doctors of law and medicine, though barred by statute from the college of Anziani, were full members of the ruling oligarchy of fifteenth-century Lucca.

The presence in the General Council of 117 merchants whose names fail to appear among the Anziani raises rather different problems. First it must be noted that the figure is artificially high. Fifty-seven of these merchants (49 per cent) were first elected to the Council only in the 1480s—twenty-five of them only in the 1490s. Many were clearly young men at the beginning of their careers; many would no doubt later appear among the Anziani well into the sixteenth century.[105] At least seven of the remaining

[102] ASL Biblioteca (Manoscritti), 65, Pietro Carelli, Sommario delle Cronache, fo. 123^r.

[103] Whether the brief political career of the surgeon Michele di Domenico da Anchiano should be attributed to the discontent of those upon whom he operated must remain an open question: AN 702 (ser Benedetto Franciotti), p. 284; 704, pp. 167, 184.

[104] Rif. 16, p. 377.

[105] Michele di Pietro Burlamacchi, e.g., was elected to the General Council from 1491, and became Anziano for the first time in 1495. Giovanni Paolo Gigli was a member of the General Council in 1493, but did not become Anziano until 1509.

sixty died soon after their first election to the Council, five of them during the early months of their first term of office.[106] Some cases—like that of Matteo di Giovanni Dati[107]—are explained by prolonged absence in the commercial colonies; Azzo and Nicolao di Lazzaro Guinigi were affected by long periods of banishment for political crimes;[108] some men quickly forsook politics for the life of a Franciscan friar or of a canon regular of S. Frediano.[109] Due allowance paid to these facts of chronology, mortality, and mobility, the fact remains that the General Council was demonstrably more open to newcomers and to those of declining fortunes than was the college of Anziani. Coluccino and Nicolao di Taddeo Busdraghi (both men categorized among those probably best described as merchants) were members of an ancient Lucchese merchant/banking family that had become impoverished by 1399. Both men were elected to the General Council in the 1450s, but the family was not represented in the Anzianate during the fifteenth century.[110] The same distinction can be made in the case of Francesco di Iacopo Magrini, described as a broker and *pacterio* in the 1450s and as a silk merchant by the 1480s, and of various members of the Lucchesini family, recently emerging from artisanal roots. Newcomers from Pisa (Nicolao Grasso and sundry Maggiolini) entered the Council but never penetrated the college.[111] Their fortunes were shared by men listed in Table 4.5 as *merciai*, *lanari*, and *speziali*.[112]

[106] Guglielmo Benettoni, Paolino di Nicolao Parpaglioni, Filippo di Bartolomeo di Poggio, Filippo Rapondi, Guglielmo di Giovanni Sbarra.

[107] ASL Corte de' mercanti, Cause civili, 151, fos. 4^{r}, 7^{r}, 117^{v}, 60^{r}–61^{v}, 66^{r}–68^{v}, 128^{r} ff. 133^{r}–135^{r}, 142^{r}–147^{v}, 175^{r}–177^{v}.

[108] Azzo Guinigi was elected to the General Council three times between his first exile of 1433 and his second banishment of 1444. Nicolao Guinigi was a member of the General Council at the time of his trial for treason in Apr. 1431.

[109] AN 700(4) (ser Benedetto Franciotti), 29 Jan. 1455, 3 Sept. 1456; 700(5), 12 Jan., 12 Dec. 1456; 702, p. 95 (29 Nov. 1458).

[110] M. Luzzati, 'Busdraghi', in *Dizionario biografico degli italiani*, xv (Rome, 1972), 505–7. Coluccino described himself in 1444 as a 'poor person and somewhat ignorant': Rif. 16, pp. 423–4. Nicolao Coluccino's brother was involved in various affrays in the city. He was assessed at 1 florin for the loan of 1431 (ASL Imprestiti, 21, fo. 29^{v}), and was still alive in 1488, thirty-five years after his last appearance in the General Council.

[111] The Maggiolini were made citizens by Paolo Guinigi, and their wealth is indicated by their high assessments for the forced loan of 1431: ASL Imprestiti, 21, fo. 32^{r-v}. Their rising fortunes were halted by their involvement in the Guinigi plot of 1444.

[112] e.g., the *lanaro* Nanni di Francesco da Moriano, his son Acconcio, and the sons of Nanni's brother Checcho. The distinction between these men and lesser merchants is less than clear. The mercer Giorgio di Benedetto Boccella, sentenced to death for murder whilst a member of the General Council in 1451, pardoned by the General Council on 9 Jan. 1453, and re-elected to the Council in 1457, is occasionally labelled 'merchant and citizen of Lucca': SB 165, fo. 460^{r-v}. Many mercers are also alternatively described as *cordellari*.

The composition of the General Council between 1430 and 1494, with special reference to those members described as merchants, confirms the earlier impression that in the fifteenth century no man of prominent family and of tolerable record seems to have been wilfully excluded from the higher and more coveted office of Anziano. Of course there are enigmas that we lack the evidence fully to explain. Nicolao di Bartolomeo Garzoni was a member of the Council sporadically between 1431 and 1454. His failure to rise to the highest office may well be connected with his imprisonment for debt in 1432 and with his obvious financial difficulties of later years.[113] More surprising at first sight is the case of Matteo di Bartolomeo Bernardini. Bernardini was a prominent silk merchant; he was assessed for the loan of 1431 for the substantial sum of 28 florins, and he was elected to the General Council at regular intervals thirteen times between 1430 and 1456.[114] Bernardini might truly have provided a puzzling exception, were it not for the fact of his illegitimate birth, a fact unchanged by his subsequent legitimization in 1401.

At least thirty of the Anziani elected between 1430 and 1494 may be described as artisans or as suppliers of basic foodstuffs. Twenty-eight of these appear also among members of the General Council. Together with those identified in Table 4.5, 129 members of the General Council may be grouped into a general category dominated by butchers, spinners, and weavers. Between them, these men held office 572 times (9.9 per cent of all places). No doubt others are hidden among those presented as 'unidentified'. The number includes families of wealthy weavers, such as the dynasty founded by Bartolomeo del Massaio; it also includes families of butchers like the Loccori, with their formidable record of public violence.[115] When treating of the Anzianate, it was found that membership of the college became increasingly exclusive as the fifteenth century progressed. Figure 4.5 shows membership of the General Council by men of lesser status. The firm line of the graph should not deceive. The graph is no more accurate than the fragmentary information on which it is based. But there is no reason to distrust its overall shape. As in the case of the Anzianate, there was a diminishing presence of artisans, butchers, bakers, and the rest by the late fifteenth century. But these people were always

[113] ASL Corte de' mercanti, Cause civili, 150, fos. 49^{r}–50^{v}, 66^{r}; AN 700(3), 16 Aug. 1457; 701, 27 June 1457; 702, p. 127 (21 Feb. 1459); 703, pp. 310–21 (15 Mar. 1459).

[114] ASL Imprestiti, 21, fo. 43^{v}; G. Nicolai, 'Bartolomeo di Matteo Bernardini', in *Dizionario biografico degli italiani*, ix (Rome, 1967), 178.

[115] ASL Podestà di Lucca, Inquisizioni, 5229, no foliation, Apr. 1439; SB 159, fos. 228^{r-v}, 240^{r}; 161, fos. 128^{r}–129^{v}, 134^{r-v}; 165, fos. 250^{r}–251^{r}.

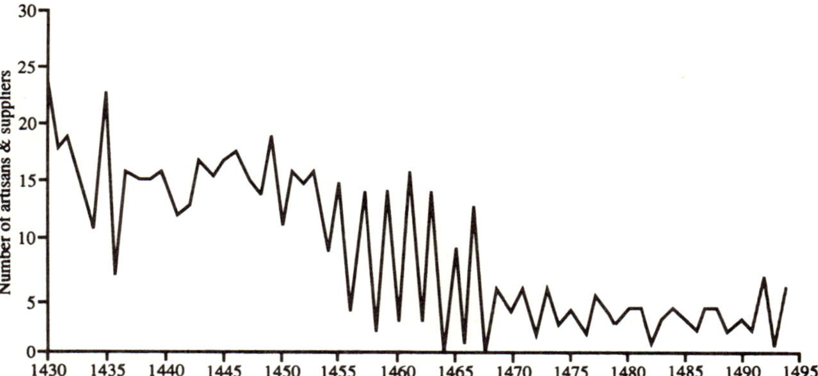

FIG. 4.5 General Council, 1430–94: participation of artisans and suppliers of basic foodstuffs. The General Council was elected in March. The year is taken as that in which the Council assumed office. This applies also to the first Councils after 1430, which were elected in October. The Council of Oct. 1432–Mar. 1434 is entered as 1432. There is no entry for 1433.

more numerous in the General Council; and their disappearance was less dramatic.

The composition of the General Council was complicated by the presence of *invitati* and *surrogati*. The first General Council of the restored republic was summoned on 13 October 1430, and was attended by nine *invitati* (three per *terziere*) themselves elected by the college of Anziani.[116] There is no record in the Riformagioni Pubbliche of the names of *invitati* and *surrogati* at the subsequent meetings of the General Council, until on 6 May 1431 the Anziani named twelve *invitati* (four per *terziere*) and thirty-one *surrogati*. The *surrogati* filled the place of eleven councillors who had died, thirteen who were absent, and seven who were present in the Council *ex officio* as Anziani.[117] Thereafter the Riformagioni Pubbliche provide a regular but by no means unbroken record of *invitati* and *surrogati*. The number of *surrogati* fluctuated considerably according to the health and whereabouts of the established membership of the Council. They were particularly numerous in a plague year like 1479 when there were many absentees, who had fled from the plague, and when many who remained had succumbed to the disease. The number of *invitati* varies over time

[116] Rif. 14, p. 41.
[117] Ibid., pp. 153–4.

between twelve (four per *terziere*) and eighteen (six per *terziere*), and the choice of these additional members fell to the college of Anziani presently in office.[118]

Berengo saw the system of *invitati* and *surrogati* as a means of ensuring the continuous presence in the Council of a small political élite of leading citizens and as a device for circumventing the *vacanza* according to which a councillor was ineligible for election to the General Council of the following year. The supernumeraries become a reflection of the real power of an inner oligarchy (and they were of course justified by the genuine disadvantage of losing, in alternate years, the services of able and experienced men).[119] To test Berengo's argument in the context of fifteenth-century Lucca, I have examined the lists of *invitati* and *surrogati* for a few specific years chosen largely at random.

The General Council of October 1432–March 1434 met thirty-four times during its eighteen-month extended life. Its membership was supplemented by a minimum of seven and a maximum of seventeen *surrogati*, by a minimum of eleven[120] and a maximum of eighteen *invitati*. One hundred and thirty-seven men[121] shared between them 389 places as *surrogati* and 475 places as *invitati* over the period as a whole. The same men were elected indiscriminately as both *surrogati* and *invitati*. Gerardo Angiorelli was chosen either as *invitato* or *surrogato* for thirty of the thirty-four Council meetings; Nicolao Burlamacchi similarly for twenty-nine; fifteen men were present at twenty or more of the thirty-four meetings. Of the 137 men chosen as *surrogati* or *invitati*, sixty had been members of the previous General Council; forty-three of these were also elected to the next General Council in March 1434. Since these members of the previous and of the next Councils were the same men who were chosen most frequently as *surrogati* or *invitati*, it is clear that the arrangement served to soften the impact of the *vacanza*. Despite the *vacanza*, men like Gerardo Angiorelli and Nicolao Burlamacchi were in fact almost always present in the General Council. But we should be cautious of talking of a narrow élite, with 137 different names appearing over an eighteen-month period. In the 1430s the election of *surrogati* and *invitati* seems to have fulfilled a

[118] The college of Anziani was permitted to nominate a maximum of eighteen *invitati* (six per *terziere*).

[119] Berengo, *Nobili e mercanti*, 23–4.

[120] The number of *invitati* is irregular for seven meetings of the General Council. Generally, for whatever reason, S. Martino was being assigned one *invitato* less than the other *terzieri*.

[121] Two of these, Matteo di Domenico Mattei and Nicolao ser Federighi, seem to represent scribal errors.

number of purposes besides the circumvention of the *vacanza*. It provided an apprenticeship and a testing time for young men of leading families. Many men who appeared first as *surrogati* or *invitati* in the Council of 1432–4 were later to enjoy long careers as regularly elected members. The system offered some political participation to leading citizens currently viewed with understandable distrust. Azzo Guinigi was chosen as *invitato* three times in 1433. Azzo, like other members of his family, was more readily admitted to high office on an *ad hoc* basis than as a permanently elected member. Finally, some of the *surrogati* or *invitati* of 1432–4 can only be described as surprising and unexpected. These include the Pisans Nicolao Grasso and Pietro Maggiolini, thirteen men who apparently were never elected as regular members of the General Council, and a liberal scattering of butchers and artisans. It seems impossible to link the presence of individual supernumeraries to the business agenda of a particular Council meeting. No doubt the presence of many lesser individuals is explicable in terms of personal links with members of the electing college of Anziani. Such patronage links remain very difficult to locate.[122]

To test the representativeness of the Council of 1432–4, I have looked at the composition of the forty-three meetings of the General Council elected in March 1474,[123] at the forty meetings of the Council of 1488–9,[124] and at the twenty meetings during the plague year of 1479–80.[125] The choice of *surrogati* and *invitati* in 1474–5 shows little change from 1432–4. In 1474–5 fifty-four men named as *surrogati* or *invitati* had been elected as permanent members to the General Council of the previous year (42 per cent of the total, compared with 44 per cent in 1432–4). Of these, forty-two were present in the Councils of both the preceding and the succeeding years (32 per cent compared with 31 per cent in the earlier period). This group of forty-two held 48 per cent of all the places as *surrogati* and *invitati* in 1474–5, compared with 56 per cent in 1432–4. For both Councils

[122] The appearance of the obscure Betto Bettini in the General Council of 1430–1 and as an *invitato* in Sept. 1433 may be connected with his association with Iacopo Arnolfini.

[123] One name is missing from the list of *surrogati* for 27 Sept. 1474. The names of all the *invitati* are missing for 26 May 1474, and of all but one of the *invitati* for 1 June. As with all the years sampled, the lists of *invitati* do not always reflect an equal number of representatives for each *terziere*.

[124] The lists of *invitati* and *surrogati* are missing from the Riformagioni Pubbliche from Jan. 1489. The calculations are therefore based on the first thirty-four Council meetings of the year. On 21 and 25 Sept. 1488 the same name appears in the lists of both *surrogati* and *invitati*.

[125] No meeting of the General Council is recorded during the summer of the plague year, from May to Oct. 1479.

certain men were chosen automatically for meeting after meeting. In 1474–5 there is a very clear link between less automatically nominated *surrogati* and *invitati* and the specific college of Anziani that named them. The Councils of both periods were supplemented by a significant number of men (thirteen in 1474–5) who were never elected to the General Council as regular members. The Councils of both periods gave early political experience as *surrogati* or *invitati* to young men (Benedetto Buonvisi and Lodovico Garzoni, for example, in 1474–5) who were later to become frequent members of the General Council. Much the same pattern is repeated in the Council of 1488–9. But there seems to be a gradually increasing tendency for *surrogati* and *invitati* to be drawn from the ranks of regularly elected councillors. Of all the places of *surrogati* and *invitati* in 1488–9, 61 per cent were held by men who were elected to both the preceding and the succeeding Councils.[126] This tendency is particularly pronounced in the plague year of 1479. In that year no less than 72 per cent of the places of *surrogati* and *invitati* were filled by men who had been elected in 1478 and who were to be elected again in 1480. At a time of crisis, when as many as thirty-five *surrogati* were required to replace the dead and absent, successive colleges of Anziani resorted to the political experience of men who had been elected to the General Council of the previous year.[127]

Surrogati and *invitati* also supplemented the composition of the Council of Thirty-Six. During the course of the present chapter the Thirty-Six have been encountered as a forum for the direct and indirect election of officials—and indeed, not just to offices of the highest political significance. The Thirty-Six also had certain administrative functions, delegated to them by the General Council. During the fifteenth century they were particularly active in the hearing of appeals. Twelve members of the Council of Thirty-Six (four per *terziere*) were designated *gonfalonieri*, and these had responsibilities relating to local defence and public order. After the revolution of 1430, the Council of Thirty-Six was quickly re-established on 30 August by the same *balìa* of twelve that, a few days earlier, had named the first college of Anziani. The Thirty-Six of October

[126] The calculations for 1488–9 are affected by the absence of names for the six meetings of the General Council held Jan.–Mar. 1489. On a larger scale than in previous years, individual *invitati* and *surrogati* of 1488 were found to bear the names of regularly elected members of the 1488–9 General Council. Throughout these lists there is reason to suspect some carelessness in transcription.

[127] In 1479–80 there is a very marked tendency for the same list to be duplicated from meeting to meeting. This is particularly true for the term of office of each succeeding college of Anziani.

1430 were appointed for four months.[128] A new Council was elected by the Anziani and by the *balìa* of twelve *Riformatori* to hold office for six months from January 1431.[129] By March 1432 it was established that the Council of Thirty-Six was to be renewed every six months: in March and September.[130] From the 1430s each new Council of Thirty-Six was elected by the current Anziani and by twelve members of the outgoing Council of Thirty-Six (chosen by the Anziani). In March the same twelve members were involved in the election both of the General Council and of the Council of Thirty-Six. A change took place at the end of 1474, apparently as a result of friction caused by electoral procedures.[131] Thereafter each Council of Thirty-Six was elected by its predecessor, joined by the current college of Anziani.[132] In view of the importance of the Council of Thirty-Six both in its own right and also in the election of the Anziani and of the General Council, it is appropriate to conclude an examination of the formal constitutional structure of fifteenth-century Lucca with a brief examination of the composition of the Thirty-Six.

Between 1430 and 1494, 543 different men were elected to the Council of Thirty-Six. Sharing between them 4,644 posts over the period as a whole, each holder held office for an average of more than eight terms. Since the *vacanza* for the Thirty-Six was only six months, many individuals returned annually to the Council. Figure 4.6 reveals the almost total overlap between membership of the college of Anziani and the Council of Thirty-Six. Of the men elected to the Thirty-Six, 81.8 per cent (holding 90.7 per cent of places) had also been drawn as Anziani prior to 1494. The percentage would be even higher if we included members who only began to be elected as Anziani after the end of the present study. Figure 4.6 also shows the importance of the doctors of law and medicine, these constituting 7.6 per cent of the members and holding 6.6 per cent of the places in the Thirty-Six. The *dottori* may have been excluded by statute from the Anzianate, but elsewhere they were omnipresent in the ruling councils of the republic. A tiny minority of twelve men appear only in the ranks of the Thirty-Six, each holding office on only one occasion.

128 Rif. 14, pp. 31–2.

129 Ibid., p. 86.

130 The Council of July 1431 was extended until the following March: Anz. Temp. Lib. 5, fos. 60ʳ–61ʳ. For the Council of Mar. 1432, see Rif. 14, pp. 227–8.

131 Rif. 20, pp. 252–3, 308. *Invitati* and *surrogati* for the Thirty-Six at the election of the new Council were now to be chosen by the General Council rather than by the Anziani. This latter arrangement only lasted for a year.

132 Elections were delayed until Oct. in 1477, 1479, and 1486 ‘because of plague’. The seriousness of the situation in 1479 necessitated irregular election procedures: Rif. 21, p. 62.

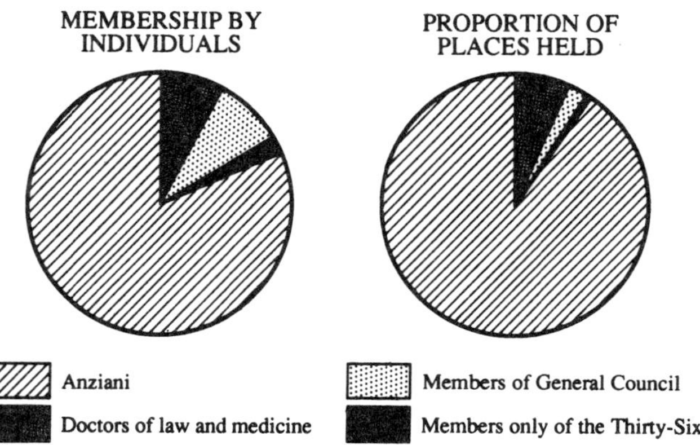

FIG. 4.6 Composition of Council of Thirty-Six, 1430–94.

Five of these date from 1430–1, three from the period after 1490. Almost all can be explained by early death or by the accident of their appearance right at the end of the period surveyed. Mortality and chronology also explain many of the forty-six cases of men (excluding the *dottori*) who appear both in the lists of the Thirty-Six and the General Council but never (before 1494) as Anziani. This category also includes the powerful, but illegitimate, Matteo Bernardini, who was a member of the Thirty-Six nineteen times between 1431 and 1455. It includes Azzo Guinigi, between periods of exile for involvement in the Guinigi plots, and also (for one term of office each) wealthy weavers like Bartolomeo del Massaio and Antonio Baldini, who were familiar faces in the General Council but never quite graduated to the college of Anziani.

In recent years Lucchese scholarship has shown some inclination to focus beyond the traditional organs of government and to stress that the real locus of power lay in the extraordinary magistracies and unofficial convocations.[133] To a degree the point is clearly well made. There can be no question of the importance (together with the Anziani) of a series of *balìe* established to extricate Lucca from the political and military crisis following Guinigi's fall. At the time of the *Otto di Balìa* in 1436 the conventional political records of Lucca virtually disappear altogether. Later the Anziani regularly summoned *invitati* to *Colloqui* where a wide range of business, often of a sensitive nature, was discussed and settled. It

[133] Luzzati, 'Politica di salvaguardia', 543–5.

remains less obvious that these extraordinary councils significantly alter the picture of Lucchese government as established in the present chapter. It is difficult to subject bodies so transitory and so variable to statistical analysis. The *Colloqui* might be attended by a dozen men, or they might be large gatherings of more than 100.[134] Of those summoned, absentees might well be in a considerable majority. But looking generally at the composition of the early *balìe* and at the later *Colloqui*, it is unambiguously clear that the core membership consisted of the same men who were elected time and again to the college of Anziani and who often headed the college as Gonfaloniere di Giustizia, joined by an inner group of *dottori di legge*.

When Benedetto di ser Stefano degli Opizini da Ficecchio, *scolare in ragione civile*, petitioned for Lucchese citizenship in 1448, he was moved to explain his request as emanating from a desire to live henceforth under a government of such unparalleled virtue.[135] Yet the constitutional structure of Lucca in the fifteenth century was essentially the same as that which—in the fourteenth century—had disintegrated into the factions leading to the Guinigi *signoria*. The statutes that limited the number of members of a single family eligible for a particular office were—in the sixteenth century—to be one of the main grievances leading to the great conspiracy of the di Poggio.[136] The relative success of the Lucchese constitution in the fifteenth century owes less to wise laws than to the fact that most men were willing to co-operate to make the system work. It has been shown above that Lucca was ruled by an oligarchy of perhaps 150 men, involving little more than 500 individuals over the period 1430–94 as a whole. This oligarchy was less devoted to endemic factionalism than might have been anticipated from the general Italian historiography; certainly they showed limited enthusiasm for pursuing a vendetta or discomforting rival families. They were open to newcomers, once legitimized by time and wealth. At the same time, admittance to the ruling councils was always limited, and became even more restricted as the fifteenth century progressed. By the fifteenth century a General Council of ninety had come to replace the Council of 1308 with its membership of 550. Prosperous artisans were never well represented on the governing councils of the restored republic; they became less common by mid-century. Office was open only to citizens, and few citizens played an active political role. Yet the cohesion

[134] Cf., e.g., ASL Colloqui, 1, pp. 5 and 64.
[135] Rif. 16, p. 781.
[136] Berengo, *Nobili e mercanti*, 83–99.

within the ruling oligarchy was matched by the passivity of the *popolo minuto*.

In search of an explanation first for the new-found political restraint of Lucca's leading families, some help might be anticipated from comparative and comparable studies. Randolph Starn has written of a changed society and judicial system in the fifteenth century, where individuals rather than whole clans became the targets of confiscation and condemnations for political offences.[137] Against this it might be noted that Lucchese chroniclers, such as the Dalli, constantly invoke the fear rather than the impotence of family power when explaining why leading Lucchese citizens were so anxious to temporize and conciliate in their dealings with powerful offenders and their families.[138] Samuel Cohn has argued for the forging of a cohesive ruling class identity in fifteenth-century Florence after the salutary experience of the Ciompi revolt.[139] But the contemporary Lucchese patriciate was guided by no such painful memories in their immediate past history. Lucchese moderation seems to have been prompted by more local considerations. First, there was the ever present external threat to Lucchese independence. Foreign bribes might lure individuals into treasonable acts. With the memory of Lucca's shameful fourteenth-century past and with the all too obvious perils of the present, most members of Lucca's leading families could have had few illusions as to the likely outcome of renewed factional strife. The same remained true in the rather different circumstances of the sixteenth century. Secondly, attention must be drawn to the economic background. It seems that Lucca (perhaps Italy as a whole) entered into a period of economic recovery and restored prosperity after the early decades of the fifteenth century. This is the subject of the next chapter. Throughout Italian history the fight for offices of honour and profit, the impulse to monopolize office and to exclude rivals, can be closely identified with moments of economic dislocation and uncertainty. The fifteenth-century rhetoric placing 'the good of the community' over personal advantage and the reasonably tolerant attitude to new families (of noble origin) are both features entirely compatible with the more relaxed economic climate of the post-Guinigi years.

The political passivity of the bulk of Lucca's population has been remarked in earlier chapters. The present chapter has made it clear that

[137] Starn, *Contrary Commonwealth*, 108–19.

[138] BSL MS 710, Salvator Dalli, Croniche, fo. 142ᵛ; MS 939, Gio: Lunardo Dalli, Cronache, pp. 191, 200, 260.

[139] Cohn, *Laboring Classes in Renaissance Florence*.

this passivity can hardly be attributed to a wide dispersal of political participation. It is true that the emphasis has been placed entirely on the ruling councils. But findings are not sensibly changed by extending the enquiry to the consultative and administrative committees and appointments that, mushrooming in fifteenth-century Lucca, have been taken as the very defining characteristic of the Renaissance state. Election to offices of profit and honour, often held for six months, was generally made by the college of Anziani and the Council of Thirty-Six. Administrative posts and seats on leading commissions were monopolized by precisely the same names that have appeared throughout the present chapter. Other offices became the preserve of the notariate. In the 1490s it was decided to take some offices away from notaries, for the support of other poor citizens. Such offices included the *Offizio dell'Esattore*, the *Offizio delle Generali in gabella maggiore*, the *Offizio del fondaco*, the *Offizio del Cancelliero dell'Entrate*, and the *Offizio di Porta S. Donato*. The expressed aim was to aid well-born and honourable citizens from many noble families. Less honourable posts were often filled with foreign stipendaries. The question of popular passivity in Lucca merges into the wider problem of the quiescence of fifteenth-century Italy as a whole, after the heady days of the late fourteenth century.

Again, some help might be expected from comparative and comparable studies. For Susan Reynolds the problem is a creation of an 'anachronistic teleology'. She dismisses the delusion of twentieth-century historians that 'the many poor must be frustrated if they are not able to exercise their democratic rights', and assures us that 'the principles which determined the structure of urban governments were controversial neither to townsmen nor to thoughtful observers from outside'. In this less complicated world it was self-evident to everyone that high office should be entrusted to those of sufficient discretion and wealth.[140] The point becomes more convincing in the context of what Guidubaldo Guidi calls 'la democrazia per partecipazione'.[141] Political eligibility in fifteenth-century Lucca involved a more demanding commitment than the occasional turn-out at the polling booth. It entailed incarceration for two months in the palace of the Anziani or compulsory attendance at the regular meetings of the General Council. Most men had neither the leisure nor the resources for such sustained involvement, and their reticence

[140] S. Reynolds, *Kingdoms and Communities in Western Europe, 900–1300* (Oxford, 1984), 184–98.

[141] Guidi, *Il governo della città-repubblica di Firenze*, i. 48–9.

becomes no more difficult to explain than the perennial lack of competition for the work of parent–teachers associations or of (most) university committees. The burden of explanation shifts to those rare moments of dislocation when a large section of the urban community became sufficiently antagonized to demand a voice in the settling of grievances.

Some historians have been less willing to abdicate the 'burden' of explanation. For Vincent Ilardi, fifteenth-century populations, and not only those of princely states like Milan, were rendered apathetic by long exclusion from the circle of power; 'the public spirit had been thoroughly suppressed'.[142] Recently a great deal of attention has been paid to the role of civic ritual in defining and legitimizing the existing order.[143] Both Florentine and Venetian sources would seem to provide more fruitful material for such an enquiry. It remains clear that Lucca, like the other republics, was alert to the disruptive potential of unregulated processions.[144] And it would be reasonable to assume, from the experiences of others, that events such as the elaborately ritualized procession of Anziani with their court and military escort behind the *cappella de' musici del Palazzo* and the *Massieri* bearing the silver mace or the highly structured annual procession in honour of the Volto Santo were moments of high significance in delineating an accepted political order and in rendering 'the political order both mystical and sanctified'.[145] Others have been inclined to seek an explanation of fifteenth-century deference less in the gentle conditioning of civic processions than in the harsher attentions of informers and secret police.[146] That Lucca was alive with informers has been fully established in earlier chapters, and the use of torture is frequently attested in the court records. The coercive forces at the disposal of the Lucchese state are probably more useful in explaining the failure of a series of ill-planned noble conspiracies than they are in

[142] V. Ilardi, 'The Assassination of Galeazzo Maria Sforza and the Reaction of Italian Diplomacy', in L. Martines (ed.), *Violence and Civil Disorder in Italian Cities 1200–1500* (Berkeley, Calif., 1972), 101–3.

[143] Most important here is the work on Venice of E. Muir, *Civic Ritual in Renaissance Venice* (Princeton, NJ, 1981), and that on Florence of Trexler, *Public Life in Renaissance Florence*.

[144] Rif. 16, p. 159.

[145] Muir, *Civic Ritual*, 186.

[146] This has been a major focus of Venetian revisionist literature. See, e.g., G. Cozzi, 'Authority and the Law in Renaissance Venice', in J. R. Hale (ed.), *Renaissance Venice* (London, 1973), 293–345. For an explanation of Venetian stability more firmly rooted in the nature of Venetian society and corporate organization, see R. Mackenney, *Tradesmen and Traders: The World of the Guilds in Venice and Europe c.1250–c.1650* (London, 1987), esp. 1–36.

explaining popular acquiescence in the rule of a narrowing mercantile oligarchy.

In reconciling the absence of *furor populi* with the equally marked absence of *popolani* from the organs of fifteenth-century government, four points seem to me particularly pertinent. The first again anticipates the chapter on trade, banking, and manufacture. If Reynolds's complaisant medieval urban populations were occasionally aroused to challenge the constituted order, the imperative was invariably provided by restrictive measures adopted by town governments in the face of economic difficulties. Lucca's stability in the fifteenth century owes not a little to a flourishing silk industry and to the profits of international finance. The point is not irrelevant to the stability of other fifteenth-century Italian societies. Secondly, bitter experience (and perhaps a sense of justice) had taught Lucca's ruling oligarchy to accommodate the population in things that really mattered. We have already spoken of the need to ensure adequate grain supplies and to control food prices. Here it might be noted that in November 1431, in the interests of equality and justice, two artisans and one notary were added to the six citizens (all of leading families) already elected to assess citizens and other inhabitants of Lucca for an imposition of 3,000 ducats needed for the war with Florence.[147] Thirdly, popular inertia was intimately intertwined with what has been said earlier of patrician restraint. Throughout the fourteenth century, popular movements were at least facilitated by factional strife. In fifteenth-century Lucca members of the ruling councils were so anxious to avoid factional strife that they refused to enquire too diligently into those implicated in treasonable affairs, and resolutely protested their unequivocal faith in the loyalty and virtue of the near relatives of men convicted of the most heinous crimes. Finally, the only real qualification for political office in Lucca was Lucchese citizenship. There was none of the institutionalized conflict between greater and lesser guilds that marked the history of Florence. Artisans and retailers not infrequently appear in the lists of *surrogati* and *invitati*—often, no doubt, because of personal links with the patricians who elected them. Lesser families might continue to aspire to the ruling councils, though even the most ambitious artisans and butchers seldom rose beyond the ranks of the General Council or (less frequently) the Council of Thirty-Six.

[147] Anz. Temp. Lib. 5, fos. 77^{v}–78^{v}, 85^{v}.

5

THE ECONOMY OF FIFTEENTH-CENTURY LUCCA: MANUFACTURE, TRADE, AND BANKING

The sources available for quantitative research into the economic fortunes of fifteenth-century Lucca are very limited indeed. The registers of the *Gabella Maggiore* simply disappear in the early decades of the fifteenth century.[1] The local *gabelle* have provided useful material for a later chapter on relations between communities of the Lucchese state and the hegemonic city, but hardly contribute a sound framework for an overview of the wider Lucchese economy. The account books of merchants, so plentiful in other Italian archives, are virtually non-existent in Lucca. Such evidence survives in Lucca only in the form of (sometimes extensive) extracts copied as evidence in the proceedings of court cases before the *corte de' mercanti*. Yet there remains a considerable amount of evidence, both direct and indirect, to suggest that Lucca was prospering in the post-Guinigi years. Prosperity owed something to the well-being of the industry that had been the foundation of Lucca's wealth for centuries: the manufacture of silk cloth.[2]

That the Lucchese silk industry enjoyed a resurgence in the fifteenth century has been generally assumed by historians; though the assumption rests on no sound statistical base, and the dating of the revival is a matter of some controversy. The Lucchese patrician Attilio Arnolfini, writing at the end of the eighteenth century on the manufacture of silk cloth in Lucca, sought the origins of economic revival in the political events of 1430. For Arnolfini it was axiomatic that the recovery of political liberty should lead to a recovery also of the economic welfare of

[1] Bongi, *Inventario*, ii. 33–6.

[2] For the silk industry, see M. E. Bratchel, 'The Silk Industry of Lucca in the Fifteenth Century', in *Tecnica e società nell'Italia dei secoli XII–XVI: Centro italiano di studi di storia e d'arte Pistoia, Atti dell'undicesimo Convegno di studio tenuto a Pistoia nei giorni 28–31 ottobre 1984* (Pistoia, 1987), 173–90.

Lucca's citizens.[3] Arnolfini's republican enthusiasm may no longer convince, but his chronology assumes some credibility from the close association that Lucchese historiography has traditionally drawn between the difficulties of the silk industry and the flight of silk merchants and artisans as refugees from political strife and faction fighting. There is some evidence that after the fall of Paolo Guinigi, and particularly after the devastation of the Florentine wars of the 1430s, the authorities were reasonably successful in attracting back Lucchese exiles and in drawing silk weavers to Lucca from neighbouring states.[4] Yet Florence Edler de Roover would delay the revival of the Lucchese silk industry to the period following 1480.[5]

The latter date would seem too late in relation to the flourishing external market for Lucchese silk cloth and with reference to evidence of consumption both at home and abroad. The period of the Renaissance generally, and particularly the fifteenth century, has been identified as a time of conspicuous consumption, an era marked by a vigorous demand for luxury goods.[6] The mercantile dimension of the fifteenth-century fairs of Lyons and Geneva was dominated by the sale of silk cloth, especially that of expensive *auroserici*.[7] In England, Edmund Fryde has argued that the import of luxury wares by Italians 'seems to have reached its climax in the fifteenth century'.[8] Throughout the fifteenth century the Valois dukes of Burgundy maintained a court of extraordin-

[3] ASL Arte della Seta, 33, p. 45. Another copy of the Arnolfini MS is preserved in ASL Archivio Arnolfini, 138.

[4] Bratchel, 'Silk industry of Lucca', 175–6.

[5] F. Edler de Roover, 'Lucchese Silks', *Ciba Review*, lxxx (1950), 2913. Certainly by the 1480s we hear of more than 100 silk weavers attending a meeting called in the church of S. Cristoforo: BSL MS 62, Memorie diverse di Lucca, p. 275.

[6] R. A. Goldthwaite, 'The Renaissance Economy: The Preconditions for Luxury Consumption', in *Aspetti della vita economica medievale: Atti del Convegno di Studi nel X Anniversario della morte di Federigo Melis, Firenze–Pisa–Prato, 10–14 marzo 1984* (Florence, 1985), 659–75; Miskimin, *Economy of Early Renaissance Europe*, 92–105; M. E. Bratchel, 'Italian Merchant Organization and Business Relationships in Early Tudor London', *Journal of European Economic History*, vii (1978), 5–32; *idem*, 'Regulation and Group-Consciousness in the Later History of London's Italian Merchant Colonies', *Journal of European Economic History*, ix (1980), 585–610; M. F. Mazzaoui, *The Italian Cotton Industry in the Later Middle Ages 1100–1600* (Cambridge, 1981), 132–3.

[7] M. Cassandro, 'Strategia degli affari dei mercanti-banchieri italiani alle fiere internazionali d'oltralpe (secoli xiv–xvi)', in *Aspetti della vita economica medievale*, 140–50; R. Gascon, *Grand commerce et vie urbaine au XVIe siècle: Lyon et ses marchands*, 2 vols. (Paris, 1971), i. 47–9.

[8] E. Fryde, 'Italian Merchants in Medieval England, *c*.1270–*c*.1500', in *Aspetti della vita economica medievale*, 216. Rather different conclusions have been reached by J. L. Bolton, *The Medieval English Economy 1150–1500* (London, 1980), 311–14. Bolton's views are expressed more fully in his thesis, 'Alien Merchants in England in the Reign of Henry VI,

ary splendour, Charles the Bold spending £38,830 in equipping his courtiers with garments of silk cloth for his meeting with the Emperor Frederick III.[9] In France, the new monarchy of Charles VII and Louis XI was established and legitimized by a lavish and elaborate ceremonial. Malcolm Vale has chronicled how the expenses of Charles VII's household more than doubled between October 1450 and March 1461.[10] Doublets of black satin of Lucca are specifically mentioned among the attire of that king's immediate associates for the May Day festivities in 1459.[11] And in Lucca itself throughout the fifteenth century the General Council frequently recorded its concern over the ills likely to follow from the growing adornment of clothing and jewelry worn by both men and women in the city and state. It was such concerns that promoted the very comprehensive decree of 1473 which, among other things, prohibited any woman from possessing more than two silk dresses.[12]

Evidence of growing conspicuous consumption—even evidence of a flourishing market for silk cloth—offers less than proof of the healthy condition of fifteenth-century Lucchese silk manufacture. It is established that one feature of the fifteenth century was the extension of the Italian silk industry, first to Florence and later to any number of new centres of manufacture. It has been argued that the market for silk in the fifteenth century favoured lightweight silks rather than the traditional brocades and heavy velvets of Lucca.[13] Yet Lucca's luxury cloths continued to be unrivalled on international markets in the sixteenth century.[14] And in specific cases there can be no doubt that it was Lucchese merchants and Lucchese wares that satisfied growing demand. Building on the close relationship forged in Flanders by Dino Rapondi with the Burgundian dukes Philip the Bold and John the Fearless, Lucchese silks were to dominate the Bruges market at least until the mid-1460s. Raymond de Roover has shown that Giovanni Arnolfini was the main supplier of silks to the Burgundian court throughout the period 1445–64.[15] Arnolfini was later to rise in the service of Louis XI of

1422–61' (Univ. of Oxford B.Litt. thesis, 1971). I am very grateful to Dr Bolton for allowing me to obtain a microfilm copy of this thesis.

[9] R. Vaughan, *Valois Burgundy* (London, 1975), 175.

[10] M. G. A. Vale, *Charles VII* (London, 1974), 219.

[11] Ibid. 223.

[12] Rif. 20, pp. 25–6, 49–52.

[13] Mazzaoui, *Italian Cotton Industry*, 132–3.

[14] Gascon, *Grand commerce et vie urbaine*, i. 57–8, 114.

[15] R. de Roover, *Money, Banking and Credit in Medieval Bruges: Italian Merchant-Bankers Lombards and Money-Changers, A Study in the Origins of Banking* (Cambridge, Mass., 1948), 20–1; *idem*, *The Rise and Decline of the Medici Bank 1397–1494* (Cambridge, Mass., 1963), 190, 446.

France.[16] Of course, Lucca had lost the monopoly in the production of silk cloth that she is reputed to have held in previous centuries. But it seems clear that Lucca benefited fully from conditions favouring Italian silk production. In the absence of statistics, it seems probable that the eighteenth-century Arnolfini was right to date a revival of the Lucchese silk industry to the period of relative tranquillity following Paolo Guinigi and the Florentine wars.

The healthy condition of the Lucchese silk industry resulted from expanding markets, from political conditions, and from the maintenance of high traditional standards of production. The statute of the court of merchants of 1376, which immediately followed a petition protesting the deplorable state of contemporary silk manufacture in Lucca,[17] was primarily concerned with the restoration of statutory norms. In later centuries the moribund state of Lucchese silk production would come to be attributed to the elaborate restrictions surviving from the Middle Ages ('la pesante bardatura medioevale').[18] At the end of the fourteenth century it was felt (perhaps rightly) that renewal could be achieved by a restatement of the old ordinances—modified if necessary as in the provisions of 1381.[19] Consequently, the fifteenth-century revival was largely unaccompanied by changes in production techniques or in the type of cloth produced. Indeed, by the fifteenth century, Lucchese cloths had also lost that originality of design that had characterized earlier centuries. The products of Lucca become exceedingly difficult to identify or to date.[20] And at the same time, there was an evident disinclination to pursue the promising technological innovations of an earlier age. Nowhere is this more apparent than in the processes of silk spinning (*filatura* and *torcitura*).

Florence Edler de Roover has argued for the construction in thirteenth- and fourteenth-century Lucca of sophisticated water-powered silk throwing-mills that were in every respect comparable with the mills described in the mid-eighteenth century by the German traveller

[16] De Roover, *Medici Bank*, 190; P. M. Kendall, *Louis XI: '. . . the universal spider . . .'* (London, 1974), 101, 109, 129.

[17] *Lo Statuto della corte dei mercanti in Lucca del MCCCLXXVI*, ed. A. Mancini, U. Dorini, and E. Lazzareschi (Florence, 1927), pp. xiv–xv, xxv, 2–3. According to the petition, in 1376, 'dicta ars sete quasi est in dicta civitate ad nichilum deducta'.

[18] ASL Arte della Seta, 33, pp. 60–1; R. Mazzei, *La società lucchese del seicento* (Lucca, 1977), 17–27.

[19] *Statuto della corte dei mercanti*, 175–201.

[20] Edler de Roover, 'Lucchese Silks', 2924–30; E. Callmann, *Beyond Nobility: Art for the Private Citizen in the Early Renaissance* (Allentown, Pa., 1980–1), 112–13.

Christopher Martin.[21] A Lucchese named Borghesano perhaps built a throwing-mill (*filatoio*) driven by water in Bologna *fuori di Porta Castiglione c.*1272.[22] Borghesano's knowledge was transmitted to his son, who in 1341 received a licence from Bologna to build a *filatoio* in the parish of S. Biagio. For fourteenth-century Lucca itself, Florence de Roover found descriptions in the notarial archives of a number of fully mechanized *filatoi* and *torcitoi*,[23] with storeys (*valichi*) of reels and spindles.[24] Clearly there was no reversion in fifteenth-century Lucca to the labour of hundreds of *torcitori* equipped only with hand tools. But equally, the early technological precocity of the Lucchese silk industry was not maintained. The future was rather to lie with the silk mills 'alla bolognese', differing from an earlier technology only in minor respects perhaps, yet more perfectly mechanized and employing—at least by the seventeenth century—large semi-skilled work-forces under one roof.[25]

Whether we should speak of a reversal of earlier developments or merely of technological stagnation in fifteenth-century Lucca rests on the uncertain foundations of the earlier evidence.[26] The notarial protocolli provide enough descriptions of fifteenth-century throwing-mills to establish that these were modest affairs, entirely compatible with small-scale domestic production by independent artisans. It is difficult to reconcile descriptions of these spinning mills with the requirements of

[21] Edler de Roover, 'Lucchese Silks', 2915–19.

[22] Though it was suggested by G. Livi, 'I mercanti di seta lucchesi in Bologna nei secoli xiii e xiv', *Archivio storico italiano*, 4th ser., vii (1881), 32, that the *filatoio* of Borghesano may have been 'a mano', despite the proximity of running water. See also R. Maiocchi, 'La macchina come strumento di produzione: il filatoio alla bolognese', in G. Micheli (ed.), *Storia d'Italia*, Annali 3 (Turin, 1980), 13; A. Vasina, 'Borghesano da Lucca', in *Dizionario biografico degli italiani*, xii (Rome, 1970), 579–80.

[23] Edler de Roover explains how warp threads 'were often doubled after the first throwing (on the *filatoio*) and then sent to the *torcitoio* for a second twist in the opposite direction': 'Lucchese Silks', 2919.

[24] See also the description of 1330 printed by T. Bini, *I lucchesi a Venezia: Alcuni studi sopra i secoli xiii e xiv*, 2 vols. (Lucca, 1854–6), i. 54.

[25] C. Poni, 'All'origine del sistema di fabbrica: tecnologia e organizzazione produttiva dei mulini da seta nell'Italia settentrionale (sec. XVII–XVIII)', *Rivista storica italiana*, lxxxviii (1976), 444–97.

[26] Poni correctly perceives that difficulties stem from what he calls 'il rapporto parola-cosa': ibid. 445. Edler de Roover's assumption that words have identical meaning irrespective of time and place is hardly convincing. The problem is compounded by Maiocchi, who generally treats 'filatoio', 'filatoio idraulico', and 'mulino da seta alla bolognese' as synonyms, only belatedly recognizing that 'le macchine piú grandi dovevano essere mosse ad acqua, ma le piú piccole potevano essere azionate da un sol uomo': 'La macchina come strumento di produzione', 24. On the other hand, the *filatoio da seta* to be built in Bologna by Bolognino di Borghesano da Lucca in 1341 was unambiguously a 'filatoio idraulico': Livi, 'I mercanti di seta lucchesi', 51–2. And the *fosse* of Lucca undoubtedly

the *filatoio idraulico*, or to believe that mills situated in houses in *seconda* and *terza ruga del borgho*—or beyond the walls in the parish of S. Giovanni capo di borgo—were particularly well-placed to utilize hydraulic power.[27] The rent of a house equipped with both *filatoio* and *torcitoio* ranged from 8 to 13 florins per year;[28] both *filatoio* and *torcitoio* were sold in 1454 for 36 florins.[29] That the equipment could be sold without reference to house or location is testimony to its scale. At 36 florins *filatoio* and *torcitoio* represented a greater investment than a weaver's loom, but are not incomparable to a fully equipped loom, which might cost as much as 24 florins.[30] There would also appear to be some evidence of the continued practice of hand-spinning by women. In 1457 both the wife of Bartolomeo Bacci and the widow of ser Buonagiunta da Lucca were claiming wages for silk spun from the spinner Bartolomeo da Moriano.[31]

Technological conservatism in the processes of silk spinning is particularly notable precisely because of the coming adoption in the new centres of the industry of mills 'exactly alla bolognese'.[32] The latter were not only fully mechanized water-powered throwing-mills, but involved the incorporation of *incannatoi meccanici* for the winding of silk on to the reels. By contrast, in Lucca this work continued to be performed manually by women called *maestre* or *incannatrici*. Even in the eighteenth century the tract of Attilio Arnolfini shows clearly that silk winding in Lucca remained a time-consuming skill practised by women working in their own homes.[33] Evidence relating to the *maestre* becomes more plentiful in the sixteenth century, at which time it appears that these women were—at least on occasion—employed directly by silk

provided a very considerable source of power: one which, I am told by Professor Louis Green of Monash University, was extensively used for grain mills at the time of Castruccio Castracani. There are problems here that would repay further study.

[27] AN 702 (ser Benedetto Franciotti), p. 193; 406 (ser Matteo di Giovanni de' Nobili), fos. 52^{v}–53^{r}; 259 (ser Simone Alberti), fos. 237^{v}–239^{r}.

[28] AN 702, p. 193; 406, fos. 52^{v}–53^{r}. The former relates to a *filatoio* of four *valichi*, sixty reels (*guindoli*), and 190 spindles (*fusi*), the latter to a *filatoio* of four *valichi*, seventy-one *guindoli*, and 324 *fusi*.

[29] AN 597 (ser Luviso di Antonio Buonaccorsi), fo. 65^{r}. The purchasing spinner of this contract lived in a house in the *contrada* of S. Agostino: ibid., fo. 348^{v}.

[30] AN 700(4) (ser Benedetto Franciotti), 13 Aug. 1456. Generally the price of looms in the 15th-cent. Lucchese protocolli range from 13 to 24 florins, depending on type and equipment.

[31] ASL Corte de' mercanti, Cause civili, 152, fo. 11^{r-v}. These entries appear to relate to spinning rather than winding.

[32] Defined by Poni, 'All'origine del sistema di fabbrica', 447.

[33] ASL Arte della Seta, 33, pp. 8–9, 13–14.

spinners.[34] The statute of 1376 assumes that the silk for winding would be supplied by merchants, and this assumption finds support in fragmentary references in the fifteenth-century court records.[35] The spinners themselves were obliged to receive their raw materials from men registered before the court of merchants as merchants *dell'arte della seta*, as were silk boilers (*cocitori*), dyers (*tintori*), and weavers (*testori*).[36] All these artisanal groups were composed of small masters owning (or, in the case of spinners, often renting) their equipment and operating within a domestic setting. The materials to be used by silk boilers and dyers, the length of the loom-reed (*pettine*), and the number of teeth (*denti per legatura*):[37] all were meticulously fixed by statute and subject to regular inspection. In every department, already by the fifteenth century, Lucchese silk manufacture presents a face of massive technological and organizational stability.

In part this stability must be attributed to what has been called 'the conservative and retrogressive consequences of merchant capitalism'.[38] In a well-quoted passage, Marx wrote that the emergence of the producer as merchant and capitalist

> cannot bring about the overthrow of the old mode of production by itself, but rather preserves and retains it as its own precondition. Right up to the middle of this century, for example, the manufacturer in the French silk industry, and the English hosiery and lace industries too, was a manufacturer only in name. In reality he was simply a merchant, who kept the weavers working in their old fragmented manner and exercised only control as a merchant; it was a merchant they were really working for. This method always stands in the way of the genuine capitalist mode of production and disappears with its development.[39]

Since Marx, a long series of theoretical and empirical studies have developed the theme that any revolutionary transformation or reorganization of industrial production presupposes the appearance of a class of industrial capitalists: manufacturers who draw their profits from industrial processes rather than, primarily, from trade.[40] I believe the

[34] Bratchel, 'Silk Industry of Lucca', 182.

[35] *Statuto della corte dei mercanti*, 130–1; ASL Corte de' mercanti, Cause civili, 151, fo. 30^{v}. In the latter citation the Lucchese patrician Pietro Dati gave 7 lb. of silk to a *maestra* for winding, which was allegedly returned to him 5 oz. short.

[36] *Statuto della corte dei mercanti*, lib. IV, xiii, xxxviii, xlviii.

[37] Ibid., lib. IV, x, xi, xv ff.

[38] E. Fox-Genovese and E. Genovese, *Fruits of Merchant Capital: Slavery and Bourgeois Property in the Rise and Expansion of Capitalism* (Oxford, 1983), 15.

[39] K. Marx, *Capital*, 3 vols., Penguin edn. (Harmondsworth, 1976–81), iii. 452–3.

[40] M. Dobb, *Capitalist Enterprise and Social Progress*, 2nd edn. (London, 1926), 308; *idem*, *Studies in the Development of Capitalism* (London, 1946); R. Brenner, 'The Origins of

point to be helpful for an understanding of contrasting developments within the Italian silk industry.

To speak of merchant capital as adapting to its cultural and socio-economic environment restores us from the heady world of economic theory to the realities of fifteenth-century Lucca. Production processes in Lucca appear to have been peculiarly fossilized by prevailing social attitudes and political assumptions. Writing of the Lucchese silk industry against the background of its manifest eighteenth-century decline, Attilio Arnolfini attributed the problems of his own day to a lack of competition resulting from contemporary convictions that silk production should be restricted to members of the nobility. Arnolfini sought solutions to eighteenth-century ills through the opening up of the industry to *popolari cittadini*.[41] But three centuries earlier there are traces of the attitudes of which Arnolfini complained. Outside fifteenth-century Lucca there is evidence of the emergence of specialist entrepreneurs within the silk industry, the *setaiuoli*: men who were distinct both from the international merchants from whom they acquired their raw materials and from the artisanal groups who served them.[42] By contrast, in Lucca even the word *setaiuolo* (or its immediate equivalents) appears most infrequently in fifteenth-century sources. Nicolao Lucchesini was described in court records as *mercator serici*.[43] There are further references specifically to silk merchants in the notarial protocolli of ser Paolo Michele Federighi Bianchi da Massa.[44] Election as consul or member of the general council of the *corte de' mercanti* was governed by divisions into *arti*, an arrangement which ensured the preponderance of representatives of the *arte della seta* (including the representatives of the *Mercanzia maggiore*).[45] But in reality precisely the same men were elected

Capitalist Development: A Critique of Neo-Smithian Marxism', *New Left Review*, civ (1977), 54–71; H. Otsuka, *The Spirit of Capitalism: The Max Weber Thesis in an Economic Historical Perspective* (Tokyo, 1982), 3–35. I have found particularly useful the introductory remarks of P. Hudson, *The Genesis of Industrial Capital: A Study of the West Riding Wool Textile Industry c.1750–1850* (Cambridge, 1986), 3–24.

41 ASL Arte della Seta, 33, pp. 107–12.

42 See, e.g., P. Massa, *Un'impresa serica genovese della prima metà del cinquecento* (Milan, 1974), 17–27.

43 ASL Corte de' mercanti, Cause civili, 151, fo. 44^r. Nicolao Lucchesini must be regarded as atypical in that he was very much a new man, the son of a silk weaver named Checcio. For Checcio Lucchesini, see ibid. 150, fos. 43^r, 67^r.

44 AN 371 (ser Paolo Michele Federighi Bianchi da Massa), fos. 11^r, 15^r; 366, fos. 40^v, 55^r. Those named as *mercatores serici* include: Iacopo di Nicolao Puccinelli, Carlo di Bartolomeo de' Buzzolini, Giovanni di ser Guidone da Pietrasanta, Bartolomeo di Giannino Fatinelli, Michele di Iacopo Gratta, and Migliore Guiducci.

45 *Statuto della corte dei mercanti*, lib. I, i–iiii.

indiscriminately: sometimes as representatives of the *arte della seta*, sometimes as representatives of the great silk merchants, sometimes as bankers, and sometimes as wool merchants. Generally the men who controlled the fifteenth-century Lucchese silk industry were not explicitly identified with silk; they are labelled merely as 'citizens and merchants of Lucca'. By the sixteenth century these same men had come to prefer the title 'noble'.[46]

The importers of raw silk and founders of silk shops may be fully identified with members of the ruling political élite as described in the previous chapter. Their factors, the keepers of the books, and the managers of the *botteghe dell'arte della seta* often appear as young men drawn from the same ranks, at a particular stage of their general business apprenticeship.[47] These same men will be met in the next chapter as landowners, often with very extensive landed interests. Their commercial and manufacturing investments might be very mixed, extending far beyond silk. In the fifteenth century, as later in the days of Attilio Arnolfini, Lucca was inextricably bound to silk by ties that were both historic and emotional. Silk was the foundation of Lucca's historic prosperity, and the basis of her present reputation. Consequently, silk manufacture was materially and emotionally too important to be left to outsiders. The continued control of silk manufacture by members of a political, landed, mercantile élite goes far towards explaining the technological conservatism of the industry. It was profoundly to affect the organization of production processes.

To a degree we can speak unambiguously of mercantile controls and of exploitative relationships. Artisanal corporations such as that of the silk weavers might enjoy a certain limited autonomy,[48] but were in fact firmly subordinated to the court of merchants. The court of merchants itself, through statutes governing election to both its *Consolato* and its *Consiglio*, was dominated by patrician merchants representing the *arte della seta*. The court thus constituted exercised extensive jurisdiction over manufacture, and particularly over the silk industry. Weavers specifically were required regularly to swear an oath that they would obey the statutes and work diligently.[49] No broker, spinner, silk boiler,

[46] For the changing self-image, see Berengo, *Nobili e mercanti*, 31–53, 245–63; G. R. Baker, 'Nobilità in declino: il caso di Siena sotto i Medici e gli Asburgo-Lorena', *Rivista storica italiana*, lxxxiv (1972), 584–616.

[47] The early career of Piero di Conte de' Guidiccioni is particularly well documented: ASL Corte de' mercanti, Cause civili, 151, fos. 90^r, 113^r ff.

[48] Tommasi, 'Storia di Lucca', Documenti, ser. ii, pp. 66–87.

[49] *Statuto della corte dei mercanti*, lib. I, viiii.

dyer, or weaver was able to work any silk cloth on his own account.[50] The looms of weavers were subject to sequestration for debt, and artisans who were in debt or who had been advanced money by one merchant were prohibited from seeking employment from another.[51] The notarial and merchant court records provide testimony to the web of indebtedness in which an individual silk worker might find himself entangled. Checcho di Simone del Vagheggia and his sons, weavers of silk cloth, were imprisoned in 1457 for the substantial accumulated debt of 60 florins owed to Iacopo and Nicolao Turrettini.[52] Other weavers found themselves constrained to work, on terms specified in great detail, in the shop of a patrician silk merchant for the repayment of accumulated debts, for the purchase price of a house, and—most frequently—for the instalments due on the cost of a loom.[53] The silk company of Silvestro di Gregorio and Cristoforo Trenta appears particularly frequently in transactions of this nature.[54]

There is another perspective. Whether because of the intrinsic qualities of mercantile capital or because of the special ethos of Lucca's leading manufacture, the statutes not only entrenched pervasive mercantile controls but also a limited artisanal independence and the prerogatives of individual mysteries. To protect the rights of artisans, no one was permitted to work out of his own mystery.[55] No person might weave silk cloth who was not inscribed in the *scuola de' testori*.[56] Weavers on the one hand were forbidden to enter into partnership agreements with merchants, and on the other received extensive protection at law against their own workers.[57] The Lucchese records are full of references to small companies formed between dyers or spinners or silk boilers—for periods of up to five years—perhaps one partner providing the equipment and the other the labour.[58] Dyers specifically figure as purchasers of substantial quantities of raw materials in the form of expensive dye-

[50] Ibid., lib. IV, xxxviii. See also lib. IV, xiii.

[51] Ibid., lib. I, viii; lib. II, iiii.

[52] ASL Corte de' mercanti, Cause civili, 152, fo. 34r. For silk weavers detained for smaller sums, see ibid., fos. 35v, 36r. The latter case is elucidated by AN 700(3) (ser Benedetto Franciotti) 19 Nov. 1457. All references to AN for the remainder of the chapter are to the protocolli of ser Benedetto Franciotti unless otherwise stated.

[53] AN 700(3), 10 May 1457; 700(4), 23 Jan. 1455, 13 Aug. 1456 (two documents); 700(5), 16 July 1456; 706, pp. 23–5 (12 Jan. 1461).

[54] All but one of the examples cited above involve the Trenta company.

[55] *Statuto della corte dei mercanti*, lib. IV, xxxviii.

[56] Tommasi, 'Storia di Lucca', Documenti, ser. ii, pp. 69–70.

[57] Ibid. 70–3.

[58] Typical in this respect is the company formed for silk boiling in 1459 by Piero di Giovanni Novellucci, his son Nicolao, and Piero di Antonio Iacopucci: AN 702, p. 272.

stuffs, though they seem to have acquired their supplies on the Lucchese market rather than as direct importers.[59] A more general solicitude for artisanal interests (amongst less disinterested motives) was expressed in measures prohibiting the import of semi-worked materials and in the provision that artisans might not be paid in cloth.[60] With the recovery of the Lucchese silk industry, protected by statute, and with limited fixed capital requirements, it is by no means difficult to construct biographies of prospering artisans. The fifteenth-century fortunes of the Lucchesini family provide one example; another is suggested by the career of the weaver Bartolomeo Pieri.[61]

The organizational structure of Lucca's dominant manufacture is not unrelated to the passive political acquiescence of the *popolo minuto* identified in earlier chapters. In a wide-ranging study Richard Mackenney has argued that 'a pervasive commercial ethic . . . was compatible if not always comfortable with vigorous guild life'.[62] In the best traditions of Venetian historiography, Mackenney is inclined to associate Venetian stability with limited artisanal independence, in a society where 'the balance between bosses and work-force was kept by the law'.[63] The distinctiveness of Venetian guild structures fails to obscure the obvious parallels. The conditions that permitted the harmonious coexistence of merchant and master artisan were not immutable. In the early sixteenth century the dislocation of Lucchese trade routes by war was adversely to affect silk production. A special magistrature was appointed to remedy the situation, and the restrictive measures emanating from this group were to cause disaffection among Lucchese silk workers, which exploded in the revolt of the *Straccioni*.[64] The fifteenth century offers no such conjuncture.

Lucca's own identification of silk as the key both to economic prosperity and to social and political stability contains, therefore, a great deal of truth. Particularly striking is the extent to which other crafts were

[59] In 1460, e.g., the dyer Ansano di Bartolomeo Nocchi promised payment of 48 florins for 48 lb. of indigo sold to him by Agostino di Giovanni da Ghivizzano: AN 704, p. 205.

[60] *Statuto della corte dei mercanti*, lib. IV, xliii, lxv.

[61] The Lucchesini in the mid-15th cent. were represented by the silk spinner Giusto di Andrea: AN 702, 31 Oct., 6 Nov. 1458, 19 May 1459; 703, 2, 13, 16, 30 Dec. 1458, 8 Aug. 1459, 14 Jan. 1460; 704, 14 Jan., 23 Aug., 4 Nov. 1460. The family's rapid rise is detailed in BSL MS 142, Racconto del principio e del progresso della famiglia Lucchesini. Bartolomeo Pieri had the resources to assign his daughter the very large artisanal dowry of 210 florins: AN 700(3), 22 Aug. 1457.

[62] Mackenney, *Tradesmen and Traders*, 80.

[63] Ibid. 82.

[64] Berengo, *Nobili e mercanti*, 117–46.

orientated to the service of silk manufacture. The *calderai*, organized under *capitano* and *consigliere* in an early statute of 1273, manufactured the great copper cauldrons used for the boiling of silk.[65] The *calderai* resident in fifteenth-century Lucca—Antonio di Bernardo; Bernardo, Giovanni, and Venturino di Benedetto; and Bonino di Martino—were all northerners, from Como. The sons of Benedetto at least, like so many foreign artisans with special and necessary skills, had been granted citizenship. By the 1450s they appear as fully integrated inhabitants of Lucca, occupying a shop in S. Michele in foro and purchasing a perpetual lease on a house in S. Maria Corteorlandini from S. Donato extra muros. They sent money by exchange to the company of Michele Arnolfini in Bruges; they engaged in a variety of commercial deals, including the purchase of copper; they sold mules and horses; and they entered into agreements *ad collariam*.[66] Of special interest is the agreement by which Venturino obtained lime and bricks in payment of the relatively small sum of £25. 12*s*. owed to him by Andrea di Guaspare Lemmucchi of Montuolo, whilst a little later the price of a horse sold by the same Venturino was requested partly in charcoal.[67] The silk industry was more directly serviced by the goldsmiths and by the *battiloro* who provided the precious threads of silver and gold. These too were likely to be foreigners. The prominent mid-fifteenth-century goldsmith Arrigo di Giovanni Tinti hailed from Pisa;[68] the Venetian *battiloro* Luizo Vectorii, after spending some months in Lucca exercising his art and teaching the locals, was emboldened to request a public subsidy to encourage him to continue with his good work.[69]

Competition for artisanal skills between neighbouring states led to the granting of many privileges to encourage the return of exiles and to attract new talents. The ferocious measures enacted to prevent the export of skills and techniques were matched by a parallel determination to poach the skills of others. A just appreciation of their worth, to Lucca and to Lucca's rivals, equipped individual artisans with substantial bargaining potential. The proximity of the border was a further force for

[65] M. Tazartes, 'Osservazioni sulle arti e corporazioni a Lucca nel xiv secolo', *Actum Luce*, xi (1982), 45.

[66] AN 700(2), 22 Dec. 1455; 700(3), 21 July 1457; 700(4), 12 May, 7 Nov., 22 Dec. 1455, 19 Jan., 9 Mar., 22 June, 15 Sept. (two documents), 25 Oct., 30 Oct. 1456; 700(5), 22 June 1456; 702, pp. 202, 228, 292; Rif. 16, p. 430.

[67] AN 702, p. 117; 704, p. 26.

[68] AN 700(2), 15 Nov. 1455; 700(3), 13 Apr. 1457 (two documents); 700(4), 23 Sept. 1455; 701, 1 Dec. 1457; 702, pp. 122–3, 265; 703, p. 148; 704, p. 180.

[69] Rif. 20, p. 20. Earlier Francesco di Iacopo Minutoli had been granted concessions to the same end: Rif. 16, p. 457.

the preservation of artisanal independence. At the same time, like the silk workers themselves, those craftsmen who supplied materials for silk manufacture were closely regulated by the *arte della seta* through the *curia dei mercanti*. The soap-maker Bartolomeo d'Andrea Nicholetti from Prato was embraced by Lucca as a valuable immigrant;[70] as a provider of soap to Lucchese silk boilers he was constrained by detailed instructions regarding ingredients, the soap only to be added by the *cocitori* in the presence of the merchant or his agents.[71] The work of goldsmiths and *battiloro* was regulated by equally meticulous constraints.[72]

If we are justified in tracing the tentacles of the *arte della seta* widely throughout the manufacturing sector, it remains true that there was an economic life in Lucca beyond silk. A petition of September 1433 presents what appears to be a fairly comprehensive list of the leading crafts and retail trades practised in the city.[73] This list, supplemented by the more general evidence of notarial and court sources, bears witness to a hive of activity largely directed towards the housing, clothing, and—in its retail dimensions—feeding of the city's inhabitants. At base are the primary labours of sand-diggers[74] and stone-cutters, the latter likely to be migrants from Carrara and further north. Thence on the path from extraction to manufacture lie various companies formed, often with an infusion of merchant capital, for the production of basic materials like bricks. An example is the short-term company formed in 1458 for the manufacture of bricks by the wool merchant Lorenzo di Piero da Prato and the *fornacerius* Lunardo di Andrea da Menabbio. Lunardo was to provide his labour and furnace (presumably in Pontetetto), whereas Lorenzo provided the capital, and was responsible for sales and accounts. At the end of the partnership Lorenzo was to recover his expenses, after which profits and losses were to be equally divided.[75] More centralized, more permanent, and much less typical was the workshop in Lucca for the manufacture of glass, sold, with its

[70] BSL MS 38, Martino Bernardini, Ricordi Storici, fo. 233r.

[71] *Statuto della corte dei mercanti*, lib. IV, x.

[72] Ibid., lib. IV, lv–lxii.

[73] Rif. 14, pp. 399–400.

[74] There is reference to a *renaiuolo* as witness to a notarial act in Apr. 1460: AN 705, p. 111.

[75] AN 702, p. 56. For an earlier contract establishing a similar company for one year between the same Lunardo and Domenico, Nanni, and Francesco di Piero da Prato, see AN 700(3), 7 May 1457. For an appeal for greater flexibility in manufacturing specifications, see Rif. 15, p. 516.

equipment, in 1461 by the heirs of Raffaele Tegrimi for more than 436 florins.[76]

The building industry was a substantial employer of labour if we are to judge from the number of men described as *muratori* repairing houses, building ovens, constructing wells. Incidental references again indicate a particularly mobile work-force, masons being drawn to Lucca from Como, Pisa, Camaiore, Florence, and Poggibonsi. Quantitatively less prominent are the specialist roofers and the house-painters, the latter often indistinguishable in the sources from artists of a finer talent. Individual *muratori* sometimes appear in the records alternatively described as carpenters.[77] Mid-fifteenth-century contracts suggest that carpenters were likely to spend an apprenticeship of three years during which they might expect to earn about 6 florins per annum, their fathers remaining responsible for clothing and expenses.[78] Details of payments made to master carpenters themselves are not readily translatable into annual incomes.[79] Less obviously than the masons, the carpenters confirm the impression of a labour force in the building industry which was drawn widely from northern and central Italy. Other craftsmen in wood—turners, coopers, and tub-makers (*bigongiai*)—reveal a presence only in petty contracts and in the witnessing of legal documents.

A further range of economic activities in quattrocento Lucca centred on the working of metals. The metalworkers extend from men generally described as smiths—*fabbri*, *ferraiuoli*—to blacksmiths, locksmiths, anvil-makers, and armourers. Impressionistically it would appear that if the building trades attracted a shifting work-force, smiths working in Lucca were more likely to be drawn from the surrounding countryside, whilst the more specialist workers in metal were invariably immigrants from the great centres of the north: Milan and Como. The essential equipment of a smith—anvil, hammers, tongs, apron, and so forth—is detailed in the lease at 6 florins for one year of a comprehensive selection of such equipment by Nicolao di Giovanni da Camporgiano to a pair of smiths operating from S. Pietro a Vico.[80] Smiths were appointed

[76] AN 706, pp. 14–17. The details are limited, but the implications are of a manufacture on a larger and more integrated scale than is typically found in the organization and culture of work in 15th-cent. Lucca.

[77] Antonio Chellucci is thus described both as master mason and carpenter.

[78] AN 700(4), 12 July 1454; 702, p. 191.

[79] Antonio Chellucci received 22½ ducats for repairs to a house and hospital belonging to the church of S. Donato; Iacopo di Guerruccio da Terriciuola was paid 5 florins by two weavers for work done: AN 706, p. 190; ASL Corte de' mercanti, Cause civili, 152, fo. 29^{r}. Without a context, such figures defy application.

[80] AN 704, p. 24.

arbitrators when one of their number became involved in a dispute with an anvil-maker (of Milanese birth) over the quality of an anvil supplied.[81] A company established for the art of locksmith bears all the hallmarks of other comparable artisanal associations with its capital investment of 79 ducats, its principle of unlimited responsibility, and with the respective inputs of capital and labour by the investing artisans.[82]

Turning to workers in a softer medium, skinners and pelterers should perhaps in part be treated among the servants of silk manufacture, for which they provided the trimmings. The leather-workers proper, because of their noisome art, were confined to the quarter of S. Tomeo, one of the few examples of residential segregation within the medieval city.[83] The restriction did not apply to workers with tanned leather: saddlers (including makers of pack-saddles), shoemakers, and cobblers whose shops can be identified throughout the city. Shoemakers and cobblers appear to constitute one of the larger artisanal groupings; the equipment of one such shop (together with the contents of the house of which it formed part) is inventoried in a civil case before the court of the *Podestà* of 1457.[84] A few years later the *cuoiai*, through the captains of their art, protested that, whilst they were prohibited from making shoes, the shoemakers since 1435 had been permitted to exercise both mysteries, to the impoverishment of the tanners. As a result of this protest of 1464, it was granted that no tanner might form a partnership with a shoemaker, that the arts be kept separate, and that nobody participating in the one art was to engage in the other.[85] This act is important in part because it provides another fragmentary glimpse of the multiplicity of corporate groupings that vitalized the shadowy artisanal world. More important, we see here another example of 'the defence of a culture of work that had been inherited and that had to be handed down to subsequent generations, the safeguarding of an identity, and the conservation of a status', as explored recently by Carlo Poni with

[81] AN 702, p. 213. [82] AN 700(4), 8 July 1454.

[83] The clustering of tanners and tanneries in the *contrada* of S. Tomeo is shown in ASL Podestà di Lucca, Curia Civile, 1176, fos. 78^{r}–79^{r}. The point is confirmed in numerous notarial references.

[84] Ibid. 1309, fos. 185^{v}–186^{v}. Besides the relatively frugal contents of the bedroom, main room, and cellar of the house in *contrada* S. Sensio, the contents of the shop included a table for cutting leather, 100 pairs of shoe-lasts both large and small, the means to hold the same whilst stitching, and benches. These premises were leased by their Lombard occupant for a rent of 10 florins a year from the apothecary Baldassare di Giovanni da Montecatini. See also ibid., fo. 103^{r-v}.

[85] Rif. 18, pp. 704–5.

reference to shoemakers some centuries later in Bologna.[86] Outside the disciplines of the *arte della seta*, we are left with a teeming world of independent artisans, small traders in raw materials, retailers in manufactured goods, privileged within their own mysteries, like Poni's Bolognese well versed in the strategies of attack and defence.

The rest of the manufacturing sector can be loosely grouped under textiles. At base are the weavers of linen cloth and those employed in the various stages in the manufacture of woollen cloth.[87] Followers of the former craft were to a noteworthy degree alien immigrants drawn to Lucca from north of the Alps. Of the twenty-four linen weavers for whom I have compiled biographies, two were immigrants from France, three were German, and one was from Flanders. A similar prominence of aliens is found when we move from textile manufacture to garment making and repair. The tailors resident in Lucca were peculiarly cosmopolitan. Their numbers included German craftsmen like Corrado di Arrigo and Giovanni di Rinaldo, the Flemish tailor Teodoricus, and a sprinkling of settlers from Milan and Piedmont.[88] Their social world is captured in such passing incidents as the agreement by which the wife of Guglielmo di Giovanni of Piedmont, granted the right to occupy a house in the *contrada* of S. Maria Corteorlandini by the terms of her father's will and finding her brother mightily upset by the arrangement, accepted an annual payment of 3 florins for every year that she kept out.[89] For the rest we speak of hosiers, doublet-makers, and mattress-makers, with a faint trace of a local lace industry. With some licence we might extend the category to embrace the *cordellari* with their shops in S. Sensio and S. Alessandro maggiore.[90]

Finally, removed from manufacture proper, there were the providers of essential goods and services. Most obviously there were the processors and distributors of foodstuffs: cheese-makers, butchers, and bakers; vintners and corn merchants. There were also the prostitutes and the slaves. From the time of the mid-fourteenth-century plagues, measures had been taken to protect prostitutes with the intention of discouraging

[86] C. Poni, 'Norms and Disputes: The Shoemakers' Guild in Eighteenth-Century Bologna', *Past & Present*, cxxiii (1989), 80–108. The quotation is taken from p. 83.

[87] A convenient summary of the steps of woollen cloth manufacture appears in F. Edler, *Glossary of Medieval Terms of Business: Italian Series 1200–1600* (Cambridge, Mass., 1934), 324–30.

[88] ASL Corte de' mercanti, Cause civili, 150, fo. 68ʳ; AN 700(3), 14 June 1457; 700(4), 10 July, 11 July, 17 Sept. 1454, 25 Sept. 1455, 24 Feb. 1456; 702, 6 Jan. 1458, p. 245; 703, p. 372; 704, p. 159; SB 159, fo. 164ʳ⁻ᵛ; 161, fo. 153ʳ; Rif. 15, p. 495; 16, pp. 491, 791.

[89] AN 700(4), 25 Sept. 1455.

[90] AN 700(4), 21 Sept. 1455; 702, p. 231.

'greater evils' (sodomy).[91] This link was specifically made again in an enactment of October 1456.[92] In August 1440 the law that prostitutes might only leave the brothel on Saturdays was amended to permit them to pass freely, and justice before the courts according to the statutes was guaranteed to them.[93] In 1448, in response to the petition of the local *stufaiolo*—German by birth, like so many of his clients—it was conceded that prostitutes might freely accompany men to the public baths.[94] Prostitutes, as might be expected, appear frequently in the court records in cases involving assault and verbal abuse;[95] a very large number of them were foreigners.[96] Perhaps the most enterprising of all Lucchese prostitutes was Pellegrina of Milan who was engaged in a small way in 1459 in the trade between Siena and Bologna via Lucca.[97] From prostitutes to slaves is not a meaningless juxtapositioning. Exclusively female, drawn largely from Russia,[98] often acquired in the markets of Pisa, slaves were most likely to achieve historical record either when bearing the children of their masters or when attracting the sexual attentions of their master's neighbours.[99] It may be noted that when a slave was assaulted and lost a tooth, the damage was adjudged to be to her; when made pregnant, the damage was to her owners.[100] Acknowledgement that 'Our Redeemer took flesh that we might be restored to pristine liberty' resulted in frequent acts of manumission, especially

[91] Bongi, *Inventario*, i. 213–14.

[92] Rif. 18, p. 809.

[93] Rif. 15, p. 490.

[94] Rif. 16, p. 811.

[95] SB 159, fo. 312^{r-v}; 162, fos. 255^{r-v}, 280^{v}–281^{r}; 165, fos. 201^{r-v}, 317^{r}–318^{v}, 320^{r-v}, 336^{v}–337^{r}, 442^{r-v}, 545^{r-v}.

[96] AN 405(6) (ser Matteo di Giovanni de' Nobili), fo. 40^{r-v}; SB 159, fo. 312^{r-v}; 162, fos. 57^{r-v}, 255^{r-v}; 165, fos. 336^{v}–337^{r}. The case in SB 162, fos. 106^{v}–107^{r}, itself involves the reception of two German prostitutes into the public baths. If many of the residents of the brothel were aliens, others were drawn from elsewhere in Italy, including Ancona, Rimini, and the Regno.

[97] AN 702, p. 186. The matter relates to carriage charges payable to the mule-drivers responsible for the transport of merchandise from Siena to Lucca and from Lucca to Bologna. Payment was due on safe arrival of the goods in Bologna.

[98] Others were described as Tartars and Bulgars. The predominance of domestic service and the general sense of provenance are compatible with the findings of Domenico Gioffrè for Genoa, particularly from the 1430s: *Il mercato degli schiavi a Genova nel secolo xv* (Genoa, 1971). I have found no references to male slaves in Lucca.

[99] ASL Archivio Guinigi, 151, Michele Guinigi, Memorie e note, fo. 61^{v}; SB 161, fos. 309^{r}–310^{r}; 162, fo. 309^{r-v}; 165, fos. 546^{v}–547^{r}; 171, fo. 79^{r}; 202, fo. 98^{v}; ASL Podestà di Lucca, Curia Civile, 1308, fos. 26^{v}–27^{r}.

[100] Cf. SB 165, fo. 142^{r-v}, with ASL Podestà di Lucca, Curia Civile, 1308, fos. 26^{v}–27^{r}.

when the owner's mind was concentrated by the approach of death.[101] Freed slaves might receive dowries and the consequent possibility of marriage with local artisans.[102] Others might receive their freedom only on harsh conditions, which could include a commitment to long-term future service.[103] Traces of tension are suggested by occasional acts of theft, and more overtly by the murder of Bartolomeo Testa by his slave Caterina.[104]

Services of a rather different order were provided by the porters, who constituted another of the more violent elements on the streets of Lucca, and by the brokers whose activities were strictly regulated in the statutes of the *corte de' mercanti*.[105] The *università* of barbers, organized under two *capitani* of their art, pledged themselves in 1449 not to work after the sounding of the Angelus on Saturday evening, and requested specified penalties for those who were not matriculated in their art.[106] Apprenticeship as a barber might involve being taught to read and write in Italian.[107] Barbers, like the followers of comparable mysteries, were likely to form relatively short-term partnerships among themselves for the exercise of their trade—in one case for a period of five years;[108] a glimpse of their working environment is provided by a case before the *Podestà* of Lucca where a certain stone for the sharpening of razors was stolen from a shop under the palace of the *Podestà* in the piazza S. Michele in foro where the barber Bartolomeo Andrea of Gallicano shaved his

[101] AN 576(1) (ser Nicolao di Pietro da Camaiore), fo. 38v; ASL Archivio Arnolfini, 2, fo. 56v; Archivio Guinigi, 151, Michele Guinigi, Memorie e note, fo. 50v. Alternatively a testator might bequeath his slave to his wife: AN Originali Testamenti, 11 (ser Domenico Ciomucchi), fo. 74v.

[102] AN 597 (ser Luviso di Antonio Buonaccorsi), fo. 320r–v; ASL Archivio Guinigi, 151, Michele Guinigi, Memorie e note, fo. 61v. One of the familiar street brawls between Lucchese women in 1450 involved two freed slaves: SB 165, fo. 263r–v.

[103] One Russian slave, Lucia, was freed in 1435 on condition both that she continued to serve the family faithfully for a further four years and that she nurtured and raised the illegitimate child that she had borne one of her owners. In a postscript, Lucia, allegedly of her love and free will, agreed that at the end of the four-year period she would remain in the house for a further two years, serving without any pay: AN 548(1) (ser Ciomeo Pieri), fos. 11r–12r. For whatever reasons, Lorenzo Buonvisi granted to his slave Margarita and her children freedom on the understanding that Margarita would not stay in the cities or territories of Lucca or Genoa: AN 385 (ser Massino di Bartolomeo da Pietrasanta), fo. 148r.

[104] ASL Podestà di Lucca, Inquisizioni, 5232, fos. 29r–31r; SB 162, fos. 143v–144r; Rif. 16, pp. 89, 171, 475.

[105] *Statuto della corte dei mercanti*, pp. xlii–xliii.

[106] Rif. 17, pp. 116–17.

[107] AN 704, p. 179. Other acts of apprenticeship contracted by barbers admittedly contain no such provision.

[108] AN 405(6) (ser Matteo di Giovanni de' Nobili), fo. 72r.

customers.[109] Similarly servicing the economically productive community are the surgeons, whose misfortune it is to be remembered largely through the complaints of their less satisfied patients.[110] The picture finds completion in the professional world of grammarians, notaries, and doctors of law and of medicine.

By definition, many of the groups latterly discussed were exclusively concerned with local markets, local needs, and a local clientele. Presumably the skilled goldsmiths, in the jewelry dimension of their craft, looked hopefully to a wider market. The German tinsmith, Piero Aldibrandi da Argentina, resident in Lucca, he said, because of the presence of the Volto Santo and the bodies of many saints, obtained permission freely to export all quantities of tin that he might work within the city.[111] Leather-workers obtained supplies of leather from local butchers,[112] but also turned to the great mercantile companies for imported raw materials.[113] That imported leather, including leather from Ireland, was obtained from Lucchese merchants trading through Pisa or purchased directly from Pisan companies would seem to indicate that the manufacture of leather goods in Lucca transcended local needs and looked to the wider market for quality products. Throughout the fifteenth century a number of Lucchese patricians advanced schemes, largely abortive, for the establishment of paper manufacture in favourable locations within the Lucchese state.[114] But when the governing councils contemplated the encouragement of alternative industries to reduce Lucca's dangerous dependence on silk, it was the manufacture of fine woollen cloths that seemed to offer the most attractive possibilities.

Lucca had always provided a market for imported woollen cloth. A record of the involvement of leading Lucchese merchants in the trade in English cloth is preserved in the earliest extant brokerage book, which dates from 1409.[115] Subsequent volumes make mention of cloths of

[109] ASL Podestà di Lucca, Inquisizioni, 5229, 30 Apr., 7 May 1436; SB 161, fo. 36^{r-v}.

[110] AN 702, p. 284; 704, pp. 167, 184.

[111] Rif. 16, pp. 485, 788.

[112] ASL Podestà di Lucca, Curia Civile, 1309, fo. 203^{r}; AN 704, p. 27.

[113] ASL Corte de' mercanti, Cause civili, 151, fos. 22^{r}–23^{v}, 30^{r}, 42^{r}, 103^{v}; 152, fo. 35^{r}; AN 700(4), 31 Oct. 1454, 15 July 1456. For Lucchese merchants transporting leather, including Irish leather, through Pisa at the end of the 15th cent., see Archivio di Stato, Pisa, Archivio del Comune di Pisa, Divisione C, 90/1, Gabella Maggiore o Dogana, fos. 1^{r}–18^{r}. Leather figures prominently in the accounts of Lucchese brokers: Corte de' mercanti, Libri de' sensali, 94–9 (1409–82).

[114] R. Sabbatini, 'La cartiera Buonvisi di Villa Basilica XVI–XIX secolo', *Archivio storico italiano*, cxl (1982), 263–5.

[115] ASL Corte de' mercanti, Libro de' sensali, 94, fo. 73^{r}. For an overview of the pattern of Italian cloth exports from England, particularly after 1370, see E. Fryde, 'The English Cloth Industry and the Trade with the Mediterranean *c.*1370–*c.*1480', in M. Spallanzani (ed.),

London and of England (the colours sometimes specified), cloth of Bruges and Ypres and others more generally described as *oltremontani*, and cloths from Lombardy. When Silvestro di Matteo Trenta left pious legacies in his will to the convent of S. Agostino and to poor girls for their dowries, his widow Mattea made payment largely in the form of cloth, sometimes identified as kerseys or as cloths of London.[116] Incidental references to the retailing of kerseys appear not infrequently in the mid-fifteenth-century Lucchese records.[117] Cloth figured largely amongst the exports of Lucchese companies based in London.[118] In Lucca the shops of *pannari* were stocked not only with the products of local manufacture, but with woollen cloth from Lombardy, Bruges, and London. In 1432 one company of *pannari*, of which the partners were Simone Luporini, Cristoforo Ricciardi, and the late Angiolo di Giorgio, was indebted to Nicolao and Michele Burlamacchi for woollen cloths to the sum of 302 florins.[119] In part payment of this debt, the company's entire stock of woollen cloth, valued at 175 florins, was consigned to the Burlamacchi by Simone Luporini. Details are recorded of the cloth thus consigned. Of the fifty-two cloths in the shop of Luporini and Ricciardi, twelve are described as of Bruges, eight as of London. Local Lucchese manufacture was represented, as were the products of Verona and Como.[120]

Like any medieval city, Lucca was also the seat of a local woollen industry primarily servicing the needs of her own population. Throughout the fifteenth century this industry was fed by supplies of imported raw materials. The fifteenth-century brokerage books contain frequent references to wool from Provence, to *lana francesca* (probably English), to *lana barbarescha*, and to *lana di Marolicha*. Impressionistically, from *c.*1450 the brokerage books seem to attest to the increasing appearance in Lucca of *lana San Mattea*. The shop of the *pannari* Luporini and Ricciardi contained one piece of dark cloth manufactured in Lucca from

Produzione commercio e consumo dei panni di lana (nei secoli xii–xviii), Istituto internazionale di storia economica 'F. Datini' Prato: Atti della 'seconda settimana di studio' (10–16 aprile 1970), ii (Florence, 1976), 343–67.

[116] AN 700(3), 5 Jan., 6 Apr., 30 Apr., 1 Aug., 16 Sept. 1457; 700(4), 21 Aug., 30 Aug., 24 Sept., 27 Sept., 1 Oct., 19 Oct. 1456. Part payment of these small dowries was made also in grain, oil, and wine.

[117] See, e.g., ASL Corte de' mercanti, Cause civili, 152, fo. 11^{r}; AN 700(3), 21 Apr. 1457; 700(4), 22 June 1456; 704, p. 178.

[118] ASL Corte de' mercanti, Cause civili, 151, fos. 60^{r}–61^{v}, 66^{r}–68^{v}, 142^{r}–147^{v}, 163^{r}–164^{v}.

[119] The 302 florins in current money are described as part of a larger sum of 385 florins in old money owing to Nicolao for cloths (*panni*) sold by him to the said company.

[120] ASL Corte de' mercanti, Cause civili, 150, fo. 75^{r-v}.

Catalonian wool.[121] And the same source provides other references to Lucchese cloth made of fine, carded wool. But we are given no indication of values, neither here nor in a comparable inventory of the contents of the shop of the *lanaro* and *farsettaio* Simone Giovanni da Cuciglano.[122] In the absence of more conclusive data it must be assumed that throughout the fifteenth century the Lucchese woollen industry was regularly producing fine woollen cloth of medium quality and price. The industry was represented in the *corte de' mercanti* by one of the seven ruling consuls (technically drawn also from the *arte dei panni lini*) and by five representatives on the general council.[123] The industry was dominated by industrial entrepreneurs bearing the designation *lanari*.[124]

The first, most striking feature of the *lanari* of fifteenth-century Lucca is the extent to which these men tended to be newcomers. The point is illustrated by their names: Bartolomeo di Domenico da Prato, Filippo di Piero da Mantua, Gabrielle di Michele da Pisa, Giovanni di Guelpho de' Lanfranchi da Pisa, Iacopo di Giovanni da Genova, Lorenzo di Piero da Prato, Nanni and Nicolao di Piero di Simone Genti da Pisa, Nicolao and his father, ser Gerardo, da Pisa, Vanni di Pietro de Malaventre da Pisa, together with others whose names indicate recent arrival from the neighbouring communities of Calci, Decimo, Moriano, and Villa. The ranks of the *lanari* offer further testimony to the encouragement of immigration by fifteenth-century governments, in Lucca as elsewhere, against a background of successive outbreaks of plague. More specifically, the prominence of Pisans is a reminder of the exodus of merchants and artisans from Pisa following the Florentine conquest of 1406, and of the prejudicial consequences of Florentine hegemony for the Pisan woollen industry.[125] *Lanari* controlled the production of woollen cloth for the market, though the various manufacturing processes remained largely in the hands of independent artisans. There are traces of capitalist organization in the miscellaneous mysteries discussed above, notably in the case of glass. But with wool we return to the putting out of materials in an organized production process by entrepreneurs who eventually recovered and sold the finished product. Indeed, the pattern

[121] Ibid., fo. 75^{r}. [122] Ibid. 151, fos. 50^{r}–51^{r}.

[123] *Statuto della corte dei mercanti*, lib. I, i–iiii.

[124] For a definition of *lanaro* (*lanaiuolo*), see Edler, *Glossary of Medieval Terms of Business*, 148.

[125] M. Mallett, 'Pisa and Florence in the Fifteenth Century', in N. Rubinstein (ed.), *Florentine Studies: Politics and Society in Renaissance Florence* (London, 1968), 403–41. For the concentration of Pisan exiles in Lucca in the mid-15th cent., see ASL Corte de' mercanti, Cause civili, 151, fo. 17^{r-v}.

of control presents an instructive comparison with that in the *arte della seta* with which the present chapter began.

The court records contain periodic references to the small debts of one or two florins owing to *lanari* by wool combers and carders. The presumption must be that, as elsewhere, these men worked for wages in a central workshop, though the agreement made (and later dishonoured) by the *scardassatore* Nicolao da S. Gennaro that he would work off a loan of 2 florins seems to indicate that such men might freely contract their labour with several woollen manufacturers.[126] The wool comber Antonio Giovanni held Lucchese citizenship. His will is a simple, uninformative instrument, but that of his widow Caterina details property which included a farm in S. Gennaro.[127] In these stages of woollen manufacture the image is hardly that of an impoverished proletariat, for which Florentine studies of combers and carders have prepared us. Here again the need to attract skilled workers—to a city whose fortunes were not traditionally tied to wool—may provide partial explanation; the comber Antonio Giovanni himself was the son of a Bolognese. References to the spinning of wool, though too infrequent to be conclusive, seem to point both to the prominence of women and also to low rates of remuneration.[128] But the weavers were largely male and often immigrants, many being described as Germans (probably from the Low Countries). One of these Germans, Giovanni di Tommaso, possessed a house in Pisa. This fact, together with the implication that Giovanni might one day return to Pisa, suggests that at an artisanal level also the Lucchese woollen industry was a beneficiary of the vicissitudes of fifteenth-century Pisan history.[129] Members of Lucca's larger community of silk weavers themselves sometimes turned their labour to wool, as in the work done by Giovanni Pieri for the wool company of Giovanni di Guelpho de' Lanfranchi and Iacopo da Peccioli.[130]

Weavers of wool, like their counterparts in the silk industry, were clearly independent masters, owning their own looms and working at home for piece wages. Earlier stages of wool manufacture were at least

[126] ASL Corte de' mercanti, Cause civili, 151, fo. 30^{v}.

[127] AN 700(2), 8 Oct. 1455; 700(5), 13 July 1456. Both wills show indifference to place of burial and funeral arrangements.

[128] e.g., the wife of Piero Antonio who was expected to pay off a debt of 23 bolognini within three months by spinning wool for Iacopo ser Cambi (a further 22 bolognini to be paid in cash within ten days): ASL Corte de' mercanti, Cause civili, 152, fo. 23^{r}.

[129] AN 700(5), 5 Jan. 1456.

[130] ASL Corte de' mercanti, Cause civili, 152, fo. 30^{r}. In this case, dating from 1457, Giovanni Pieri sought 80 bolognini which he claimed were owing to him by the partners for weaving *panni*.

potentially more conducive to centralized wage labour than is readily apparent in silk. Against this, many of the more rigid institutional restraints of the *arte della seta* are missing. Truly there were the supervisory attentions of the *provveditori* and *misuratori* of linen and woollen cloths; and the provisions to ensure the return of debts and of worked materials were extended to cover weavers of woollen cloth.[131] But silk workers were required to obtain their materials from registered silk merchants, and were prohibited from working silk on their own account. The more relaxed regime governing wool is suggested by the 40 lb. of wool given to the weaver Piero da Corsagna by the barber Andrea di Francesco for the making of a bedspread.[132]

The finishing processes were undertaken by independent masters, but also in establishments that were more obviously distinctive to woollen manufacture. Among the former were the dyers, who formed small companies in partnerships between themselves and sometimes with *lanari*.[133] These men appear primarily as dyers of cloth rather than of yarn; and for their services might become creditors of *lanari* for not inconsequential sums of money, perhaps accumulated over a substantial period.[134] There is a particularly curious reference to an open cauldron for dyeing cloth which was situated in the shop of the wool dyer Papo da Arezzo. Half this cauldron belonged to the prominent Lucchese merchant Piero di Giovanni da Ghivizzano, from whom Papo leased it for five years at an annual rent of 1½ florins. The other half belonged to the *arte della lana* of Lucca.[135] Into this same familiar category of independent master craftsmen with private shops must be placed shearmen like Bartolomeo di Piero Taissi, of whom we catch occasional glimpses purchasing the instruments of his art and operating from his shop in the *contrada* of S. Sensio.[136] More distinctively characteristic of woollen manufacture were other processes that demanded a special environment or large-scale establishments beyond the private resources of the individual master, such as the washing, scouring, stretching, and drying of cloth, all mysteries which at least on occasion were exercised by

[131] *Statuto della corte dei mercanti*, lib. I, xiiii; lib. II, iiii. Wool workers were also covered by the protection of the provision that they were not to be paid for their labours in cloth: ibid., lib. IV, lxv.

[132] ASL Corte de' mercanti, Cause civili, 152, fo. 4^{v}.

[133] Ibid. 150, fo. 38^{r}; 152, fos. 14^{r}, 15^{v}, 19^{v}, 20^{r}, 23^{v}, 39^{r-v}.

[134] Ibid. 151, fo. 36^{v}.

[135] AN 704, 2 Jan. 1460.

[136] AN 700(3), 21 Apr. 1457; 700(5), 19 July 1456; 703, pp. 268–71.

the same company.[137] The statutes prohibited the use of olive presses for the stretching of cloth, whilst generally sanctioning the use of the rightful equipment on condition that things were done according to good mercantile practice.[138] In fact, for the tentering of cloth, recourse was often made to the *tiratoio* of S. Martino, of which, in the 1450s, Iacopo del Guffo, *tiratore*, was master.[139] Both a *tiratoio* and a *purgo* were attached to the monastery of S. Frediano, which, as the proprietor of the plant, was party to the formation of a company for the art of *purgatura* and *tiratura* between Iacopo del Guffo and Raineri di Raineri da Empoli in November 1456.[140] Before stretching, cloth was fulled, a process that presumed the availability of running water. The fulling mills were situated some distance from the city, at Vorno in the foothills of the Monti Pisani.[141]

It is clear that throughout the fifteenth century Lucca was a centre of woollen cloth manufacture of some consequence. The prominence of immigrant entrepreneurs and artisans, particularly refugees from Florentine expansionism, suggests throughout the century a potential for quality production. Anxious to correct Lucca's dangerous economic dependence on silk, from the 1430s the Lucchese authorities made frequent attempts to encourage the woollen industry. In 1435 the importation of cheap foreign cloth was prohibited, and although other cloth (including English cloth) might be imported on payment of the usual *gabelle,* no Tuscan cloth was to be imported into Lucca without a licence.[142] Temporary relaxation was offered in 1440, dictated by the twin concerns of public policy both to supply the poor of Lucca with cheap woollen cloth and also provide due protection for local industry.[143] A little later Giorgio di ser Piero Orselli, long resident in Venice, was negotiating the terms by which he might return to Lucca, promising to engage in the manufacture of fine woollen cloth and offering to bring

[137] Iacopo di Nanni alias Guffo (da Pisa) is variously described as *purgatore* and *tiratore*. With his partner, the *purgatore* Raineri di Raineri da Empoli, he formed a company in 1456 for the art of *purgatura* and *tiratura*: AN 700(4), 26 Nov. 1456. Apprentices contracted to Raineri might expect wages of 26–8 florins a year, part payable in cloth: ibid., 14 Oct. 1454, 12 Aug. 1456. In the case of other companies of *purgatori* there is reference to a *purgo* only: ASL Corte de' mercanti, Cause civili, 151, fos. 40^{r}, 42^{v}, 43^{r}. The first reference cited relates to a claim for damages against an apprentice who burnt wood in vain whilst making a fire for a cauldron, with the resulting loss of both time and wood.

[138] *Statuto della corte dei mercanti*, lib. IV, lxiii.

[139] ASL Corte de' mercanti, Cause civili, 151, fo. 45^{r}.

[140] AN 700(4), 9 June, 26 Nov. 1456.

[141] See, e.g., ASL Corte de' mercanti, Cause civili, 152, fo. 30^{v}.

[142] Rif. 14, pp. 732–3.

[143] Rif. 15, pp. 513–14. See also Rif. 17, pp. 308, 324.

with him up to forty master weavers for the purpose.[144] Efforts were intensified from mid-century. In October 1459 Giovanni Bernardi was to complain in *Colloquio* of the great sums of money leaving Lucca to pay for Florentine woollen cloth. The money would remain in Lucca were she to produce her own fine cloth, and a commission of three men was appointed to look into the matter.[145] Statutes and ordinances framed to implement these aspirations were to follow at regular intervals for the rest of the century.[146] In part these measures repeated earlier attempts to prohibit the importation of foreign cloth; in part they looked to quality control in decrees reminiscent of the statutes governing the manufacture of silks. Weavers were forbidden to exercise the art of wool for themselves or in partnership with others.[147] More positively, subvention was offered both for the production of a sufficient quantity of cloths and for the establishment of the appropriate plant. Alderigo Trenta received subvention for the building of a *purgo* and *tiratoio* in 1485.[148] And on a smaller scale the records of the General Council are full of references to grants, including grants of citizenship, made to entrepreneurs and to artisans engaged in the various processes of woollen manufacture.

In practice, the manufacture of woollen cloth in fifteenth-century Lucca seems to have rested with a group of *lanari*, who were likely to be immigrants, and who were unlikely to figure prominently in the political annals of the city. The dreams of Lucchese self-sufficiency and of a local woollen industry to rival that of neighbouring Florence were harboured in the councils of the *corte de' mercanti* and by the patrician élite that dominated both mercantile and political affairs. The names of Giorgio Orselli, Giovanni Bernardi, and Alderigo Trenta have been cited above. By the 1490s those who (in this dimension of their business activities) were calling themselves *lanaioli* include Giovanni Guinigi, Lunardo Rapondi, and Giovanni Battista Bernardi. There is little evidence that this attempt at diversification met with spectacular success. Throughout the later decades of the fifteenth century measures against the importation of cloth had to be suspended because of the limitations of local production. In seeking explanation for Lucca's failure in this regard,

144 Rif. 16, pp. 587–8.

145 ASL Colloqui, 1, p. 42.

146 Rif. 19, pp. 170–4; 20, pp. 215–16, 217, 222–3, 236, 288, 309, 312–13, 558–9, 566–7, 572, 573–6, 788; 21, pp. 139–40, 389–91, 466, 493, 673; BSL MS 38, Martino Bernardini, Ricordi Storici, fos. 217^{v}, 224^{r}, 233^{v}.

147 Rif. 20, p. 312.

148 Rif. 21, pp. 650, 708.

Luzzati invokes the 'quasi monopolio fiorentino'.[149] It is ironic that Luzzati should stress the pernicious economic impact of Florentine power whilst persistently denying the more obvious political threat. In fact, testimony to the latter is explicit and overwhelming,[150] whereas direct proof of the former is entirely lacking. But no doubt the competition of the established woollen and leather industries of Florence was a prime factor in thwarting Lucca's attempts to find an industrial future beyond silk.

Whether we speak of silk or wool or leather, Lucchese industries (like those of Italy generally) were what have been described as 'transplanted' industries. The silk industry specifically was almost entirely dependent on imported raw materials. Certainly, there are references to mulberry trees scattered throughout the fifteenth-century records of the Lucchese state. The exportation of mulberry leaves was being prohibited in May 1461.[151] Court cases relating to damage to property in the 1490s suggest significant mulberry cultivation in the area around Villa Basilica.[152] The Japanese historian Hidetoshi Hoshino collected references in the Lucchese brokerage books to silk coming from the Appennino modenese, from the valley of the Serchio, and probably from Valdinievole.[153] Long ago Vincenzo Santini attempted to trace mulberry cultivation in the territory of Pietrasanta to the earliest years of the fifteenth century, though Pietrasanta's importance as a centre of sericulture was really delayed until the sixteenth century, and was to coincide with the period of Florentine rule.[154] Despite a number of such references, it is difficult to believe that locally raised silk was used in any significant quantities by Lucchese manufacture before the sixteenth century.[155] The surviving fifteenth-century brokerage books indicate that only between 1 and 2 per cent of the silk traded in the city was of local origin; confirmation of this impression—at least for the early decades of the fifteenth century—is

[149] Luzzati, 'Politica di salvaguardia', 548. By mid-century the Florentine industry seems to have recovered from the difficulties of the 1420s and 1430s: H. Hoshino, *L'arte della lana in Firenze nel basso Medioevo* (Florence, 1980), 231–82.

[150] See esp. Ch. 3 above.

[151] Anz. Temp. Lib. 6, 30 May 1461.

[152] SB 202, *passim*. This volume, which is dominated by pasturing and other minor rural offences, also records (fo. 488^r) an action against certain men of Menabbio for the illegal exportation of mulberry leaves.

[153] H. Hoshino, 'La seta in Valdinievole nel basso medioevo', in *Atti del Convegno su artigianato e industrie in Valdinievole dal Medioevo ad Oggi: Buggiano Castello, giugno 1986* (Buggiano, 1987), 47–59. I am grateful to the late Professor Hoshino for sending me an offprint of this paper.

[154] Santini, *Versilia centrale*, ii. 195–6; v. 66, 171.

[155] For mulberry cultivation in 16th-cent. Lucca, see Berengo, *Nobili e mercanti*, 309–10.

provided by a detailed inventory of the stock of the silk shop of Bartolomeo di Franco da Montechiaro.[156] As in the earliest days of Lucchese silk production,[157] Lucca at the beginning of the fifteenth century was receiving large quantities of *seta leggi* and *seta talani*, silks from the East originating from the area of the Caspian Sea. But the fifteenth century was to witness changes. With the end of 'the Mongolian peace' and the offensive of the Ottoman Turks, traditional trade routes became threatened, and supplies traditionally imported from the East became increasingly produced within Christendom itself. Already by 1409 as much as 36 per cent of the silk and thread entered in a brokerage book of that year (as measured by weight) is described as Spanish.[158] During the next half-century, Spanish silk was to be increasingly ousted by southern Italian silk from Calabria and Sicily. Spanish silk had long realized high prices on the Lucchese market; Calabrian silk was much less highly prized at the beginning of the post-Guinigi era. The imbalance had largely disappeared by the end of the century.[159]

Similarly for supplies of dye-stuffs and precious metals, for fine wools and high-quality leather, Lucchese industry was entirely dependent on imported raw materials. As manufacturer of luxury wares, Lucchese products were destined primarily for foreign courts and international markets. Both the provision of raw materials and the distribution of the finished product necessitated the services of merchant bankers with representation throughout Europe; and within Lucca this entrenched the control of merchants over the leading sectors of the Lucchese economy. Blomquist has argued that, at an early date, artisans in the silk industry were truly independent masters, purchasers of their own materials, and sellers of the work of their own hands.[160] If such a state ever existed, it was soon transformed by dominant mercantile interests. At home, the qualified concentration of both political and economic power has been discussed in Chapter 4; throughout the fifteenth century the political careers of the Lucchese patriciate continued to be punctuated (particularly in their younger years) by periods of service in the commercial colonies overseas.

[156] AN 375 (ser Paolo Michele Federighi Bianchi da Massa), fos. 10^r–28^v, 54^v–63^r.

[157] T. W. Blomquist, 'Trade and Commerce in Thirteenth-Century Lucca' (Univ. of Minnesota Ph.D. thesis, 1965), 85.

[158] ASL Corte de' mercanti, Libro de' sensali (1409), 94.

[159] For a more detailed review of the evidence, see Bratchel, 'Silk Industry of Lucca', 178–81.

[160] Blomquist, 'Trade and Commerce', 83. Blomquist makes the point specifically with reference to dyers 'who actually owned the cloth which they worked'.

It is not suggested that Lucchese merchants were necessarily active at the source of supply. Blomquist's work has shown how in the thirteenth century Lucchese merchants were not present in the Eastern centres of sericulture, but rather obtained their supplies of silk on the Genoese market.[161] In the fifteenth century, with the growing importance of Spanish silk, there are traces of a Spanish presence in Lucca. One Spaniard, described as a vagabond and thief, appears not as a supplier of thread but as a purchaser, for 68 florins, of silk cloths, including velvets, from the silk shop of Giovanni Guidiccioni and partners. The case involves both the use of a false identity and the surreptitious switching of the box in which the Spaniard's pledge was deposited with the Guidiccioni company.[162] Generally Spanish silk seems to have been supplied less by Spaniards than by Genoese merchants established in Pisa,[163] and perhaps by Pisan and Florentine companies in Spain.[164] Later in the century, with the growing importance of southern Italian silk, the brokerage books reflect the presence in Lucca of Neapolitan merchants, often purchasing kerseys in Lucca in exchange for supplies of southern silk.[165] On the distribution side, there are frequent references to Lucchese silks despatched for sale to non-Lucchese (often Florentine) firms in the north.

All this merely testifies to a vital and interdependent commerce. Lucchese merchants themselves had long since established a sophisticated mercantile/banking network stretching from the eastern Mediterranean to northern Europe. Like other Tuscans, the Lucchese from the late fourteenth century were operating the *sistema d'aziende* of juridically autonomous companies, largely familial in character and united by the participation and capital investment of the pre-eminent partner(s).[166] In a series of studies Paolo Pelù has gone further to argue that, long anticipating Florentine developments, Lucca had established principles of limited liability in the *società in accomandita* by the very beginning of

[161] Blomquist, 'Trade and Commerce', 37–55, 82.

[162] ASL Capitano del Contado, 55, 1st foliation, fos. 5^{r}–8^{r}; AN 700(3), 28 May 1457.

[163] ASL Corte de' mercanti, Libro de' sensali, 96, fo. 37^{r}; 98, fos. 13^{r}, 34^{r}. See also M. Luzzati, 'Lorenzo Buonvisi', in *Dizionario biografico degli italiani*, xv (Rome, 1972), 334. Earlier in the century the Pisan merchant Giovanni Maggiolini appears prominently as a supplier of Spanish silk (and also of Spanish leather). For the Maggiolini, see ASL Biblioteca (Manoscritti), 125, B. Baroni, Famiglie Lucchesi, p. 312.

[164] AN 705, 19 Mar. 1460.

[165] ASL Corte de' mercanti, Libro de' sensali, 99, fos. 11^{v}, 12^{r}, 14^{r} ff., 17^{r}, 54^{v}, 55^{v}–56^{r}; see also Corte de' mercanti, Cause civili (1517), 187, fo. 125^{v}.

[166] The operation of the system in practice is abundantly illustrated in the numerous Lucchese entries in the *Dizionario biografico degli italiani* penned by Michele Luzzati.

the fifteenth century.[167] Trade remained inextricably linked to financial activity, and the continuing works of Thomas Blomquist have firmly identified Lucca as a precocious centre both of deposit and transfer banking and also of international exchange.[168] By the fifteenth century dealings in foreign exchange remained a prominent (perhaps the most visible) function of Lucchese companies at home and abroad; though the *campsores* themselves seem to have lost their clear corporate identity. The label *campsores* now merely served to locate members of the Lucchese patriciate in yet another of their multitudinous economic activities.[169]

At home, details of Lucchese companies, their titles, partners, *fattori*, and *garzoni* are recorded in the single Libro dei mercanti surviving for the post-Guinigi period, that of 1488.[170] Vaguely, and appropriately, these companies are often described as being formed for the art of silk and exchange and all other business ('per l'arte della seta et cambi et ongni altra mercantia' or 'per l'arte della seta et ogni altra arte che meglio ci paresse'). Besides entrepreneurial and commercial activities and the dealings in foreign exchange, there are traces (rare only because of the nature of the sources) of the local deposit and transfer facilities provided

[167] P. Pelù, *Priorità della mercatura lucchese in alcune forme collettive di investimento aziendale nel xiv e xv secolo* (Lucca, 1974); *idem* (ed.) *I libri dei mercanti lucchesi degli anni 1371, 1372, 1381, 1407, 1488* (Lucca, 1975); *idem*, 'Dalla Compagnia tradizionale al sistema d'azienda: conquiste della mercatura lucchese nei sec. xiv e xv', *La Provincia di Lucca*, xvi, no. 1 (Jan.–Mar. 1976), 30–5; *idem*, 'Figure della vita economica medievale lucchese: Michele di Lazzari Guinigi', *La Provincia di Lucca*, xvi, no. 3 (July–Sept. 1976), 13–19. Pelù's findings are essentially an extended commentary on the conclusions of F. Melis, *Tracce di una storia economica di Firenze e della Toscana in generale dal 1252 al 1550* (Florence, 1966–7), 47 ff.

[168] T. W. Blomquist, 'Commercial Association in Thirteenth-Century Lucca', *Business History Review*, xlv (1971), 157–78; *idem*, 'The Castracani Family of Thirteenth-Century Lucca', *Speculum*, xlvi (1971), 459–76; *idem*, 'The Dawn of Banking in an Italian Commune: Thirteenth-Century Lucca', in *The Dawn of Modern Banking*, Center for Medieval and Renaissance Studies, University of California, Los Angeles (New Haven, Conn., 1979), 53–75; *idem*, 'La famiglia e gli affari: le compagnie internazionali lucchesi al tempo di Castruccio Castracani', in *Castruccio Castracani e il suo tempo: Convegno Internazionale, Lucca 5–10 ottobre 1981*, published as anni xiii–xiv, nos. 1–2, of *Actum Luce* (1984–5), 145–55.

[169] The *campsores* (together with goldsmiths and gold-beaters) continued to constitute one of the groups represented on the consulate and council of the *corte de' mercanti*. But there seems something rather arbitrary about the choice of a particular individual to represent banking rather than the *arte della seta*. Of course, from the beginning Blomquist has shown both the involvement of patrician families in deposit banking and the participation of *campsores* in non-banking activities, particularly trade and landed investment.

[170] ASL Corte de' mercanti, Libri de' mercanti (1488), 86. A transcription has been published by Pelù, *I libri dei mercanti lucchesi*, 185–205.

by leading merchants like Matteo di Bartolomeo Bernardini.[171] Provision of credit, including 'consumption' loans, mentioned briefly above as a mechanism of mercantile control, finds more convenient discussion in the next chapter.

Outside Lucca lay a nexus of partnerships and interlocking interests of bewildering complexity. In the late 1420s Aldibrando di Francesco de' Guidiccioni, long resident in Venice but now briefly in Bruges, formed companies with Paolo di Francesco Miliani and Lorenzo di Stefano di Poggio, two Lucchese merchants then resident in London.[172] At the same time Paolo Miliani from London was also partner in Lucca of a company formed there with Landuccio Bernardi.[173] In this early period the Lucchese communities in London and Bruges provided an outlet not only for Lucchese wares but also for silk manufactured in Venice by the substantial Lucchese community established in that city.[174] Lorenzo di Poggio, who in 1429 was required to operate from London, Bruges, Paris, or Venice as determined by the other two partners,[175] was in fact to live out his life in London. He provides a link of continuity with the Lucchese community in England, as revealed when the records of the *corte de' mercanti* recommence in mid-century.[176] Then, as earlier, there was considerable interchange between London and the much larger Lucchese community in Bruges.[177] From mid-century Lucchese finan-

[171] Explicit references generally relate to the deposit of money on behalf of religious foundations for subsequent disbursement for expenses and repairs: AN 700(4), 9 July, 24 July, 9 Sept. 1456. See also ibid. 700(5), 15 Oct. 1456; 706, p. 137. The implication of deposit transactions and of transfer banking is present in a large number of contracts.

[172] ASL Corte de' mercanti, Cause civili, 151, fos. 142^r–147^v, 163^r–164^v. The case provides valuable details of company formation, and hints at the financial dealings of the London company, the importation of silk cloth and jewels, and the exportation of woollen cloth, wool, and tin.

[173] Ibid., fo. 164^{r}. The expressed concern was that the accounts of the two companies might become muddled. Miliani also had other moneys apart from the two companies.

[174] Thus, e.g., the Cristofani silk shop maintained factors in Bruges and London: ibid., fo. 3^{r}.

[175] Ibid., fo. 143^{v}.

[176] In the later years of his life, Lorenzo di Poggio was partner of Matteo Dati: ibid., fos. 60^{r}–61^{v}, 66^{r}–68^{v}; 128^{r}–135^{v}, 175^{r}–177^{v}, 142^{r}–147^{v}, 163^{r}–164^{v}. In the 1430s and 1440s Matteo Dati had been *giovane*—later *fattore*—of Piero Guidiccioni in Venice: ibid., fos. 4^{r}, 7^{r}, 117^{v}. This series of lawsuits also serves to locate in mid-15th-cent. London two Guidiccioni factors (Filippo Pini and Andrea Gratiani), Lazzaro di Poggio (soon to depart for Venice), and Carlo de' Gigli. Francesco Micheli, detained in England in 1450, was prominent in the export of English cloth in the 1460s: Fumi (ed.), *Regesti*, 1229; ASL Corte de' mercanti, Libro de' sensali (1453–68), 98, fos. 131^{r}, 141^{v}, 142^{r}; AN 732, 1 Oct. 1474.

[177] Nicolao de' Gigli, partner in Bruges with Francesco Sandei, travelled to London to sell silk cloth to the royal wardrobe on commission for Nicolao ser Federighi. Gigli's mission was facilitated by the presence in London of his brother Carlo: ASL Corte de' mercanti, Cause civili, 151, fos. 52^{r}–53^{v}. Accounts preserved among the records of the merchants' court show

cial and commercial activity in both centres was to be closely associated with the great houses of Cenami,[178] Guinigi,[179] and Buonvisi.[180]

Further south, the opportunities offered to Italian bankers by papal finance are reflected in the Avignon company of Raffaele Tegrimi and Galeotto Franciotti,[181] a company and bank represented in Geneva by Stefano ser Federighi. We hear of silk cloth and letters of exchange despatched to Geneva and of the dealings of the Geneva company with merchants in Lucca, Florence, Valencia, Avignon, Rome, and Bologna.[182] Léon Mirot has studied the Lucchese community in fifteenth-century Paris, a community perhaps increasingly diverted by honours, offices, and landed property—certainly one that appears

intensive mercantile contacts in the 1450s between the company of Girolamo and Francesco Guinigi of Bruges and that of Matteo Dati and Lorenzo di Poggio in London: ibid., fos. 60^{r}–61^{v}, 66^{r}–68^{v}. For the history of the Bruges community, see Eugenio Lazzareschi's introduction to his edition of *Libro della comunità dei mercanti lucchesi in Bruges* (Milan, 1947), pp. xv–xxxix. The central importance of the Arnolfini presence in Bruges from the 1420s is discussed by Ovidio Capitani in his article on Giovanni Arnolfini in *Dizionario biografico degli italiani*, iv (Rome, 1962).

[178] Already in the 1370s Giusfredo Cenami was partner in a Flanders company with Dino Rapondi, Betto Schiatta, and Francesco Martini. Two of his sons were resident in Bruges, and one of them later more permanently in Paris. Prominent in Bruges from the mid-15th cent. was the company of Giusfredo's grandson Martino, represented on occasion by Martino's cousin Rodolfo. See particularly the articles on 'Cenami' and 'Pietro Cenami', in *Dizionario biografico degli italiani*, xxiii (Rome, 1979).

[179] The Guinigi were represented in London and Bruges from the early decades of the 14th cent. In the 1450s this representation took the form of the company of Francesco and Girolamo Guinigi of Bruges, of which Lorenzo Buonvisi was an unnamed partner: ASL Corte de' mercanti, Cause civili, 151, fo. 61^{v}. For the Guinigi involvement in England in the late 15th and early 16th cent., see ibid. 186 (1515), fos. 2^{r} ff., 334^{r} ff.; 187 (1517), fos. 26^{r} ff., 97^{r} ff., 170^{r} ff., and *passim*; AN 1519 (ser Michele di Giovanni da Mommio), fos. 242^{r}–249^{v}; 1789, (ser Lazzaro Franchi), fos. 45^{r-v}, 81^{r} ff.; 1929, (ser Giuseppe Piscilla), fos. 91^{r}–92^{r}, 130^{r}–132^{r}; AN Originali Testamenti, 16 (ser Benedetto Franciotti), fos. 220^{r}–225^{r}; S. L. Thrupp, *The Merchant Class of Medieval London (1300–1500)* (Chicago, 1948), 221.

[180] Members of the Buonvisi family were present in both Bruges and London in the 1380s, in London as *fattore* of the Guinigi: Lazzareschi (ed.), *Libro della comunità dei mercanti lucchesi in Bruges*, 86, 100. They were prominent in English trade in the 1470s: Public Record Office, London, Exchequer K. R. Customs Accounts, E122/194/19, m. 11^{v}, 12^{v}; E122/194/20, m. 4^{r}, 7^{r}, 13^{v}; E122/194/22, m. 5^{v}; E122/194/24, m. 8^{v}. From this same period there are the beginnings of a number of companies in London bearing the Buonvisi name: AN 731, fo. 133^{v}; 732, 5 Dec. 1474; AN Originali Testamenti, 15 (ser Benedetto Franciotti), fos. 248^{v}–249^{v}. For the later history of the Buonvisi as merchants and bankers in London, see M. E. Bratchel, 'Alien Merchant Communities in London, 1500–1550' (Univ. of Cambridge Ph.D. thesis, 1975); *idem*, 'Italian Merchant Organization'; *idem*, 'Regulation and Group-Consciousness'.

[181] ASL Corte de' mercanti, Cause civili, 151, fos. 85^{r}–88^{v}. In 1454 Guglielmo Monetti of Avignon was living with Franciotti in Lucca: AN 700(4), 10 July 1454. For Franciotti's career in papal service, see ASL Podestà di Lucca, Curia Civile, 1307, fos. 128^{r}–131^{v}.

[182] ASL Corte de' mercanti, Cause civili, 151, fos. 85^{r}–88^{v}.

relatively infrequently in the commercial records.[183] But in distant Nantes there are traces of a Lucchese mercantile community.[184] And by the 1470s there is abundant evidence of the new importance of the Lyons market for Lucchese merchants.[185] In Italy itself, besides the massively important interchange with Venice and besides the contacts with Ferrara, Modena, and Bologna—all to some extent an offshoot of the Venetian connection—traditional links with Genoa were maintained, whilst there are numerous references to Lucchese merchants in Milan as acquirers of Milanese fustians and woollen cloth (and presumably armaments).[186] Ancona remained a centre for Lucchese exiles.[187] In southern Italy, the growing importance of the Regno as a source of raw silk encouraged Lucchese intervention.[188] For the more adventurous the community in Venice provided a springboard for the markets of the East, though it is unlikely that many Lucchese hastened to follow the Guerrucci in their journeys within the eastern Empire[189] or, for that matter, to join Gerardo Spada in Scio.[190] As in the East, so also in the far

[183] L. Mirot, *Études Lucquoises* (Paris, 1930). The point should not be overstressed. Girolamo di Lorenzo Trenta, as a young man, clearly in Paris, 'did various things as a merchant': AN 385 (ser Massino di Bartolomeo da Pietrasanta), fos. 158^{r}–159^{r}. Even this case relates to a deposit of pearls. When Nicolao di Bartolomeo de' Martini appointed his brother Francesco to settle matters relating to their late father's inheritance in France, Burgundy, and Savoy, the concern was explicitly for goods in France, especially around Paris: AN 700(5), 8 Mar. 1456. See also AN 597 (ser Luviso di Antonio Buonaccorsi), fos. 312^{r}–313^{r}, for the collection of debts due in Paris and elsewhere in France to the late Bettino Dati. Almost all the commercial references to Paris that I have found in the AN and in the Archivio Diplomatico relate to the immediate post-Guinigi years.

[184] AN 706, pp. 69–76.

[185] ASL Archivio Guinigi, 29, Girolamo Guinigi, Libro di ricordi, fos. 16^{r} ff.

[186] Particularly interesting are the credits owing in Genoa to the heirs of Guaspare Ridolfi: AN 385 (ser Massino di Bartolomeo da Pietrasanta), fos. 198^{r}–201^{r}. Besides the direct links between Lucca and Milan, the nexus of interests is again indicated in the 1450s with Galeotto Franciotti—described as a merchant and citizen of Lucca usually living in Venice—sending, under his sign, 10 bales of spices to a Milanese merchant Gabrielle Baldi in Milan. The goods were to be carried by a mule-driver of Cremona, and were assigned to another Lucchese merchant, Manfredo Nocchi (sometime of Geneva): AN 700(5), Oct.–Dec. 1456. See also ASL Corte de' mercanti, Cause civili, 152, fos. 7^{r}, 8^{v}.

[187] Most prominently Chello d'Antonio di Poggio, whose efforts to establish *l'arte della seta* in Ancona provoked a large fine and confiscation of goods: Rif. 16, p. 104.

[188] The Lucchese presence in Sicily can, of course, be traced back a very long way: G. Fallico, 'La presenza dei lucchesi in Sicilia in epoca castrucciana', in *Castruccio Castracani e il suo tempo: Convegno Internazionale, Lucca 5–10 ottobre 1981*, published as anni xiii–xiv, nos. 1–2, of *Actum Luce* (1984–5), 173–85; S. Sambito Piombo, 'Una famiglia lucchese a Palermo nei primi decenni del secolo xiv', *Rivista di archeologia, storia e costume: Istituto storico lucchese*, ix, no. 3 (1981), 37–44. For the later period, see Bratchel, 'Silk Industry of Lucca', 180–1.

[189] ASL Cause Delegate, 2. But see Podestà di Lucca, Curia Civile, 1180, fos. 82^{r}–83^{r}.

[190] Spada's son was born in Scio. In 1503, Girolamo Guinigi's son Lodovico was sent via

west. For the fifteenth century I have found no convincing evidence of any substantial Lucchese presence in Spain. It is true that the saintly Giovanni Buonvisi is supposed to have begun his career as a merchant in Spain.[191] But in the few references found to the Spanish trade, Lucchese merchants appear rather to favour the services of Florentine and Pisan companies set up in Barcelona.[192] It may be significant that in forming the London company between Paolo Miliani and Lorenzo di Poggio, di Poggio was authorized to act according to his own discretion except for trafficking with Spain, for which he required specific approval.[193]

The history of Lucchese merchants *all'estero* is a large subject that cannot be justly treated in the context of the present work. No detailed study is required in order to establish for the fifteenth century the continued commitment of Lucca's ruling patriciate to the profits and rigours of international trade. The evidence is overwhelming, but the *ricordi* of Girolamo Guinigi speak to this theme with compelling eloquence.[194] A member of the house that ruled Lucca until 1430, in July 1433 Girolamo accompanied his kinsman Pietro di Nicolao Guinigi to Genoa 'per garzone'. He remained in Genoa until March or April 1435. Pietro himself retired from Genoa following that city's rising against the Duke of Milan, and during the latter months of his stay Girolamo remained behind in order to attend to Pietro's affairs. Back in Lucca, in December 1436 Girolamo went to stay with Raffaele Tegrimi, whom he then accompanied to Venice and thence to Avignon, where he kept the accounts of Tegrimi's bank. After some months, Girolamo Guinigi went to stay with Bartolomeo di Mariano Cinucchi da Siena in Avignon, and remained with him until 3 November 1438. He was back in Lucca by 6 December, returning by way of Genoa in the company of Bartolomeo and of Silvestro Trenta, and continuing on to Siena in the service of Bartolomeo. His ill-treatment by the Sienese merchant was to be the subject of bitter comment in later years. The above itinerary provides no explanation of how, on 27 January 1437, Girolamo Guinigi found himself in Ferrara, where he took minor orders. Back in Lucca again in

Scio to join Giovanni di Gerardo Spada in 'Turchia' ('al governo di Giovanni di Ghilardo Spada'): ASL Archivio Guinigi, 29, Girolamo Guinigi, Libro di ricordi, fos. 57^{r}, 59^{v}.

[191] U. Nicolini, 'Giovanni Buonvisi', in *Dizionario biografico degli italiani*, xv (Rome, 1972). Luzzati, in his article on 'Lorenzo (di Neri) Buonvisi' in the same volume, questions the evidence for Giovanni Buonvisi's sojourn in Spain. Luzzati is also inclined to stress the extent to which the Spanish trade was in the hands of intermediaries.

[192] AN 705, pp. 69–70.

[193] ASL Corte de' mercanti, Cause civili, 151, fos. 142^{r}–147^{v}, 163^{r}–164^{v}.

[194] ASL Archivio Guinigi, 29.

1440, in March of that year Guinigi left for Palermo, in Sicily, where he joined the company of Mariano and Nicolao Tomaxii da Siena, a company governed in Sicily by yet another Sienese. In 1443 Girolamo married Pippa, daughter of Lorenzo Buonvisi, and in the following years was to engage in a number of business partnerships with his Buonvisi in-laws and their Martini associates. The marriage brought no immediate end to Girolamo's travels. Many years later he was to mutter about unrequited services to the Buonvisi when, at the beginning of his relationship with them, he not only sorted out their writings, which were in a tangle, but served them in Palermo, Naples, Rome, Venice, Bruges, and London. The date of these activities is unclear; certainly by the end of the 1440s Girolamo Guinigi seems to have been permanently established in Lucca. The career of Girolamo's brother Francesco followed a rather different pattern. Alternately appearing in Bruges and London, Francesco was accompanied to these northern stations by his wife, a daughter of Pietro Cenami. In March 1457 Girolamo received news from Francesco in London of the birth two months earlier of a son Tommaso. A daughter, 'creata a Bruggia e nata a Lucca', was to follow in January 1461. Restless to the end, Francesco died in Rome on 12 June 1468.

From the 1470s Girolamo Guinigi's attention turned to chronicling the ventures of his nephews—and later of his own sons. In October 1470 Giovanni and Francesco di Michele were travelling to Lyons, where from March 1472 they established a company together with messer Nicolao da Noceta. Francesco di Michele died in Lyons on 28 July 1473, his brother returning safely to Lucca in December of the same year. In 1474 another nephew, Tommaso di Francesco, was sent to London by his maternal kinsmen the Cenami to join Lodovico Buonvisi. Tommaso was back in Lucca in September 1492, where he married a daughter of Luiso Guidiccioni, returning to London by way of Lyons in January of 1493. He was back in Lucca again by May 1496, this time bringing with him from London Nicolao di Paolo Buonvisi and his young kinsman Michele di Giovanni Guinigi. When Tommaso returned to his London post in October 1496, he was accompanied, at least on this occasion, by his wife Ginevra. Tommaso died in London at the end of 1500, and was buried there in the church of the Austin friars. Letters advising of the death of Tommaso followed hard on the news of the death, also in London, of Francesco di Pietro Guinigi, son of Girolamo's earliest business mentor. Francesco di Pietro had been in the employ not of the company of Giovanni di Michele Guinigi and Tommaso Guinigi, but rather of another Lucchese company in late fifteenth-century London, that of the Gigli. The Guinigi company itself, following Tommaso's death, was to be managed by Tommaso's brother, yet another Francesco. This Francesco di Francesco had spent some time in London prior to 1499. In July 1499 he returned to Lucca, where he married a daughter of Nicolao Micheli. Hastening back to London in February 1501 to take up the affairs of the London company, he was accompanied by Giovanni Battista Guidiccioni, the latter charged with bringing Tommaso's widow (Guidiccioni's sister) back home to Lucca.[195] With regard to Girolamo Guinigi's own sons, Giovanni was despatched to London in January 1493 to join his cousin Tommaso, remaining there until August 1500. Giovanni di Girolamo was back in Lucca between December 1501 and April 1502 to visit his father before returning for yet another spell of duty with the London company. On 17 April 1498 Girolamo sent his son Piero Angelo to Lyons, where he was to serve the company of Lorenzo Dati. Girolamo noted Piero Angelo's 'return to see us' in 1500 and 1503. On 16 June 1501 another of Girolamo's sons, Lodovico, left Lucca for Genoa, whence he was to take ship for Scio and from there find and obey Giovanni Spada. The voyage was abortive. But the project was renewed in May 1503 when Michele Micheli and Giovanni Guinigi came to Girolamo's house. Lodovico was sent to join Spada in *Turchia* for two years at the expense of Michele Micheli and Giovanni Guinigi, and at the end of the two-year period was to participate in the profits.

The evidence of the *ricordi* of Girolamo Guinigi is no more than skeletal, and indeed can easily be filled in from other sources. No other source provides so complete a picture over so long a period of the commercial involvement of a leading Lucchese family. The rest is fragmentary. But the fragments confirm that the Guinigi story is by no means atypical. We find the same relentless mobility in the career of Pietro Dati in the decade 1446–56.[196] In Dati's case it is impossible to disentangle how far he was travelling on state business, how far about his own affairs. No doubt the distinction was always somewhat blurred. Finally there is the path to riches of Piero Guidiccioni, in this case distinguished by a period at the *studio* in Bologna.[197] From the totality of

[195] For Francesco di Francesco di Giovanni Guinigi's will, drawn up in anticipation of his journey to London and containing some useful information on the Buonvisi and Guinigi companies in London, see AN Originali Testamenti, 16, fos. 220^{r}–225^{r}.

[196] ASL Podestà di Lucca, Curia Civile, 1306, fos. 35^{r}–37^{v}, 91^{r}–93^{r}.

[197] Details for a biography of Piero Guidiccioni are scattered throughout ASL Corte de' mercanti, Cause civili, 151.

the sources there emerges a regular rhythm according to which young men aged 16 or 17 might expect to be sent abroad to serve a commercial apprenticeship. Thereafter they might return to Lucca, to conduct their affairs primarily from home. Others never returned, a fact often though not inevitably to be explained by early death. The Arnolfini brothers Giovanni and Michele di Arrigo chose to live out their lives in Bruges, where—in 1472—they died within little more than a month of each other, the one without legitimate issue, the other leaving behind him three sons and five daughters.[198]

The dangers and uncertainties emerge very poignantly from the Guinigi *ricordi*. There is great pathos in the trepidation with which Girolamo Guinigi watches the departure of a young son or nephew, the joy with which he greets his return. With what justification, the *ricordi* provide ample testament. And the dangers extended beyond life to property. No doubt Lucchese merchants—the young travelling with the more experienced—were sophisticated, and consequently less vulnerable than the travelling 'Lombards' who appear repeatedly in the Lucchese criminal records as victims of transparent trickery, conned out of their possessions or lured to shady places where they became targets for robbery and murder.[199] But for the most experienced the dangers remained, particularly when institutionalized in the form of reprisals. In October 1442 Lucca was warning her merchants in Venice and Bruges of the reprisals against Lucchese goods issued by Genoa at the instigation of Tommaso Ravaschieri.[200] The affair was to have consequences not only for Lucchese merchants. With his silk cloth sequestered in Genoa, Paolo di Poggio in turn demanded of the authorities at home 'reprisals against the city of Genoa and the men of the said city and against all and every district and subject of the said city of Genoa and against their goods to the sum of 1,000 gold ducats with expenses, damages, and interest'.[201] In terms of the sentence of the Lucchese court, di Poggio refused to part with 210 gold ducats that he owed for merchandise received from Aluysio Taglacarne da Levanto. Such reprisals and counter-reprisals were clearly immensely damaging to regular commercial intercourse. Lucca was haunted by fears of new Genoese reprisals in

[198] ASL Archivio Guinigi, 29, Girolamo Guinigi, Libro di ricordi, fo. 21^{v}.

[199] ASL Capitano del Contado, 51, 1st foliation, fos. 43^{r}–48^{r}; SB 165, fos. 131^{v}, 134^{r}, 391^{r}–394^{v}; 171, 2nd foliation, fos. 53^{r}–56^{r}; 202, fos. 212^{r}–214^{v}, 263^{r}–265^{v}; ASL Capitano del Contado, 97, 2nd foliation, fos. 25^{r}–31^{v}.

[200] Fumi (ed.), *Regesti*, 848.

[201] Ibid. 1183, 1192, 1210, 1249, 1351, 1449; ASL Podestà di Lucca, Curia Civile, 1307, fo. 183^{r}.

1460.[202] In 1474–5 great anxiety was felt lest the bankruptcy of Adriano Burlamacchi, and specifically debts owing to merchants of the house of Grimaldi, should lead to the issue of reprisals against Lucchese merchants returning from Lyons.[203] More seriously, the reprisals granted against Lucchese goods by the Duke of Savoy at the behest of Stefano ser Federighi were to cause major problems for Lucchese merchants *en route* for the fairs of Lyons. The Ser Federighi affair was sporadically to worry the Lucchese authorities for nearly three decades.[204] The interruption of the land route northward was presumably an important factor in encouraging Lucca to improve and upgrade the via da Montramito and to develop the port of Viareggio as a substitute for Motrone which had been lost during the post-Guinigi wars.[205]

Sea communications presented new dangers in the attentions of corsairs, particularly Catalans active in the western Mediterranean. But far more ominous was the encroachment of the Turks in the east. Included in the large file of mercantile and personal letters preserved in Lucca as a consequence of the Guerrucci conspiracy of 1460 are some fascinating letters relating to Lucchese travels within the eastern Empire. Giovanni Guerrucci had been in Constantinople in the 1440s,[206] but much more interesting are the travels of his son Michele in the years immediately before the Turkish conquest. Business letters from Venice and Broussa are interspersed with extravagant expressions of love and concern.[207] Letters sent after Michele's return to Venice in 1452 not surprisingly show the pressing concern for news about the Turks. It is my impression—and the material certainly exists for further study—that the fall of Constantinople marks a turning-point in the long history of the Lucchese mercantile community in Venice. It was precisely in the 1450s that representatives of families long associated with Venice began to drift back to Tuscany. Michele Guerrucci's own return provided both

[202] ASL Colloqui, 1, p. 67.

[203] ASL Archivio Guinigi, 29, Girolamo Guinigi, Libro di ricordi, fos. 25ᵛ–26ʳ; Lazzareschi (ed.), *Regesti*, 115, 123–4, 126–7, 129, 165, 167, 169–71, 176.

[204] References in ASL Consiglio Generale, Riformagioni Pubbliche from vol. 19, as well as in the *Regesti* and elsewhere, are too numerous to permit citation. For the origins of the affair, see Ch. 3, n. 158. The severe consequences for the passage of Lucchese silks into France are spelt out in a petition of the court of merchants of 15 Feb. 1470: Rif. 19, pp. 574–5. The matter was not finally settled until 1491, though serious commercial dislocation seems to have been limited to the period up to 1474, with further disruption in the year 1481.

[205] Rif. 19, pp. 573, 639, 700, 747; 21, pp. 136–7, 143–5, 549–50, 669.

[206] ASL Cause Delegate, 2, pp. 15–16.

[207] Ibid., pp. 73–136.

the occasion and (more obscurely) the context of his bid for lordship in 1460.[208]

The present chapter began with the proposition that the period 1430–94 was in general a time of economic recovery for Lucca. The proposition rests on no sound statistical base, and the same lack of statistical evidence renders it very difficult to postulate patterns of growth and decline within the wider period. It is easy to list individual bankruptcies, but the philosophizing of Antonio Diodati on the rising and falling fortunes of merchants[209] might warn us against translating individual misfortunes into general crises. Commerce was clearly interrupted with the Florentine army at the gates in 1430, and by the 'most cruel siege' of 1438.[210] In fact, with reference to the later period, we are specifically told that silk could not be sent out of Lucca because of the war.[211] In the 1430s, and periodically throughout the rest of the century, Lucca suffered from severe visitations of the plague. Since the Lucchese authorities attempted to counter the plague by restricting movement, the plagues too must have had a dislocating impact. The quite remarkably unreliable Gio: Lunardo Dalli tells, for the year 1448, of four Lucchese merchants going to the fairs of Bolzano without health certificates ('bollette della sanità'), who were captured and condemned to death, but spared on the intervention of Pietro da Noceta, *Segretario* of Pope Nicholas V, then fortuitously returning from a mission to England.[212] There is reference to the 'penuria' of the present year (1457).[213] The serious consequences for Lucchese trade of the Ser Federighi reprisals in Savoy have already been discussed. It is against the background of those reprisals that we find reference in 1474 to the near destitution of the people of Lucca because of the decline in silk manufacture.[214] However devastating in themselves, all the above are mere incidents of necessarily limited and short-term import. Italian historians have generally argued that the 1470s and 1480s as a whole were a period of deep and lasting depression. The evidence offers little opportunity to test the applicability of such findings to the Lucchese situation. Despite spectacular events like the bankruptcy of Agostino

208 See above, pp. 68–74.
209 Rif. 16, p. 46.
210 Rif. 15, p. 224.
211 Ibid., p. 272.
212 BSL MS 939, Gio: Lunardo Dalli, Cronache, p. 217.
213 ASL Podestà di Lucca, Curia Civile, 1309, fo. 33ʳ.
214 Rif. 20, p. 215. The same period saw the failure of Adriano di Michele Burlamacchi.

Rapondi in 1483,[215] all the pointers seem to indicate an active commercial life for the last decades of the fifteenth century, based on the growing demand in the northern kingdoms for Lucchese luxury products.

The uncertain contours of Lucca's economic prosperity in the fifteenth century make it virtually impossible to link changing economic fortunes to the great events of Lucchese history as described in earlier chapters. Political turmoil clearly coincided with economic hardships and fiscal exactions in the 1430s. But the forces for disruption in the first decade of the restored republic are plainly too numerous and too complex to be reduced to a single source. In later decades it is often possible to locate the material grievances of interest groups and political conspirators. But these grievances are invariably too personalized and idiosyncratic to fit comfortably into a pattern of economic cycles. In a more general sense, however, economic structures and reality do provide the necessary and revealing background for the socio-political life of the republic.

At a time of severe manpower shortage, we see the easy and liberal accommodation of newcomers at all levels. The point relates both to economic and to political life, though there was a hardening of attitude both towards the indigent and towards skilled competitors from the 1470s onwards.[216] In 1471 measures were taken against the *muratori*, identified above as overwhelmingly foreigners, who saved their money and despatched it home to Lombardy to the prejudice of Lucca.[217] We see, further, the entrenchment in Lucca of quasi-independent artisanal groups, men well versed in Poni's stratagem of self-defence with regard to the preservation of status and corporate identity.[218] This is true of the small craftsmen servicing the local economy. It is true, with qualifications, of the labour force assembled under the guidance of merchant capital to produce for international markets. The same corporatism protected the retail traders—the mercers and the spice-merchants—who, even more than individual artisans, played a meaningful if subordinate role in the political life of the city. Thus in 1445 we find the mercers demanding the protection of the state against certain foreigners who, on Saturdays, set up stalls in the piazza without paying rent ('senza

[215] Rif. 21, pp. 483–5, 519, 538, 615–16.

[216] Rif. 20, pp. 228, 235, 476, 484. In 1491 nine dyers of silk, speaking of the long-established honour and utility of silk manufacture to the inhabitants of Lucca, petitioned against foreigners coming to exercise that art in Lucca: Rif. 22, pp. 674–5.

[217] Rif. 19, p. 696.

[218] Poni, 'Norms and disputes', *passim*.

pagare pigione di bottegha').[219] If artisans and retail merchants enjoyed considerable powers of self-regulation, real political and economic power lay in other hands, and the power of wealth was firmly rooted in international trade. The families that ruled fifteenth-century Lucca had not withdrawn from industry and trade. These families comprised very mobile individuals still able to anticipate great profits from trade and banking.

The image is therefore created of the kind of politically illegitimate and ignoble merchant community of which Richard Trexler has written in the context of contemporary Florence.[220] Whether the imagery of 'a festively bedecked but tawdry skiff among princely galleons' is appropriate to fifteenth-century Florence lies beyond the concern of the present study. For Lucca the impression of a bourgeois order is clearly too limiting. The inevitable association of all Tuscans with commercial, financial, and industrial enterprise seriously distorts the range of interests—even the leading preoccupations—of the Lucchese patriciate, and indeed of all levels of Lucchese society. In recent years Philip Jones has done much to establish the profoundly aristocratic ethos of the Italian city-states; the pervasive influence of the land on all cities, no matter how mercantile, and on all classes, no matter how tied to trade.[221] General texts are now forced to wrestle with the complex links between the interrelated communities of town and country and with the 'artificial distinctions [traditionally] drawn between the expected activities of the bourgeoisie and those of the nobles and peasantry'.[222] The renewed interest in the land is amply justified by the Lucchese case-study. In previous chapters party formation in the restored republic was explained largely in terms of traditional clan loyalties, both within and beyond the city walls. Early in the present chapter the course of Lucchese industrial development was placed in the context of a prevailing aristocratic mentality. That mentality, together with the connected themes of urban relations with and attitudes towards the countryside, will be examined more fully in Chapter 6.

[219] Rif. 17, pp. 509–10.

[220] Trexler, *Public Life in Renaissance Florence*, 42–3, 279.

[221] P. J. Jones, 'Economia e società nell'Italia medievale: il mito della borghesia', in *Economia e società nell'Italia medievale* (Turin, 1980), 3–189. The article was originally written for the Einaudi *Storia d'Italia*.

[222] D. Hay and J. Law, *Italy in the Age of the Renaissance 1380–1530* (London, 1989), 47–74. The quotation is taken from p. 53.

6

URBAN SOCIETY AND THE COUNTRYSIDE: PATTERNS OF INTER-DEPENDENCE AND CONTROL

The origins of Lucca's leading families are as obscure as the early history of families elsewhere in Italy. The energies of Lucchese genealogists, and especially of G. Vincenzo Baroni, provide invaluable—and generally verifiable—information from the fourteenth century. Their ventures backwards from the thirteenth century seldom carry much conviction. Thus the Balbani claimed to derive from Ariperto, King of the Lombards;[1] the Buonvisi from a councillor of the Emperor Otto III.[2] There is no doubt that in the twelfth and thirteenth centuries Lucca, in tune with the aspirations of other communes, entered into treaties with the nobility of the surrounding countryside. These treaties, in an assertion of power, detailed the (military) services due, and imposed residential requirements whereby the nobles were obliged to spend a specified part of each year within the city.[3] In March 1310 the *capitani*, *nobili*, and *militi* of the Versilia, from whom so many of Lucca's greater families claimed to derive, were required to spend the months of March and April in the city.[4] Others arrived by less public act: the Guidiccioni apparently in the early thirteenth century from their native Verrucola in Garfagnana.[5] The drift from the countryside was relived in each new generation, and is as much a feature of the fifteenth as of earlier centuries. Some families achieved identity only in the urban milieu, often through the *notariato*, that classic

[1] BSL MS 2598, Antonio Iova, Annali Historici, p. 101.

[2] L. Tettoni and F. Saladini, *Teatro Araldico ovvero Raccolta Generale delle Armi ed Insegne Gentilizie delle più illustri e nobili casate che esisterono un tempo e che tuttora fioriscono in tutta l'Italia*, 8 vols. (Milan, 1841–8), vi, 'Bonvisi di Toscana'; ASL Biblioteca (Manoscritti), 20, B. Baroni, Alberi di Famiglie, pp. 108, 201; Raccolte Speciali: G. B. Orsucci, 28, Note di Casati e Famiglie Lucchesi, p. 312.

[3] BSL MS 2598, Antonio Iova, Annali Historici, pp. 342, 347.

[4] Santini, *Versilia centrale*, i. 88–92.

[5] T. W. Blomquist, 'Lineage, Land and Business in the Thirteenth Century: The Guidiccioni Family of Lucca', *Actum Luce*, ix (1980), 7–29.

instrument of social advancement in southern European, Roman-law societies.[6] Whether we speak of the legacy of the ancient world and the intrinsically aristocratic quality of the early Italian commune,[7] of the processes by which the great noble clans of the countryside were inexorably drawn into the economic and political life of the city, of the parvenu's single-minded search for respectability through marriage and landed investment, there was an intense interchange between town and countryside which renders it very difficult to think in traditional terms of two alien and conflicting worlds.

The contrast potentially finds sharpest expression with regard to the surviving powers of feudal lordship in the more distant, more mountainous parts of the state. The Lunigiana to the north-west of Lucca, an area subject to Lucca at the beginning of the fourteenth century and claimed anew by the forces of Castruccio Castracani,[8] was peculiarly the domain of petty feudal principalities held by the numerous branches of the Malaspina family. Still, at the end of the fifteenth century, fiefs were ruled jointly or in rotation by brothers who held their lands in common.[9] Local communities functioned under the supervisory agents of their lord, though individual communes like Madrignano might obtain exceptional privileges, and the more oppressive features of unfree tenure had disappeared from the Lunigiana by 1500.[10] The scene of some of Piccinino's campaigns in the 1430s, the province had largely passed out of the Lucchese sphere of influence by the fifteenth century. The western lands became a battleground between the contending forces of Milan, Florence, Genoa, and the Campofregosi family, the east disputed by Milan and Florence. In the east particularly, Florence successfully pursued a policy of extending its 'protection' over local *signori*. This was

[6] M. B. Becker, *Medieval Italy: Constraints and Creativity* (Bloomington, Ind., 1981); P. J. Jones, 'An Italian Estate, 900–1200', *Economic History Review*, 2nd ser., vii (1954), 21; Berengo, *Nobili e mercanti*, 56–64. Despite the search for a more distinguished pedigree, the first clear reference to the Buonvisi family relates to ser Lorenzo di Ranieri, who was a notary and chancellor to the Lucchese tyrant Castruccio Castracani in 1327. Ser Lorenzo's son Neri married a daughter of the notary ser Nicolao Turinghelli. And Neri's own sons included Lodovico, who was to marry the daughter of ser Risico di Paolo Risichi: Green, *Castruccio Castracani*, 91 n. 32; Baroni, Notizie genealogiche, MS 1108, fos. 27^r, 41^r.

[7] K. Marx, *Pre-Capitalist Economic Formations*, ed. E. J. Hobsbawm (London, 1964), 77; P. Anderson, *Passages from Antiquity to Feudalism*, Verso edn. (London, 1978), 166; C. Wickham, *Early Medieval Italy: Central Power and Local Society 400–1000* (London, 1981); *idem*, 'The Other Transition: From the Ancient World to Feudalism', *Past & Present*, ciii (1984), 3–36; Jones, 'Economia e società'.

[8] Green, *Castruccio Castracani*, 123–5.

[9] Branchi, *Lunigiana feudale*, i. 232–3.

[10] Ibid., i. 565–7; ii. 157–65.

achieved through the naming of guardians for the minor heirs of fiefs and by taking over fiefs when, through death without heir, they fell vacant. The Marchesi Malaspina themselves achieved distinction as the *capitani* of the great powers on the wider Italian scene. Yet Lucchese influence in the Lunigiana was not entirely a thing of the past by 1430. Little was achieved in October 1431 when Lucca sentenced Antonio Alberico, Marchese Malaspina di Fosdinovo, to death and confiscation of property (*in absentia*) for occupying a number of Lucchese strongholds, including Carrara, Moneta, and Massa, during the Florentine wars.[11] The sentence failed to discourage Antonio Alberico from giving renewed support to his Florentine allies in 1436; nor did it prevent him from seizing and holding more Lucchese territories after he was formally freed from the 'bando di ribellione' in 1442.[12] But another branch of the vast Malaspina clan, represented by Tommaso and Fioramonte Malaspina di Villafranca, was at this same time submitting to Lucchese protection, promising obedience and military support in return for Lucca's defence of their castles and lands. The grant of protection involved the Malaspina in that most symbolic ritual acknowledgement of Lucchese authority: the offering of candles at the vigil of Santa Croce.[13]

If some feudatories like the Malaspina filled a world clearly distant from the rhythm of urban life, others played a more ambiguous role. We think of the de' Nobili di Pugliano, distinguished (wrongly) by Baroni from the de' Nobili d'Albiano.[14] On the one hand, there was ser Giovanni di

[11] SB 160 fo. 106^{r-v}.

[12] Antonio Alberico was freed 'to please the Florentines', and at their request: Rif. 16, pp. 156–7. For Antonio Alberico's Florentine connections and the continuing problems that he posed for the Lucchese state, see Branchi, *Lunigiana feudale*, iii. 539–51, 759–61; Fumi (ed.), *Regesti*, 360, 491, 508, 612, 642, 654, 676, 763, 833, 847, 910; MAP, vi. 6; xi. 207, 410; xii. 84.

[13] Rif. 14, pp. 583, 586–9. For Tommaso and Fioramonte, see Branchi, *Lunigiana feudale*, ii. 64–7. In terms of the agreement, both were required to assist in the recovery of Pietrasanta in 1436, when Pietrasanta rebelled against Lucca, its 'propria madre e fondatrice': Fumi (ed.), *Regesti*, 771. Tommaso died in 1438, but Fioramonte survived to the age of 90, and was little disturbed in his possessions until after 1449, when he was faced by the rising power of the Campofregoso. It is far from clear what part the agreement with Lucca played in securing a period of relative tranquillity for these Malaspina lands, which did not actually include Villafranca itself but were centred around castles such as Panicale and Virgoletta.

[14] Baroni, Notizie genealogiche, MS 1123, fos. 12^{r}, 370^{r}, 374^{r}. Baroni says that the Nobili d'Albiano went to live in Pietrasanta, and came to be called degl'Albiani. But it appears clearly in the records of Casoli oltre Giogo that Bartolomeo di Lorenzo de' Nobili was known variously as di Pugliano and d'Albiano: ASL Podestà di Casoli oltre Giogo, Atti Civili, 31. Baroni's notes confuse Albiano della vicaria di Minucciano and Albiano, Val di Magra. For the Albiani of Pietrasanta, see Santini, *Versilia centrale*, vi. 126–30. A useful history of the de' Nobili di Pugliano and d'Albiano is found in C. De Stefani, *Storia dei comuni di Garfagnana* (Modena, 1923; repr. Pisa, 1978), 89–93.

Lorenzo de' Nobili di Pugliano, citizen of Lucca, married to a daughter of Piero Balbani, who made a will in 1437 in which he asked to be buried 'nel suo sepolcro presso la Pila dell'acqua benedetta' in the church of S. Maria in Via.[15] On the other, in the mountainous far northern reaches of the Lucchese state, a civil case before the *podestà* of Casoli oltre Giogo provides invaluable insights into the life in Albiano and Pugliano of Bartolomeo di Lorenzo de' Nobili d'Albiano (sometimes called di Pugliano), almost certainly brother to ser Giovanni. The case, which involves an interesting side dispute over whether Bartolomeo was entitled to the legal privileges of Lucchese citizenship, since he lived in Albiano and not in Lucca, shows Bartolomeo served in his wedding festivities by Giovanni di Ottolino, who accompanied his entourage to and from Massa and played at the celebrations upon the *ceramella*.[16] Giovanni himself was

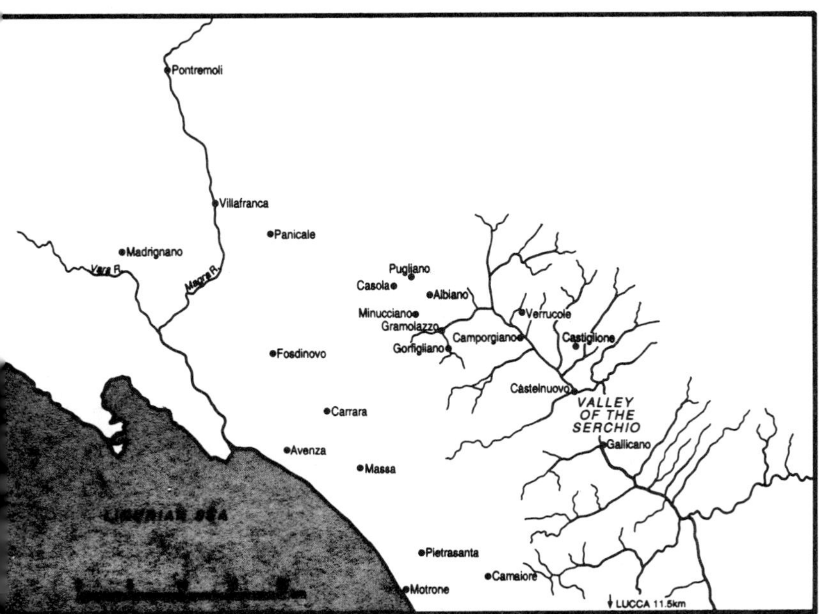

FIG. 6.1 Territory to the north of Lucca: Lunigiana, Garfagnana, and Versilia.

[15] Baroni, Notizie genealogiche, MS 1123, fo. 370r. I have not seen the original will, dated 18 Aug. 1437 in the hand of ser Michele Giovanni Pieri. But for ser Giovanni's son and heir, Piero, see AN 702 (ser Benedetto Franciotti), p. 254.

[16] A wind instrument, probably a bagpipe.

clearly a man of some property, but entangled in debts to Bartolomeo de' Nobili, and therefore often in the great man's pay, not only at the lengthy wedding rituals, but pruning his vines and (through Giovanni's wife) wet-nursing his son. We cannot know what pressures, other than the promise of 4 florins per month, induced Giovanni's father Ottolino to take over the management of Bartolomeo's plague-stricken and dying household whilst Bartolomeo himself fled to the safety of his Pugliano house.[17] But the influence and powers at the disposal of these men stand revealed in the case of Nicolao di Lorenzo de' Nobili d'Albiano (presumably another brother) who was sentenced to death in 1451 for leading an armed band of *compagni* against the *castello* of Pugliano.[18] In denying the charge and in requesting that the sentence be reversed, it is no less significant that Nicolao was supported in his appeal to the General Council of Lucca by the representatives of the communes of Albiano, Sermezzana, Gorfigliano and Gramolazzo, Pugliano, Bergiola, and Agliano, all chorusing that favours granted to Nicolao be regarded as favours granted unto themselves.[19]

Powers of lordship were not the sole prerogative of the wild nobles of the Lunigiana, or even of the hardly less wild nobles of Albiano and Pugliano who bridged the gap between Lucca and her remotest territories. Nicolao di Dino Avvocati appears in one guise as a prominent citizen frequently represented on the ruling councils of Lucca. In another, as count palatine, *consorte*, and descendant of the *domo Advocatorum*, he claimed certain hills and pastures in the parish of S. Pancrazio by virtue of Imperial grant and privilege. A very ordinary dispute over the ownership of pasture between Nicolao and the commune of Matraia is transformed into something more interesting when Nicolao claimed that the men of Matraia had no right to form a commune, since they were in fact his *subditi* and *vassalli*.[20] Others might acquire through purchase the kind of prerogatives that Nicolao Avvocati asserted by ancient right. When Bartolomeo di Andrea del Portico purchased land that had been

[17] ASL Podestà di Casoli oltre Giogo, Atti Civili, 31, fos. 3^{r-v}, 9^{v}–10^{v}, 19^{r-v}, 25^{r-v}, 47^{r}–48^{v}. For a fuller account of Ottolino's experiences, see Ch. 1.

[18] SB 165, fo. 408^{r}.

[19] Rif. 17, p. 507. Nicolao, by special grace, was freed from the sentence of execution and from confiscation of his goods, dependent on his paying 150 florins to the *camera* within six months, the confiscated goods meanwhile to be held as security.

[20] ASL Podestà di Lucca, Curia Civile, 1180, fos. 14^{r}–16^{v}. The *Podestà* in fact recognized the credentials of the syndics of Matraia who, whilst not disputing any Imperial judgment, continued to maintain that the pastures had always been held to belong to the commune of Matraia. For the Avvocati family and their private civil and criminal jurisdiction in the area of Col di Pozzo, see D. Osheim, *An Italian Lordship: The Bishopric of Lucca in the Late Middle Ages* (Berkeley, Calif., 1977), 33–6; Green, *Castruccio Castracani*, 93–4, 98.

confiscated from the ousted Paolo Guinigi, he assumed the rights over lands and communities that Paolo himself had acquired from the inheritance of Castruccio di Orlando de' Antelminelli.[21] By these earlier acts Guinigi—in his own name, and not as lord of Lucca—received not only lands, *ville*, and *castri*, but rights of lordship and jurisdiction confirmed by the oaths of loyalty of the men or vassals of the same. Thus on 9 February 1409 the men of the commune of Veghiatoia in the vicariate of Pietrasanta met in a *parlamento*, and, learning of the donation of the Antelminelli inheritance to Paolo Guinigi, promised to send now to Guinigi the annual perpetual rent of 18 *staia* of good dry grain, for observance of which they obligated all their goods present and future. These rights passed to the commune of Lucca on confiscation of Guinigi's possessions, and were subsequently purchased from Lucca by Bartolomeo del Portico.[22] We know of agreements and disputes over pasture between the Cenami and the *comunità* of Balbano.[23] The possessions of noble citizens might assume international implications if, as in the case of the di Poggio *castello* of Sorico, they formed enclaves of territory beyond the political boundaries of the Lucchese state.[24] In the countryside citizens might command the loyalty of 'multos armatos' as when in 1487 the Trenta and the Bernardi contended for possession of S. Gemignano.[25] The true dimensions of such vestiges of seigneurial power remain obscure. That the resources, ethos, and mental conditioning of a turbulent countryside constitute the essential backcloth to the tensions of urban politics analysed in earlier chapters is beyond question.

Urban investment has proved a more popular theme than lordship and seigneurial jurisdiction among historians of the Italian countryside. Lucchese citizens inherited and purchased land; but not only land. Castruccio Castracani had been granted all the iron and silver deposits ('tota vena ferri et argenti') in the territory of Pietrasanta.[26] These extensive mineral rights subsequently passed from the Antelminelli to Paolo Guinigi, who in turn granted them in 1411 to Gregorio Trenta.[27] In the post-Guinigi period Dino di Fondora, sometime lessor (with his

21 AN 327(4) (ser Antonio Morovelli da Castelnuovo), loose unfoliated instrument dated 23 Jan. 1409, fos. 10^{v}–35^{r}.

22 ASL Archivio Arnolfini, 2, fos. 14^{v}–16^{v}, 19^{v}–22^{r}.

23 Baroni, Notizie genealogiche, MS 1110, fos. 43^{r-v}, 63^{r}.

24 MAP, vi. 229.

25 Rif. 22, pp. 30–1.

26 ASL Capitoli, 7, fo. 17^{r}; Santini, *Versilia centrale*, ii. 25; iii. 265.

27 ASL Biblioteca (Manoscritti), 38, Giuseppe Civitali, Storia di Lucca, fo. 391^{v}; BSL MS 939, Gio: Lunardo Dalli, Cronache, pp. 60–1.

brother Nicolao) of the Lucchese mint, petitioned the General Council to grant him a lease for life to exploit the mineral resources of the entire Lucchese state.[28] Less ambitiously, in 1446, Lazzaro Cagnoli, himself sometime lessor of the Lucchese mint, received (together with Francesco Natali da Ragusa) specified mining rights in 'locis silvestribus' of the vicariate of Valdilima and within the Sei Miglia.[29] Cagnoli's grant was for ten years, with the condition that rights would revert to the commune if after two years he was not employing at least four men in the search for minerals. The fruits of such ventures are difficult to assess.

More certain returns were promised by the rich fishing resources of the Lucchese state. To the north-west, in the territory of Pietrasanta, the lago di Porta Beltrame (lago di Perotto), replenished by sea-water, was a particularly valuable source of fish. The lake, and the area thence to the sea, was held in the mid-fourteenth century by Imperial grant to the Streghi 'in feudo honorevole', from whom possession was to pass to their di Poggio creditors. The di Poggio in turn sold the lake to the hospital of the Misericordia in Lucca, which retained possession from 1406.[30] Lucca's loss of Pietrasanta in the mid-1430s complicated relationships.[31] The continued material value of the lake to the hospital of the Misericordia is detailed in a contract of 1439 whereby three men of Pietrasanta leased from the hospital's representative, also a native of Pietrasanta, all the fishing rights for a period of two years. The lease covered the lake itself, together with the ditches and waterways connecting it to the sea. The hospital was to receive as rent half of the money derived from the sale of fish, and in return was bound to maintain four fishing vessels for the use of the lessees.[32] By the fifteenth century that other great expanse of marsh and water to the south-east—the lago di Sesto or Bientina, formed by the changing course of the river Arno—was also largely in corporate hands. This too was an area of disputed jurisdiction: between Lucca and Florence. But here ownership was not concentrated in a single body, whatever the importance of the Abbazia di Sesto. The canons of the cathedral of S. Martino of Lucca owned the lake in that part called

[28] Rif. 15, pp. 38–9, 213–16; 16, p. 110.

[29] Rif. 16, p. 601.

[30] Baroni, Notizie genealogiche, MS 1133, fos. 168r–171v; MS 1134, fos. 246r–261r. See also MS 1126, fo. 314v.

[31] Baroni, Notizie genealogiche, MS 1105, fo. 382r; ASCP, I 2, Atti dei Genovesi (1433–82), fo. 51r.

[32] NAC, N 116 (ser Nicolao di Coluccio di Pellegrino da Pietrasanta, 1435–9), 6 Jan. 1439. The rent is elsewhere specified at 90 florins and 100 fish per annum: Baroni, Notizie genealogiche, MS 1134, fos. 254v–255r.

Carpinochio, and in 1493 both the canons and their lessee (Matteo Antonio da Colle) were damaged to the sum of 3 florins through the theft by certain men of Altopascio of 200 lb. of fish.[33] Not that the interests of private families were entirely subverted by monastic and charitable foundations: on lago di Sesto itself fisheries formed part of the Guinigi inheritance; Francesco di Stefano di Poggio acquired the 'peschiera di acqua lungha' from Camaiore; in 1428 the Burlamacchi obtained part of lago di Massaciùccoli.[34] Wherever ownership might lie, the Lucchese authorities themselves were to prove vigilant guardians of the natural resources under their jurisdiction. A series of laws sought to prevent the contamination of lakes, rivers, and streams; to stop the catching of undersized fish; and to ban fishing with illegal equipment.[35]

Flowing waters offered economic returns beyond fish. The previous chapter located certain branches of the Lucchese textile industries in the foothills of the Lucchese plain where fast-flowing streams could be harnessed for hydraulic power. Mills in the vicariates were often communal property, monopolies, and a chief source of communal revenue.[36] Mills built on the canals around Lucca were themselves public property, and leased to millers by the commune.[37] Where mills were built by private individuals, permission was required because of the wider potential consequences of interruption and diversion of water supplies. Despite the restrictions, the fifteenth-century records suggest a constant interest in the building and leasing of mills by citizens and urban foundations. Interest was expressed by members of the great patrician families: Bartolomeo Arnolfini possessed a mill on the Serchio at S. Pietro a Vico; ser Monello Bertini an olive press (*frantoio*) in Camaiore which was apparently water-powered.[38] Piero Guidiccioni received permission to build a mill in pieve S. Stefano in 1466, Piero Trenta a mill and *frantoio* at Mutigliano in 1487.[39] Two years later Stefano and Sebastiano Turchi

[33] SB 202, fos. 160^{v}–161^{v}.

[34] AN 771 (ser Giovanni Roffia, 1468–70), fo. 72^{v}; Biblioteca (Manoscritti), 30, Pellegrino di Bartolomeo Pellegrini da Camaiore, Libro di Memorie, fo. 30^{v}; BSL MS 62, Memorie diverse di Lucca, p. 397.

[35] Rif. 16, p. 499; 20, p. 53. For prosecutions under these statutes, see, e.g., SB 165, fo. 188^{r}.

[36] See, e.g., ASG MS 6, pp. 62–4. For the lease of a mill by the commune of Camaiore, see AN 702 (ser Benedetto Franciotti), p. 35; 703, pp. 52–5.

[37] Anz. Temp. Lib. 5, fo. 56^{v}; Rif. 16, pp. 66–7; ASL Podestà di Lucca, Curia Civile, 1309, fo. 180^{r}; ASL Archivio Arnolfini, 2, fo. 22^{r}; SB 159, fo. 178^{r}.

[38] ASL Capitano del Contado, 52, fo. 15^{r-v}; AN 597 (ser Luviso di Antonio Buonaccorsi), fo. 297^{r}.

[39] Rif. 19, p. 165; BSL MS 38, Martino Bernardini, Ricordi Storici, fo. 229^{v}.

negotiated the construction of a mill for making paper at Quiesa.[40] But mills were not the sole prerogative of wealthy merchants. Antonio di Baldino, a weaver of the suburbs, owned a mill and *frantoio* in the territory of S. Gennaro.[41] Here too we find the interests of urban monasteries and charitable foundations. The hospital of the Misericordia became embroiled with the commune of Pietrasanta not only over the lago di Perotto, but also over the possession of *frantoii*.[42] The canons regular of S. Frediano were engaged in a long dispute with Buono di Bernabo, citizen of Lucca, purchaser from the monastery of a mill at Vorno called il Battiferro.[43]

Clearly Lucchese citizens were aware of riches beneath the soil, of the benefits to be derived from lakes and rivers, of the cheap labour, particularly that of female silk winders, available in the surrounding countryside.[44] Overwhelmingly the notarial contracts preserved in the vast notarial archives of Lucca reflect merely the endless rhythm of land transactions: the buying, selling, and leasing of land, sometimes in the city or suburbs, but more often agricultural land with or without buildings in the wider Lucchese state. To identify more accurately the salient features of urban investment in land, I have taken the protocolli of a single notary, ser Benedetto Franciotti, for the years 1451–61. These years are covered in eleven volumes, and with some duplication.[45] Like all notaries, ser Benedetto Franciotti was favoured by specific individuals and institutions—which in Franciotti's case included the monastery of S. Frediano. But there is no reason to believe that the results achieved from this small sample are in any way distorting. Indeed, they offer little enough that is surprising. The results of this survey are set out in Table 6.1.

The survey takes note only of the landed transactions of Lucchese citizens and of urban-based religious foundations. I have ignored casual references to landed possessions, in which the sources abound; and have also ignored reference to land in dowries, testaments, and pledges, in arbitration awards, and in acts of entering into possession—in all of which the details are often less specific than in land contracts *per se*. I have included land that changed hands by exchange, and (as purchases) land acquired as payment for a specific debt. I have not entered a separate recording of lease in those frequent instances when (concealing an

[40] Rif. 22, p. 289.
[41] ASL Podestà di Lucca, Curia Civile, 1306, fo. 53ʳ.
[42] ASCP Libro di Consigli (1435), fo. 17ʳ.
[43] ASL Raccolte Speciali: S. Frediano, 20 no. 11; 21 no. 8.
[44] Bratchel, 'Silk Industry of Lucca', 181–2.
[45] AN 700–6 (ser Benedetto Franciotti); 700 itself consists of five separate vols.

effective loan at interest) land was leased by buyer to seller for a number of years pending a future offer of resale. The volumes used contain many examples of two copies of the same contract: I believe that the duplications have been eliminated. When contracts were entered into by a procurator, the transaction has been recorded in the name of the principal. Here there is considerable room for error, since the identity of the true purchaser is sometimes not revealed in the original contract. Women acting (with consent) in their own right have been grouped socially with their husbands or with their fathers in the case of minors and of women married to non-citizens. In fact, 5.5 per cent of the principals were women, often widows. Women of course also appear regularly in land contracts as the guardians of the minor heirs of their deceased husbands. To achieve a more detailed breakdown of patterns of landholding within the Lucchese state would involve methodological problems of daunting proportions. The consistent application of somewhat arbitrary principles of selection provides, in Table 6.1, an overview which is adequate for present purposes.

Almost 45 per cent of all land transactions involved men described as merchants and citizens of Lucca: the same group, including an inner patriciate, that dominated the political life of the republic. If we add the notaries, lawyers, and doctors of medicine—socially indistinguishable from the merchants and often of the same families—we reach 56 per cent of all landed transactions. Over the ten-year period these groups were purchasing land more frequently than selling land, in the ratio of five to three. The next most important grouping comprised churches and monasteries (including *opere*, altars, and chapels), as well as confraternities, together accounting for 24 per cent of all land transactions. Leases account for 65 per cent of the contracts on behalf of religious institutions; for the rest, the Church appears as a net seller of land, no doubt at least in part a consequence of damages suffered during the war years.[46] Individual clerics were also involved in the land market in their own names. Finally, the table reveals the stable presence of retailers (mercers, apothecaries, *lanari*, *pannari*, butchers) and artisans. At 7 per cent the number of transactions involving artisans is rather less than a range of more impressionistic evidence might have suggested. The focus on *transactions* rather than inheritance, dowries, and permanent small-holding has perhaps in some measure served to conceal the holdings in the suburbs and Sei Miglia of humbler members of Lucchese society.

[46] The devastation of church property is discussed more fully in Ch. 8.

Table 6.1. Landed transactions from the protocolli of ser Benedetto Franciotti, ASL Archivio de' Notari, 700–6 (1451–61)

Location	Type of contract	Merchants	Professionals	Retailers/ butchers	Artisans	Clerics	Unidentified individuals	Churches/ monasteries	Confraternities/ hospitals	Total
Lucca	Purchase	12	4	3	11	2	2	1	0	35
	Sale	13	3	3	0	2	2	9	2	34
	Lease	23	1	7	4	0	1	19	3	58
	Total	*48*	*8*	*13*	*15*	*4*	*5*	*29*	*5*	*127*
Suburbs	Purchase	9	4	1	1	0	0	2	0	17
	Sale	10	0	2	1	0	0	5	0	18
	Lease	8	0	0	0	0	0	21	1	30
	Total	*27*	*4*	*3*	*2*	*0*	*0*	*28*	*1*	*65*
Sei Miglia	Purchase	75	34	13	13	5	1	18	1	160
	Sale	50	12	13	14	6	1	23	0	119
	Lease	85	17	15	6	7	2	65	6	203
	Total	*210*	*63*	*41*	*33*	*18*	*4*	*106*	*7*	*482*
Vicaria di Camaiore	Purchase	21	2	0	1	0	2	1	0	27
	Sale	7	1	1	1	0	0	2	0	12
	Lease	9	4	1	0	1	1	3	0	19
	Total	*37*	*7*	*2*	*2*	*1*	*3*	*6*	*0*	*58*

Vicaria di	Purchase	12	2	0	0	1	0	0	0	15
Coreglia	Sale	1	2	0	0	0	0	0	0	3
	Lease	6	0	1	0	2	0	0	0	9
	Total	*19*	*4*	*1*	*0*	*3*	*0*	*0*	*0*	*27*
Vicaria di	Purchase	0	0	0	0	0	1	0	0	1
Valdilima	Sale	0	0	0	0	0	1	0	0	1
	Lease	0	0	0	0	0	0	0	0	0
	Total	*0*	*0*	*0*	*0*	*0*	*2*	*0*	*0*	*2*
Vicaria di	Purchase	1	0	0	1	0	1	0	0	3
Valdriana	Sale	0	0	0	0	0	0	0	0	0
	Lease	1	2	0	0	0	0	2	0	5
	Total	*2*	*2*	*0*	*1*	*0*	*1*	*2*	*0*	*8*
Outside	Purchase	1	0	0	0	0	0	1	0	2
Lucchese	Sale	7	1	0	1	1	1	1	0	12
state	Lease	2	0	0	0	0	0	1	0	3
	Total	*10*	*1*	*0*	*1*	*1*	*1*	*3*	*0*	*17*
Total		353	89	60	54	27	16	174	13	786

One hundred and twenty-seven transactions (16 per cent of the total) concern urban property situated within the walls. A relatively high proportion of house purchases in Lucca involved artisans. Sixty-five transactions (8 per cent of the total) relate to property located in the suburbs. The suburbs have been defined narrowly to refer to the *contrade* and *bracci* beyond the walls; the contracts relate both to houses in the area of urban overspill and to agrarian land. Predictably, the majority of contracts (61 per cent of the total) treat of land located within the Sei Miglia, that area of intensive grain cultivation of the plain, but rising to areas of olive groves and viticulture in the more immediate vicinity of the city. Berengo speaks of the Sei Miglia in the sixteenth century as fragmented into small and medium-sized farms belonging to citizens and urban monasteries.[47] The 1450s reveal a not dissimilar pattern, though frequent contracts within the Sei Miglia between *contadini*—not evident from Table 6.1—warn against exaggerating the totality of urban control. Landed transactions involving citizens and religious foundations in the files of ser Benedetto Franciotti are widely scattered between more than 110 separately specified locations; but there were areas of clearly focused urban investment. Thirteen per cent of transactions within the Sei Miglia were within the peripheral ring of what were to become designated *comuni suburbani*.[48] A further 41 per cent of transactions relate to the area east of the city which today constitutes the commune of Capannori: particularly around Capannori itself, Lammari, Lunata, Marlia, Matraia, pieve S. Paolo, S. Gennaro, Segromigno, Tassignano, and Vorno. Other dealings are distributed quite evenly throughout the Sei Miglia. The twenty-five contracts relating to the wine and olive belt around pieve S. Stefano (including Castagnori, Forci, and Greco) show this already to be an area of considerable patrician interest. A slightly smaller number of contracts concerned land in the episcopal Iura to the north of Lucca. In 1460 the notary ser Ciomeo di Piero Ciomei received a licence from the bishop to purchase land in S. Quirico di Moriano from certain residents of Moriano.[49]

Beyond the Sei Miglia, the Franciotti files confirm very limited citizen involvement. There is no indication at all of citizen holdings in the upper valley of the Serchio or in the mountainous northern extent of the Lucchese state. Many of the references to the vicariates come from the

[47] Berengo, *Nobili e mercanti*, 294.

[48] Monte S. Quirico, Pontetetto, S. Alessio, S. Casciano a Guamo, S. Cassiano a Vico, S. Lorenzo a Picciorana, S. Pietro a Vico, S. Vito di Picciorana, and Sorbano.

[49] AN 704 (ser Benedetto Franciotti), pp. 172–3.

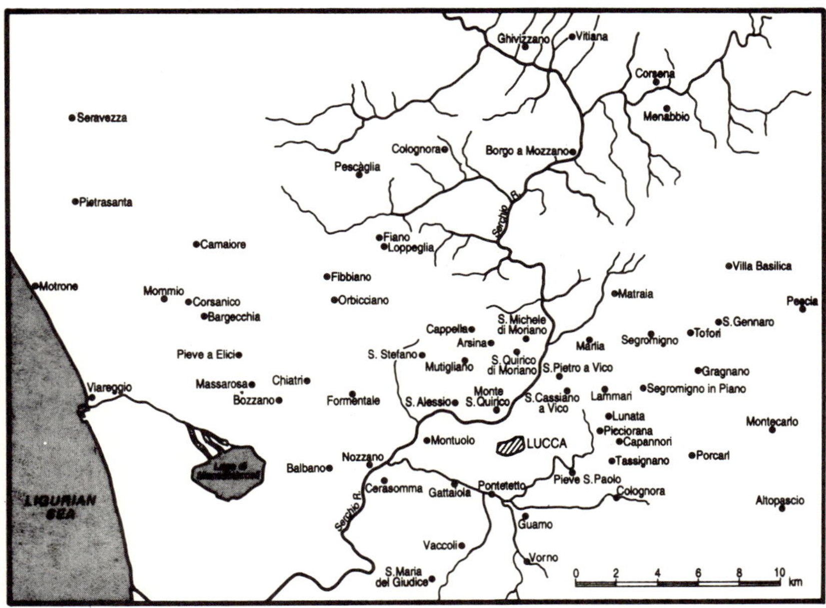

FIG. 6.2. Landed transactions: Lucca, the Sei Miglia, and the southern vicariates.

ambiguous border areas: from Porcari, for example, which was part of Valdriana following the loss of Montecarlo to Florence, but was later joined to the Sei Miglia. An exception must be made for the wine and olive belt stretching from Camaiore to pieve Elice, which, in the fifteenth century as in the sixteenth, was an area of considerable citizen investment. Abundant casual references confirm the extent of Lucchese landholding in the area around Camaiore. More surprising is the number of contracts relating to the vicariate of Coreglia, as far north as Ghivizzano and Vitiana. The Coreglia figures are partly, but only partly, explained by the continued interest of the prominent merchants da Ghivizzano in the land of their family's origin. A different statistical base would have revealed the involvement of Domenico Bertini in his native Gallicano.[50] The small number of references to land transactions, particularly the selling of land, outside the political borders of the Lucchese state are largely explained by the political and military vicissitudes of the early fifteenth century. For the

[50] Baroni, Notizie genealogiche, MS 1105, fos. 380ʳ–445ᵛ.

most part these lands are located in Carrara, Montecarlo, Pietrasanta: all lost to Lucca in the 1430s and 1440s. In Pescia, where Lucchese rule was a more distant memory, di Poggio lands were being sold—clearly to the representative of local men—in the summer of 1460.[51]

More than 40 per cent of the contracts that we have been analysing were leases. Urban property was invariably let for a money rent, as indeed was pasture-land very often. Thus Giusfredo Cenami let woodland and pasture in the commune of Balbano and in the pieve of Massaciùccoli to Giuliano di Nicolao da Vico Pancellorum of the vicariate of Valdilima, from October 1460 to May 1461, for 10 florins payable in two instalments.[52] Agrarian lands were equally invariably let for rent in kind, as had been the practice in Italy for centuries.[53] In one respect, however, Lucca was distinctive, especially with regard to her immediate Tuscan neighbours. Whilst grain cultivation elsewhere in fifteenth-century Tuscany had become very largely associated with *mezzadria* contracts, in Lucca share-cropping leases involving grain were very rare indeed.[54] There are occasional exceptions in the early protocolli of Franciotti, as in the acts redacted by other notaries. One share-cropping contract specifying rent in grain relates to land as close to Lucca as *contrada* S. Anna; an improvement lease on land in Capannori provided for an initial year 'ad medium' whilst the land was being brought into cultivation.[55] But these are isolated exceptions to a rule that was all but universal.

Not that *mezzadria*-type contracts were particularly unusual in the fifteenth-century Lucchese state. They occur very frequently when rent was demanded in nuts or fruit, and especially when rent was specified in wine and olive oil. In a revealing contract (taken from our present statistical base), the heirs of Silvestro di Matteo Trenta leased one of their farms in S. Gemignano di Moriano for two years. The lessee promised to pay half of the oil, wine, and other fruits issuing from the mountainous parts; and 6 bushels (*staia*) of grain per *coltra* for those parts on the plain.[56] In border areas of mixed cultivation this combination of fixed rent in grain

[51] AN 705 (ser Benedetto Franciotti), pp. 167–8.

[52] AN 704, p. 180.

[53] Money rents had dominated from the 9th and 10th centuries, but rents were again in kind by the 12th–13th cent.: Wickham, *Early Medieval Italy*, 112–14. More specifically for Lucca, see Osheim, *An Italian Lordship*, 101–3; L. A. Kotelnikova, 'Il ruolo dello sviluppo delle città e delle relazioni mercantili-monetarie nei mutamenti delle condizioni economiche e sociali dei contadini toscani nei secoli xii–xv', in *Studi in Memoria di Federigo Melis*, 5 vols. (Florence, 1978), i. 411.

[54] Pinto, *La Toscana*, 225–6.

[55] AN 700(5) (ser Benedetto Franciotti), 16 July 1456; 702, p. 66.

[56] AN 700(4), 8 Nov. 1455. The heirs kept for themselves all the Trebbiano wine.

together with half the wine and the oil is quite common, though in other leases the amount of wine and oil was also expressed as fixed rent. The range of possible permutations was extended by the *caseario* Nanni di Lorenzo who, together with Pasquino di Martino da S. Pietro a Vico, leased land in Fiano in return for $2\frac{1}{2}$ *some* of wine per annum and one-fifth of the oil.[57] *Mezzadria*-type contracts were also prominent in leases involving not land but livestock. Citizens often leased cows, sheep, and goats to countrymen, who pastured them at their own expense in return for half the cheese, half the wool, and half the progeny. Thus Marchesio di Guglielmo de' Gigli in September 1458 leased five goats, worth 90 bolognini, to a resident of Petrognano in return for half their produce, specifying cheeses, the goats to be returned to de' Gigli at the end of the year.[58] Similarly, Matteo di Iacopo da Aquilea in the episcopal Iura leased for five years from Michele di Giovanni Guinigi a two-year-old cow *in soccidia*, the produce to be divided in half.[59] By contrast, citizens rented oxen, and very occasionally horses, to countrymen in return for a set rent in grain. These contracts included clauses to ensure appropriate care of the animals. The distinction between oxen and other livestock is neatly drawn in an agreement involving a resident of S. Quirico di Moriano who was indebted 15 ducats to the monastery of S. Frediano, the sum owing for a mule (with bell and rope). Unable to pay, the debtor in May 1457 handed over to S. Frediano an ox, twenty-nine goats, and six lambs. The animals were duly leased back to their owner: the ox for 8 ducats, payable in one year, and for 6 *staia* of grain payable in August; the goats for half their cheese and fruits.[60]

Whether the kind of share-cropping agreements that were so common in the wine- and olive-producing areas of the Lucchesia can properly be defined as *mezzadria* contracts has recently become the subject of considerable debate. The debate hinges on a list of defining qualities through which historians have come to distinguish *mezzadria classica* from contracts *ad medium* or *colonia parziaria*.[61] The details of individual leases

[57] AN 702, p. 273.

[58] AN 702, p. 66.

[59] AN 700(3), 20 Oct. 1457.

[60] AN 700(3), 2 May 1457.

[61] B. Andreolli, 'Considerazioni sulle campagne lucchesi nella prima metà del secolo xiv: paesaggio, economia, contratti agrari', in *Castruccio Castracani e il suo tempo: Convegno Internazionale, Lucca 5–10 ottobre 1981*, published as anni xiii–xiv, nos. 1–2 of *Actum Luce* (1984–5), 277–301. The essential text is G. Giorgetti, 'Contratti agrari e rapporti sociali nelle campagne', in *Storia d'Italia*, v, pt. 1 (Turin, 1973), 699–758, esp. 702–16. M. Ginatempo, *Crisi di un territorio: il popolamento della Toscana senese alla fine del medioevo* (Florence, 1988), 17, 148, 206–7, 232, 484, shows clearly that in southern Tuscany the *mezzadria*

in the Lucchesia varied widely. Often there was the provision of a house, equipment, olives, and vines; obligations of residence on the tenant and his family; and specific provisions to ensure that the tenant worked hard and well. Always we are speaking of leases of brief duration. Obviously, the confining of *mezzadria* contracts in the Lucchesia to areas of vine and olive cultivation distinguishes the Lucchese contracts from the *podere mezzadrile* that were spreading at this time throughout the rest of Tuscany. Many of the Lucchese examples embrace so many of the structural features of *mezzadria* that I am disinclined to withhold use of the term.

By the third decade of the fifteenth century, two-thirds (in value) of the Florentine countryside was in citizen hands. Significant *proprietà contadina* survived only in the high hills and mountains.[62] For Lucca it is impossible to produce comparable figures. Berengo has argued that by the early sixteenth century the whole of the fertile plain of the Serchio was in the possession of citizens, and organized into compact farms.[63] In 1430 that process was far from complete. But it is abundantly clear that the post-Guinigi years saw continued urban investment in the countryside, particularly in the Sei Miglia. Urban interest extended to the provision of livestock and of credit to rural individuals and communities (the credit often under the guise of landed transactions). If the urban interest is clear, the nature, motivation, and direction of that interest remain very much a matter of debate. These problems bring us to a difficult series of issues which have come to be grouped together under the phrase 'return to the land'.

Residentially, Lucchese citizens remained thoroughly urban throughout the fifteenth century. In this sense, certainly, there was no mass movement to the countryside, though some individuals, particularly newer citizens, were rather ambiguously divided between Lucca and the larger urban centres of the *contado* (Camaiore, Gallicano, and Pietrasanta). In the case of Domenico Bertini, not only did he celebrate his growing distinction by plastering his motto 'Ut vivam vera vita' throughout his native Gallicano, but he extended his energies to building work at the mineral baths of Corsena (Bagni di Lucca).[64] Indeed, before Bertini's involvement, the need to retire to the baths had become established as a

contracts of the 15th cent. can be contrasted with *mezzadria* in the modern age, and fall far short of Andreolli's defining requirements.

[62] Pinto, *La Toscana*, 158–9.

[63] Berengo, *Nobili e mercanti*, 301.

[64] Domenico Corsi, 'Domenico Bertini', in *Dizionario biografico degli italiani*, ix (Rome, 1967); Paoli Puccetti, *Di Messer Domenico Bertini*.

valid reason for absence from the political councils of Lucca. The development of Corsena as a social centre and place of retreat attracted rogues in search of rich pickings. And by the 1440s the baths were proving a promising environment for tricksters with false dice—even if the recorded victims were the inevitable gullible Lombards rather than ailing citizens.[65]

Besides Corsena, Lucchese citizens were also looking to more private centres of rural retreat; even if the villas that still adorn the Tuscan countryside are the creations of a later age. Whether for purposes of leisure or supervision, Silvestro di Battista ser Castruccio da Pietrasanta, citizen of Lucca, insisted on retaining the largest house on the property for his own use in the *mezzadria* contract by which he leased a farm in Ciciana to Marco di Filippo da Brancoli.[66] Similarly, when the mercer Ridolfo di Lorenzo leased a fully equipped farm in Busdagno for nine years, also by *mezzadria*, he too reserved one house to his own use.[67] In yet another *mezzadria* contract Iacopo di Giovanni da Ghivizzano, merchant and citizen of Lucca, leased a farm with house, land, trees, vines, olives, and so on in Massa Pisana (together with other land in S. Ambrogio da Massa) to Bartolomeo di Ceo da Calci for three years. A house and its garden was reserved to Iacopo, and the lessee was explicitly absolved from responsibility for certain plants and cuttings placed there by the owner.[68] Around Forci and Castagnori, Carolo di Iacopo Tomasini kept a house when he leased for three years all his lands there—including houses, vineyards, and olive groves—for an annual rent of 18 *staia* of grain, 2 *staia* of chestnuts, and half the wine and oil.[69] The merchant Nicolao Lucchesini maintained a house at S. Giusto di Brancoli,[70] Giovanni ser Cambio a palace and *viridario* at Massarosa.[71] On a more modest scale, Agostino di Giovanni da Ghivizzano, when leasing a farm at Capannori (for eight years at a rent of 45 *staia* of grain per annum), dictated only the retention of a room, though he did insist that no animals be kept in the house, and that the lessees refrain from building any place adjoining the house for the keeping of beasts.[72]

65 SB 165, fos. 131^{v}, 134^{r-v}.

66 AN 700(4) (ser Benedetto Franciotti), 21 Sept. 1455.

67 Ibid., 29 Nov. 1456.

68 AN 702, pp. 279–80.

69 AN 704, p. 208; 705, pp. 360–1. The contract also includes reference to a cow and calf leased *in soccidia*.

70 AN 706, pp. 129–34.

71 AN 705, p. 295.

72 AN 700(4), 11 Jan. 1455.

The above examples, all taken from the early protocolli of ser Benedetto Franciotti, illustrate a point that scarcely needs more rigorous proof: that Lucchese citizens (like their Florentine neighbours) maintained country residences as places of occasional and supervisory sojourn. In contemporary Florence, a more permanent rural base was sufficient evidence of poverty, failure, and exclusion.[73] It was also deemed undesirable. Writing of his father, who had been sent off as a child to Mugello, the Florentine Giovanni Morelli reflected in his *ricordi*: 'Think what he must have been like, having stayed in the country all or most of the time: little better than a farm labourer.'[74] Parallel attitudes were expressed frequently enough in quattrocento Lucca. There is the sad story of Galvano del Portico who, because he lacked the means to continue living in Lucca, had been forced to withdraw with his family to Cappella di S. Lorenzo in the *pieve* of Torri. In Cappella, as a non-resident citizen, he was being pursued by the officials of the *gabella* who had assessed him, for every year that he remained 'in villa', at 1 florin per mouth (*per boccha*), a sum that (allegedly) del Portico was quite unable to pay.[75] Attitudes captured in the plight of del Portico are complemented by the appeal for citizenship of Cristoforo Turinelli of Ghivizzano in the vicariate of Coreglia. That ambitious petitioner informed the General Council that he had lived in the city of Lucca for so long that he had acquired a passion for 'il vivere civile', and could no longer bear the prospect of living in the *contado*.[76] From different perspectives, both del Portico and Turinelli refute any notion that the countryside had become an attractive alternative to the city. Even the regular pattern of rural retreat and the circuit of country house living, evoked for sixteenth-century Lucca in the writings of Berengo and Cesare Sardi, seem very imperfectly established in the decades before the French invasion.[77]

There was no physical flight to the countryside. If the return to the land

[73] Kent, *Household and Lineage*, 249–52.

[74] *Ricordi* of Giovanni Morelli quoted in Trexler, *Public Life in Renaissance Florence*, 162. For the full quotation, 'Dovea avere Pagolo dieci o dodici anni; pensa, sendo istato sempre in villa, o la maggiore parte del tempo, quello che dovea essere: poco meglio ch'un lavoratore!', see Giovanni di Pagolo Morelli, *Ricordi*, ed. Vittore Branca (Florence, 1956), 145.

[75] Rif. 16, p. 789.

[76] Rif. 17, p. 179.

[77] Berengo, *Nobili e mercanti*, 245–63; C. Sardi, *Dei mecanti lucchesi nel secolo xvi* (Lucca, 1882). In this respect Lucchese development may have been somewhat retarded. Both Petrarch and, later, Boccaccio produced images of villa life that would have been entirely familiar to later generations. And see P. E. Foster, *A Study of Lorenzo de' Medici's Villa at Poggio a Caiano*, 2 vols. (New York, 1978), i. 1–34. I am grateful to Professor Meek for providing me with Lucchese examples of *villeggiatura* from the notarial protocolli for the period before 1430.

necessitates rather an eschewing of trade, the evidence remains equally intractable. The most direct attempt to seek an attempted reconversion of wealth in fifteenth-century Lucca has focused on the lands of Michele di Giovanni Guinigi.[78] Michele was the half-brother of Girolamo Guinigi, whose *ricordi* provided, in the previous chapter, some of the most telling evidence for the continued vitality of Lucchese mercantile activity throughout the fifteenth century.[79] The Guinigi diarist shows with great clarity—not only for the Guinigi, but for a wide range of associated families—the regular rhythm of commercial apprenticeship and the anxiety of successive generations of patrician fathers as they prepared their sons to leave Lucca. Of course, some individuals—even some patrician families like the Mansi—are more easily associated with the professions than with trade. And some prominent individuals appear to have combined their office-holding and landed transactions with less than high-profile careers in either the professions or trade.

More common would appear to be the path trodden by the late-fifteenth-century merchant Benedetto di Lorenzo Buonvisi, as revealed in a Terrilogio and a Libro di contratti relating to the Buonvisi family.[80] In the years following his father's death in 1460, Benedetto Buonvisi served the customary commercial apprenticeship in the Lucchese colonies of north-western Europe. Though he does not appear among the Italian merchants living in London in 1469,[81] he was named regularly in the English customs accounts between 1471 and 1473 as an exporter of English cloth and an importer of silk and alum.[82] He seems to have left London in the summer of 1473, from which date the Buonvisi were represented in the London customs by the name of Benedetto's brother, Lodovico.[83] It was in Lucca in 1474 and 1475 that Benedetto Buonvisi was described as 'gubernator' of the London company named 'Benedetto Buonvisi e compagni',[84] though at this stage of his life Benedetto was

[78] Polica, 'An Attempted "Reconversion" of Wealth'.

[79] ASL Archivio Guinigi, 29, Girolamo Guinigi, Libro di ricordi.

[80] BSL MS 3380, Terrilogio ove sono notati li beni stabili che possedeva Benedetto Buonvisi; MS 3381, Libro di contratti antichi della nobile famiglia de' Buonvisi di Lucca cominciato addì xi settembre MCCCCXXXVI finito il 1514.

[81] Public Record Office, London, Exchequer K. R. Lay Subsidies, E179/144/67. See also E179/144/68.

[82] Public Record Office, London, Exchequer K. R. Customs Accounts, E122/194/19, m. 11^{v}, 12^{v}; E122/194/20, m. 4^{r}, 7^{r}, 13^{v}.

[83] Public Record Office, London, Exchequer K. R. Customs Accounts, E122/194/20, m. 8^{r}. See also E122/194/22, m. 4^{r}, 6^{v}, 10^{r}–11^{r}; E122/194/24, m. 2^{v}, 11^{r}; E122/194/26, m. 13^{r}; E122/73/40, 9 Oct. 1478.

[84] AN 731 (ser Benedetto Franciotti), fo. 133^{v}; 732, 5 Dec. 1474; AN Originali Testamenti, 15 (ser Benedetto Franciotti), fos. 248^{v}–249^{v}.

certainly far from settled at home.[85] Very soon after 1475, however, Michele Luzzati is clearly right when he describes Benedetto as running his extraordinarily diverse international commercial and banking affairs from his house in secunda ruga del Borgo in the parish of S. Frediano.[86] The commercial biography dovetails perfectly with the man's landed investments. Between 1460 and 1470 the Terrilogio and Libro di contratti show no landed purchases at all. Then, between 1470 and 1490, Benedetto—individually or jointly with his brothers—in most years bought one or two pieces of land. In the 1490s he was much more actively involved in the land market; but the period of really intensive buying falls in the decades preceding Benedetto's death in 1515, when the purchases of individual years sometimes exceeded a value of 1,000 ducats. In view of Benedetto Buonvisi's advanced years, it is hardly surprising that the land purchases tail off somewhat in the very last years of his life.[87] The pattern linking landed investment to a merchant's life cycle was already long established by the quattrocento. We see the same trend in the thirteenth century in the case of Rugerio Castracani, the money-changer largely responsible for founding the financial fortunes of the Castracani family, who started to invest heavily in urban and rural real estate in the 1250s in the years immediately before his death.[88]

The career of Benedetto Buonvisi amply testifies that there was no contradiction between commercial/industrial activity and landed investment. His last testament, besides its detailed concern with the foundation of the Buonvisi chapel in S. Frediano, was preoccupied with the future of the commercial companies over which he ruled. The landed wealth that he bequeathed to his sons was valued (in 1520) at more than 19,431 gold ducats, and rendered an annual income of 2,380 *staia* of grain, 1,143 *libbre* of oil, 860 *some* of wine, and 142 ducats. The Lucchese patriciate retained its balanced and diverse investment portfolio. I have found no clear

[85] AN 731, fo. 28v.

[86] Michele Luzzati, 'Benedetto Buonvisi', in *Dizionario biografico degli italiani*, xv (Rome, 1972). In an example of the bonds of family solidarity in quattrocento Lucca, Benedetto and his brothers continued to live in the same house in the quarter of S. Frediano until the beginning of the 16th cent.

[87] Buonvisi's landed investments are considered in more detail in my article 'The Return to the Land'.

[88] Blomquist, 'Castracani Family', 460–2. For rather different conclusions, based on the Florentine *catasto* of 1427, see D. Herlihy, 'The Problem of the "Return to the Land" in Tuscan Economic History of the Fourteenth and Fifteenth Centuries', in *Civiltà ed economia agricola in Toscana nei secc. xiii–xv: problemi della vita delle campagne nel tardo medioevo: Centro italiano di studi di storia e d'arte Pistoia, Ottavo Convegno Internazionale, Pistoia 21–24 aprile 1977* (Pistoia, 1981), 409–12.

evidence from the fifteenth century of that contempt for all economically productive activity which was becoming increasingly common in Italy, but was muted in Lucca (if only with respect to *grand commerce*) even in the more pretentiously aristocratic sixteenth century.[89] Whether for the patriciate as a whole the fifteenth century marked a decisive shift in the balance between commercial and landed investment remains a difficult question. The limited evidence presented in Table 6.1 shows that citizens in the 1450s were buying more land in the *contado* than they were selling. Certainly we can say that there was no diminution of interest in the countryside on the part of a Lucchese patriciate which had never neglected its landed interests.

The nature of those landed interests has become a very contentious theme in Italian historiography, and forms an important component in the 'return to the land' debate. Writing of Venice, where the growing preoccupation with the *terraferma* represents a much more radical redirection than any developments in contemporary Tuscany, Richard T. Rapp has argued that the intensified interest in the countryside was merely a response to changing and rational investment opportunities.[90] Consequently, interest in land was prompted by 'an "active" spirit of acquisitiveness, not a wish to stand by'.[91] The Venetian picture is complemented by Frank McArdle's study of the former Lucchese territory of Altopascio, where 'this particular landholder showed himself to be no idle, feeble aristocrat, but the master of a team of shrewd, imaginative, and ingenious administrators who never relaxed their efforts to maximize profits'.[92] A rather different set of imperatives has lately been posited for Lucca. Duane Osheim in a recent article has reopened the difficult question of why Lucca followed a different path during those centuries which saw the spread of the *mezzadria classica* throughout the rest of Tuscany, perhaps excepting Pisa.[93] Osheim begins from the premise that *mezzadria* was a peculiarly efficient way of controlling a landlord's agricultural investments, and that the spread of *mezzadria* offers an index of landlord domination over the inhabitants of the

[89] Berengo, *Nobili e mercanti*, 255–7.

[90] R. T. Rapp, 'Real Estate and Rational Investment in Early Modern Venice', *Journal of European Economic History*, viii (1979), 269–90.

[91] Ibid. 273.

[92] F. McArdle, *Altopascio: A Study in Tuscan Rural Society, 1587–1784* (Cambridge, 1978), 127. The quotation refers to the 18th-cent. crisis, but typifies McArdle's overall vision of the impact of a Medici business mentality on estate management.

[93] D. J. Osheim, 'Countrymen and the Law in Late-Medieval Tuscany', *Speculum*, lxiv (1989), 317–37.

countryside. The absence of *mezzadria* in the Lucchesia thus becomes evidence of the strength of Lucchese countrymen *vis-à-vis* urban landlords. The distinction is explained by Osheim partly in terms of the procedure of the *Curia dei Foretani*, the court handling minor civil cases from the countryside, and the *de facto* protection that the court offered to countrymen. But the protection was made possible on the one hand by the relative strength of countrymen because of their own landholdings, the availability of diverse sources of credit, and the shield of local community spirit, and on the other hand because of the importance for landowners of smooth personal relationships of interdependence and patronage.[94] It is true that Osheim is writing primarily of the fourteenth century. The absence of *mezzadria* contracts from the Lucchese plain in the fifteenth century makes Osheim's conclusions of potential relevance to the present enquiry.

The notion of *mezzadria* grants as commercial leases peculiarly suited to the profit-orientated mentality of business-minded Italians (and leading inexorably to the 'proletarianization' of the peasantry) is, of course, well established in the Italian historiography of the countryside.[95] But the linkage has by no means gone unchallenged. Some, whilst insisting that *mezzadria* maximized the exploitation of the labour force, have emphasized also both the extremely variable status of the *mezzadro* and the essential stability in productivity and in managerial and production techniques of the *mezzadria* model.[96] The exploitation of the labour force itself, as presented for example in the earlier work of Kotelnikova, has probably been exaggerated.[97] And the example of areas of arboriculture within the Lucchese state would seem to suggest that *mezzadria* was as compatible with the comfortable, passive life of *rentiers* as any other form of commercial rent.

[94] There is, of course, a very large literature emphasizing the essentially non-monetary returns on landed investment in terms of the buying of prestige and authority. The point is neatly expressed by J. P. Cooper, 'In Search of Agrarian Capitalism', *Past & Present*, lxxx (1978), 64.

[95] P. J. Jones, 'From Manor to Mezzadria: A Tuscan Case-study in the Medieval Origins of Modern Agrarian Society', in N. Rubinstein (ed.), *Florentine Studies: Politics and Society in Renaissance Florence* (London, 1968), 193–241. L. A. Kotelnikova, 'Condizione economica dei mezzadri toscani nel secolo XV (consumo, livello di vita)', in *Domanda e consumi, livelli e strutture (nei secoli xiii–xviii): Atti della sesta settimana di studio dell'Istituto internazionale di storia economica 'F. Datini'* (Florence, 1978), 93–9.

[96] M. Aymard, 'From Feudalism to Capitalism in Italy: The Case that Doesn't Fit', *Review: A Journal of the Fernand Braudel Center for the Study of Economies, Historical Systems, and Civilizations*, vi (1982–3), 131–208. See also McArdle, *Altopascio*, 66–129.

[97] Pinto, *La Toscana*, 293 n. 177.

If there are ambiguities in the structural implications of *mezzadria*, we may add that in fifteenth-century Lucca short-term leases at fixed rent (*fitti*) proved entirely effective for land improvements, and often imposed precisely those onerous burdens on the peasantry that are usually associated with *mezzadria*. The protocolli of ser Benedetto Franciotti show from the 1450s a sustained effort by citizen landowners to bring wasteland into cultivation, particularly in the area around Capannori. The phenomenon may well testify to the beginnings of demographic growth and to renewed pressure on land after the plagues and military devastations of the late fourteenth and early fifteenth centuries. In one instance, Agostino di Giovanni da Ghivizzano leased a *podere* in Capannori to a group of brothers, natives of Parma but residents of S. Gemignano: the first year, whilst bringing the land into cultivation, they were to pay half the crop; thereafter for nine years to render a rent of 135 *staia* of grain per annum.[98] The 'ad medium' ingredient is atypical. Other leases in the area merely specify a set rent in grain for every *coltra* of land brought under cultivation. Thus when the church of S. Frediano leased land in Porcari for six years with obligation to plant vines and to build, the lease offered two years free of rent, the third at a rent of half a *staia* of grain, and thereafter a rent of 1 *staia* of grain per *coltra*.[99] In such cases it was clearly the very low rent during the years of land improvement that offered the incentive to peasant initiative. When repairs to farm buildings were required, the repairs were at the expense of the lessee, but deductible from the rent.[100] Sometimes the long list of duties imposed on lessees was enforced by a conditional promise of future lease renewal.[101] But whether leased by *mezzadria* or *affitto* the controls over peasant life and movement were often real enough. In January 1460 the merchant Nicolao di Michele ser Federighi leased a farm, with house, in Bozzano for nine years to Benedetto di Giovanni da Chiatri. The farm was divided into various pieces of land, with fields, vines, olives, and trees. The rent was fixed at 6 *staia* of grain, $4\frac{1}{2}$ *libbre* of oil, and 2 *some* of wine per annum. The lease provided that the farm could be taken away from the lessee if it were not well governed, that the lessee was bound to live in the house for the duration of the lease, and that the lessee had specified obligations annually to plant vines and olives.[102]

[98] AN 702 (ser Benedetto Franciotti), p. 66.
[99] AN 700(3), 9 May 1457.
[100] AN 700(4), 27 Jan. 1455.
[101] AN 702, p. 135 (3 Mar. 1459).
[102] AN 704, p. 9. These terms are of course precisely those that are so often seen as distinctive to *mezzadria* leases.

It is therefore unclear whether the spread of *mezzadria* provides a useful index of either aggressive urban investment or of peasant dependence; the contrast between Lucca and Florence remains unexplained. The realities of the Lucchese countryside would seem to be much more ambiguous, incorporating evidence both of paternalism and of the ruthless pursuit of profit; of rational investment, *ad hoc* opportunism, and economic withdrawal. The point is well illustrated in the case of rents. In the fourteenth century, Osheim found that landlords showed great patience before resorting to the courts for payment of rents that were often from five to eight years in arrears. The tardiness in pursuit of debts forms the central evidence for Osheim's portrayal of an essentially harmonious relationship based on 'a complex tissue of loans, advances, and favors which tended to tie landlord to tenant'.[103] The evidence of civil cases before the court of the *Podestà* in fifteenth-century Lucca impressionistically seems to point overwhelmingly in the same direction: the series would repay systematic analysis in this regard. Certainly in some notarial contracts rent arrears were completely written off before the renewal of the lease with the same tenant. When rents were paid, profits still appear relatively low. The return on rural investment seldom seems to have exceeded 6 per cent,[104] and throughout Italy for much of the fifteenth century landlords were handicapped by labour shortages and low grain prices. Against this must be set Berengo's claim that, by the sixteenth century, rents in the Sei Miglia totally absorbed grain production,[105] a situation somewhat foreshadowed by a mid-fifteenth-century lease of a *podere* in Massa Pisana, where the lessee received one *coltra* explicitly for his own use, which he could sow with millet, lupines, and other leguminous crops.[106] The plethora of small cash and grain advances from landlord to tenant in which the notarial records abound might point to ties of interdependence, but would also seem to indicate a tenantry close to the level of subsistence.

No doubt landlords realized what rents they could. Tenants were

[103] Osheim, 'Countrymen and the Law', 328, 335–6.

[104] Calculations for the mid-15th cent. are based on the usual valuation of 5 *staia* of wheat per florin.

[105] Berengo, *Nobili e mercanti*, 309. In the 15th cent. it is very difficult to determine the relationship between rent and grain production. Besides the obvious variables of fertility and harvest, grain rents were most frequently specified *per coltre* in improvement leases, which fulfilled a distinctive function. There are frequent references to 6 *staia per coltra*, falling to 2 *staia* and less in improvement leases. Berengo's average of 10 *staia per coltra* seems far too high in the light of the documents that I have examined. A *coltra* was *c*.4,000m^2; a *staio* equalled 24.42 litres.

[106] AN 702 (ser Benedetto Franciotti), pp. 279–80.

sometimes evicted from the land on expiry of their leases.[107] Lucchese merchants were an important source of credit not only to individual countrymen but also to rural communities.[108] None of these facts provides sufficient proof of rational investment as traditionally conceived. An alternative model has been argued for the extensive rural investments of Michele di Giovanni Guinigi.[109] Michele Guinigi played at best only the most peripheral of roles in commercial and industrial affairs; his business activities were devoted almost entirely to the countryside. He was an avid purchaser of land, particularly of deteriorated land to be brought back into cultivation. He kept his leases as short as possible, and on expiry frequently reallocated lands to new tenants at increased rent. He was adept at exploiting impoverished countrymen. First they were softened up by a series of loans—to pay for a marriage or to survive a bad harvest or for agricultural supplies and equipment. Then they were drawn into usurious transactions whereby they 'sold' their land for a cash advance, with the offer of redemption after a period of two or three years. For the duration of the 'sale', the peasant paid interest in the form of rent for the continued occupation of his own land. Rents were so high, and the conditions of repayment so unfavourable, that only in exceptional cases was the right of 'repurchase' realized. After 1456 most of Michele Guinigi's landed acquisitions were accomplished in this way. By all these means Guinigi was dynamically involved in rural investment; but of the rationalization and improvements often associated with the *corsa alla terra* there is no sign. He showed little interest in consolidating his scattered and fragmented properties and a great unwillingness to invest directly in farming. Sante Polica has attributed the lack of *mezzadria* contracts to this avoidance of direct involvement.[110] Profits came from usurious transactions. He increased his income through the bonding of the peasantry and by increasing the cultivable land at his disposal without improving productivity, without the commercialization of agricultural production, and without investing capital. It is for these reasons that Polica talks of backwardness and of a 'rickety farm structure'.[111] For all his frenzied

[107] e.g., AN 700(1), fo. 23^{v}.

[108] Pietro di Stefano Bernardi in 1451 lent 20 ducats to the community of Menabbio, to buy pigs: ibid., fos. 14^{v}–15^{v}.

[109] Polica, 'Attempted "Reconversion" of Wealth'. What follows is based on Polica's article. I have worked independently on Michele Guinigi, and—although the article contains some errors of detail—I am in substantial agreement with Polica's conclusions.

[110] Polica distinguishes the share-cropping agreements in the Lucchesia (*colonia parziaria*) from *mezzadria classica*, with the specific implications of the latter for landlord–tenant relations.

[111] Polica, 'Attempted "Reconversion" of Wealth', 671.

activity, Michele Guinigi's career falls far short of illustrating the diversion of an urban business mentality to the problems of estate management.

The question arises as to how far the case-study of Michele di Giovanni Guinigi reflects a mentality characteristic of the Lucchese patriciate as a whole. Michele was clearly atypical—if not unique—in his total withdrawal from trade. The withdrawal was a personal choice, unrelatable either to diminishing commercial opportunities or to the peculiar circumstances of the Guinigi family in the era after the fall of the Guinigi *signoria*.[112] Nor was Michele Guinigi typical in his aggressive exploitation of peasant debts and labour. Many Lucchese landlords were involved in the improvement of deteriorated land in the middle of the fifteenth century.[113] Most followed the path of very low rents and extended leases, at least for the years when the land was being brought back into cultivation.[114] Michele Guinigi granted no such concessions, but relied rather on his power over his peasant debtors.[115] Michele Guinigi's approach seems to have been peculiarly harsh, though there were other individuals who were equally active in land purchases with conditional redemptions, and who seem to have been at one with Guinigi in seeing this as a method of acquiring land rather than as a mechanism for the provision of credit—the names of Agostino di Giovanni da Ghivizzano, his brother Iacopo, Nicolao di Michele ser Federighi, and, perhaps, the *speziale* Mariano di Giovanni come most readily to mind.[116] It is probably no

[112] Polica tries to link Michele Guinigi's activities to the status of the Guinigi after Paolo. But Michele's abandonment of trade was paralleled in the lives neither of his half-brothers nor of his sons.

[113] A good example is provided by the medical doctor and citizen of Lucca Michele di Nicolao de' Diodati. Between 1455 and 1457 the notarial protocolli of ser Benedetto Franciotti show Diodati involved in ten acts of land purchase. Two of these contracts involved urban property in Lucca; a third in pieve S. Paolo close to the city probably concealed a loan to another Lucchese citizen. The remaining acts concerned the purchase of largely undeveloped and wooded lands to the east of Lucca in the area of Lunata and Capannori: AN 700(2–5), 17 Apr., 30 May, 20 June, 25 June, 26 June (two documents) 1455, 6 Feb., 15 May (two documents) 1456, 19 Feb. 1457.

[114] Michele Diodati (n. 113 above), on 1 Aug. 1455 leased certain lands to Nanni Giovanni alias Cerro da Capannori for six years. Nanni was to hold the land rent-free for the first three years, and thereafter was to render 2 *staia* of grain in rent *per coltra* farmed: AN 700(4), 1 Aug. 1455.

[115] Polica, 'Attempted "Reconversion" of Wealth', 692–3, where he recognizes that Michele Guinigi was probably in this regard following a different path to most of his contemporaries.

[116] Most prominent citizens were involved occasionally in this kind of transaction, and credit was offered in this form not only to countrymen but also to fellow citizens. Certain names, however, seem to appear with particular regularity in these initially fictitious sales.

accident that, his mind concentrated by the prospect of death, Agostino da Ghivizzano in his will of 3 July 1462 showed more than a little concern for the victims of his earlier confiscations. All men who had lost their lands to Agostino, through failure to meet the terms of repurchase, were to be given one year from the present notification in which to repurchase their property for the price at which the testator or his father had bought it. In cases where the time of repurchase had not already elapsed, 'sellers' were also to be given an extra year beyond that stipulated in the contract.[117]

In other respects Michele Guinigi was probably a much more representative figure. Presumably most Lucchese landowners were anxious to bind tenants to themselves. This could be achieved through the ruthless recording of debts; no less effective must have been contracts that 'generously' provided that a loan was repayable only when the tenant gave up his lease. All landlords (no matter how acquisitive in their relations with the peasantry at large) were presumably anxious to remain on good terms with their own regular and reliable tenants. Sante Polica, noting an absence of tension specifically in the relationship between landlord and tenant, assumes that tenants did not notice what Michele Guinigi was doing to them.[118] His explanation is probably too harsh a judgement on the perspicacity of countrymen. The more loquacious *ricordi* of Michele's brother Girolamo hint throughout at the presence and involvement of countrymen and women—apparently often *coloni*—in the life of this great patrician family as it passed through the natural rhythm of birth, marriage, and death.[119]

Above all, Michele Guinigi was probably entirely typical in his passive attitude towards landownership, excepting only his passions for land acquisition and for rent and debt collection. Perhaps the nature of our sources has caused historians to underestimate the amount of direct farming still taking place in Tuscany.[120] Certainly the notarial protocolli refer irregularly to agricultural wage labour—labourers usually earning 40

[117] ASL Archivio Arnolfini, 2, fo. 95^{r-v}.

[118] Polica, 'Attempted "Reconversion" of Wealth', 691 n. 121.

[119] ASL Archivio Guinigi, 29. Country-dwellers (and servants) appear particularly prominently in the lists of *compari* and *comari*, suggesting perhaps confinements in the countryside. Girolamo's kinsman Pietro di Nicolao died—suddenly, without the sacraments—on his estates in Segromigno on 17 Oct. 1469: ibid., fo. 17^{v}. It remains perilous to draw conclusions about Michele from Girolamo's *ricordi*, more especially since the *ricordi* provide the best evidence for the former's outrageously grasping nature.

[120] Polica, 'Attempted "Reconversion" of Wealth', 682. Understandably, sources that are primarily concerned with the purchase and leasing of land are silent on the matter of direct farming.

bolognini a month by the mid-fifteenth century.[121] The existence of a pool of agricultural labour is also suggested by characters such as the ploughman of Lucca, Bartolomeo Franceschi, involved in a brawl in 1451.[122] Probably Sante Polica has minimized the incidence of consolidated *poderi* in the fifteenth-century Lucchese state. The processes by which the *poderi* were formed are controversial;[123] in the quattrocento there are many examples of landowners rationalizing the borders of their lands by purchase and exchange. But there is no indication of significant capital investment in agriculture. Neither the late medieval economic crisis nor any other imperative coaxed Lucchese landlords beyond the *rentier* mentality exemplified by Michele di Giovanni Guinigi. Indeed, the urban statutory controls over the productive capacity of the countryside may well have rendered the introduction of capitalist agriculture impossible.[124]

That in practice individual tenants must have coexisted harmoniously with their landlords palliates none of the contempt felt by urban society for rustics in general. The unwillingness of patrician landowners to invest directly in farming was compatible with the entanglement of individual *contadini* and rural communities in a morass of debts and dependence. The political history of post-Guinigi Lucca testifies to the countryman's image of leading citizens as ravaging wolves.[125] The tensions are so visible that it is appropriate to pause for qualification. In positing a structural antipathy between the residents of town and countryside, it might be noted that in a dispute of 1460 between the merchant Piero di Giovanni da Ghivizzano and his *mezzadro* Piero di Antonio the arbitrators appointed were two countrymen: Lorenzo Mannini da S. Alessio and Appollonio di Gerardo from Decimo but resident in S. Alessio.[126] Piero da Ghivizzano claimed that Piero di Antonio, a native of Pontito though living in Monte S. Quirico, had failed to work his land according to the terms of their agreement. Reviewing the evidence, the arbitrators not only found in

[121] On one occasion, two residents of S. Cassiano di Moriano, Giovanetto di Piero da Valdottavo and Antonio di Coluccio da Mammoli, having leased from the church of S. Frediano land in Acquacalda for four years, then leased their labour to the church for two years at wages of 1 florin per month: AN 702 (ser Benedetto Franciotti), p. 277. Other cases seem to refer to genuine agricultural wage labour.

[122] SB 165, fo. 384ᵛ. Earlier, another ploughman living in Lucca was accused of stealing wood to make a plough: SB 161, fos. 311ᵛ–312ᵛ.

[123] See Osheim's pertinent comments in *An Italian Lordship*, 107–13.

[124] Aymard, 'Feudalism to Capitalism in Italy', 145–6, 191–6; Polica, 'Attempted "Reconversion" of Wealth', 680–1, 697–8.

[125] See above, pp. 66–7, 71–2.

[126] AN 704 (ser Benedetto Franciotti), pp. 207, 213.

favour of the merchant, but imposed very heavy penalties on his *mezzadro*: 11 *staia* of grain for the seed lent to Piero di Antonio during the past year for sowing on da Ghivizzano's land; 24 *staia* of grain in damages, since Piero di Antonio had not worked the land well and in good time, whereby the land would not bear fruit that year; 6 *staia* in damages and interest, since Piero di Antonio had failed to reap the grain sown on the land under *mezzadria*, which was then damaged by water. Such penalties were imposed on Piero di Antonio not by an unsympathetic urban court but by men who were apparently his peers.

Parallel nuances are suggested in a case brought before the *Capitano del contado* in 1476.[127] At first sight the case appears to be a clear example of aggression by members of a rural community against a Lucchese citizen. Ser Eustachio Mei, notary and count palatine, claimed that in April 1476 six men of Saltocchio had threatened him and had offended against his person. He demanded that the rural commune of Saltocchio be compelled to provide sureties of £500 not to offend against him in future. A little later a seventh man, 'Lazaretus Lumbardus', was alleged to have threatened ser Eustachio. The case was initially complicated when one of the accused, Lorenzo di Pereto de la Scessa, claimed (successfully) to be a Lucchese citizen, and consequently not subject to the jurisdiction of the *Capitano del contado*. All the accused were then released so that they might return to work. Their release was at the petition of Girolamo di Giovanni Guinigi and Nicodemo di Piero da Ghivizzano, who promised to present them again before the *Capitano* at his request. When duly presented on 27 April, four of the accused promised not to offend ser Eustachio in person or property, under pain of a fine of £125. And Guinigi and da Ghivizzano obligated themselves for this sum on behalf of the Saltocchio men. In his *ricordi* Girolamo Guinigi protested that ser Eustachio had detained Andrea and Pasquino di Bartolomeo di Simo da Saltocchio and the others against all right, and that 'a loro preghiere' he had come to their assistance.[128] Guinigi believed that ser Eustachio had been guilty of dishonest dealings with the commune, and that his action had resulted from spite (*per dispetto*). The Guinigi possessed a great deal of land around Saltocchio; the case shows not so much the innate hostility between citizens and *contadini*, but rather the bonds of sympathy and support binding a local community to a major local landowner.

[127] ASL Capitano del Contado, 79, fos. 21^{r}–24^{v}, 34^{r-v}.

[128] ASL Archivio Guinigi, 29, Girolamo Guinigi, Libro di ricordi, fo. 30^{v}. Guinigi did not deny the threats; it seems to have been on the legal technicality of the Saltocchio men's detention as 'sospetti' that Guinigi protested.

In reality the Lucchese court records provide a very fragile source for the analysis of relations between citizens and *contadini*. The records are richly illustrative of actions (including violent actions), but are very deficient when it comes to probing motivation. The series Sentenze e bandi is full of examples of damage to citizen-owned lands by pillage, trespass, and the activities of grazing animals large and small. Some of these acts were patently devoid of malice, as with the two boys who stole pears from the estate of Bartolomeo Bettini in pieve Segromigno[129] or even Antonio di Antonio da Sillicano, who started a fire on his own land in Marlia which spread to burn down houses belonging to Pietro di Francesco Accettanti in S. Pietro a Vico.[130] The general range of petty rural offences were not of necessity directed against citizens by rural dwellers, but as frequently involved contiguous communities, near neighbours, and even fellow citizens.[131] A Lucchese merchant, Piero di Giovanni Rapondi, and a resident of Marlia, Andrea Granucci, might unite to protest against damage done to their respective lands by cows of the men of Marlia.[132] When grazing beasts wandered on to the cultivated lands of citizens, the immediate victim was the tenant who had sown the crop and whose capacity to meet his obligations was jeopardized; often it was the tenant rather than the urban landlord who demanded redress.[133] Certainly there were some spectacular acts of devastation caused by pigs: the pigs of citizens on the lands of *contadini*, the pigs of *contadini* on the

[129] SB 161, fos. 53^{v}, 69^{r}. The two men of S. Colombano, pieve Segromigno, fined for cutting wood on the land of Piero di Giovanni Rapondi not unreasonably protested that nobody lived in that place excepting themselves and one other, a foreigner: ibid., fo. 290^{r}; Rif. 15, p. 497. These same men were clearly taking advantage of their isolation, since they were also accused by Lodovico di Guglielmo de' Gigli of stealing his grapes: SB 161, fos. 207^{r}–208^{r}.

[130] The fire was allegedly started deliberately, for which Antonio was sentenced to death *in absentia*. But it could hardly have been targeted at Pietro Accettanti: SB 161, fo. 53^{r-v}. In a similar case from Massa Macinaia, a *colono* of Nicolao Avvocati started a fire that burnt down a house belonging to Nicolao Garzoni: SB 162, fos. 322^{v}–323^{r}.

[131] A comprehensive survey of SB 202, for 1493, reveals, unsurprisingly, that in the vicariates (except perhaps in Camaiore), disputes over damages were overwhelmingly between local residents, and that in the Sei Miglia the damaged property was likely to belong to a Lucchese citizen. Throughout the period the owners of the offending animals were very likely to be Lucchese butchers: SB 161, fos. 54^{v}, 59^{v}, 64^{r}, 229^{r-v}, 295^{v}–296^{r}, 332^{v}.

[132] SB 161, fos. 219^{r-v}, 240^{r-v}, 287^{r-v}.

[133] See, e.g., ibid., fo. 192^{r-v}, where Nanni di Domenico of Acquacalda accuses Nanni di Colombano of S. Lorenzo a Picciorana of damaging, with his twenty-four cows, lands (including vineyards) in Monte S. Quirico that the accuser leased from the wife of Stefano di Poggio. See also ibid., fos. 282^{r-v}, 295^{v}–296^{r} (which also refers to a farm in the suburbs leased from Stefano di Poggio by Nanni di Domenico of Acquacalda), and 311^{r-v} (where the lessee was himself a Lucchese citizen and silk weaver).

lands of citizens.[134] The court records amply illustrate the threat posed in the Lucchesia by pigs.[135] It is difficult to identify a pattern, and impossible to forge this material into evidence of rural resistance to encroaching urban capital. It is equally difficult to show that in such cases the claims by citizens for damages were treated overly sympathetically by the courts.[136]

It is often difficult to identify a clear polarity of forces even in cases where *contadini* stand accused of deliberately attacking the persons of citizens (or their tenants) or of disturbing the peaceful possession of citizens. In 1492 Bartolomeo Angiorelli employed Antonio Martelli da Fibbialla, 'laborator et colonus', to collect chestnuts on his land in S. Frediano a Piazzano. He was shown the borders of the lands claimed for his employer by Bartolomeo's former *colono*, Lazzaro di Berto da Piazzano, and the next day showed the confines to two of his daughters before leaving them to collect chestnuts. But the girls were rapidly chased off the land by three men of Piazzano led by Paolo di Marco Malsangue, and a few days later the father was similarly threatened with violence should he harvest chestnuts on behalf of Bartolomeo Angiorelli—threats that were effective enough to cause Antonio and his family to leave the land.[137] On the one hand, the lines of division are complicated by the witness of a local man—a neutral who, according to the formula, was friend to both parties, neither creditor nor debtor nor 'famulus' nor 'colonus' nor 'operarius' of the said Bartolomeo—who insisted that

[134] Men of Capannori were accused of doing great damage with their pigs, which they kept 'in great multitudes and quantities' in the area bounded by a triangle from Porcari to Montecarlo to S. Martino a Colle: ibid., fos. 130^{r}–131^{v}. Plaintiffs and defendants were alternately citizens and *contadini* in two juxtaposed cases both involving pigs in chestnut groves: ASL Cause Delegate, 3, pp. 43–5. Assaults on pig-keepers were presumably most likely to arise from the pig-keepers' negligence in the care of their charges. For unspecified reasons, Andrea di Bartolomeo Fantezzi of S. Lorenzo a Picciorana came to words with the *porchario* Guglielmo di Antonio, whom he hit with a wooden stick (*bastone*) on the lands of Nicolao Busdraghi: ASL Capitano del Contado, 51, 1st foliation, fos. 63^{r}–64^{r}; SB 165, fo. 481^{r-v}.

[135] Legislation to control the keeping of pigs was motivated both by the damage that they caused and also because of the perceived health hazard: Rif. 16, pp. 418, 434–5, 724, 744–5. For attempts to implement this legislation, see ASL Capitano del Contado, 51, 1st foliation, fos. 70^{r} ff.; 2nd foliation, fos. 29^{r} ff.; and the unfoliated sections of both this volume and Capitano del Contado, 52. Of all cases before the *Capitano del contado* between 1441 and 1461, 37 per cent involved the keeping of pigs in prohibited places: Casali, 'Aspetti della criminalità nel contado lucchese', 4–6.

[136] Citizens themselves were often found guilty of causing damage, whilst suits brought by citizens were often dismissed, particularly if vague: SB 159, fo. 84^{r-v}; 161, fos. 194^{r}–195^{r}, 328^{v}–329^{v}; Rif. 17, p. 147.

[137] SB 202, fos. 386^{r-v}, 410^{r}; ASL Podestà di Lucca, Inquisizioni, 5362, fos. 222^{r}, 234^{r}–236^{r}, 245^{r}.

Bartolomeo Angiorelli had held and possessed the land in Piazzano for thirty years. On the other hand, the division of forces is complicated by the fact that the three men of Piazzano were found not guilty and absolved.

Apart from the involvement as principals of an urban landowner and a group of men from the *contado*, the dispute regarding Angiorelli's land is indistinguishable from any number of other conflicts over possession—from a case in Saltocchio, for example, where Paolo di Francesco di Piero del Cima da Saltocchio, seeing Biagio di Piero da S. Gemignano with his son working a piece of land which Paolo claimed belonged to his father, ordered them to stop, and, when they failed to do so, attacked them with a stick (*bastone*).[138] In 1457, Nicolao di Domenico of Saltocchio, armed with an iron *clavarina* with wooden *scotata* (called a *clavarina pistorensis*), killed a horse belonging to ser Eustachio Mei which was on Nicolao's *podere*.[139] Does the case show rural hostility to Lucchese citizens? or the more specific tensions between the community of Saltocchio and ser Eustachio Mei noted above? or merely a vigorous defence of the millet sown on Nicolao's farm, upon which the horse was clearly grazing? We simply do not know why a man of Vallecchia set fire to property of the heirs of Francesco Sbarra in Vallecchia[140] or why a man of Fivizzano followed the pregnant wife of a citizen to her house in Mommio, where he stabbed her with a lance (*lancia*) so that she aborted.[141] The court records provide no trace of the motivation for the attempt to kill ser Massino di Bartolomeo da Pietrasanta in Nozzano;[142] or for the threat to the person and property of Francesco di Poggio by a resident of the vicariate of Camporgiano.[143]

The Lucchese court records illustrate the endemic violence of the countryside; but the message of individual cases is usually highly ambiguous. Beyond the ambiguities, we find countrymen willing to testify on behalf of citizens and citizens testifying to the honesty and diligent service of *contadini* defendants. Countrymen often obtained favourable verdicts before the law administered from the city. We know of the bands of armed men maintained by citizens in the countryside.[144] Just as in the

[138] SB 161, fo. 191^{r-v}. In a further possible permutation, the Lucchese apothecary Quirico Viviani, with his son and another relative, drove ser Iacopo da Fiano from his land, and took his hemp, in another of these interminable disputes over possession: SB 162, fos. 85^{r}–86^{r}; Rif. 16, pp. 65–6.

[139] ASL Capitano del Contado, 55, 1st foliation, fos. 11^{r}–13^{v}. The weapon was clearly a small club, heavy and gnarled.

[140] ASL Podestà di Lucca, Inquisizioni, 5224, fo. 5^{r}.

[141] SB 161, fo. 220^{r-v}.

[142] SB 162, fos. 148^{r}–149^{r}.

[143] ASL Capitano del Contado, 79, fo. 35^{r}.

[144] Rif. 22, pp. 30–1.

city horizontal and vertical allegiances might, in practice, coexist in the same mind, so in the countryside attacks on individual citizens may well mask the rivalries of urban patrons. Individual relationships conformed to no simple pattern. Yet the stereotyped attitudes are unmistakable, as is the underlying atmosphere of tension between rural dwellers and the privileged citizens with whom contact was so often on economically disadvantageous terms.

When on 29 October 1438 the restored republic turned its attention to the problem of disorder in the countryside with the appointment of ser Bartolomeo de' Paraventi di Todi as *Capitano del contado*, the concern was specifically 'to curb the pride of rustics'.[145] The early 1440s saw quite a lot of attacks on citizens and their tenants. Most notably in September 1440, no less a person than the doctor of decretals, vicar of the bishop of Lucca, Lazzaro Guinigi, was hit about the body by Benedetto di Frediano of the *contrada dei sobborghi* SS. Annunziata who, armed with a billhook (*roncola*), chased Guinigi up to the walls of the suburbs (with the intention of hitting him again).[146] It may well be no coincidence that only a month later the Gonfaloniere di Giustizia explained in the General Council that because of the arrogance and malice of rustics the possessions of many citizens lay uncultivated, and that measures were necessary to combat this evil.[147] In the 'Ordines contra rusticos' that followed on 27 October 1440, a fine of £100 was provided for anyone who threatened tenants or workers of the land or who in any way discouraged *coloni* or agricultural labourers from remaining on the land, working or leasing it.[148] Further penalties were stipulated for threatening words and conduct, the fines graded according to whether the parties involved were citizens, non-citizens, or foreigners.

The ordinances passed in 1440 clearly had a limited effect. Antoniaccio Marchioni was murdered in July 1442 on the piece of land in the territory

[145] 'Utile et necessarium videtur esse, quod provideatur de uno Capitano Comitatus ad refraenandas superbias rusticorum, qui per impunitatem delictorum in dies magis molesti efficiuntur Civibus suis': Rif. 15, pp. 298–307. For the history of the office and its change of emphasis from the protection to the control of *contadini*, see Casali, 'L'amministrazione del Contado Lucchese'. For the origins of the office, see also Leverotti, 'Ricerche sull'amministrazione della vicaria di Massa', 140–1.

[146] SB 162, fo. 64^{r-v}. Benedetto was fined the very high sum of £200 for the first offence and £50 for the second. Although the conviction of *contadini* was far from a foregone conclusion, when convicted, offences against citizens commanded higher penalties than offences against *contadini*.

[147] Rif. 15, pp. 512–13.

[148] Ibid., pp. 518–20.

of Camaiore that he leased from Giovanni Sbarra.[149] But the real *cause célèbre* was the murder in September of the same year of the merchant and citizen of Lucca Cione Guerci. Tensions may initially have arisen when Giorgio Fantossi and other men of S. Lorenzo a Picciorana grazed their cows and oxen on Cione Guerci's land.[150] The pasturing offence presumably preceded the more dramatic, though entirely unexplained, dispute over grapes and other fruits on Cione's land. Interestingly, Cione was personally harvesting the fruits of his land. Seeing him, Giorgio Fantossi, now described as of the commune of S. Vito a Picciorana, turned to his sons, Matteo, Lorenzo, and Francesco, and instructed them: 'Unyoke the oxen, leave your work, and go to gather those grapes.' Thereupon they took up various weapons, went to the field where Cione was working, and attacked and killed him. Wisely, the men of Picciorana failed to turn up for their trial. Giorgio was banished from the Lucchese state under pain of death and confiscation of property. His sons were sentenced to death. From their goods, £200 was to be paid in compensation to the sons and heirs of the murdered man.[151] Father and sons clearly fled to the haven of Pietrasanta, from where in 1446 the Florentine notarial records show them appointing Giorgio's brother Bartolomeo (still living in S. Lorenzo a Picciorana) as procurator to make peace with Cione's son and other kin.[152]

So blatant an act of aggression against a Lucchese citizen called for an immediate response from the highest level. The very next day, the murder was being discussed in the General Council. The first object of the Council's wrath was obviously the delinquents themselves. To remove all doubts, the Council approved the razing of the murderers' house. Two citizens per *terziere* were elected who, together with the Anziani, were to have power against Giorgio and his sons; whatever they proposed was to have the force of law. But the wider challenge to the city and to right order was not lost on the city's rulers. They were acting 'ad terrorem rusticorum et foretanorum seu comitatinorum'. The general object was to teach countrymen a lesson for offending against citizens. The same two citizens per *terziere* were to make statutes and ordinances to this effect. Further, from henceforth, in perpetuity, the Anziani were granted full powers to deal with any countryman or foreigner who offended against a citizen in

[149] SB 162, fo. 277^{r-v}.
[150] Ibid., fo. 325^{r-v}.
[151] Ibid., fos. 321^{r}–322^{r}.
[152] NAC, N 115 (ser Nicolao di Coluccio di Pellegrino da Pietrasanta, 1409–68), fos. 163^{v}–164^{r}.

civil or criminal matters; whatever they might decree was to have immediate force, with this condition that they were not able to impose lower penalties than those contained in the statutes.[153]

The official records are scattered with measures designed to keep countrymen in their place; the prevailing attitude is one of fear tinged with distaste. Countrymen were not slow to take advantage of their official image. In appeals against adverse judgments they defended their illegal acts in terms of their inborn ignorance and stupidity. The image stemmed from a disregard that is probably more revealing than the occasional overt acts of violence. One case in particular neatly sums up the meeting of the two worlds. In the summer of 1449 the wife of a Lucchese citizen, Giuntino di maestro Guido da Campi, was going to Parmatorato to the house of Vanni Nicolai dei borghi, her nephew, 'to pass the time'. Travelling with her female companions, she crossed a *podere* belonging to her nephew, where the ladies stopped to pick cherries. The action aggrieved Vanni's *salani*, men of Parma, who not unreasonably told the ladies that they did wrong to pick the fruit on the farm for which they were paying the rent. Giuntino's wife replied by speaking slightingly of the *salani* as Lombards. To which (they claimed) they answered that if they were Lombards, she was *pratessa*; though she believed that they had said *pretessa*. Whereupon the lady rushed to complain to her husband, who accused the *salani* of 'injurious words' before the court of the *Podestà*. There is the inevitable qualification. Giuntino was unable to establish his case; the countrymen were found not guilty; and it was the citizen who was fined for having failed to prove his accusation.[154]

For all the qualifications with regard both to Lucchese justice and to the nuances of the specifically landlord–tenant relationship, we are left with the urban stereotype of the *contadino* as ignorant, malicious, troublesome, and dangerous. The image of citizens as 'ravaging wolves' probably had a currency in the countryside beyond the bold public utterances of individuals. The wolves were men with deep roots in the countryside, and show little resemblance to any model of the agrarian capitalist bent on turning the rural world upside down. Citizens could still be ruthlessly acquisitive and harshly exploitative, as shown above through the career of Michele di Giovanni Guinigi. They might pose no more of a threat than the thoughtless depredations in the cherry orchard of the wife of Giuntino

[153] Rif. 16, pp. 212–13.

[154] Rif. 17, p. 147. *Pratessa* probably refers to a native of the plains rather than a lady of Prato. The case therefore also provides interesting testimony to tensions between people of the hills and lowlanders. *Pretessa* means priest's concubine.

da Campi and her entourage. For countrymen it was no doubt difficult to distinguish between Lucchese citizens and the state which they controlled. It was for this reason that rural conspirators looked to political revolution and to the restoration of princely rule.[155] But there is no simple identification of the interests of the state with the private interests of the leading citizens who dominated its councils. The relations between Lucca and its *contado*, and particularly the relations between the ruling city and the larger centres of population within its state, constitute an important theme in its own right. It is the subject of the next chapter.

[155] e.g., SB 162, fo. 365ᵛ.

7

THE HEGEMONIC CITY AND ITS SUBJECT COMMUNITIES

The close intertwining of urban and rural interests is paralleled in the relationship between city and state. In the first instance the countryside was the source of food, and particularly of grain. In years of scarcity, provisions for the import of grain were predicated on the most vigilant attempts to stem exports. Thus in 1442, when food shortages were alleged to threaten Lucca's very liberty, all licences to export wheat and other grain were prohibited. Four citizens *sopra l'abbondanza* were elected to ensure adequate grain supplies for the city and to prevent the illegal export of grain from Lucchese territory.[1] The same heightened sensibilities reappeared regularly from the 1460s. In 1463 a committee of nine citizens was elected who, together with the Anziani, were to review the statutes and ordinances for retaining grain within the Lucchese state and to reassess the penalties imposed for its export.[2] In 1473 heavy penalties were imposed on anyone carrying chestnut flour out of the state;[3] and in the difficult year 1483 the attention of Lucchese legislators was focused indiscriminately on all manner of victuals.[4] The Anziani were granted express powers to search the houses of all citizens and *contadini* for food supplies and to arrange for the bringing of victuals to the city. Efforts to monopolize the produce of the dependent territories were supplemented by a concern for effective land utilization. Noting the great expense of acquiring grain from outside Lucchese territory and also the danger of reliance on foreign imports, the General Council in June 1467 decreed that all uncultivated land 'in locis marittimis', suitable for cultivation, must be handed over to the commune

[1] Rif. 16, pp. 203–4. The decrees against exporting grain were again confirmed in Aug. 1444: ibid., p. 418.

[2] Rif. 18, pp. 612–13.

[3] Rif. 20, p. 116. Because of shortages, the *gabella* due on chestnut flour was suspended at this time.

[4] Rif. 21, pp. 491–2.

of Lucca 'a livello perpetuo'.[5] In directing the produce of the countryside to the needs of the city, adequate grain storage within the city walls became a constant of urban policy. In the provisions made in the summer of 1460 for grain storage, specific emphasis was placed on millet because of its better preservative qualities.[6]

The Lucchese state was also a source of revenue. The direct taxes, the individual compositions, and the *gabelle* on mercantile and legal transactions have implications for the relationship between Lucca and its subject communities that will reappear throughout the present chapter. Here it suffices to note three points. First, the inhabitants of Lucca, its suburbs, and the Sei Miglia were exempt from the general obligation to buy a fixed amount of salt per annum.[7] Secondly, the *estimo*, which for citizens was the base for the assessment of forced loans, was in the *contado* an instrument for the collection of that direct taxation which Lucchese citizens had successfully resisted.[8] Finally, in the vicariates and *contado* the *gabelle*, traditionally imposed on the movement of goods between vicariates and on internal transactions, were being replaced in the 1440s by individual agreements with Lucca for the annual payment of a fixed *canone* by the subject communities.[9] The geographical possessions of Lucca were in themselves a source of profit. Herders passing through the Lucchese state brought dues. The dilemma of the General Council in May 1438, when the territories controlled by Lucca were much reduced in the renewed Florentine wars, was that merchants and animals passing from Pisa to Pistoia could so easily evade Lucchese territory altogether that it had become necessary to review local transit dues.[10] The point is important beyond the level of transhumance. Lucca was the centre of a major road network connected with the via Francigena linking France with Rome, which passed through Lucca. The control of the *contado* was intimately linked with the control of roads, and thus of the passage of merchandise.[11] The loss of Castelnuovo to Ferrara, for example, enabled the Marquis of

[5] Rif. 19, p. 281.

[6] ASL Colloqui, 1, p. 50.

[7] From 1388 there had been an attempt to extend the forced distribution of salt to the city: Meek, *Lucca 1369–1400*, 69–70. Bongi confirms that 'in antico' forced distribution was sometimes extended to the communes of the Sei Miglia and of the Suburbani: *Inventario*, ii. 120.

[8] Bongi, *Inventario*, ii. 127.

[9] Ibid. 77.

[10] Rif. 15, pp. 243, 294, 400–1.

[11] There is a particularly useful discussion of this point in Osheim, *An Italian Lordship*, 6–9.

Ferrara to reach an agreement with the men of Barga (by the fifteenth century long lost by Lucca to Florence)[12] for the diversion and tolling of merchandise and animals then passing of necessity through those territories towards Lombardy.[13]

To the economic and fiscal importance of the Lucchese state we must add its military importance. The successful defence of individual castles never, of course, prevented the devastation of the surrounding countryside or the appearance of an enemy army at the very gates of Lucca. But the holding of great fortresses like Nozzano was seen as essential for the defence of the city. The importance of Castiglione and Gallicano to Lucca can be found defined in primarily military terms.[14] The rocca di Bargiglio, called 'the eye of Lucca' because of its strategic importance, was rebuilt and refortified in 1468.[15] More generally, the countryside was a source of military recruits. The universal obligation for military service of all adult males extended in the fourteenth century to both the city and the state. By the end of the fourteenth century the peasant militia had come to be called the *cerne*.[16] The history of the *cerne* in fifteenth-century Lucca is very obscure indeed. The participation of men from the *contado* was encouraged from the 1440s in the crossbow competitions instituted to raise the general level of military preparedness of the population.[17] When, towards the end of the century, attention shifted to gunpowder, parallel tournaments were held in the vicariates to encourage skill in shooting with *archiburgi*.[18] For local defence, many small local communities presumably followed the example set in the statutes of Gallicano: that all over the age of 14 were obliged 'fare le guardie'.[19] Occasionally we see evidence of the *cerne* as a substantial military force raised in the countryside, as in the sending in 1450 of 500 *fanti* and

[12] After some vicissitudes the Barghigiani finally placed themselves under Florentine rule from the 1340s: P. G. Camaiani, 'Le magistrature di Barga dal XV secolo alle riforme leopoldine', in Carla Sodini (ed.), *Barga medicea e le 'enclaves' fiorentine della Versilia e della Lunigiana* (Florence, 1983), 13–14.

[13] MAP, xii. 273.

[14] Rif. 17, p. 517; 18, p. 218.

[15] Rif. 19, pp. 367–8; Polica, 'Attempted "Reconversion" of Wealth', 680.

[16] Bongi, *Inventario*, i. 247.

[17] Rif. 16, pp. 323–4.

[18] Rif. 22, p. 24.

[19] ASG MS 6, p. 64. All males failing to do so were bound to pay 20 bolognini per annum to the *entrata* of the commune of Gallicano. Failure to pay was to be punished by a fine of 1 florin per offence, half of the fine going to the commune of Gallicano and half to the vicar and notary. The statute applied to all people of Gallicano, whether living there or not. Exempt was anyone who had left Gallicano to learn a trade or to learn to read. These were freed for the period that they were away from Gallicano for these purposes.

cerne for the recovery of places in Garfagnana.[20] A head of faction in the Garfagnana with 200–300 men under his command is described as 'formerly head of the *cerne*'.[21] At other times the word seems to be used of the men sent by local communities to Lucca for the illumination of Santa Croce, in symbolic recognition of Lucchese authority.[22] The compositions with the vicariates in the 1440s suggest that the idea of a general military obligation at Lucca's discretion continued to have force.[23] In practice Lucca fought with her own, and often with borrowed, armies of foreign mercenaries. Many men from the wider Lucchese state clearly made a career out of military service to Lucca, but in a paid, professional capacity.[24]

The subject communities were important to Lucca. But throughout the 1430s it is impossible to talk of a Lucchese state as a stable and coherent geographical entity. During the last months of the *signoria* of Paolo Guinigi the Florentines seized most of the eastern parts of Lucca's state, excepting the stronghold of Montecarlo, and they besieged Lucca. The coming of Francesco Sforza in July 1430 brought relief, though with dire consequences for Guinigi rule. The sieges of Lucca and Montecarlo were raised. But then Sforza was bought off by the Florentines, and the Florentine offensive was renewed. By the autumn of 1430 the *castello* of S. Gennaro had fallen, and Lucca was again vigorously besieged. Once more assistance came in the form of a *condottiere* despatched by Milan/Genoa: Niccolò Piccinino was sent to Lucca's aid by Genoa, and won a great victory over the Florentines near S. Anna on 3 December. After his triumphant entry into Lucca, Piccinino began the systematic recovery of territory, moved into the Lunigiana, besieged Pontremoli, and sent men to re-enforce the guard of Montecarlo. But Piccinino was recalled by the Visconti soon after he had taken Pontremoli and Calci in 1431, and Lucca was again left to face the Florentines bereft of significant external support. During these last years of the war, only the visit of the Emperor Sigismund to Lucca in May–June 1432 provided Lucca with a brief respite. There

[20] Anz. Temp. Lib. 532, no. 32, fos. 88ᵛ, 98ᵛ. According to Martino Bernardini, Ricordi Storici, 300 *cerne* were brought to Lucca as a precaution at the time of Iacopo da Ghivizzano's negotiations with the Duke of Milan in May 1446: BSL MS 38, fo. 134ᵛ.

[21] ASL Podestà di Lucca, Inquisizioni, 5270, fo. 108ᵛ.

[22] ASL Gabelle del contado e delle vicarie: Gabella di Pietrasanta 80(11), no foliation. For a much earlier reference to the *cerne* of Pietrasanta, see ASCP MS I, 161, Memorie della Versilia di V. Santini, vol. ii, no foliation.

[23] Rif. 17, pp. 92, 93. The importance of the *cerne* in 15th-century Lucca, beyond the raising of men in an emergency, seems to have been that it enabled Lucca to levy men for specific guard duty: see, e.g., ibid., p. 98.

[24] Anz. Temp. Lib. 6 shows the prevalent granting of *condotte* to men of the vicariates.

were abortive conspiracies to hand over individual castles to Florence: Pedona in the vicariate of Camaiore in May 1431,[25] Montecarlo in October 1432.[26] In the west, Nozzano held out, though all the surrounding countryside was ravaged. The entire vicariate of Massa suffered terribly throughout these wars. The general picture is of a few well-garrisoned castles, particularly in the west, held securely for Lucca whilst the surrounding lands were periodically overrun and sacked. Lucca itself was again besieged, both before and after the visit of the Emperor Sigismund. There were some Lucchese victories towards the end of 1432. Then in March 1433 both Cune and Decimo fell to soldiers in Lucca's pay who had been suborned by the Florentines.[27] The peace of April 1433 must have come as a great relief to Lucca. By its terms, Florence promised to return all lands, particularly in the vicariates of Valdriana, Valdilima, and Coreglia, seized from Lucca since 1428.[28]

Deteriorating relations of Milan with Genoa, the Papacy, and Florence brought Lucca (as Milan's ally) into renewed conflict with Florence in 1436. The war began well for Lucca. Niccolò Piccinino swept through Pisan territory, entered the Lunigiana, and seized Sarzana. At the beginning of 1437 he turned his attentions against Barga, where he suffered a major reverse. By May 1437 Piccinino had been recalled to Lombardy by the Duke of Milan, and Lucca was left exposed to the full fury of the Florentines. This time Lucca's losses were much more comprehensive. Francesco Sforza, again in the employ of Florence, took Sarzana, Massa, and Camaiore. Now even the great fortresses of Montecarlo and Nozzano were lost by Lucca, and yet again the city itself was besieged. At the time of the peace negotiations of 1438 nothing much was left of the Lucchese state beyond the city walls, apart from a few castles: Castiglione, Coreglia, and Lucchio. The last was only saved for Lucca by the ingenuity of two young peasant girls.[29]

By terms of the peace of 28 April 1438, Florence returned to Lucca all the communes of the Sei Miglia excluding Nozzano and Ruota, the fate of these last to be decided by Sforza. Of the vicariates, Castiglione was to be restored to Lucca, excepting Sassi. Coreglia was to remain with Lucca, but the fate of

[25] SB 159, fos. 168^{r}–170^{v}, 175^{r}.

[26] Ibid., fos. 210^{r}–211^{v}.

[27] SB 160, fos. 242^{r}–243^{r}.

[28] There are full MS accounts of the war in BSL MS 2599, Antonio Iova, Annali Historici, pp. 841–84, and in BSL MS 939, Gio: Lunardo Dalli, Cronache, pp. 88–154. Both accounts contain manifest errors. The war is treated briefly in Tommasi, 'Storia di Lucca', 311–19, and in Mazzarosa, *Storia di Lucca*, ii. 5–11.

[29] Rif. 15, p. 322. For a description of this incident, see BSL MS 26, Alessandro Spada, Storia di Lucca, fo. 99^{v}.

Ghivizzano and the rest of the vicariate of Coreglia was left to Sforza. Ghivizzano was still held by Sforza in April 1440.[30] For the period 1438–41 Lucca's power was effectively confined to the area of the Sei Miglia. Better terms were achieved in the league made with Florence in March 1441, according to which Lucca was promised all the lands that she had lost since 1428. Sforza restored the vicariate of Coreglia, and on 14 May 1441 representatives of a long list of communes in the vicariate of Coreglia swore loyalty to Lucca.[31] Camaiore was duly returned in 1442, though not—apparently—without some attempt by the local Florentine authorities to persuade the inhabitants to opt for Florentine rule.[32] In the west, distant Montignoso was recovered,[33] and in the east, Villa Basilica and the Valdriana. Negotiations were set in motion for the restoration of Massa and Camporgiano. Only in the case of Motrone and Montecarlo, now both lost permanently to Lucca,[34] did the Florentines prove inflexible. Motrone was Lucca's port; Montecarlo controlled approaches from the east. Both were of great importance to Lucca; they were described as 'the keys to Lucca' during the negotiations.[35] Nevertheless, in territorial terms Lucca's losses to Florence as a result of the wars of 1428–38 were very modest. To other enemies, and to erstwhile allies, territorial losses were more considerable.

On 17 December 1429 the Marchese Niccolò d'Este of Ferrara received the submission of the communes of Silico and Bargecchia. By the end of the month, he had acquired most of the vicariate of Gallicano; much of the vicariate of Castiglione, including Castelnuovo but excluding Castiglione itself; and Eglio in the vicariate of Camporgiano. In February 1430 all these lands were united in a new Estense vicariate centred on Castelnuovo.[36] Estensi acquisitions in the Garfagnana appear to have been achieved in part through the activities of Niccolò's agents, in part because of local rivalries and grievances. In later years the idea was fostered that Ferrara intervened in the Garfagnana to preserve these places for Lucca against the forces of Florence.[37] The Este correspondence would seem to indicate that, whilst

[30] Rif. 17, p. 44.

[31] Rif. 16, pp. 55–7.

[32] ASL Biblioteca (Manoscritti), 26, M. Bianco Bianchi, Historie della terra di Camaiore, no foliation or pagination; 30, Pellegrino di Bartolomeo Pellegrini da Camaiore, Memorie, fo. 2r.

[33] Sforza, *Montignoso*, 41–4.

[34] Motrone was lost to Florence by treachery in July 1437: SB 161, fos. 170r–171v. Motrone was temporarily recovered by Lucca for a brief period after 1496.

[35] MAP, xi. 418.

[36] De Stefani, *Garfagnana*, 171–7.

[37] e.g., BSL MS 26, Alessandro Spada, Storia di Lucca, fo. 94r; MS 38, Martino Bernardini, Ricordi Storici, fo. 395r; MS 939, Gio: Lunardo Dalli, Cronache, p. 96. Dalli

playing his own hand, the ruler of Ferrara acted as an ally more of Florence than of Lucca.[38] However aligned, it soon became clear that Niccolò d'Este had no intention of relinquishing his new possessions. Following the peace of 1433, and again after 1438, Lucca made every effort to include the places of the Garfagnana in the general restoration of lands to pre-1429 boundaries. On 19 June 1434 nine Lucchese citizens were appointed to recover castles and lands held by the Este during the late war.[39] In 1435 and again in 1440 the old enemy Florence was petitioned to use her influence with Ferrara for the restoration of Lucchese lands.[40] Not only were these moves unsuccessful, but when, under the terms of the peace, Florence attempted to restore the reluctant men of Camporgiano to Lucchese rule, Leonello d'Este took advantage of the troubled state of the region to add the vicariate of Camporgiano to the Ferrarese state, in 1446.[41] Gallicano and its surrounding communities[42] restored themselves to Lucchese obedience in 1450; Camporgiano and Castelnuovo were recovered very briefly by Lucca in 1512. Apart from the territory of Gallicano, Lucca's losses to the Este in the 1430s and 1440s were to prove permanent.

A rather less independent northern challenge to the Lucchese state came from the Malaspina. Marchese Antonio Alberico Malaspina di Fosdinovo, as ally of Florence, had occupied the vicariate of Camporgiano at the end of 1429.[43] On 17 October 1431 Antonio Alberico was sentenced to death and confiscation of property for his attacks against Carrara, Moneta, Ortonuovo, Massa, Casoli oltre Giogo, and Minucciano.[44] Attacks on Carrara, Ortonuovo, and on rocca Moneta were indeed led by men of Carrara in the service of the Malaspina of Fosdinovo.[45] But the Lucchese sources draw only the haziest distinction between the Florentines and their Malaspina ally, Antonio Alberico in fact having obtained Florentine citizenship for himself

argues that Niccolò d'Este feared the threat to Ferrara occasioned by the Florentine advance into the Garfagnana, and therefore took the rest of the province under his protection, 'con protesta di ritenerli a devotione de Lucchesi'.

[38] De Stefani, *Garfagnana*, 175–7. Certainly Este links were closer with the Guinigi than with the new republican regime. Later Castelnuovo became an important centre for Lucchese exiles, and Niccolò d'Este was suspected of favouring the ambitions of Ladislao Guinigi.

[39] Anz. Temp. Lib. 5, 19 June 1434; De Stefani, *Garfagnana*, 188–91.

[40] MAP, xi. 418; xii. 108.

[41] BSL MS 47, Antichità di Lucca, fo. 299^{r}; MS 91, Storie di Lucca, fos. 98^{r}–100^{v}; MS 939, Gio: Lunardo Dalli, Cronache, p. 207; De Stefani, *Garfagnana*, 192–200.

[42] Gallicano, Verni, Bolognana, Perpoli, Fiattone, Lupinaia, Trepignana, and Riana.

[43] De Stefani, *Garfagnana*, 173.

[44] SB 160, fo. 106^{r-v}.

[45] Ibid., fos. 11^{r-v}, 129^{r-v}; ASL Vicario di Massa Lunese, Atti Criminali, 261, fos. 2^{r}–3^{r}.

and his descendants in 1429.[46] It was to Florence that, of their own free will, the men of Minucciano, Agliano, and Renzano offered submission in December 1429, and thereafter Minucciano was under the custody of a constable of Florence.[47] All these lands—which in the distant past had belonged to the Malaspina—were returned to Lucca under the terms of the peace of 1433. Things were to change during the second Florentine war, when the Florentines, on reconquering the Garfagnana in 1437, apparently handed over the *podesterìa* of Casoli, including Minucciano, to their Malaspina ally.[48] A letter of 10 January 1439 to Cosimo de' Medici hints at Antonio Alberico's reluctance to return to Lucca the lands that he was holding.[49] In an apparently spontaneous act of submission in March 1442, Casoli, Minucciano, and the surrounding communes gave themselves to the Malaspina.[50] Minucciano, Renzano, and Agliano rebelled against Antonio Alberico's successor in 1449, and returned to Lucca.[51] Casoli remained with the Malaspina, passing to Florence at the end of the century.

More permanent gains were made by the Malaspina in the west. The Florentines had conquered Massa in 1437. In this arena too they were closely allied with Antonio Alberico Malaspina di Fosdinovo. In Massa, as elsewhere, negotiations between Lucca and Florence for the restoration of lands were delayed by internal divisions. On 8 December 1442 a public parliament of the commune and vicariate of Massa accepted an agreement between their representatives and Antonio Alberico whereby the men of Massa swore obedience to the Malaspina, and in return the Marchese promised to govern and defend them.[52] In 1473 Carrara, Avenza, and Moneta—lands acquired by Genoa/Milan during the second Florentine war and subsequently ruled by members of the Campofregoso family, sometime doges of Genoa—were consigned by the Duke of Milan to the Marchese di Massa.[53] Genoa's most important gain from Lucca had been Pietrasanta, which had rebelled against Lucca in 1436.[54] The vicariate of Pietrasanta, excluding the territory of Montignoso, was ruled by Genoa,

[46] Branchi, *Lunigiana feudale*, iii. 546–7.

[47] De Stefani, *Garfagnana*, 171, 178; ASL Podestà di Casoli oltre Giogo, Atti Civili, 31, fos. 50^r–51^v, 52^v; NAC, N 115 (ser Nicolao di Coluccio di Pellegrino da Pietrasanta, 1416–34), 2nd foliation, fo. 32^r.

[48] De Stefani, *Garfagnana*, 191.

[49] MAP, xi. 207.

[50] De Stefani, *Garfagnana*, 195.

[51] Ibid. 200–1; Rif. 17, pp. 161, 167–9.

[52] AS Massa, Pergamene, 349/374, 8 Dec. 1442.

[53] AS Massa, Archivio dei Malaspina di Fosdinovo Marchesi di Massa, 1, nos. 7, 15, 30; Branchi, *Lunigiana feudale*, iii. 757–72.

[54] See below, pp. 243–50.

later by the Banco di San Giorgio, until captured by Florence in 1484. Like Carrara and Massa, Pietrasanta was permanently lost to Lucca from the 1430s if we exclude a couple of decades of renewed Lucchese control following the French intervention of 1494.

Throughout the 1430s the Lucchese state was a fragile and transitory entity. Former Lucchese territories were to be contested between Lucca's neighbours throughout the rest of the century. For Lucca herself the negotiations with Florence of 1438–41 brought a new stability. With the regaining of Minucciano in 1449 and of Gallicano in 1450, Lucca attained the boundaries that, with minor adjustments, were going to endure. To the west was the detached enclave of Montignoso; to the north, Minucciano, Castiglione, and Gallicano. For the rest, the late fifteenth-century Lucchese state was compact and cohesive, if considerably smaller than the territory ruled over by Castruccio Castracani. In essentials it differed little from the state portrayed in the map of 1569 by Alessandro Resta which now hangs in Lucca in the Archivio di Stato.[55]

The political vicissitudes of the Lucchese state provide a context for the miseries and dangers endured by its inhabitants. Particularly in the 1430s, but periodically thereafter, Lucca's territories suffered from the movement of armies and from the planned devastation that accompanied siege warfare. Their experience firmly refutes Machiavelli's vision of fifteenth-century warfare as private quarrels between principalities which exempted civilian populations from the traditional harshnesses of war.[56] Certain atrocity stories were to become firmly embedded in Lucca's historical consciousness. Notable here were the sacking and burning of Collodi by the Florentines in 1432, whence scarcely 200 people were able to save themselves by fleeing to Lucca. The same year saw the sack of Villa Basilica and the burning down of the church and bell-tower in Borgo a Mozzano, where many people, including women, had taken refuge.[57] More generally, a high proportion of appeals for mercy and concessions over the next twenty years were to cite losses and injuries suffered during the Florentine wars.[58] The offenders were not always in the employ of the

[55] The Resta map, which has been reproduced as the frontispiece, also provides the base for Figure 7.1. The map contains serious distortions of scale and direction, but it remains an invaluable guide to the boundaries of the Lucchese state at the end of the 15th cent.

[56] Nicolo Machiavelli, *Florentine History*, trans. W. K. Marriott (London, n.d.), 183–4.

[57] A graphic account appears in BSL MS 2599, Antonio Iova, Annali Historici, pp. 881–2. Iova also tells the story of the alleged letter sent by Florence in 1437 to their commissioners in the field instructing them to kill those from Lucca whom they captured; but if women, to cut their noses and their clothes to the waist and let them go: ibid., pp. 902–3.

[58] Rif. 14, p. 626; 15, pp. 48–9, 243; 16, pp. 280, 473, 711; 17, pp. 57–8, 85.

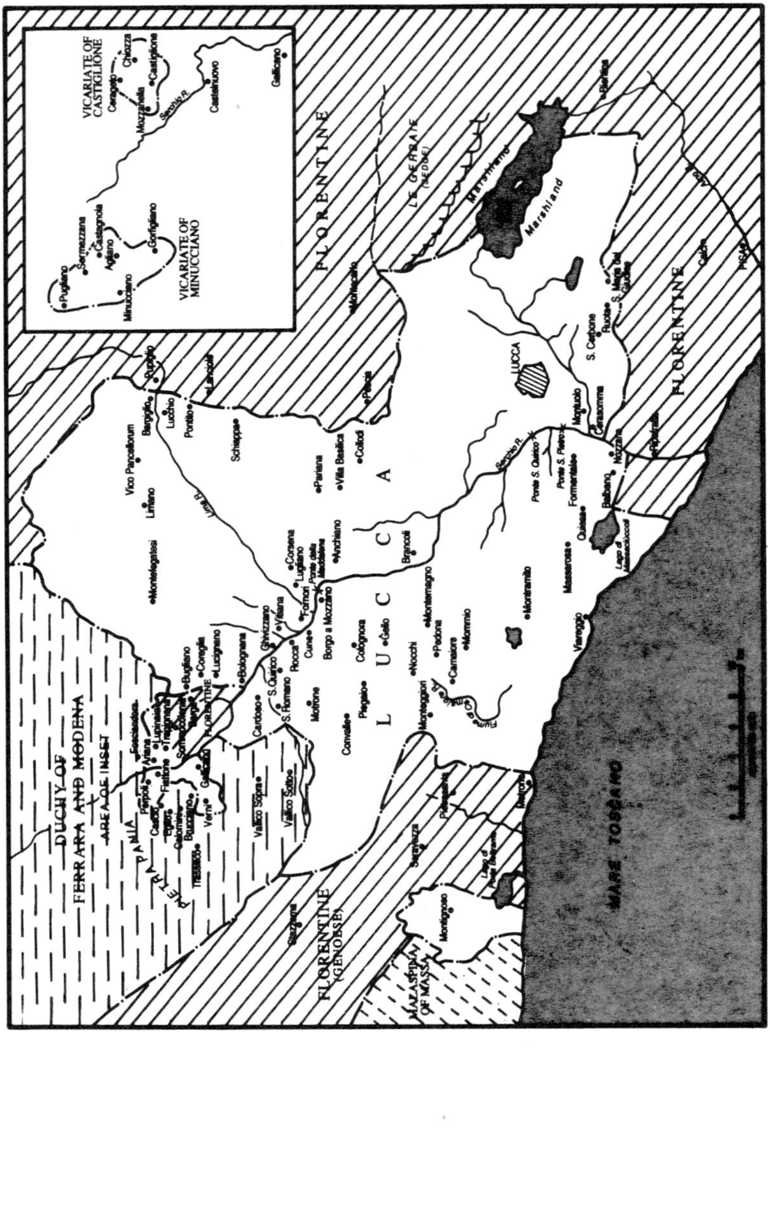

FIG. 7.1. The Lucchese state: approximate boundaries at the end of the fifteenth century.

enemy. Damages were often attributed rather to the allied forces of Niccolò Piccinino and other stipendiaries of Lucca.[59] The criminal records show a large population of foreign mercenaries brawling among themselves. They, and wandering ruffians, made men fearful of journeying by road where, if taken, they were likely to be robbed and killed.[60] Things improved after 1440, though news of troop movements continued to awaken fears throughout the second half of the century.[61] Localized conflict did not end with the peace of 1438. Following the rebellion of Gallicano in 1450, considerable damage was done to Lucchese territory by Estensi forces based in Castelnuovo;[62] and to the west, in 1479, escalating tensions between Lucca and Florence resulted in the sacking of the countryside around Quiesa.[63] More serious, because a more permanent feature of rural life, were the endless acts of destruction committed between contiguous communities: most obviously between the men of Camaiore, Pietrasanta, and Montignoso.[64]

For communities open warfare might mean the loss of crops, the destruction of houses, and a cramped and precarious life within the walls of the *rocca*. Bridges at Moriano, S. Quirico, S. Giustina, and S. Pietro were destroyed in the war with Florence, and had to be replaced.[65] Rents went unpaid.[66] Livestock and personal goods were secreted away, often with uncertain chance of recovery.[67] For individual men and boys there was the very real danger of being abducted from Lucchese territory by marauding troops.[68] Ransoms, and more specifically the loans raised to pay them, were to tax individuals long after the conclusion of hostilities.[69]

[59] Rif. 14, p. 692; 15, pp. 293, 406, 445; ASL Podestà di Lucca, Inquisizioni, 5229, no foliation.

[60] The point is explicitly made, e.g., NAC, N 115 (ser Nicolao di Coluccio di Pellegrino da Pietrasanta, 1409–68), fo. 88^{r-v}.

[61] In 1460 it was determined to bring supplies of grain into Lucca because of rumours of troop movements: ASL Colloqui, 1, p. 57. BSL MS 2599, Antonio Iova, Annali Historici, pp. 954, 958, records damage caused by foreign troops crossing Lucchese territory in both 1478 and 1482. The archives of Pietrasanta show that community, in 1449, offering a gift to the magnificent captain Giovanni da Tollentino, on the understanding that he would not remain on their plain and would do as little damage as possible: ASCP Libro di Consigli (1449), fo. 17^{v}.

[62] Anz. Temp. Lib. 532, no. 32, fo. 106^{r-v}.

[63] ASL Biblioteca (Manoscritti), 38, Giuseppe Civitali, Storia di Lucca, fos. 445^{v}–446^{r}.

[64] Santini, *Versilia centrale*, ii. 103–5.

[65] Bongi, *Inventario*, i. 315–16.

[66] NAC, N 115 (ser Nicolao di Coluccio di Pellegrino da Pietrasanta, 1432–4), fo. 34^{v}.

[67] ASL Podestà di Lucca, Curia Civile, 1177, fo. 73^{r-v}; Podestà di Casoli oltre Giogo, Atti Civili, 31, fos. 20^{r}–21^{r}, 56^{r}–57^{v}, 59^{r}–62^{v}.

[68] Rif. 14, p. 493; SB 159, fos. 373^{v}–374^{v}; 165, fos. 460^{v}–461^{r}.

[69] ASL Podestà di Casoli oltre Giogo, Atti Civili, 31, fos. 50^{r-v}, 52^{v}; NAC, N 115 (ser

Some of the most plaintive individual expressions of loss came from holders of *proventi*. In 1433 Nanni di Papi, called Nannino della barca, purchased for eight years the *provento* of the ferry across the Serchio at Monte S. Quirico. First, Nannino was unable to operate the ferry for fear of the men of arms of conte Luiso dal Verme; then came Niccolò Piccinino, who took the boat away from him; finally Nannino himself was captured by the enemy.[70] A similarly sad history was related by a certain Domenichino who held the *provento* of the tavern at ponte S. Pietro. Again, trouble came with conte Luiso dal Verme, whose men occupied the tavern and took provisions without payment. The advent of Niccolò Piccinino and the war made things worse. And Domenichino found no relief after the peace, for the rebellion of Pietrasanta caused travellers to stop using the route serviced by the tavern.[71] Parallel difficulties, recounted in less detail, faced the lessee of a hospice in Montignoso.[72]

Temporally and causally, to war was linked plague. Thus Agliano, sacked by the Florentines contrary to agreement, had been abandoned by its defenders because of the outbreak of plague among them.[73] The fullest description of the interlocking woes faced in the countryside comes from the same region. Michele di Pietro da Casoli oltre Giogo, suffering from *aposteme pestilenziose*, in 1431 was expelled by his neighbours who feared contagion. Removed to a place called 'alla lama' and sensing the approach of death, Michele decided to make his testament. But the notaries—and indeed, all men who could write—had already fled from those parts because of the plague. Michele was therefore reduced to declaring his intentions verbally to a group of men who were perhaps themselves members of the quarantined community. To the obvious problems of an unwritten will was added the further difficulty that one of the witnesses, Giovanni Simonini *fabbro* of Agliano, was subsequently captured by the Florentines and lay a prisoner in Minucciano.[74] The impact of plague, like that of war, was not limited to the immediate post-Guinigi period. There were serious epidemics in the countryside in the late 1440s and in the period 1476–80. Whether these 'plagues' were 'true plagues' is unclear.

Nicolao di Coluccio di Pellegrino da Pietrasanta, 1409–68), fo. 280^{r-v}; (1432–4), fo. 32^{r-v}; N 116 (1428–32), fos. 56^{v}, 74^{r-v}, 95^{v}; LA 88, fo. 17^{r-v}.

[70] Rif. 15, p. 293.

[71] Ibid., p. 406.

[72] NAC, G 163 (ser Gherardo da Pietrasanta, 1430–5), fo. 16^{r}.

[73] ASL Podestà di Casoli oltre Giogo, Atti Civili, 31, fo. 51^{r-v}.

[74] NAC, N 115 (ser Nicolao di Coluccio di Pellegrino da Pietrasanta, 1432–4), fos. 3^{r}–6^{r}, 30^{v}–31^{v}.

The Lucchese evidence would seem to counter arguments that plague was becoming an urban phenomenon by the fifteenth century;[75] though in the fifteenth century, as in the fourteenth century, citizens continued to flee to the countryside when the plague struck in Lucca.[76]

To the vulnerabilities of life in the Lucchesia we might add the periodic floodings of the river Serchio[77] and the dangers of fire to primitive wooden village constructs.[78] The Lucchese authorities were far from insensitive to the trials of their subjects. It is difficult to see how Lucca could have responded insensitively to the frequent petitions of the officials of local communities when they protested that only one or two inhabitants remained in deserted villages now quite incapable of fulfilling their traditional obligations.[79] Following the peace of 1433, Lucca offered a range of concessions and pardons in reward for the loyalty and sufferings of the men of Massa, Pietrasanta, Camaiore, Montignoso, and Coreglia.[80] Castiglione and Coreglia were similarly favoured for their loyalty after 1438.[81] From the late 1440s revenues due to Lucca from the subject territories, which had been collected previously in the form of various *gabelle* on legal and commercial transactions, were consolidated, by a series of individual compositions, into fixed payments. All these compositions acknowledged that times had changed, and that the capacity of the vicariates to pay had been diminished by depopulation and war.[82] Following these compositions, local communities enjoyed notable successes in winning further concessions by drawing new factors and difficulties to Lucca's attention.[83] In the negotiating process the distant, strategically important, and vulnerable territories of Montignoso, Gallicano, and Minucciano won for themselves very special exemptions and

[75] For an assessment of the role of bubonic plague in the epidemics of Renaissance Italy and for evidence that the countryside was increasingly spared the scourge of plague, see A. Carmichael, *Plague and the Poor in Renaissance Florence* (Cambridge, 1986).

[76] ASL Colloqui, 1, p. 18.

[77] e.g., ASL Archivio Arnolfini, 2, fo. 55^{r-v}.

[78] Schiappa in the vicariate of Valdriana, first devastated by war, was largely burnt to the ground on the morning of Santa Croce in 1445: Rif. 16, pp. 473, 535, 706–7.

[79] The general problem is considered in Rif. 15, p. 490.

[80] Rif. 14, pp. 324, 430, 435, 494, 495, 593; ASL Capitoli, 7, Libri di Sentenze, p. 63.

[81] In May 1438, in recognition of their fidelity, the community of Castiglione was freed for three years from all 'oneribus realibus' excepting the salt tax: Rif. 15, p. 243. The loyalty of that community was acknowledged in the sympathetic composition made with Castiglione in 1456: Rif. 17, pp. 827–8. For the due reward of the men of Coreglia, who lost everything defending the *rocca* of Coreglia from the Florentines, see Rif. 17, pp. 57–8.

[82] Rif. 17, pp. 86–7, 91, 99–101, 103–5, 111, 105–6.

[83] Ibid., pp. 87, 91, 101, 202. The concern for equity was allegedly behind the decision to reform the *estimo* of the *contado* in 1457: ASL Colloqui, 1, p. 7.

privileges.[84] Lucca was prepared to make considerable concessions to ensure the continued loyalty of these precarious outposts.

In many respects the interests of Lucca and of her subject territories were indivisible. Lucca could hardly fail to support her own in conflicts with the subjects of foreign princes. Thus on 7 November 1483 the Anziani were writing to Marchese Alberico Malaspina of Massa to protest a breach of boundary agreements between the men of Massa and those of Montignoso.[85] The bond was somewhat compromised by Lucca's insistence in the same letter that conflict between princes ought not to be generated by the peasant ignorance of subject communes ('per la rusticità de' comuni subditi').[86] Less ambiguously, Lucca responded very positively to appeals from the men of Montignoso that foreigners not be allowed to purchase land in their territory.[87] Mutual interests were served by the various plans formulated in Lucca to preserve woodland, to improve marshland, and to protect the countryside from the flooding of the Serchio.[88] The needs of the fisc lay behind the statute of 1441 that *contadini* were not to be molested inside or outside Lucca for any public debt when coming to Saturday market.[89] Local communities themselves were not slow in identifying Lucca's self-interest. Appeals against the judicial sentences of local men frequently pointed to the impoverishment and depopulation of their home communities. Banishments and imprisonments would further reduce the capacity of those communities to meet their obligations towards Lucca.[90]

The demands and controls placed by Lucca upon her subject territories remained potentially onerous. The extent to which ruling cities drew disproportionate revenues from the countryside and from subordinate

[84] Sforza, *Montignoso*, 166–8, 262–9; ASG MS 5, Libro delle Compositioni e Gratie concesse dall'Eccellentissima Repubblica di Lucca al Castello e Huomini di Gallicano e sua Vicaria fino nell'anno 1450 (copy of 1668 'dal libro vecchio'); Rif. 17, pp. 167–9, 181.

[85] AS Massa, Archivio dei Malaspina di Fosdinovo Marchesi di Massa, 2, no. 4. The background to this dispute is explained: ibid. 1, no. 38 (six documents).

[86] A similar ambiloquy characterizes Lucca's support of Camaiore and Montignoso in their periodic boundary disputes with the Genoese territory of Pietrasanta.

[87] Rif. 22, p. 128. The interests both of the Lucchese state and of Castiglione were cited as reasons for repurchasing woodland in Castiglione which had been sold to certain Lombards: ASL Colloqui, 1, pp. 11, 28. For background, see Rif. 16, pp. 280, 397; Vicario poi Commissario di Castiglione, Atti Criminali, 722, fos. 4r–11r, 24r–31r, 39r–43v, 49r–53v.

[88] Rif. 16, pp. 705–6; 19, pp. 583–4; 21, pp. 254–5, 448, 499–503, 515–16; 22, pp. 633–4; ASL Colloqui, 1, pp. 51, 63; Biblioteca (Manoscritti), 65, Pietro Carelli, Sommario delle Cronache, fo. 115r. 'Because of the sterility of the country', the men of Ruota were granted special licence to cut and work their woods without need for permission: Rif. 22, pp. 25, 46–7.

[89] Rif. 16, pp. 584–5. For the more detailed provisions of 1487, see Rif. 22, pp. 118–20.

[90] Rif. 15, p. 500; 16, p. 475.

centres of population is one of the most controversial themes in the history of Renaissance Italy. In Lucca two series of documents, introito-esito of the Camarlingo Generale and Ragionieri della camera e del comune, have made it possible to calculate and analyse state revenue.[91] Neither series survives for the period after 1430. Unquestionably Lucca's subjects bore very heavy burdens during the war years 1429–33. The circumstances were exceptional, and these were years of deprivation and repeated forced loans for the citizens of Lucca herself. The very comprehensiveness of Lucca's territorial losses in the war of 1436–8 ensured that little real succour could be obtained from the subject communities. Only from the 1440s is it possible to assess the normal public revenue demands of the hegemonic city. In 1447 the men of Montefegatesi recorded that, apart from unspecified obligations to the vicar of Coreglia, for the past ten years they had paid an annual composition of 15 florins (40 bolognini per florin) to the *camera* of Lucca, a sum which they regarded as too high.[92] In the compositions of 1449, the vicariate of Coreglia was assessed to contribute 800 florins per annum towards administrative and ordinary expenses (reduced on appeal to 600 florins per annum);[93] for the commune of Coreglia the assessment was 50 florins *auri in auro largos*, 'et hoc pro quinquaguinta testis taxatis hominum dicti communis ad rationem bol. iiii.[or] in mense per qualibet testa'.[94] Montefegatesi was assessed at a similar rate, amounting to 20 ducats a year;[95] the vicariate, city, and suburbs of Camaiore now owed 560 ducats *auri in auro largos* at 48 bolognini per ducat.[96] These figures are placed in some perspective if we recall that at this very time Count Francesco Sforza was asking Lucca for a loan of 4,000–5,000 ducats.[97] A little later, in a composition of 1452 with the Sei Miglia and the *comuni suburbani*, the inhabitants of the same were required to contribute 20 bolognini per head (exempting those not eligible by reason of age or other just cause); property (excluding the property of

[91] See Meek, *Lucca 1369–1400*, 48–76.

[92] Rif. 16, p. 711.

[93] Rif. 17, pp. 86–8. In the revision, the free gift of 300 *staia* of salt from Lucca to the vicariate was reduced to 200 *staia*.

[94] Ibid., pp. 91–2. In a later modification it is specified that where the composition speaks of 50 gold *ducats*, the men of Coreglia ought to pay at the rate of 45 bolognini per florin.

[95] Ibid., p. 93.

[96] Ibid., pp. 99–101. As a result of local complaints, the sum was reduced from 560 ducats to 550 florins (at 40 bolognini per florin). The gift of salt to Camaiore was commensurably reduced from 250 to 200 *staia*: ibid., pp. 101, 220. The vicariate of Valdilima was assessed at 425 florins per annum (40 bolognini per florin), later reduced to 400 florins; the vicariate of Valdriana was assessed at 225 florins *auri in auro*: ibid., pp. 103–6.

[97] Ibid., pp. 95–6. The actual loan raised amounted to only 2,500 ducats: ibid., pp. 112–13.

citizens and of religious foundations) was to be taxed at the rate of 2 florins for every 100 florins evaluated.[98]

It is difficult to place the above compositions within the total revenues of the Lucchese state, revenues that in the late fourteenth century averaged 65,000–70,000 florins per annum.[99] It is equally difficult to link the fixed assessments of 1449 to the real fiscal contribution of the vicariates. The assessments related to the payment of salaries and ordinary expenses. They excluded extraordinary levies and obligations. The agreements specified a range of duties that Lucca could expect from her subjects, largely relating to local defence. All communities were subject to the highly symbolic levy for wax for the illumination of Santa Croce. *Gabelle* on external transactions remained in place, and countrymen could be called upon for many services including road-building.[100] In the preambles to the compositions of 1449, the Council spoke of the great expenses that Lucca had incurred for the administration and defence of the state; the new assessments were justified as an equitable contribution of the vicariates towards their own expenses. Even in the most favourable years it would seem unlikely that Lucca, in fiscal terms, drew great profits from the vicariates. In the late fifteenth century the disappearance of internal *gabelle* and of the obligation to purchase fixed quantities of salt removed two of the most frequent sources of tension between Lucca and her subjects.[101] The Sei Miglia was a greater potential source of revenue; but around Lucca much of the land was in the possession of Lucchese citizens, churches, and monasteries, and therefore exempt from *imposte*.

With or without fiscal exploitation, the interests of the *contado* were undeniably subordinated to those of the ruling city. Grain production was channelled to meet the needs of Lucca; prices were fixed at times of harvest shortage. Raw materials—notably mulberry leaves and silk cocoons—could not be exported from the Lucchese state.[102] And a very considerable body of legislation restricted artisanal activity beyond the walls of Lucca. Some acts were designed to restock the manpower needs of the city. Thus in 1451 an attempt was made to force artisans of the *contado*

[98] Ibid., pp. 367–9. Special terms were offered to the men of Nozzano and Collodi because of the additional military and other services expected of them.

[99] Meek, *Lucca 1369–1400*, 48–54.

[100] In 1471 powers were granted to the *Sei Cittadini sopra le Entrate* to raise money from *contadini* to finish the via di Montramito: Rif. 19, p. 700. Men of Valdilima were fined for having failed to repair the bridge at Calavorno: Rif. 16, p. 474.

[101] See, e.g., the long list of men from the vicariate and borghi of Camaiore fined for offences against the *Gabelle* and the *Dovana salis* in 1442: Rif. 16, p. 428.

[102] Rif. 14, pp. 721, 733; 16, pp. 419, 706; BSL MS 38, Martino Bernardini, Ricordi Storici, fo. 205ʳ.

to exercise their trades in Lucca.[103] Three years later further measures to this end included the provision that *contadini* with three sons were required to send one to Lucca to learn some *arte*.[104] Clearly the Lucchese authorities were never so unrealistic as to envisage the exclusion of all crafts even from the Sei Miglia. The main force of the legislation, beyond the incentives given to artisans to settle in Lucca, was to limit and define those activities that were permissible in the countryside. In 1484 the inhabitants of the Sei Miglia were confirmed in their right to inn-keeping, to the weaving and tailoring of rough woollen cloth called *albagi*, to certain of the blacksmith's arts (particularly relating to the repair of implements), and to the weaving of linen cloth on payment every six months to Lucca of a fee of 1 florin (36 bolognini per florin) per loom.[105] The interests of artisans in Lucca and the interests of the *entrate* of the city of Lucca typically had been cited together by the tanners of Lucca in the 1440s when petitioning against the continuance of tanning in the *contado*.[106] A more relaxed regime prevailed in the vicariates where industries servicing local needs were permitted and even protected. In relations with her subject territories as a whole, Lucca's most pressing concern was to retain the urban monopoly over luxury manufacture for export markets, and particularly over all the processes of silk manufacture.[107] These prohibitions must have had a fairly limited impact on subject communities, which, for the most part, lacked the skilled manpower and resources to produce goods for more than primitive and strictly local needs.

The collection of revenue, the enforcement of Lucchese statutes, and the preservation of good order within and between communities presuppose instruments of local government and control. The area immediately around Lucca—the Sei Miglia—was ruled directly from the city. Each commune was required by statute to appoint a *guardiano* and officials to denounce ills and damages; the failure of the men of S. Colombano to do so in 1441 resulted in the imposition of a fine.[108] In the vicariates even small communes like Lucignana were defined as communities living by and governing themselves.[109] But the perimeters of self-government were very narrow, and the freedoms were matched by the

[103] Rif. 17, p. 372.
[104] Ibid., pp. 561–2.
[105] Rif. 21, pp. 585, 590–1.
[106] Rif. 16, p. 486.
[107] Legislation to this effect recommenced in 1433: Rif. 14, pp. 404–6.
[108] SB 162, fo. 207^{r-v}. For the election and powers of the syndics of Saltocchio, see AN 705 (ser Benedetto Franciotti), pp. 3–8.
[109] Rif. 17, pp. 44–5.

perils of joint responsibility. The whole community of Vico Pancellorum was fined £10 for failing to make payments which they had been condemned to pay in August and September 1442 by Guaspare Bandini, then vicar of Valdilima.[110] The *sindaco*, commune, and men of S. Vitale were fined *in absentia* for failing to report a fire put to the vineyard of Lunardo di Domenico da Lavacchio of the same commune.[111] Even more unfortunate were the men of Pariana, fined by the vicar of Valdriana for the export of mulberry leaves—an act allegedly committed, unbeknown to the men of Pariana, by two natives of the neighbouring Florentine state.[112] Local officials continued to handle local affairs like the selling of communal land for the repair of a church;[113] goods sequestered by Lucchese officials were entrusted to the safe keeping of local men, who also remained responsible for reporting offences; the men of the whole vicariate might on occasion be required to send representatives to a *parlamento*.[114] Generally Lucchese historians have seen the period from the end of the fourteenth century as a time when local communal organization was retreating before the expanding powers of the central administration, represented in the localities by a vicar or *podestà*.[115]

This picture of a growing concentration of power in the hands of the agents of central government has much to recommend it. To the work of the vicars in their vicariates and to the vigilance of the officials of the *curia del fondaco* and others in the Sei Miglia must be added the elastic authority of the *Capitano del contado*. This man had a wide jurisdiction in the Sei Miglia against the sheltering of *banniti*, gambling, the illegal carrying of arms, and the defrauding of the state; in the vicariates he exercised the same extensive powers as the *Podestà di Lucca* himself. Jurisdictions were tangled and overlapping, but the careful restatement of the powers of the *Capitano del contado* in the statutes of 1446–7 has been interpreted as a determined attempt on the part of Lucca to impose order and discipline on

110 SB 544, no foliation.

111 ASL Vicario di Massa Lunese, Atti Criminali, 266, fos. 3^{r-v}, 21^{r-v}.

112 Rif. 16, p. 706.

113 At a convocation of the men of the commune of Nozzano summoned by its officials, it was agreed to sell common land for 3 florins to pay for repairs to the local church: AN 431 (ser Domenico Arrighi), fos. 13^{r}–14^{r}.

114 In 1434 the men of many communes in the vicariate of Valdilima were fined for not obeying a summons to a *parlamento* by the vicar of same: Rif. 16, p. 474.

115 This transition has been discussed for Massa by Leverotti, 'Ricerche sull'amministrazione della vicaria di Massa'; *idem*, *Massa di lunigiana*, 3–5.

the *contado*.[116] Certainly the agents of central government were sometimes cautious about offending powerful local interests. In the admittedly difficult circumstances prevailing in Massa Lunese in 1431, when the servants of the vicar wounded and arrested a man in execution of their duty, the vicar, Giovanni Turchi, temporized because the offender was head of the Guelph party in those parts.[117] In so acting, the local vicar was merely responding to the same interests of the public good that so often influenced the General Council and the Council of Thirty-Six in Lucca when hearing appeals. But there was little opportunity for the forging of bonds of interest between officials and the communities over which they ruled, as happened in other developing states of early modern Europe. The *Podestà di Lucca* and the *Capitano del contado* were foreigners in terms of the statutes; vicars were elected for only six months, no one could be elected vicar for a vicariate in which he had made his residence, and the office was often seen as a great burden, particularly for such distant outposts as Montignoso.[118] The power of the centre in the Lucchesia was limited rather by the dictates of discretion and by a range of practical constraints related to distance, terrain, settlement patterns, and community structures.

The criminal records provide abundant evidence of local resistance to Lucca's rule, characterized both by a passive refusal to co-operate and also by attacks on the persons and property of Lucchese officials. The war years of the 1430s saw *contadini* plotting to advance the enemy cause. In 1451 the men of Cerageto entered into negotiations to give their land to the Este.[119] But most acts of resistance were more spontaneous, with less sharply defined aims. Often they consisted of no more than a natural determination to minimize dues and losses. Antonio di Vincenzo of Massa sent warning of troop movements not to advise the enemy (though this was the effect), but rather so that his two sons might be removed from the area of conflict.[120] The men of Massa and of Pietrasanta were singled out for false returns on the *estimo*, defending their lands from tax obligations by

[116] For the development of the office, and the growing 15th-century emphasis on the control rather than the protection of the *contado*, see Casali, 'L'amministrazione del Contado Lucchese'; *idem*, 'Aspetti della criminalità nel contado lucchese'.

[117] Rif. 14, pp. 327–8; ASL Vicario di Massa Lunese, Atti Criminali, 261, fos. 4^r–5^r, 8^{r-v}.

[118] In 1448 ser Benedetto di ser Bartolomeo del Guarguaglia, *podestà* of Montignoso was confirmed in his office for a full year (with a salary of 8 florins per month to be paid by the men of Montignoso) because of the difficulty of finding a replacement: Rif. 16, p. 822. Montignoso was exceptional, but the Riformagioni Pubbliche generally show that the office of vicar or *podestà* was often difficult to fill.

[119] ASL Capitano del Contado, 52, fos. 3^r–8^r.

[120] ASL Vicario di Massa Lunese, Atti Criminali, 260, no foliation.

pretending to have sold them to Lucchese citizens and to ecclesiastics.[121] Bartolomeo di Iacopo of Dallo in the vicariate of Castiglione, being among those instructed by the vicar to apprehend men taking animals through the territory of Castiglione without *bulletta* to the defrauding of the *gabelle*, immediately warned the shepherds and herders so that they might avoid the territory.[122] Such evasions led naturally to violence or threats of violence against Lucchese officials entrusted with the assessment and collection of revenues. When ser Benedetto del Guarguaglia arrived in Bugliano in the vicariate of Coreglia in 1445 as *estimatore* to evaluate their lands, local men climbed the bell-tower and sounded *a martello* four times to summon men to arms to drive off the unwelcome visitors.[123]

Violence most frequently erupted when Lucchese officials attempted to make arrests, sequester property, or capture *banniti*. In the Sei Miglia the victims were often officials of the *curia del fondaco* acting against illegal manufacture or agents of the *vice-podestà* pursuing countrymen for debts.[124] Vicars might be physically attacked, the vicar of Massa with his *nuncius* by an armed man in the piazza of Antona in 1434.[125] The *nuncius* of the vicar of Castiglione was threatened with a *lancia* by the consul of Corsiglano when he went to the consul to demand a pledge;[126] agents of the vicar of Camaiore were attacked by five men of Monteggiori whilst they were taking to Camaiore animals found causing damage to property.[127] Most acts of violence relate to the *Capitano del contado*: testimony, no doubt, to the effectiveness of that office. A survey of crimes handled by the *Capitano del contado* shows that between 1441 and 1461, 9.5 per cent of all cases were acts of 'disobbedienza' of varying degrees of gravity.[128] In 1450, when servants of the *Capitano del contado* went to investigate frauds against the *gabelle*, they met a man of Villa Basilica with a laden ass, whom

[121] Rif. 14, p. 584.

[122] SB 161, fo. 336^{r-v}.

[123] Rif. 16, pp. 615–16. In Aug. 1441 Giovanni di Domenico alias Elmorca of Massaciuccoli was attacked by a man of Quiesa 'dum ponebat ipse Iohannes imposita et extimas hominibus dicti communis' as he was bound to do by virtue of his office: SB 162, fo. 156^{r-v}.

[124] SB 161, fos. 276^{r}–277^{r}; 165, fos. 43^{r}–44^{r}; Rif. 15, pp. 404–5.

[125] ASL Vicario di Massa Lunese, Atti Criminali, 266, fos. 11^{r-v}, 24^{r-v}. NAC, N 116 (ser Nicolao di Coluccio di Pellegrino da Pietrasanta, 1435–9), 5 Feb. 1435. For a case in Camporgiano, see SB 161, fo. 4^{r-v}.

[126] The pledge related to a composition that the commune was bound to pay to Lucca; but when the *nuncius* was sent by the vicar of Castiglione to receive it, Guaspare Fasini, consul and official for the commune of Corsiglano, refused to pay, saying, 'Io non voglio e cosi divieto che tu non pigli alcuno pegno': SB 165, fos. 253^{v}–254^{r}.

[127] SB 202, fos. 513^{r-v}, 538^{r-v}.

[128] Casali, 'Aspetti della criminalità nel contado lucchese', 6, 16–19.

they attempted to arrest, but who was protected by a group of men from Villa Basilica armed with various weapons.[129] A year later the officials and whole community of Vico Pancellorum were alleged to have come to the armed assistance of the *banniti* Simone di Piero and Piero di Antonio, convicted of the murder of Bartolo of Vico Pancellorum, when Simone's house in Vico was surrounded at night by the *Capitano del contado* and his forces.[130] In the 1490s the *Capitano*, his notary, and nine servants claimed to have been attacked by twenty men and women of Fernello, Aiola, and Silivano, all armed, when they came to collect a fine imposed in a civil case.[131]

In order to give meaning to these countless acts of public violence, it is necessary to consider the bonds and loyalties that influenced the actions of men in rural society. In the city we have spoken of the pervasive power of kinship. It has become part of historical orthodoxy that wider kinship bonds held no such attractions in the surrounding countryside.[132] This view needs to be reconsidered. It is certainly true that in the countryside (as in the city) the most immediate kinship relationships were the most vital. In conflicts—whether with his neighbours or with the representatives of urban authority—a man might expect the support of his sons and brothers. Typical is the case of two brothers who travelled from the territory of Pistoia to wreak vengeance on a man of S. Alessio who had struck their father.[133] Paradoxically, the high incidence of domestic violence probably also points to the centrality of the father–son, brother–brother relationships.[134] But as in the city, there is evidence of wider and vaguer kinship bonds. The Lucchese statutes designed to handle and contain disputes between *consorti* had full application in the countryside;[135] sentences for high crimes might include a man's sons and all his descendants in the male line.[136] Such acts of the Lucchese administration might merely reflect the imposition on the countryside of

[129] ASL Capitano del Contado, 51, 1st foliation, fos. 3^{r}–4^{v}; SB 165, fos. 295^{r-v}, 300^{r}.

[130] The condemned men were rescued through the roof of their dwelling: SB 162, fo. 182^{v}; Rif. 17, pp. 98–9. For a similar incident, in which the *Capitano* lost his principal horse, see Rif. 20, p. 39.

[131] SB 202, fos. 84^{r}–85^{v}, 98^{r-v}. See also ibid., fos. 475^{r-v}, 515^{r-v}, 536^{r-v}.

[132] The argument is made for Lucca by Berengo, *Nobili e mercanti*, 345–6.

[133] ASL Capitano del Contado, 51, 2nd foliation, fos. 2^{r}–3^{v}.

[134] The potential for violence, particularly between brothers living in the same house, was very high: SB 202, fos. 134^{r-v}, 178^{v}, 463^{r}.

[135] One case in Casoli in which the statutes relating to *consorti* were invoked involved the son of one daughter and the uncle of another: ASL Podestà di Casoli oltre Giogo, Atti Civili, 31, fos. 37^{r}–38^{v}.

[136] SB 160, fo. 129^{r-v}; Rif. 16, p. 461.

urban norms. Other evidence is less ambiguous. When Pellegrino di Bernardo of Pontremoli, assisted by his brother Matteo and by many men of Farneta where the two brothers were living, came armed to a garden in Maggiano from which he abducted (and subsequently raped) Caterina, the daughter of Antonio Prete of Pontremoli, the Farneta men were forced to release the girl because a great clamour of people came after them, the kindred (*consanguinei*) of the said Caterina.[137] A very complex group of kinsmen were collected together in Pietrasanta in 1434, to make peace with the murderer of one of their number.[138] And the same year sees men of Pariana speaking the language of the patrilineage, admittedly—as in all these cases—a language filtered through the experience and formulae of the recording notary.[139]

The examination of witnesses shows clearly the web of blood-relationships binding together members of the smaller communities of the *contado*; courts were concerned to learn to which party a witness believed himself to be more closely related.[140] Naturally, there are cases where the ties of kinship were ruptured.[141] But generally kinship intermingled with neighbourhood in forging the turbulent loyalties of the countryside. These were the groupings confronted by the *Capitano del contado* as he pursued *banniti* and attempted to execute sequestrations and arrests. It is far from self-evident that resistance to the *Capitano del contado* was of a fundamentally different order from the no less frequent cases in Lucca itself where Lucchese citizens snatched friends and kinsmen from the agents of the *Podestà*.[142]

The communes of the vicariates—particularly in the high mountains—were nevertheless distinctive and self-reliant communities whose percep-

[137] ASL Capitano del Contado, 55, 2nd foliation, fos. 18ʳ–20ᵛ, 23ʳ–24ʳ. The affair was settled by marriage and the payment of a dowry. Since Pellegrino was the only one of the armed band to rape the girl, the incident was probably an elopement designed to force a marriage.

[138] NAC, N 115 (ser Nicolao di Coluccio di Pellegrino da Pietrasanta, 1432–4), fo. 39ʳ.

[139] NAC, G 163 (ser Gherardo da Pietrasanta, 1430–5), fos. 4ʳ, 8ʳ. The latter citation relates to men of Massa. For the general problems of notarial sources, see J. Kirshner, 'Some Problems in the Interpretation of Legal Texts re: the Italian City-states', *Archiv für Begriffsgeschichte begründet von Erich Rothacker*, xix (1975), 16–27.

[140] See, e.g., ASL Podestà di Casoli oltre Giogo, Atti Civili, 31, fos. 43ʳ–46ʳ.

[141] The widow Comina, daughter of Guidone Cionelli of Aiola, seems to have disinherited her male relatives in favour of the woman with whom she was living in Gallicano: NAC, N 116 (ser Nicolao di Coluccio di Pellegrino da Pietrasanta, 1428–32), fo. 22ʳ. An old couple of Cascio in the vicariate of Gallicano handed over the greater part of their worldly goods to a man of Fiattone, with whom there was no obvious blood-relationship, in return for being appropriately looked after by him during their lifetimes and properly buried on their deaths: ibid., fos. 23ᵛ–24ʳ.

[142] Cf., e.g., SB 161, fos. 6ʳ–7ᵛ; 165, fo. 424ʳ⁻ᵛ; 202, fos. 466ʳ⁻ᵛ, 494ʳ–495ʳ.

tions of central government were shaped by the latter's distance and by its uncertain attentions. Even in the far north, the *podesterìa* of Casoli oltre Giogo could claim its own doctors and teachers;[143] the effectiveness and number of these men may be gauged by a pervasive illiteracy.[144] A strong community life was not incompatible with considerable internal violence. The greater part of the acts of violence recorded in the criminal records involved men and women of the same commune, though here we must include that large floating population of foreigners so prominent in the fifteenth-century countryside.[145] But energies could soon be more profitably channelled by a common cause and a common enemy. The whole of the fifteenth century is riddled with armed conflicts between adjacent communities over the apportioning of dues and obligations, and over boundaries, fishing rights, water resources, and pastures. These quarrels might take place between the subjects of Lucca and those of other states: between the men of Camaiore, Monteggiori, and Montignoso and those of Pietrasanta (Genoa);[146] between the men of Montignoso and Castiglione and those of Massa (Malaspina);[147] between the men of Gallicano and those of Barga (Florence)[148] and of Vallico Sopra (Ferrara).[149] Political boundaries may have exacerbated conflict, but for the most part the fight over resources paid little heed to the external borders of the state or to the internal boundaries of the vicariates.[150] The men of Camaiore were engaged in interminable disputes with the small communities of the *vicinanza*.[151] Conflicts between Coreglia, Ghivizzano,

143 ASL Podestà di Casoli oltre Giogo, Atti Civili, 31, fos. 79ᵛ, 82ʳ.

144 Ibid., fos. 60ʳ–63ʳ.

145 The registers of SB as a whole give a strong impression that most acts of violence involved men and women of the same community. The impression is confirmed by Casali, 'Aspetti della criminalità nel contado lucchese', 8–9.

146 Rif. 20, pp. 608, 612, 614; ASL Biblioteca (Manoscritti), 26, M. Bianco Bianchi, Historie della terra di Camaiore, no foliation; 30, Pellegrino di Bartolomeo Pellegrini da Camaiore, Memorie, fo. 36ᵛ; ASCP, I 2, Atti dei Genovesi (1433–82), fos. 20ᵛ–21ʳ; E 3, Libro di Consigli (1479–84), fo. 47ʳ⁻ᵛ; Santini, *Versilia centrale*, ii. 103, 223; ASF Signori—Legazioni e Commissarie, 19, fos. 142ʳ–147ʳ.

147 SB 202, fos. 506ʳ⁻ᵛ, 547ʳ; AS Massa, Archivio dei Malaspina di Fosdinovo Marchesi di Massa, 1, nos. 38, 40; 2, nos. 3, 4; Sforza, *Montignoso*, 46–7.

148 ASG MS 13, fos. 42ʳ, 179ᵛ, 182ʳ, 225ᵛ, 227ᵛ–228ʳ. Further south, other subjects of Florence, those of Bientina, caused damage to the abbey of Sesto: SB 165, fo. 336ʳ⁻ᵛ.

149 ASG MS 13, fos. 96ʳ, 100ʳ, 137ᵛ–138ʳ, 166ᵛ, 193ʳ⁻ᵛ.

150 At the same time, the vicariates were more than arbitrary administrative divisions. In 1447 the men of the commune of Montefegatesi threatened to abandon their lands and go elsewhere should they be placed under the vicariate of Valdilima. The men of Valdilima had sacked and undone them during the late wars: Rif. 16, p. 711.

151 ASL Biblioteca (Manoscritti), 30, Pellegrino di Bartolomeo Pellegrini da Camaiore, Memorie, fo. 20ᵛ; BSL MS 939, Gio: Lunardo Dalli, Cronache, p. 390.

and Lucignana were to occupy the Lucchese authorities for much of the century.[152] There were boundary disputes in mid-century between S. Quirico (Valdriana) and Aramo, and between Pescaglia, Fiano, and Loppeglia.[153] At the end of the century a large armed band from Gello launched an attack on certain men of Vetriano;[154] forty men of Menabbio, armed with various weapons, assaulted the shepherds of Sante di Guaspare of Cutigliano.[155]

Disputes between subject communities were to be settled by Lucchese commissioners at the expense of the parties involved.[156] It is significant that some of the attacks on the *Capitano del contado* were committed less against the representative of Lucca than against a man caught in the middle of these local conflicts (or believed to have taken sides in these local disputes). The *vice-capitano* was attacked by the men of Pescaglia when he came to settle border issues between that commune and the men of Fiano and Loppeglia.[157] The men of Capannori were really arming to launch an attack on neighbours in August 1493 when the *Capitano del contado* arrived on the scene.[158] The *estimatore* ser Benedetto del Guarguaglia was attacked by the men of Bugliano in the first instance because he was accompanied by the *sindaci*, consuls, officials, and men of Monti di Villa, also in the vicariate of Coreglia, whom they did not wish to estimate the value of their property, more especially since these latter had designs to unite the commune of Bugliano to their own.[159]

One final factor helps to explain passive and active resistance in the Lucchese countryside. The immediate post-Guinigi period was dominated by war, when very considerable powers were granted to local constables and commissioners. The disobedient claimed—probably truthfully—that they were motivated only by a healthy sense of self-preservation.[160] It is difficult not to sympathize with the man of S. Cassiano a Vico who, when ordered as late as 1449 to allow foot-soldiers and cavalry to cross his land, refused and threatened the official.[161] Generally the 1440s, and the half-century thereafter, was a period of

[152] Rif. 17, pp. 44–5; 20, pp. 573, 593–4; Colloqui, 1, p. 3.

[153] Rif. 16, pp. 594–5; 17, pp. 96–7.

[154] SB 202, fo. 5r–v.

[155] Ibid., fos. 32r–v, 53r–v.

[156] Rif. 20, p. 590; Anz. Temp. Lib.: Appelli agli Anziani, 674, unfoliated.

[157] Rif. 17, pp. 96–7.

[158] SB 202, fo. 475r–v.

[159] Rif. 16, pp. 615–16.

[160] See, e.g., the excuses given for failing to obey the instructions of the *podestà* of Nozzano to provision Castiglioncello: Rif. 15, p. 461.

[161] SB 165, fo. 224r–v.

peace. Now one of the greatest threats came from the *famigli* of the *Podestà* and of the *Capitano del contado*. These men were of extraordinarily mixed provenance; their acts of theft and their violent and unruly behaviour is richly documented in the Lucchese criminal records. It may be noted that when they were attacked whilst executing their duty, Lucchese courts very often showed a degree of sympathy for the accused, and found that the agents of the law had given at least as much as they got. Details are lacking, but we can well imagine the circumstances in which Francesco Neri, *castellano* of Montefegatesi, 'killed because of a woman', met his end.[162] Nor was the conduct of the highest officials of the Lucchese state always beyond reproach. Antonella Casali's study of the registers of the *Capitano del contado* for 1441–61 has shown how far 'disobbedienza' was likely to have resulted from petty acts of tyranny and corruption.[163] These abuses of power (which the central government was clearly anxious to remedy) must be added to the fiscal demands and the economic and administrative controls, and to local solidarity—particularly in the vicariates—in the face of any external intervention. Together these ingredients often engendered a highly suspicious attitude towards Lucchese rule.

Marino Berengo has seen brigandage in the Lucchese countryside of the cinquecento as a natural product of the contradictions of the rural economy and of the deep and mysterious cleavages of rural society.[164] Naturally, and rightly, the Lucchese authorities most feared the appearance of armed gatherings, whether in the city or in the *contado*, during times of grave shortages.[165] It is not difficult to find examples where local communities banded together to protect *banniti* from pursuit and capture. But Berengo is clearly right to resist any Robin Hood imagery in his treatment of the robber bands that were as characteristic of the fifteenth- as of the sixteenth-century Lucchesia. Throughout the 1440s Simone di Piero of Vico Pancellorum, thief, murderer, and miscreant, usually alone but sometimes with others, committed crimes remarkable for both their number and their variety. His victims included the

[162] Baroni, Notizie genealogiche, MS 1122, fo. 164^{r-v}.

[163] Matteo di Vanni of pieve S. Stefano was fined 25 *libbre* by the *Capitano*, and subsequently protested that the *Capitano* 'solo questo ha facto perché esso Mactheo si dolse a M. Signori della iniuria che Lui et il suo notaio li volevano, che esso Capitano del mese di dicembre 1451 li mandò a casa sua il notaio et tre famigli et quine stenno giorni due a tucte spese di dicto Mactheo, et non vastando questo, volsero havere bol. 6. Et di tal cosa si dolse al Vostro Exactore et insieme con dicto Exactore si dolse a M. Signori della iniuria et al dicto Mactheo furono renduti dicti bol. 6 dal Capitano'. For this and similar cases, see Casali, 'Aspetti della criminalità nel contado lucchese', 7, 17–19.

[164] Berengo, *Nobili e mercanti*, 346–56.

[165] Rif. 19, pp. 183–4, 191.

inevitable travelling Lombards, but his first recorded murder victim was Bartolomeo di Domenico of Vico, and most of his robberies (usually of grain and other provisions) were from houses in Vico and its neighbouring communes.[166] In 1471 the men of Vico Pancellorum were given a *podestà* to settle their problems, but five years later Lucca was still seeking a solution to the 'huomini schandolsi' of Vico.[167] In December 1489 a number of exiles from Vico and Fibbialla (together with men of Pistoia) returned to Lucchese territory with the intention of killing two men of Vico Pancellorum and another of Pontito.[168] And this same period saw action taken against a robber band—perhaps better described as a fluid group of companions in crime centred on Berto di Bernardo of Permesana (or Lenazano) of the district of Parma, though living in Saltocchio—for at least fifty serious crimes committed over the previous two decades. In some ways the pattern is very much the same: the robbing and murder of Lombards and casual thefts committed over a wide area of the Sei Miglia, in the Garfagnana, and beyond the borders of the Lucchese state. Not only did Berto confess under repeated torture to a range of crimes from rape to defrauding the *gabelle* to coining false money (in Pontecosi), but he and his companions also clearly found employment as professional assassins. Men secured their services to attack a neighbour or to remove an enemy. Political boundaries were of no consequence to the likes of Berto di Bernardo.[169] And they were the enemies of Lucca only in the sense that they were a threat to any public order and constituted authority.

To advance beyond these generalities, it is useful to look at two case-studies: Pietrasanta, which rebelled against Lucca in 1436 and placed itself under the rule of Genoa, and Gallicano, which rebelled against the Este in 1450 and returned to Lucchese obedience. Neither case is typical. Pietrasanta was especially distinctive: a significant economic and political community within a Lucchese state that was markedly lacking in subordinate centres of population of any size or importance. But both cases offer opportunities to explore local attitudes towards Lucchese rule which are of more than local relevance.

166 ASL Capitano del Contado, 51, 1st foliation, fos. 43r–48r; SB 165, fos. 391r–394v.

167 Rif. 19, pp. 770–1; 20, pp. 452–3.

168 SB 202, fos. 351r–v, 358r–v. The intruders attacked Domenico di Paolo of Pontito, but when the men of Vico learnt that they were on Lucchese territory, they fled to Limano, and thus evaded them.

169 ASL Capitano del Contado, 97, 2nd foliation, fos. 25r–31v; SB 202, fos. 212r–214v, 263r–265v, 426r–v, 449r–450r, 475v, 484r–v. As usual, the criminal records give no real hint of motivation, but the 'political' crimes—most notably the murder of ser Girolamo da Casoli in the district of Parma—seem to involve long-standing private *vendette* against prominent local men in the very enclosed world of the rural communes.

The importance of Pietrasanta stemmed largely from its geographical position. Its origins are very controversial, but the growth of Pietrasanta can certainly be dated to the decision of the *podestà* Guiscardo da Pietrasanta in 1255 to resettle the inhabitants of Corvaia and Vallecchia in the new Lucchese town that was to be named after him.[170] Thereafter the region centred on Pietrasanta was to be fiercely contested with Pisa. The territory was of vital concern to Lucca, not only because it straddled the road network north to Genoa and beyond to France, but also because through Pietrasanta Lucca was connected to the sea at Motrone. In a letter to the Duke of Milan in 1431, Pietrasanta was described as 'the noblest place in our territory, and in a special sense our port through which we obtain provisions'.[171] The registers of the *gabella* of Pietrasanta for 1429–36 show the lively commercial interchange between Motrone and Pietrasanta, and beyond to Camaiore.[172] They show the role of Motrone in the 1430s as the final port for the despatch inland of provisions and industrial materials shipped or trans-shipped from Genoa, La Spezia, Portovenere, Pisa, and Livorno.[173] And they show the passage through Pietrasanta of goods sent by land from Genoa, Milan, and the whole of Lombardy.[174] The Pietrasanta *gabelle* also establish the importance for the Lucchese treasury of the passage of animals seasonally through the vicariate: inland from the marina and along a north–south axis from Lombardy into Pisan territory[175]—a passage worth 120 florins, £86 13*s.* 6*d.*, in dues in the peak month of October of 1429.[176] Naturally the local

[170] These events form part of the general 13th-cent. communal offensive against the nobility of the surrounding countryside, for which the basic source is the *Annals* of Ptolemy of Lucca. Santini, *Versilia centrale*, ii. 5–9; Green, *Castruccio Castracani*, 23; M. Piloni, *Pietrasanta e i Medici (1255–1513): ipotesi di ricerca* (Pietrasanta, 1983), 9–10; O. Cervietti, 'Pietrasanta dalla fondazione al Lodo di Leone X', *Rivista di archeologia, storia, economica, costume*, v, no. 2 (1977), 31–3.

[171] Fumi (ed.), *Regesti*, 123: 'il più nobil luogo del nostro territorio, et veramente è il Porto nostro, del quale caviamo vettovaglia'.

[172] ASL Gabelle del contado e delle vicarie, Gabella di Pietrasanta, 80(2), fos. 2^{r}–15^{v}, 38^{r}. For further references of note, see ibid. 81(2), fos. 6^{r-v}, 8^{r}; 81(4), *passim*; 81(6), fos. 2^{r} ff.

[173] Many of the references speak only of goods received from those places by sea. For the internal water links between Pisa and Motrone, see A. Bartelletti, 'Boschi ed incolti nel paesaggio, nell'economia e nella cultura del medioevo. I. Il caso della pianura Pisano-Versiliese', *Studi Versiliesi*, ii (1984), 28. For clear evidence of reshipment through Motrone, see ASL Gabelle del contado e delle vicarie, 80(1), fo. 4^{r}; 81(2), fos. 7^{r} ff.

[174] The land route is indicated: ASL Gabelle del contado e delle vicarie, 80(2), fos. 14^{r}, 15^{v}; 80(4), fo. 8^{r}; 81(2), fo. 15^{v}; 81(4), fo. 6^{r}; 81(6), fo. 6^{v}.

[175] Ibid. 81(4), esp. fos. 5^{v}, 6^{r}; 81(6), fos. 3^{r}, 4^{r-v}, 5^{v}. For patterns of transhumance, see Bartelletti, 'Boschi ed incolti', 32–4.

[176] ASL Gabelle del contado e delle vicarie, 80(1), Libro del camarlingo della gabella di Pietrasanta, fos. 51^{r} ff.

gabelle reveal very little about the transit of goods to Lucca through the territory of Pietrasanta. A series of licences to transport goods to Lucca free of customs include references to raw silk and cheeses from Messina.[177] Some record is preserved in the notarial protocolli of goods that actually changed hands in Pietrasanta: for example, the two *fardelli* of Spanish silk purchased there for £1,315 7*s.* 8*d.*, money of Genoa, by Giovanni da Ghivizzano from the agent of the Genoese merchant Catanio Spinola.[178]

The territories of Pietrasanta drew their importance not only from their geographical situation, but also from the richness of their natural resources. First, there were the mineral deposits. True, the search for gold and silver seems to have been unsuccessful;[179] and there are only the most occasional references to the export of lead.[180] But the area was traditionally noted for its iron, and the *arte* of iron-smelting was called the sustainer of this place ('quella la quale mantiene questa terra').[181] Large quantities of unworked iron (together with nails and horseshoes) were being sent out of Lucchese territory from Pietrasanta in the 1420s and 1430s.[182] Local iron of *vena silvestra* was, however, of indifferent quality. In 1479 iron made from a mixture of local and imported ore, according to the Genoese vicar, 'was found almost for the greater part to be useless and unmerchantable'.[183] Much earlier, during the last years of Lucchese rule, a good deal of iron ore from Elba was already being imported to feed the industry of Pietrasanta and its surrounding villages.[184] Under Genoa there was a sustained, and never entirely successful, campaign to impose the use of iron from Elba, which led to the total prohibition of the use of *vena silvestra* in 1467.[185] Pietrasanta had also long benefited from the exploitation of local marble, the quarries at Ceragiola being the most

[177] Ibid. 81(2), fos. 119ʳ–122ᵛ.

[178] NAC, N 116 (ser Nicolao di Coluccio di Pellegrino da Pietrasanta, 1428–32), fos. 66ʳ–67ʳ.

[179] Santini, *Versilia centrale*, ii. 25; iii. 265.

[180] ASL Gabelle del contado e delle vicarie, 81(2), fo. 16ʳ.

[181] ASCP, E 3, Libro di Consigli (1479–84), fo. 8ᵛ.

[182] ASL Gabelle del contado e delle vicarie, 80(2), fo. 38ʳ; 81(5), fos. 60ʳ–61ʳ; 81(6), fos. 40ᵛ–41ʳ, 44ᵛ–45ʳ.

[183] ASCP, E 3, Libro di Consigli (1479–84), fo. 8ᵛ: 'quasi per la magior parte si ritrovava inutile et non mercantile'.

[184] ASL Gabelle del contado e delle vicarie, 81(4), fo. 4ᵛ; 81(5), fo. 70ʳ; 81(6), fos. 44ʳ–45ᵛ. NAC, N 115 (ser Nicolao di Coluccio di Pellegrino da Pietrasanta, 1409–68), fos 29ᵛ–31ᵛ; N 116 (1428–32), fos. 67ʳ–68ᵛ.

[185] ASCP, A 6, Filze giusdicenti (1467), fos. 339ᵛ–340ʳ; I 2, Atti dei Genovesi (1433–82), fos. 19ʳ⁻ᵛ, 21ᵛ, 25ʳ–27ᵛ, 32ʳ–33ʳ, 95ʳ; E 3, Libro di Consigli (1479–84), fos. 8ᵛ–9ʳ; Santini, *Versilia centrale*, ii. 122; iii. 283–7. In 1481 the representatives of Pietrasanta petitioned the Genoese for a licence that some merchants from Piombino might come and settle in the *terra*: ASCP, I 2, Atti dei Genovesi (1433–82), fo. 51ᵛ.

important at the beginning of the fifteenth century.[186] Local wool and leather were by-products of the pastures of Palatina and the marina. Some wool was still being exported at the end of the Guinigi period.[187] And the butchers of Pietrasanta continued to supply a local leather industry.[188] By the fifteenth century, better-quality leather, like higher-grade iron ore, was imported.[189] The sea, rivers, and lakes, even up to the walls of Pietrasanta itself,[190] offered a plentiful supply of fish.[191] Before the rebellion, conflicts arose over the leasing of fishing rights;[192] afterwards there were the problems of rival jurisdictions.[193] Finally the whole region was famous for its fruits—oranges, lemons, melons, figs, pears, cherries, and so on—though mulberry cultivation was probably developed only under Medici rule in the next century.[194]

Thus favoured, Pietrasanta had developed by the fifteenth century into a town of 989 mouths, excluding a resident population of 146 foreigners.[195] A list of artisans and *bottegai* of 1401 shows Pietrasanta possessed of precisely the kind of local and service industries that one would expect of a community of this size.[196] Distinctive are the workers in marble,

[186] Santini, *Versilia centrale*, iii. 146–9.

[187] ASL Gabelle del contado e delle vicarie, 81(2), fo. 15ᵛ.

[188] NAC, N 115 (ser Nicolao di Coluccio di Pellegrino da Pietrasanta, 1409–68), fo. 89ᵛ. All references to NAC for the remainder of the chapter are to the protocolli of ser Nicolao di Coluccio di Pellegrino da Pietrasanta unless otherwise stated.

[189] ASL Gabelle del contado e delle vicarie, 80(4), fos. 6ᵛ, 8ʳ; 81(2), fo. 6ʳ and *passim*; 81(4), fo. 6ᵛ and *passim*; 81(6), fos. 2ʳ, 6ʳ. The tanner Paolo di Cristoforo bought Spanish leather from the Lucchese merchant Meo di Biagio: NAC, N 116 (1425–7), 17 July 1426.

[190] NAC, N 115 (1409–68), fo. 307ᵛ.

[191] ASL Gabelle del contado e delle vicarie, 80(2), fo. 4ᵛ and *passim*; 81(2), *passim*; NAC, N 115 (1409–68), fos. 29ʳ, 58ʳ; ASCP, A 6, Filze giusdicenti (1467–8), no foliation: case against Michele dele puto; Santini, *Versilia centrale*, v. 6, 111.

[192] ASCP, E 3, Consiglio (1429), fos. 235ᵛ–236ʳ.

[193] ASCP, I 2, Atti dei Genovesi (1433–82), fo. 51ʳ. Even after the rebellion the spedale di S. Luca of Lucca had continued to lease fishing rights on the lago di Perotto to men of Pietrasanta: NAC, N 116 (1435–9), 6 Jan. 1439.

[194] Santini, *Versilia centrale*, ii. 199; v. 11, 171; NAC, N 115 (1409–68), fos. 307ᵛ, 313ᵛ, 316ᵛ.

[195] ASL Amministrazione delle comunità soggette e delle vicarie, 38, fo. 27ᵛ. A little earlier, in Sept. 1435, the population of the whole territory of Pietrasanta was estimated at 1,440 mouths, excluding babies of less than 2 years and *c.*500 foreigners: ibid., fo. 20ʳ. The same source speaks in Pietrasanta of 258 'testes', of whom 83 were poor: ibid., fo. 32ᵛ. A total of 419 households were listed in Pietrasanta for the *estimo* of 1407, of which 46 were headed by women, and 29 were 'heirs of': ASL Estimo, 126. The oath of loyalty of the men of Pietrasanta of 31 Mar. 1496 lists 419 men (including 13 priests and 11 Augustinian friars). The men of the vicariate of Pietrasanta (Seravezza, Stazzema, Stettoia, Farnocchia, Pomezzana, Terrinca, Pruno, Volegno, Ruosina, Ratignano, Linigliano, Azzano, Basati, Minazzana, Fabiano, Cappella, and Giustagiana), who swore the oath at the beginning of Apr. 1496, numbered altogether 838: ASL Capitoli, 7, pp. 109–17.

[196] Santini, *Versilia centrale*, ii. 85–6.

particularly Riccomano di Guido and his son Leonardo, who were employed on the churches of Pietrasanta in the last years of Lucchese rule.[197] Other artisanal activities were of more than local significance. We know relatively little about the woollen industry; probably, as in Lucca itself, the periodic attempts to revive it met with only limited success,[198] though there is certainly evidence from the surrounding countryside of fulling-mills driven by mountain streams.[199] The linen manufacture that was clearly taking place in and around Pietrasanta has also left relatively little trace beyond the names of individual weavers (notably Francesco da Milano) and fragmentary details of exports.[200] But it is possible to follow more confidently the career of the tanner Paolo di Cristoforo da Albiano, who took Antonio di Giorgio Pedrimoli as apprentice for five years in 1431,[201] and who, two months later, sublet a tannery in ruga sottana di sotto to two other tanners of Pietrasanta.[202] Paolo was a man of substance: the purchaser for 125 florins of a house in Pietrasanta from Lorenzo di Lazzaro Guinigi.[203] As such, he was indistinguishable socially from a group of merchants, mostly bearing the title *speziali* or *caseari*, who supplied the ironworkers of the surrounding countryside with materials and sold their wares.[204] Indeed, the tanner Paolo entered into a partnership for the manufacture of leather with the *speziale* Filippo di Michelino

[197] NAC, N 115 (1409–68), fo. 97^{r}; N 116 (1428–32), fos. 71^{r}–72^{v}. The Riccomani took a boy from Gragnano as apprentice, among other things to cut marble for them, in 1444: N 115 (1409–68), fo. 126^{r}.

[198] Santini, *Versilia centrale*, ii. 91, 131–2; ASCP, I 2, Atti dei Genovesi (1433–82), fo. 63^{r}.

[199] NAC, N 115 (1409–68), fo. 181^{v}; N 116 (1435–9), 2 Jan. 1439. There are various references to shearing shops in Pietrasanta: e.g., that of Piero del trighiaro of Pisa: N 115 (1409–68), fo. 187^{v}.

[200] ASL Gabelle del contado e delle vicarie, 81(2), fo. 119^{r}; 81(4), fo. 6^{r} and *passim*; 81(6), fos. 6^{r}, 40^{r}; ASCP, A 6, Filze giusdicenti, Causarum civilium (1411), fos. 30^{r}, 37^{v}; NAC, N 115 (1409–68), fo. 166^{v}; N 116 (1428–32), fo. 77^{v}.

[201] NAC, N 116 (1428–32), fo. 53^{r}.

[202] Ibid., fo. 57^{r-v}.

[203] Ibid., fo. 83^{r-v}.

[204] NAC, N 115 (1409–68), fos. 29^{v}–31^{v}, 35^{r}, 89^{r}, 324^{r}; (1432–4), fo. 14^{r}; N 116 (1428–32), fos. 67^{r}–68^{v}, 79^{r}, 81^{v}; (1435–9), 9 Feb., 23 Feb. 1436. The iron manufactories were situated in the countryside, where they benefited from local fuel and hydraulic power. Useful inventories appear in N 115 (1409–68), fos. 271^{r}, 282^{v}; (1432–4), fos. 15^{r-v}, 38^{r-v}, 40^{v}–41^{r}; N 116 (1428–32), fos. 93^{v}–95^{r}; (1435–9), 17 Mar. 1436. Similar installations in the countryside included lime-kilns and tile manufactories: ASCP, A 6, Filze giusdicenti, Causarum civilium (1411), fo. 30^{r-v}; NAC, N 115 (1409–68), fo. 268^{v}. The furnace for making tiles was owned by builders of Pietrasanta; the iron furnaces were normally owned by local men. But there are examples of the latter directly owned by merchants of Pietrasanta: N 115 (1409–68), fo. 324^{r}; N 116 (1425–7), 28 Oct. 1426, the 1426 contract relating to temporary ownership of goods assigned.

Iacobi.[205] Above the local hierarchy of tanners, butchers, *speziali*, and *caseari* were men of more ambiguous status who enjoyed the privileges of Lucchese citizenship. Merchants and citizens of Lucca included Tommaso di Arrigho Simi, with his palace above the shop fronting on the public piazza,[206] and Battista di ser Castruccio di ser Francesco, whose father was assessed at the very large sum of £895 in the *estimo* of 1407.[207] The interests of these men might be finely divided between Pietrasanta and Lucca. Battista di ser Castruccio was a partner of the Lucchese company of the *pannaro* (and leading conspirator against Paolo Guinigi) Nicolao Neri.[208] The business life of his son Silvestro is more closely associated with Lucca than with Pietrasanta, a fact probably only partly determined by the events of 1436. Similarly, notaries of Pietrasanta with Lucchese citizenship, like ser Nicolao di Coluccio and ser Gherardo Bartolomei, forged careers for themselves as much in the employ of Lucca as in the service of their fellow Pietrasantesi.[209]

The society of Pietrasanta was complicated in the early 1430s by the very large number of resident and visiting foreigners: members of the Genoese garrison; artisans from Liguria, Lombardy, and all over Tuscany; merchants from Genoa and Pisa;[210] and scions of the great feudal families of the north like the Cattani of Massa and the Malaspina of Lunigiana.[211] It was complicated by the Lucchese citizenship of leading local merchants and professionals and by Lucchese citizens themselves who possessed palaces in Pietrasanta and vineyards and olive groves in the

[205] Paolo invested 460 florins in the company, partly in money and partly in materials; Filippo placed 225 florins, and promised a further 235 florins to be paid in iron. The tanning was to be done by Paolo, but Filippo promised to provide Paolo with a master craftsman to cut and make shoes. Filippo was also to keep the books. Money was to be kept in a chest, of which both partners were to have keys. The partnership was to maintain two shops: one for the tanning of leather, the other for the making of shoes, one shop supplied by each partner. At the termination of the partnership, capital and profits were to be divided equally: NAC, N 115 (1409–68), fos. 84ʳ–85ᵛ, 89ᵛ.

[206] Ibid., fo. 88ᵛ.

[207] ASL Estimo, 126, fo. 53ʳ. Only M. Pezzino Colucci (£1,026 10*s*.) was assessed for more.

[208] NAC, G 163 (ser Gherardo da Pietrasanta, 1430–5), fo. 5ʳ.

[209] The office-holding of ser Nicolao di Coluccio under Paolo Guinigi and under the restored republic can be traced through his surviving protocolli in Florence: NAC, N 115 and N 116.

[210] The Pisan Marco Maggiolini appears regularly in the registers of the *gabelle* for the late 1420s and early 1430s. For Genoese merchants operating in Pietrasanta before 1436, see NAC, N 115 (1409–68), fo. 23ᵛ; N 116 (1428–32), fos. 67ʳ–68ᵛ.

[211] The Cattani of Massa had property in Pietrasanta in the 1430s, and were living there in the 1440s: NAC, N 115 (1409–68), fos. 55ʳ, 129ʳ. Giorgio di d. Lunardo Marchese Malaspina da Lunigiana was resident in Pietrasanta in Aug. 1433: G 163 (ser Gherardo da Pietrasanta, 1430–5), fo. 2ᵛ.

surrounding countryside.[212] But within Pietrasanta there was a group of leading families comparable within their own small world, in their activities and their attitudes, to the Lucchese patriciate itself. Men like the *speziale* Nicolao di Giovanni Nuti combined their commercial activities with extensive landholding within and beyond the walls of Pietrasanta.[213] The butcher Antonio di Michele Narducci received money *in deposito* from the hospital of S. Antonio of Pietrasanta.[214] Other butchers, including Duccino di Bartolomeo Gherardi—with his brother ser Gherardo—were prominent in the leasing of animals *in soccidam* and *ad collariam* to country-dwellers.[215] Duccino himself, with Nicolao Nuti and Filippo di Michelino Iacobi, was active in granting presumably usurious loans based on the fictitious sale of property.[216] The scorn of the men of Pietrasanta for the 'rudes et illiterati' inhabitants of the countryside fully echoes attitudes discussed earlier in consideration of Lucchese investment in the rural world.[217] Reminiscent of the great families of Lucca too is the holding of land undivided between brothers for some years after the father's death,[218] the employment of wet nurses,[219] and the endowment of altars.[220] The wills of the leading men and women of Pietrasanta replicate those of the Lucchese patriciate both in the concern to be united with deceased members of the *casa* and in a characteristic late medieval

[212] The property of Lucchese citizens is usually hidden from the records of the *estimo*. But see ASL Estimo, 131, fragments which include Paolo Guinigi himself. There are abundant references in the notarial protocolli to the urban palaces and houses of the Guinigi, Rapondi, Arnolfini, Gigli, Parghia, Schiatta, Busdraghi, etc. and to the holding of land in the surrounding countryside by Lucchese families.

[213] For the assessment of his father's lands, see ASL Estimo, 126, fo. 56ʳ.

[214] NAC, N 115 (1409–68), fo. 75ᵛ.

[215] NAC, N 115 (1409–68), fos. 21ᵛ, 24ʳ; (1416–34), fo. 21ʳ⁻ᵛ; (1432–4), fo. 40ʳ; N 116 (1425–7), 8 Sept., 10 Sept. 1426; (1428–32), fo. 96ʳ.

[216] NAC, N 115 (1409–68), fos. 93ʳ, 270ʳ⁻ᵛ; (1432–4), fos. 6ᵛ–7ʳ; N 116 (1426–32), fos. 75ʳ⁻ᵛ, 82ʳ⁻ᵛ, 92ᵛ, 95ᵛ; T 573 (ser Paolino di Tomuccio Tomucci), 22 June 1437. One contract with offer of resale was not a disguised loan to countrymen, but involved rather Nicolao di Lorenzo Neri, banker and *pannaro* of Lucca (as 'purchaser') and the Lucchese citizen Nicolao di Sbarrino Sbarra of Pietrasanta (as 'seller'): N 116 (1425–7), 7 July 1426. For direct loans from urban merchants and landlords, sometimes to their own tenants, see N 115 (1409–68), fo. 108ʳ; N 116 (1425–7), 24 Aug. 1426.

[217] The idea of 'rudes et illiterati' ironworkers, always suspicious of the intentions and good faith of the merchants in Pietrasanta who supplied them, actually emanates from the Genoese authorities: ASCP, I 2, Atti dei Genovesi (1433–82), fo. 27ʳ. But it summarizes decades of distrust chronicled in the Pietrasanta records.

[218] NAC, N 115 (1409–68), fo. 123ʳ; N 116 (1425–7), 14 July 1426.

[219] NAC, N 115 (1409–68), fo. 201ᵛ.

[220] Ibid., fo. 345ᵛ; Santini, *Versilia centrale*, iv. 83, 91.

emphasis on works.[221] It is hardly surprising that the political institutions of Pietrasanta clearly reflect those of the mother city.

The Lucchese administration in Pietrasanta was headed by a vicar who held office for six months. With his five servants and his salary of 24 florins per month, the post was by far the most attractive of the vicarial appointments.[222] The establishment in the court, *gabelle*, *cancellaria*, and *camera* of Pietrasanta was also far more elaborate than for any other vicariate, as befitted its importance.[223] Beneath the vicar, and responsible to him, were the local organs of representation and self-government. Five Anziani, the chief of whom was called a prior, ruled Pietrasanta under Lucchese supervision. As in Lucca, the *tasca* of Anziani was renewed every two years; it was prepared by eight men nominated by the General Council of Pietrasanta together with the vicar. Names were divided into colleges and locked in a chest, from which they were drawn by the vicar at the appropriate time.[224] The Anziani held office for three months, and each new college, on taking office, took an oath to maintain the dominion, jurisdiction, and honour of Lucca; to preserve the castle and lands of Pietrasanta with its vicariate; and to report anything contrary to the interests of Lucca to the Anziani of Lucca or their officials.[225] The General Council of Pietrasanta was made up of twenty-four *consiglieri*, three per *ruga*.[226] Members of the Council held office for six months, and the *tasca* was renewed every eighteen months. The *tasca* for the General Council was prepared at a meeting in the *cancellaria* of Pietrasanta of the Anziani

221 See esp. the wills of ser Castruccio di ser Francesco and of his widow Giovanna: NAC, N 116 (1428–32), fos. 41^{r-v}, 70^{r-v}. Also ibid., fos. 41^{v}–42^{v}, 43^{r-v}, 47^{r-v}; (1435–9), 4 Mar. 1436. It is interesting that some of the same flavour attaches to the will of Salvuccio di Vanuccio, an immigrant from the Papal states and herder or shepherd to two butchers of Pietrasanta: N 116 (1416–34), fos. 22^{r}–23^{r}.

222 The vicar of Camaiore had three servants and a salary of 12 florins per month: Anz. Temp. Lib. 5, fo. 80^{v}.

223 Again, cf. the five notaries servicing Pietrasanta with the two appointed for Camaiore: ibid., fos. 81^{v}, 83^{r-v}. These appointments were also for a term of six months. The court of the vicar was served by *avvocati assessori*: for procedures, see ASL Vicario di Pietrasanta, Atti Criminali, 233, *passim*, and also AN 504(12) (ser Antonio Nuccorini), fos. 232^{r} ff. The modern foliation of the latter volume is in some confusion.

224 Unfortunately, most of the evidence relates to the Genoese period, but changes instituted then make reference to earlier customs: ASCP, I 2, Atti dei Genovesi (1433–82), fos. 44^{v}, 46^{r}; Libro di Consigli (1447), fo. 10^{r}; E 3, Libro di Consigli (1479–84), fos. 9^{v}, 58^{r-v}. When the number of active Anziani was so reduced by sickness that it became difficult to govern the commune or to carry out the instructions of the vicar, the remaining Anziani nominated replacements for the approval of the General Council: ASCP Libro di Consigli (1431), fos. 6^{v}–7^{r}.

225 ASL Amministrazione delle comunità soggette e delle vicarie, 38, fo. 2^{r}.

226 Ruga Sottana di sotto, sottana di sopra, maestra di sopra, maestra di sotto, soprana di sopra, soprana di sotto, terra nuova di sotto, terra nuova di sopra.

together with one representative per *ruga*; these eight representatives (presumably chosen by the Anziani) each named nine men, and these seventy-two men were divided into three groups, to provide the members of the next three Councils of twenty-four.[227] The Anziani and General Council sat together, sometimes in the great hall of the vicar's palace, sometimes in the *cancellaria*.[228] The Council was enlarged by the presence of *invitati* chosen by the Anziani—sometimes as many as thirty-two *invitati* when important business was being discussed.[229] Councils were sometimes attended by representatives of Cappella and Seravezza. All the communes of the vicariate had their own officials who were responsible to the administration in Pietrasanta, though they might attempt direct appeals to the ruling city. Much business in Pietrasanta was delegated to *Colloqui*, a word used for any *ad hoc* body summoned by the Anziani with the authority of the General Council.

The names of the Anziani in the early 1430s are those of Pietrasanta's leading merchants, artisans, and notaries, as recorded in the commercial and notarial records. With a *tasca* of seventy-two names, the membership of the General Council must have embraced all adult male Pietrasantesi of property. These men were responsible for the election of local officials: most prominently the *camarlingo generale*, but also including the doctor and the schoolmaster. They were responsible for the imposition of the salt tax and for local levies. With the revenues received they paid the salaries of the vicar, notary, chancellor, and local officials. These salaries included £30 owing every trimester to each college of Anziani. They paid the expenses of their frequent ambassadors to Lucca, the expenses due on the feast of Santa Croce, and costs for such miscellaneous materials as the paper and wax required for the chancellor.[230] The records of the Libri di Riformagioni e Consigli are characterized by lively and sometimes acrimonious debate. It is true that for all its administrative responsibilities, the Council of Pietrasanta had few real powers of government. The commune even needed the express permission of Lucca to impose a

[227] ASCP Libro di Consigli (1431), fo. 3^{v}; Libro di Consigli (1446), fo. 1^{v}.

[228] The rough distinction seems to be between meetings summoned by the vicar to notify them of instructions from Lucca or to handle matters of political importance and meetings concerned with basic administrative detail.

[229] ASCP Libro di Consigli (1435), fo. 23^{r-v}. This General Council was in fact described as a meeting of 'the greater and saner part' of the men of Pietrasanta. For other meetings where large numbers of *invitati* were present, see ASL Amministrazione delle comunità soggette e delle vicarie, 38, fos. 21^{r}, 23^{r}, 25^{r}, 28^{v}, 31^{r}.

[230] ASL Gabelle del contado e delle vicarie, 81(11), 81(12).

datia to cover its basic expenses and obligations.[231] Within very narrow confines, Pietrasanta in the 1430s enjoyed sophisticated powers of self-government, comparable with neighbouring Camaiore,[232] but unusual throughout the rest of the Lucchese state.

On 28 September 1430 Lucca received a loan of 15,000 *fiorini d'oro* from Genoa for purposes of local defence in the Florentine war. As security, Carrara, Avenza, Pietrasanta, and Motrone were pledged to Genoa. Local revenues and administration remained with Lucca, but these fortresses all received Genoese garrisons at Lucca's expense.[233] Lucca itself was required to appoint a Genoese *Podestà*. The loan, which was for three years, was subsequently extended.[234] And the Genoese still occupied the *rocca* of Pietrasanta in 1436. In March of that year the men of Pietrasanta, carrying a banner, paraded through the piazza and the rest of the town shouting 'Viva San Giorgio', 'Mora le gabelle', and 'Viva libertà'. They seized and imprisoned the vicar, Alessandro Rapondi, with the other Lucchese officials; appointed their own administration; and gave Pietrasanta with its territory to the Genoese.[235] At the beginning of April the General Council of Lucca approved the imposition of a forced loan of 1,200 ducats, to be used exclusively for the recovery of Pietrasanta.[236] In May two leading Pietrasantesi, ser Nicolao Colucci and ser Nicolao Giusfredi (Morroni), described as 'li principali fondatori di questo tractato', were taken whilst on an embassy to Genoa by certain foot-soldiers, and were handed over to Lucca.[237] They were subsequently

[231] ASL Amministrazione delle comunità soggette e delle vicarie, 38, fo. 13^{v}. Taxes were levied on the basis of the *estimo*. The book of the *estimo* was the work of men sent from Lucca, but the Anziani of Pietrasanta might appoint men to review the work of the *estimatore* and, if necessary, appeal to the Anziani of Lucca for redress: ASCP Libro di Consigli (1435), fo. 16^{r-v}.

[232] In Camaiore the 'Anziani' were called 'Capitani': ASL Biblioteca (Manoscritti), 30, Pellegrino di Bartolomeo Pellegrini da Camaiore, Memorie, fos. 25^{r}–26^{r}, 40^{r-v}. For both Pietrasanta and Camaiore the difficulty was to produce a *tasca* that was large enough to satisfy local aspirations, but not so large that it became impossible to find suitable candidates.

[233] ASL Capitoli, 7, pp. 53–6.

[234] Ibid., pp. 57–8.

[235] SB 161, fos. 84^{r-v}, 91^{r}, 86^{r-v}, 89^{r}; Podestà di Lucca, Inquisizioni, 5230, no foliation. Civitali names the authors of the rebellion as ser Nicolao Colucci, Pardino Celli, ser Nicolao Giusfredi, and Duccino Bartolomei: ASL Biblioteca (Manoscritti), 38, Storia di Lucca, fo. 427^{r}.

[236] Rif. 15, pp. 36–7, 39. A second forced loan was approved at the beginning of May, to be repaid from the goods and lands of the rebels of Pietrasanta: ibid., p. 47.

[237] Ibid., p. 52; Anz. Temp. Lib. 532, no. 31, fos. 99^{v}–100^{r}.

released, clearly in exchange for Lucchese prisoners in Pietrasanta.[238] Early expeditions resulted in the recovery of Motrone,[239] but not of Pietrasanta; more was hoped of Niccolò Piccinino in January 1437.[240] But Piccinino soon diverted his army against Barga,[241] and after his retreat, Lucca was in no position to hold on to what she possessed, far less undertake the reconquest of lost lands. With the coming of peace, Lucca in June 1438 offered protection to the goods and persons of all subjects of Genoa in the city and territory of Lucca.[242] For nearly half a century an uneasy truce prevailed, punctuated by the early refusal of the Pietrasantesi to pay their rents to Lucchese landowners[243] and by interminable border conflicts.[244] The conquest of Pietrasanta by Florence in 1484 revived Lucchese hopes; the French invasion of 1494 resulted in Lucca's brief recovery of Pietrasanta, before it fell finally under Florentine rule in the sixteenth century.[245]

The impact of these events should not be exaggerated. They are reflected in the short-lived lacuna in the notarial protocolli.[246] Even in September 1436 conte Luiso dal Verme had been able to negotiate on behalf of Lucca a truce for the cultivation of land by the men of Pietrasanta and by Lucchese subjects.[247] By 1438 the Pietrasantese *speziale* Filippo di

[238] ASL Biblioteca (Manoscritti), 38, Giuseppe Civitali, Storia di Lucca, fo. 427^{r-v}. It has often been repeated, by, among others, Santini, *Versilia centrale*, i. 130, that both men were executed in 1436. The extent of Santini's confusion about the affair—and indeed, on matters genealogical in general—is made plain by his notes still preserved in Pietrasanta: ASCP, I, 159–61. The career of ser Nicolao Colucci can be followed closely in his own notarial protocolli: NAC, N 115–16.

[239] Rif. 15, pp. 52, 92; ASL Podestà di Lucca, Inquisizioni, 5229, no foliation.

[240] Rif. 15, p. 121.

[241] Ibid., pp. 122–3.

[242] Ibid., pp. 256–7.

[243] Santini, *Versilia centrale*, ii. 97.

[244] ASL Capitoli, 7, pp. 69, 85–95; ASCP, I 2, Atti dei Genovesi (1433–82), fos. 8^{v}, 20^{v}–21^{r}, 63^{r}–65^{r}; Libro di Consigli (1449), fos. 8^{v}, 9^{r}; E 3, Libro di Consigli (1479–84), fo. 47^{r-v}; Santini, *Versilia centrale*, ii. 98–109, 133, 223–4.

[245] ASL Capitoli, 7, pp. 99, 109 ff.; Santini, *Versilia centrale*, ii. 113–18, 135 ff.

[246] AN 459(3) (ser Giovanni da Gallicano), fos. 15^{v}–30^{v}. Ser Giovanni seems to have been absent from his house in Pietrasanta between 1436 and 1438. He recorded (fo. 33^{v}) the making in Pietrasanta by the Genoese authorities of a public notary to be recognized in both Lucca and Pietrasanta on 27 Feb. 1439. The notary thus authorized was ser Paolino di Tomuccio Tomucci, who had been operating until 1427/8, but whose acts then disappear until 19 June 1437, with a further gap from 14 Dec. 1440 to 25 Jan. 1444: NAC, T 573–4. Clearly, in this case the problem is partly one of survival. The work of ser Gherardo da Pietrasanta is missing for the period 1436–8: NAC, G 163(1)(2). Not surprisingly, the registers of ser Nicolao Colucci contain virtually nothing for the couple of years after the revolt: NAC, N 115–16.

[247] ASL Capitoli, 7, pp. 60–1. Lucca's promises were allegedly not honoured: ibid. 35, p. 428.

Michelino Iacobi was engaged in an (albeit disrupted) attempt to buy Sicilian cheeses from Palermo in return for iron.[248] By the 1440s the notarial records are full of examples of Lucchese citizens pursuing commercial debts and unpaid rents.[249] By the 1450s Lucchese citizens were again commercially active in Pietrasanta.[250] Most prominently, Silvestro di Battista di ser Castruccio reappears as sometimes resident in Pietrasanta: taking possession of his father's lands, lending money, and forming a company with Angelo di ser Giovanni da Castiglione of Pietrasanta for retailing woollen cloth and trading in iron.[251] In 1463 the sons of the leading traitors of 1436, ser Nicolao Colucci and ser Nicolao Giusfredi, applied (successfully) for Lucchese citizenship.[252] Life continued, and geographical proximity made the true severing of ties impossible. Nevertheless, after 1436 the Pietrasantesi owed obedience to new political masters, and their fortunes became entangled with the turbulent politics of Genoa.[253]

In explaining the revolt of 1436, we may dismiss the obligatory protestations of ignorance and innocence issuing from Genoa.[254] The revolt was made possible by the Genoese garrison and by Genoese reinforcements. No doubt the Genoese offered encouragement to local ambitions in the days leading up to the revolt. For the Pietrasantesi themselves, the slogans in the piazza clearly summarized their hopes: they wanted fewer taxes and more liberty. But, equally clearly, the slogans are of little help in determining why in 1436 the leading men of Pietrasanta decided that their advantage lay with Genoa rather than Lucca. The self-justification that only through Genoese protection could Pietrasanta be

[248] NAC, N 116 (1435–9), 26 Nov. 1438.

[249] NAC, N 115 (1409–68), fo. 107^r; ASCP, A 6, Filze giusdicenti (S. Giorgio, 2 Jan.–19 Aug. 1461), no foliation. For parallel difficulties experienced by the men of Pietrasanta, see NAC, N 115 (1409–68), fo. 118^v. The 1440s also saw a number of Lucchese citizens selling their landed property in and around Pietrasanta.

[250] AN 597 (ser Luviso di Antonio Buonaccorsi), fos. 224^v–225^v; NAC, N 115 (1409–68), fos. 191^{r-v}, 298^r, 306^v.

[251] NAC, N 115 (1409–68), fos. 251^{r-v}, 254^{r-v}, 272^v, 282^r, 283^r, 284^v, 285^r, 286^r, 289^v, 296^r, 299^v, 300^v, 315^v. For Silvestro in Lucca, and for his will enacted there in the monastery of S. Giorgio, see ASL Podestà di Lucca, Curia Civile, 1309, fos. 84^r–88^r; AN 385 (ser Massino di Bartolomeo da Pietrasanta), fos. 264^v–266^v, 296^v–297^v. He was member of the General Council of Lucca once for the year 1453/4.

[252] Rif. 18, p. 639.

[253] See, e.g., the truce between the vicar of Pietrasanta for the Banco di San Giorgio, the vicariate, and the Campofregosi lords of Genoa: NAC, N 115 (1409–68), fo. 129^r. At this time in the mid-1440s, Pietrasanta passed from the rule of Genoa to that of the Banco di San Giorgio. In 1459 Tommaso Panichi was lamenting to Giovanni di Cosimo de' Medici that as a result 'delle guerre di Genova tutto questo luogo esere disfatto': MAP, ix. 521.

[254] ASL Capitoli, 7, p. 58.

protected from Florentine conquest makes little sense in the spring of 1436: it smacks of an excuse devised later, in the light of subsequent developments.[255] It is possible that men like ser Nicolao Colucci had already divined that their career prospects were diminished under the new republican regime in Lucca. The rule of Paolo Guinigi had been a time when able men from the *contado* had flourished in the service of the prince.[256] The later applications of Tommaso Panichi for Medici patronage show the importance to ambitious Pietrasantesi of employment beyond the narrow confines of Pietrasanta itself.[257] Probably urban republics like that reconstituted in Lucca in 1430 were intrinsically less sympathetic to outsiders, even to those like ser Nicolao who held Lucchese citizenship. Whether this was already apparent in Pietrasanta by 1436 remains unproven. Ser Nicolao Colucci himself, between 1430 and 1436, continued to be elected to the kind of minor legal and administrative offices in the Lucchese state that he had enjoyed under Paolo Guinigi.[258] Three contemporary realities offer less speculative grounds for revolt: the specific burdens of Lucchese rule in the early 1430s, the positive—and more particularly the negative—attractions of Genoese control, and the endemic tensions, discussed above, between conterminous communities within the Lucchese state.

Pietrasanta was treated with no less consideration by Lucca than any other part of her embattled territories. The composition with Pietrasanta of October 1433 offered a reduction in the salt tax, a review of expenses incurred on behalf of Lucca, and—in reward for the great labours and sacrifices of these 'filii et fidelissimi subditi lucani communis' on behalf of Lucchese liberty—the grant of an annual fair or market.[259] In November

[255] Ibid., p. 59; Santini, *Versilia centrale*, i. 130; ii. 95. Santini may have misunderstood comments from the long preamble to the agreement between Genoa and Pietrasanta of July 1437 which relate to the events of 1430: ASL Capitoli, 35, p. 420.

[256] Guinigi seems to have particularly favoured men from Pietrasanta. Santini's haphazard genealogies have caused him to attribute a number of unlikely candidates to Pietrasanta; the point can nevertheless be abundantly illustrated from the pages of *Versilia centrale*.

[257] MAP, viii. 352; ix. 521. For Arrigo Panichi, see ibid. v. 776.

[258] He was appointed *commissario* for Avenza in 1431: Rif. 14, p. 128. With ser Gherardo Bartolomei of Pietrasanta, he was among the notaries for the court of *sindici* and *fondaci* of Lucca in 1432: Anz. Temp. Lib. 5, fo. 84^r. His final appointment in Lucchese service was as *podestà* of Monteggiori for the whole of 1436: Rif. 14, p. 789. Ser Nicolao Giusfredi was *podestà* of Casoli oltre Giogo for the first semester of 1434: Rif. 14, p. 433.

[259] ASL Capitoli, 7, pp. 61–3; Rif. 14, pp. 414–16, 418. The salt payment was fixed at 178 florins at 40 bolognini per florin, £400 11*s*. 11*d*., at 11*s*. per bolognino due six-monthly; the salary of vicar, court, judge, *Capitano del contado*, etc. was set at 102 florins, £7 9*s*. 10*d*., for every three months.

1433 all fines against the Anziani of Pietrasanta, their agents, or private individuals for failing to obey orders during the late wars were cancelled, a remission which the Anziani were able to extend to common criminal offences.[260] Ironically, Tommaso Mathei da Carrara, one of the leading rebels in 1436, was unbanned by the republic in 1434, since his crimes had been committed under the Guinigi tyranny.[261] Despite such concessions, the political records of Pietrasanta show clearly the tensions generated by Lucca's massive financial needs during the war and in its immediate aftermath. During the war, with harvests devastated and with a large population of foreign stipendiaries to feed in Pietrasanta, Lucca was in no position to impose extraordinary charges.[262] There remained the ordinary expenses, and even these were resisted with pleas of prevailing poverty and misery.[263] More dramatically, the men of Pietrasanta clashed with their political masters over the inflow of yet more foreign troops under Lodovico Colonna and Buongiovanni Trotto. Even at this stage individual Pietrasantesi were plotting to hand the town over to the Florentines.[264] With the coming of peace, Lucca seems to have pressed rather harder for what she regarded as a legitimate contribution from her subjects. The most fractious issue was the 600 ducats demanded from Pietrasanta in 1435 for the recovery of lands held by the Este of Ferrara. Here the General Council of Pietrasanta threatened ominously, and not for the first time, that they 'will no longer be able to live at the feet of Lucca' if impossible demands are made of them. The debates over the 600 ducats offer the faintest trace of the presence within the General Council of Pietrasanta of men of more intransigent views.[265] Further problems arose over Lucca's attempt to insist on early payment for houses purchased by Pietrasanta for the use of the commune.[266] When Lucca decided to send grain from Pietrasanta to furnish her ally Genoa, there was concern that exports would leave Pietrasanta dangerously short;[267] then Lucca

[260] Rif. 14, pp. 430, 494.

[261] Ibid., p. 580.

[262] 'non l'abbiamo aggravati di spes alcuna': Fumi (ed.), *Regesti*, 123; BSL MS 91, Storie di Lucca, fo. 65^{v}; ASCP Libro di Consigli (1431), fo. 7^{r-v}.

[263] ASCP Libro di Consigli (1431), fos. 10^{r-v}, 14^{r-v}. The Pietrasantesi were admittedly not unsympathetic in May 1431 when approached by their vicar, Tiero Gentili, who had exercised his office well and with great effort, and who now sought his unpaid salary and the expenses of his administration: ibid., fo. 11^{r-v}.

[264] Fumi (ed.), *Regesti*, 123.

[265] ASL Amministrazione delle comunità soggette e delle vicarie, 38, fos. 21^{r}–26^{v}, 28^{v}–30^{r}, 30^{v}–32^{v}.

[266] ASCP Libro di Consigli (1435), fos. 13^{r-v}, 24^{v}–25^{v}; ASL Amministrazione delle comunità soggette e delle vicarie, 38, fos. 8^{r}, 9^{r-v}, 10^{v}–11^{r}, 13^{v}–14^{r}.

[267] ASL Amministrazione delle comunità soggette e delle vicarie, 38, fos. 17^{v}–18^{v}, 19^{r}–20^{v}.

prohibited grain exports which would have been very profitable for Pietrasanta.[268] The same year of 1435 saw protests against the fiscal burdens that resulted from the exemption from the *estimo* of the property of Lucchese citizens and of pious foundations.[269] In a case of fraud involving the Genoese *castellano*, the vicar Nicolao Sandei clearly felt it safer to proceed against a local scapegoat.[270] In a particularly unfortunate incident in March 1435 one of the ambassadors sent from Pietrasanta to the Anziani of Lucca, Antonio Diodati, was detained by the *Podestà* for commercial debts.[271] The whole of 1435 is full of petty haggling and bad-tempered incidents, a fitting prelude to the events of the following spring.

The Pietrasantesi turned to Genoa because they had little choice. Immediate past experience of Genoese power included the brawling in the streets of Pietrasanta of members of the Genoese garrison.[272] But commercial links with Genoa were traditionally strong; indeed, in the fifteenth century communications with Liguria were perhaps easier than with Lucca. In explaining the attractions of Genoese rule, local historians have stressed less these traditional ties than the great liberties offered by the Genoese to their new subjects. Santini believed that Pietrasanta became almost a free republic under Genoa.[273] The enthusiasm has resulted in exaggeration. All attempts by the Anziani of Pietrasanta to exercise an independent authority or petty jurisdiction were thwarted from Genoa.[274] The most minor of local ordinances were subject to the approval and revision of the *protectores* of San Giorgio.[275] The traditional responsibilities of local government for the upkeep of roads and prisons were strictly supervised;[276] the appeal to Genoa to put pressure on a tardy Pietrasantese craftsman working on the *coro* of S. Martino was hardly the act of a free republic.[277] Much remained unchanged. Attempts by the Pietrasantesi to limit expenses were met by Genoa, as by Lucca, with charges of frivolous excuses and by angry denunciations of men unwilling

268 Ibid., fos. 21^{r}–22^{r}.

269 Ibid., fo. 13^{v}. For an attempt to spread to foreigners the 'great expense in our commune that it is not possible for our men to pay', see ASCP Libro di Consigli (1435), fo. 11^{v}.

270 ASL Vicario di Pietrasanta, Atti Criminali, 236, fos. 2^{v}–5^{r} and unfoliated.

271 AN 431 (ser Domenico Arrighi), fos. 28^{v}–29^{r}.

272 ASL Vicario di Pietrasanta, Atti Criminali, 233, fos. 4^{r}–7^{r}, 19^{r}–20^{v}.

273 Santini, *Versilia centrale*, ii. 132–4. The point is frequently repeated.

274 ASCP, I 2, Atti dei Genovesi (1433–82), fos. 21^{r}, 22^{v}–24^{v}, 86^{r}.

275 Ibid., fos. 60^{r}–61^{v}; Libro di Consigli (1447), fo. 10^{r}.

276 ASCP, I 2, Atti dei Genovesi (1433–82), fos. 41^{r}–46^{v}.

277 Ibid., fo. 50^{v}.

to bear costs incurred for the defence of their own wives and children.[278] There were the usual complaints from Pietrasanta about vicars unlearned in the law, about breaches of privileges, and above all over the determination of the communities of its vicariate to avoid their share of the financial burdens.[279] At the same time, the men of Pietrasanta clearly believed themselves to have achieved favourable terms from Genoa in 1436.[280] These included commercial privileges within Genoa.[281] Genoese citizens in Pietrasanta did not enjoy the exemptions from tax and service of their Lucchese predecessors.[282] The dignity of the Anziani of Pietrasanta was augmented with the title of *domini* and with freedom from arrest for debt whilst in office.[283] The Libri di Consigli for the Genoese period suggest that local government (however closely supervised) was being conducted by the vicar in close association with the Anziani, and that the Genoese vicar occupied rather more of an intermediate position between mother city and subject community than had his Lucchese counterpart.[284]

The men of Pietrasanta rebelled in 1436 because Lucchese rule had become intolerable, and because they hoped for better things from Genoa. Local historians have stressed a third ingredient: the ancient animosity between Pietrasanta and Camaiore.[285] Pietrasanta was a favourite residence of Paolo Guinigi. His favour was to the detriment of Camaiore, not least because of the diversion of water resources. The men of Camaiore rejoiced greatly at the restoration of the republic. During the wars of the 1430s they became among the most ostentatiously loyal of Lucca's subjects. It is very tempting to attribute the loyalty of Camaiore and the

[278] ASCP, A 3, Filze giusdicenti (S. Giorgio, Vercamini vic. 1448), fo. 7^{r}; I 2, Atti dei Genovesi (1433–82), fo. 95^{r}.

[279] ASCP, I 2, Atti dei Genovesi (1433–82), fos. 3^{r}–4^{v}, 5^{r}–10^{v}, 15^{r}–16^{r}, 20^{v}, 29^{r}–31^{v}, 33^{v}–34^{v}, 49^{v}–50^{r}, 61^{v}, 64^{r}–71^{r}, 77^{r-v}, 84^{r}–86^{r}; Libro di Consigli (1449), fos. 6^{v}–7^{r}, 9^{r}, 13^{r-v}.

[280] The terms of the agreement are missing from ASL Capitoli, 7, p. 60, but a copy of the composition can be found in Capitoli, 35, pp. 419–38. For the ratification of the agreement in 1443, see ASCP, I 2, Atti dei Genovesi (1433–82), fos. 55^{r}–57^{r}.

[281] ASCP, I 2, Atti dei Genovesi (1433–82), fo. 20^{r-v}.

[282] All inhabitants were to be treated alike, despite the protest of those born in the district of Genoa that 'it seems wrong that Genoese should be treated as foreigners in a land under San Giorgio': ibid., fos. 88^{r}–90^{r}.

[283] Ibid., fos. 16^{r}, 39^{v}–40^{r}. The periodic measures to ensure that the Anziani of Pietrasanta did not act independently of vicar and General Council may, paradoxically, provide further evidence of the greater stature of the Anziani during this period: ibid., fos. 17^{r-v}, 75^{v}, 76^{v}–77^{r}, 78^{v}; Libro di Consigli (1449), fo. 6^{r}.

[284] On the one hand, there are the complaints against the vicar from Pietrasanta to Genoa: ASCP, I 2, Atti dei Genovesi (1433–82), fos. 20^{v}, 49^{v}–50^{r}, 84^{r}–86^{r}. On the other, the vicar might turn to the Anziani of Pietrasanta for support against criticism at home: E 3, Libro di Consigli (1479–84), fos. 58^{v}–59^{r}.

[285] Santini, *Versilia centrale*, ii. 50–60, 82, 221–4; iv. 184.

treason of Pietrasanta to these deep-rooted local rivalries, recently fuelled by the partial rule of Paolo Guinigi. There are two problems. First, our chief sources are two local chroniclers of Camaiore.[286] Neither chronicler had much historical or chronological sense; both were preoccupied with the outrages committed by the men of Pietrasanta against Camaiore after 1436. The differing political loyalties after 1436 exacerbated, though they did not create, the conflicts over water resources and fisheries. There is a very real danger of transferring the hatreds of the late fifteenth and early sixteenth centuries to the 1430s. Secondly, all the notarial sources show that in the real world the men of Pietrasanta and Camaiore continued to do business together, to buy and inherit land, to take wives and receive dowries, regardless of political borders.[287] But these are no more than cautionary notes. Whilst impossible to prove, there is every likelihood that Pietrasanta's loss of favoured status *vis-à-vis* Camaiore was a major irritant behind the revolt.

In November 1449 the men of Minucciano threw off the rule of the Malaspina, and returned to Lucchese obedience.[288] They were well rewarded for their new-found loyalty with a composition of 11 December 1449 which granted them quite exceptional liberties and privileges.[289] In September 1450 the example of Minucciano was followed by the men of Gallicano, thus ending a period of rule by the Marchesi d'Este that had begun in 1429. As in the case of Minucciano, it was very much in Lucca's interests to emphasize that the men of Gallicano had acted on their own initiative and of their own free will.[290] In reality, Lucca had long worked for the recovery of these lands. And on hearing false rumours of the death of Leonello d'Este at the beginning of September 1450, Lucca immediately sent 500 *fanti* and *cerne* to Castiglione to receive those places 'that wished peacefully to return to us'.[291] Lucchese possession of Gallicano was sanctioned by papal arbitration in February 1451. In May the agreement reached on 20 September of the previous year between Lucca's special *commissario*, Bartolomeo di Nicolao da Moncigoli, and the

[286] ASL Biblioteca (Manoscritti), 26, M. Bianco Bianchi, Historie della terra di Camaiore; 30, Pellegrino di Bartolomeo Pellegrini da Camaiore, Memorie.

[287] See, e.g., NAC, N 115 (1409–68), fos. 141^{v}, 153^{v}, 159^{v}, 164^{r}, 184^{r}, 200^{v}, 223^{v}, 227^{r-v}, 238^{v}.

[288] Rif. 17, p. 161; Fumi (ed.), *Regesti*, 1211–12, 1215.

[289] Rif. 17, pp. 167–9, 181. The privileges did not prevent subsequent conspiracies: ibid., p. 727.

[290] Anz. Temp. Lib. 532, no. 32, fos. 88^{r}, 89^{r-v}, 90^{r-v}, 90^{v}–91^{r}, 91^{r-v}.

[291] Ibid., fos. 88^{r-v}. By 27 Sept. Lucca could write of Gallicano: 'sonvi per noi oltre li huomini della terra fanti circa 100 per questo principio perchè intendiamo tenerlo et difenderlo'. Leonello in fact died, and was succeeded by Borso in Oct. 1450.

men of Gallicano was confirmed in Lucca in the palace of the Anziani. By this agreement Gallicano was freed from most expenses for twenty-five years; its inhabitants were pardoned past offences, and received a number of privileges, including the right to carry arms in the *contado* of Lucca and in the city of Lucca itself.[292] These concessions were renewed when the composition lapsed in 1475, as on subsequent occasions.[293] Obviously the fate of Gallicano was largely determined by military manœuvres and arbitration awards over which it had little control. Nevertheless, when the right occasion presented itself in the autumn of 1450, Lucca found within Gallicano support for the restoration of Lucchese rule. To this extent the example of Gallicano offers a useful counterpoise to events in Pietrasanta in 1436.

In 1453 the whole vicariate of Gallicano was calculated at 200 hearths, of which the men of Gallicano and Verni accounted for sixty.[294] The notarial acts for Gallicano show a small, simple, essentially rural society whose concerns at law were confined to wills, dowries, small loans, and the sale and leasing of land and livestock.[295] There was some iron smelting and manufacture in the area,[296] but generally trades and crafts were limited to the service needs of an isolated and largely self-reliant community. Lucchese rule was exercised by a vicar, as always holding office for six months, whose salary and establishment after 1460 were increased to equal those of Camaiore and Valdilima.[297] Before the Estense conquest, local power probably rested with a general *parlamento* of all adult males, summoned and headed by three elected consuls and officials.[298] The role of the *parlamento* continued, but from at least the 1460s Gallicano was ruled, under its vicar, by two *capitani*, or officials, holding office for a term of three months and by a council of *dieci buoni huomini* elected twice yearly. The *dieci buoni huomini* were elected in June and December: one by the

292 ASG MS 5, Libro delle Compositioni, fos. 1r–10r.

293 Ibid., fos. 10v–11v.

294 Ibid., fo. 9r. In 1428 forty-six parishioners of the pieve of S. Giovanni of Gallicano attended a convocation summoned by the consuls and officials of the commune: NAC, N 116 (1428–32), fos. 6v–7r. All males between the ages of 14 and 70 were obliged to attend the *generale parlamento*: ASG MS 6, Statuti (1461), 13. The *atti* for the period from 1482 show an attendance of between fifty and sixty men at most meetings in the 1480s; by the 1490s as many as sixty-eight individuals might be listed: ASG MS 13.

295 NAC, N 116 (1428–32), fos. 4r–36r; AN 459(3) (ser Giovanni da Gallicano), fos. 27r–30r. Ser Nicolao Colucci, leading conspirator of Pietrasanta in 1436, was part of the Lucchese administration in Gallicano when it fell to the Este in 1429.

296 AN 704 (ser Benedetto Franciotti), p. 160; NAC, N 116 (1428–32), fos. 15v, 18r, 20v–21r.

297 ASL Colloqui, 1, p. 52; Rif. 18, pp. 304, 305, 349, 637.

298 NAC, N 116 (1428–32), fos. 6v–7r.

vicar, one by the vicar's notary, one by each of the two officials, or *capitani*, and one by each of three men elected in turn by each of the two officials. The *capitani*, or officials, were elected for the year every December: one by the vicar, one by his notary, one by each of the two officials presently in office, and the rest by members of the council. The eight men thus elected were divided into 'colleges' of two; the names were placed in bags, and drawn as required in bizarre imitation of the electoral procedures of far larger political communities.[299] There is a surviving record from 1482 of the proceedings of the *parlamento*, of the council of *dieci buoni huomini*, and of various *ad hoc* committees summoned by the officials.[300] This, together with the statutes of 1461, would seem to suggest that the men of Gallicano had rather more control over local regulations and the punishment of offenders than had their counterparts in Pietrasanta even under the Genoese.[301] But the issues were very parochial. Beyond the election of officials and the leasing of communal lands and facilities, local government in Gallicano was concerned with the control of dogs and the regulation of the harvest.

If the economic and political structures of Gallicano were relatively simple, the passions of rival groupings within Gallicano are impossibly complex. Lucca regained control in an atmosphere of civil strife. The Lucchese victory, despite the pardoning of past offences, produced a body of exiles who were responsible for repeated attacks on the property of their enemies at home. Particularly in July 1451, and clearly with the support of Borso d'Este, the exiles of Gallicano were coming at night into Gallicano from Castelnuovo to burn crops and to destroy barns and other installations.[302] Prominent among the Gallicano exiles were Benedetto Micheli called Berrecta, his brother Giovanni, and his son Iacopo. The exiles were joined by men from Turrite and by supporters from Castelnuovo itself. Their leading targets included the lands of Chele Bartolomei and Biagio Martini. In the interests of peace, Rodolfo di Tommaso of Gallicano was pardoned in 1452, and Simone Dini in 1456.[303]

[299] ASG MS 13, fos. 14^{r}–15^{r}, 21^{v}, 31^{r}. Cf. the rather different electoral procedures described in the communal statutes of 1461: MS 6, Statuti (1461), 1–2, which also specify a vacancy of one year for both *capitani* and councillors, applying also to fathers, sons, uncles, nephews, and brothers.

[300] The vicar of Gallicano also called general meetings of the syndics and officials of Gallicano, Perpoli, Fiattone, and Verni: ASG MS 13, fos. 23^{r-v}, 178^{v}.

[301] ASG MS 6, Statuti (1461), 1, 4–5, 10–11, 14, 24–65, pp. 75–6; MS 13, fos. 10^{r}, 16^{r}, 21^{v}, 27^{v}, 100^{v}, 102^{v}, 105^{r}, 134^{r-v}, 136^{v}–137^{r}, 221^{v}, 225^{r}.

[302] SB 165, fos. 405^{r-v}, 420^{r}, 456^{r-v}, 473^{r-v}, 503^{r}; Anz. Temp. Lib. 532, no. 32, fo. 106^{r-v}; Fumi (ed.), *Regesti*, 1328.

[303] Rif. 17, pp. 400, 404–5, 818.

The following year, at the behest of the Marchese of Ferrara, Benedetto Micheli and his kinsmen were also pardoned.[304] But these acts of mercy did not dissuade Simone Dini from becoming involved in a new plot that was taking place in Gallicano in 1459. A total of eleven men[305] were implicated in a conspiracy of that year to kill Chele Bartolomei and restore Gallicano to the rule of Ferrara.[306] Even now Lucca was cautious about proceeding to extremes. The plotters were imprisoned in Lucca and tortured. They were saved in part by the intervention of Domenico Bertini, originally from Gallicano, a Lucchese citizen and humanist who appears frequently in the General Council of Lucca as spokesman for his native land. Bertini pointed out that the *parenti* of the arrested men constituted half—perhaps two-thirds—of the population of Gallicano, and offered to advise Lucca on more effective measures to end the continuing faction struggles.[307]

It is easier to assert that Lucca, Ferrara, Florence, and other powers were favoured by a fluid body of support within Gallicano than to identify the origins and nature of the divisions. Berengo has stressed the impossibility of attributing concrete identities to the *sette contadine*.[308] Members of the Bertini family had received Lucchese citizenship under Paolo Guinigi, and were resident in Lucca whilst their native Gallicano was under Estense rule.[309] One of the 'coniunctissimi' of Domenico Bertini was prominent in the restoration of Lucchese rule in 1450.[310] Chele Bartolomei was in Lucchese service by the 1430s.[311] From the 1450s he was combining employment in the high military service of Lucca with a leading role in the political life of Gallicano.[312] The granting of a *condotta*

304 Rif. 18, p. 53.

305 Francesco Bartolomei, Iacopo Colucci, Pasquino Dini, Simone Dini, Frediano Magini, Andrea Martini, Iacopuccio Martini, Andrea Melani, Frediano Micheli, Iacopo Pieri, and Giovanni Stefani alias Bonacci.

306 ASL Capitano del Contado, 55, 2nd foliation, fos. 45ʳ–46ᵛ; Colloqui, 1, pp. 26–7, 28.

307 Rif. 18, pp. 201, 218; Colloqui, 1, pp. 30, 48. The men were gradually released, under various conditions, until in June 1460 they were permitted to return to Gallicano: Rif. 18, pp. 218–21, 245, 277, 300–1, 303.

308 Berengo, *Nobili e mercanti*, 341–6.

309 Baroni, Notizie genealogiche, MS 1105, fos. 380ʳ–445ᵛ; AN 385 (ser Massino di Bartolomeo da Pietrasanta), fo. 141ʳ⁻ᵛ; Podestà di Lucca, Curia Civile, 1176, fos. 78ʳ–79ʳ.

310 Anz. Temp. Lib. 532, no. 32, fo. 88ᵛ.

311 Ibid. 442, 6 June 1434.

312 For Chele Bartolomei as constable of Lucca, see Rif. 18, p. 300; Anz. Temp. Lib. 6, unfoliated; SB 165, fos. 613ʳ–614ᵛ. He represented Gallicano in the negotiations with the Anziani of Lucca in Apr. 1453, and was one of the *statutarii* in 1461: ASG MS 5, fo. 9ᵛ; MS 6, p. 3. His son Giuliano was very prominent in the councils of the commune in the last decades of the century.

from Lucca did not ensure unswerving political loyalty to Lucca.[313] But there remains some correlation between service, favours, and political allegiance. As important were the bitter and changing personal animosities that severed the Gallicano community. The men of Gallicano contemplated the restoration of Estense rule in 1459 because they hated Chele Bartolomei. He was held responsible for bringing discord into the land,[314] though the causes of his unpopularity remain obscure. The only concrete charge relates to interference in the marriage politics of his neighbours.[315] Chele Bartolomei was the son of a blacksmith accused under the Este of being a notorious usurer.[316] But the case centred around Chele's brother Tommaso, and Rodolfo di Tommaso was one of the exiles sallying forth from Castelnuovo to burn crops and barns (including his uncle's) in 1451. The factions of Gallicano were tied, through Domenico Bertini's brother Antonio, to the Guerrucci plot in Lucca of 1460,[317] though the links now seem irrecoverable. Always in the background, in Gallicano and throughout the whole Garfagnana, were the old party labels of Guelph and Ghibelline.[318] The Lucchese chronicler Antonio Iova claimed that it was the Ghibelline party in Gallicano that rebelled against the Este in 1450, and returned that land to Lucchese obedience.[319] Alignments between local men, Ferrara, republican Lucca, Guinigi exiles, and Florence were certainly vaguely still associated with Guelph and Ghibelline identities. What the old party names might have meant in the party conflict of the Garfagnana in the mid-fifteenth century is impossible to imagine.

Throughout the fifteenth century Lucca complained of the unwillingness of her subject communities to bear a reasonable proportion of the expenses for their own administration and defence, whilst *contadini* responded with accusations of exploitation and impoverishment. Wherever the true balance lies, the examples of Pietrasanta and Gallicano show that the men of the vicariates might find themselves in quite a strong

313 Pasquino Dini, one of the conspirators of 1459, was *compagno* of Chele Bartolomei in the pay of Lucca in 1451: Rif. 18, pp. 50–1; SB 165, fo. 485^r. His fellow conspirator Iacopuccio Martini was in the employ of Lucca by 1461: Anz. Temp. Lib. 6, 30 Apr. 1461.

314 ASL Colloqui, 1, p. 30. Iacopuccio Martini is alleged to have said, 'Voi vedete quante discordie Chele mette in questa terra, tagliamolo a pezzi': Capitano del Contado, 55, 2nd foliation, fo. 48^r.

315 According to Giovanni Stefani alias Bonacci, 'Voi vedete questo Chele quanto male ci fa che non mi lassa maritare le mie figluole ne mi lassa ammoglere il mio figuolo e per questo Io lo voglo tagliare a pezzi': ASL Capitano del Contado, 55, 2nd foliation, fo. 48^r.

316 ASL Podestà di Lucca, Curia Civile, 1177, fo. 9^{r-v}. Bartolomeo was operating through the usual technique of fictitious sales. Relationships are clarified ibid. 1307, fos. 87^r–90^r.

317 ASL Colloqui, 1, p. 67.

318 De Stefani, *Garfagnana*, 162 ff.

319 BSL MS 2599, Antonio Iova, Annali Historici, p. 925.

bargaining position in the highly competitive world of inter-state rivalries. More important, these case-studies must warn against viewing the situation and aspirations of the periphery purely in terms of relations with the metropolitan power. Tensions between Pietrasanta and Camaiore may have been as important as tensions between Pietrasanta and Lucca. Similarly, it was a long-standing conflict with Castiglione, rather than any particular hostility towards Lucca, that lay behind the abortive plot of April 1451 to surrender Cerageto, Tramonte, and Verucchio to the Este of Ferrara.[320] In Gallicano the local ambitions and *vendette* of native factions were undoubtedly more important than any passionately held commitment to either Lucca or Ferrara. In Camaiore trouble festered between the local community and the powerful house of Orsucci in their midst.[321] The loss of Massa to the Malaspina in 1442 was largely occasioned by the intense unpopularity of the great local family of Cattani, which was not unconnected with their claim to the exemptions and privileges of Lucchese citizenship.[322] Obviously Lucca was the central player. But as in other late medieval societies, too rigid a focus on the centre can obscure the essential truth that the ambitions and rivalries that really mattered were likely to have been generated in the localities and to have revolved around precisely those inner dynamics of rural life which the sources so imperfectly capture.

[320] Rif. 16, pp. 673–4, 724–6, 802–3; 17, pp. 484, 512, 614–15, 733, 750–1; ASL Capitano del Contado, 52, fos. 3^r–8^r.

[321] BSL MS 939, Gio: Lunardo Dalli, Cronache, pp. 329–30, 365.

[322] Rif. 14, pp. 391, 724; AS Massa, Pergamene, 349/374, 8 Dec. 1442; Archivio dei Malaspina di Fosdinovo Marchesi di Massa, 2, no. 19.

8

THE LUCCHESE REPUBLIC AND THE CHURCH: THE CLERICAL BUTTRESS

The Church in Lucca has been well served by recent scholarship.[1] It is not the intention to mirror here Marino Berengo's sweeping overview of the Lucchese Church in the age of the Reformation.[2] The present concern is not with the history of the Church *per se*, but rather with the integration of religious and secular life in the restored republic. At the simplest level, the problems of the Lucchese Church perfectly reflect those of the republic itself during the period of plague, famine, devastation from war, and depopulation that followed the deposition of Paolo Guinigi. In times of great financial need the republic drew freely on the resources of the Church; and in return state subvention was anticipated by the city's churches. More important and more pervasive were the intangible supports provided between Church and republic. Churchmen were present to ensure both the honesty and the legitimacy of electoral procedures; the bones of the saints, which were the treasure of Lucca's churches, offered the surest guarantee of Lucca's liberty; churchmen and laity came together in the great ritual processions culminating in the illumination of Santa Croce. There were many opportunities for tension, not least because of the Church's independent jurisdiction, and because Lucca, like other cities, had long since assumed the legislative

[1] For the 14th cent. there are three important contributions to *Castruccio Castracani e il suo tempo: Convegno Internazionale, Lucca 5–10 ottobre 1981*, *Actum Luce*, xiii–xiv, nos. 1–2 (1984–5): D. Osheim, 'I sentimenti religiosi dei lucchesi al tempo di Castruccio', 99-111; E. Coturri, 'La chiesa lucchese al tempo di Castruccio', 113–24; L. Green, 'Il Capitolo della Cathedrale di Lucca all'epoca di Castruccio Castracani', 125–41. Also G. Benedetto, 'I rapporti fra Castruccio Castracani e la chiesa di Lucca', *Annuario della Biblioteca Civica di Massa* (1980–1), 73–97. For the 15th cent., see L. Nanni, 'Il clero della cattedrale di Lucca nei secoli xv e xvi', in Lamberto Donati (ed.), *Studi e ricerche nella biblioteca e negli archivi vaticani in memoria del Cardinale Giovanni Mercati (1866–1957)* (Florence, 1959), 258–84; E. Coturri, 'La canonica di S. Frediano di Lucca dalla prima istituzione (metà del sec. xi) alla unione alla congregazione riformata di Fregionaia (1517)', *Actum Luce*, iii, nos. 1–2 (1974), 47–80; Benedetto, 'Potere dei chierici e potere dei laici'.

[2] Berengo, *Nobili e mercanti*, 357–454.

responsibility to curb the Old Adam which used to be seen as the special prerogative of Protestant magistrates.[3] Above all, the Church itself in Lucca should be pleasing to God. Consequently, the city authorities were active in their encouragement of reformers, in the promotion of the Observants, and in the ousting of the Conventuals. There were numerous potential areas of Church–State conflict; occasionally tensions surfaced. Generally the relationship was a harmonious one; partly because of a manifest interdependence and interpenetration of lay and ecclesiastical society, and partly because the practical constraints on independent ecclesiastical initiatives were well understood in Lucca by the fifteenth century.

The diocese of Lucca did not conform to the unstable boundaries of the Lucchese state. The subordination of distant foundations to the bishopric of Lucca lay behind appeals from the bishop to Florence for Medici consideration and favour.[4] Parts of the Lucchese diocese now fell within Florentine territory; parts of the Lucchese state were outside the diocese. The territory of Pietrasanta, for example, was divided between Lucca and Luni, and further administrative complications arose once Pietrasanta had passed permanently out of Lucca's political control.[5] Perhaps it was during the wars with Lucca following Pietrasanta's rebellion that the lands of S. Piero of Ratignano were so damaged that the bishop of Lucca granted a licence for that church effectively to exchange chestnut woods with charcoal pits for land in Seravezza possessing mill, fulling-mill, and olive press, the exchange further complicated by an offer of resale.[6]

For some purposes state and diocese can be equated, and the Church in Lucca in the 1430s shared fully in the suffering of other Lucchese landlords: church buildings in the localities were damaged or destroyed, more especially since they and their bell-towers were the foci of local refuge and defence; church lands were devastated in the Sei Miglia and

[3] G. Strauss, 'Protestant Dogma and City Government: The Case of Nuremberg', *Past & Present*, xxxvi (1967), 38–58.

[4] MAP, x. 494, 499. For a map showing the relationship between political and ecclesiastical boundaries in Tuscany in the early 15th cent., see G. Chittolini, 'Progetti di riordinamento ecclesiastico della Toscana agli inizi del Quattrocento', in S. Bertelli (ed.), *Forme e tecniche del potere nella città (secoli xiv–xvii)* (Università di Perugia, Annali della Facoltà di Scienze Politiche—a.a. 1979–80, 16), 280.

[5] ASCP, I 2, Atti dei Genovesi (1433–82), fo. 50^{r-v}; Santini, *Versilia centrale*, ii. 81, 127; iv. 59–60. In many respects, however, the political changes made no real difference to episcopal control: NAC, N 115 (ser Nicolao di Coluccio di Pellegrino da Pietrasanta, 1409–68), 14 July 1453, fos. 90^{v}–91^{r}, 99^{v}, 159^{v}, 203^{r-v}; N 116 (1435–9), 2 Jan. 1439; AAL Cause civili della Curia (ser Ciomeo Pieri, 1453), fo. 51^{v}.

[6] NAC, N 116 (ser Nicolao di Coluccio di Pellegrino da Pietrasanta, 1435–9), 2 Jan. 1439.

elsewhere, a testimony to the helplessness of local populations watching from behind the fortifications of city or *rocca* the progress of both allied and enemy armies. The bell was taken from the tower of S. Simone of Scilivano, and placed on the torre degli Onesti in S. Martino in Freddana 'for *custodia* of the countryside in this time of war'.[7] The rector of S. Giulia was granted permission in February 1432 to absent himself from the city and diocese of Lucca because of the penury that was in the city;[8] in September 1433 the *pievano* of S. Maria of Villa Basilica was readmitted to the benefice that he had fled during the wars.[9] The church of S. Martino in Collodi was demolished;[10] the *ospedale* of S. Pietro maggiore was burnt down.[11] And in Lucca, as beyond its walls, benefices, with and without the cure of souls, were united as they ceased to command the material revenues for their support.[12] With the renewal of war in 1436 the bishop suspended all *cause civili* because of the pressure of men of arms in the city and *contado*,[13] and the renewed conflict brought with it a fresh batch of licences permitting *pievani* temporarily to abandon their benefices.[14] By 1439 S. Frediano, the great city church of the Augustinian canons, found itself so impoverished by war, depopulation, and the flooding of its possessions along the River Serchio, that one of its canons regular, Andrea di Andruccio da Marciagio, 'with tears in his eyes' successfully petitioned his prior and the remaining canons that he might 'go without sin to some other church or chapel with cure or without which will provide him with food and clothing'.[15]

The men of arms were only one of the predators faced by the Lucchese Church in the early years of the restored republic. In August 1432, on the orders of the Emperor Sigismund, the Anziani of Lucca required the clergy to raise 200 florins with which to send their bishop for the reform of

[7] Licence was granted, conditional on the bell being restored to the church within one month of the making of peace: LA 87, fos. 62ᵛ–63ʳ.

[8] Ibid., fo. 56ʳ.

[9] Ibid., fo. 70ʳ.

[10] LA 88, fo. 47ʳ.

[11] LA 87, fo. 51ᵛ.

[12] Ibid., fos. 53ᵛ, 56ᵛ–57ᵛ.

[13] LA 88, fo. 13ʳ.

[14] Ibid., fos. 18ʳ, 20ᵛ.

[15] AN 576(2) (ser Benedetto Guarguaglia, 1439–47), fo. 26ᵛ. The instrument speaks of a church so impoverished that it could scarcely support its prior with one or two others. In 1443 the bishop of Lucca received a *breve* from Eugenius IV empowering the prior and canons of S. Frediano to exchange lands to the value of 500 florins for the repair of its property damaged during the wars: ASL Raccolte Speciali: S. Frediano, 20, no. 11, fos. 21ᵛ–23ʳ.

the universal Church to the Council of Basle. A sum of 50 florins was to be paid by the clergy of Versilia and of all Lucchese territory from the monastery of Quiesa to the River della Macra, a further 50 by the exempt clergy (*clero esente*), and 100 florins in ready money through the pledging of church treasures in Lucca.[16] The goods of churches and other pious foundations were exempt from the forced loans raised to pay for the war effort: that point was stressed by the *operaio* of S. Martino in Pietrasanta when the *esattore* attempted to tax goods in the possession of the altar of the Annunciation in S. Martino as universal heir of the late Gabrielle Morlani.[17] Nevertheless, the silver chalices and crosses were taken from all the principal churches for the 'subvention of the necessities of our city' during the first Florentine war. The frequently repeated assertion of the chroniclers that Lucca was placed under an interdict for this act of impiety seems to have been based on a misunderstanding.[18] Restitution was not provided until April 1440, when the General Council converted money received by the city from fines and condemnations to that purpose.[19] The council of Pietrasanta resisted a proposal to relieve the great financial hardships of that community through the reappropriation of butchers' shops and other properties formerly granted for the maintenance of their church of S. Martino.[20] In Lucca itself there was a deeply held conviction that works undertaken for the benefit of all should be paid for by all.[21] In October 1436, as Lucca again prepared for war, the local clergy once more found it prudent to organize themselves to resist the new challenge to clerical privilege.[22]

There is a danger of exaggerating the impoverishment of the diocese and of individual foundations as a distinctive feature of the early and mid-

[16] LA 87, fos. 59v–60v. The subsidy was demanded by the Emperor through the secular authorities; its imposition was determined by a convocation of the clergy summoned by the vicars-general of the bishop. The prior of S. Frediano was unable to obey the summons to Basle because of 'many obstacles and impediments': NAC, N 115 (ser Nicolao di Coluccio di Pellegrino da Pietrasanta, 1409–68), fo. 82r. The prior and canons did, however, appoint a procurator.

[17] ASL Imprestiti, 21, loose unfoliated paper placed after fo. 58. NAC, N 116 (ser Nicolao di Coluccio di Pellegrino da Pietrasanta, 1428–32), fos. 41v–42v.

[18] BSL MS 710, Salvator Dalli, Croniche, fos. 139r, 143v; MS 939, Gio: Lunardo Dalli, Cronache, pp. 141, 162. The bull of absolution of Eugenius IV seems to relate to private mutterings of citizens against the bishop and clergy aroused by the war situation: Rif. 14, pp. 716–17.

[19] Rif. 15, pp. 455–6; 16, p. 749.

[20] ASCP Libro di Consigli (1435), fo. 13v.

[21] The principle was asserted, e.g., when Lucca decided in the interests of health to clean the ditches around the walls of the city: Rif. 15, pp. 147–9.

[22] LA 88, fo. 13v.

fifteenth century. First, many of the problems were occasioned by changes and natural hazards which were in no sense new. Changing population patterns caused old churches to be abandoned. Thus Pope Innocent VIII gave permission in 1485 for the men of Gallicano to knock down the old deserted baptismal church of S. Giovanni Battista, which was situated in the woods outside the walls of the settlement ('posta nelle selve fuor delle mura del castello'), and to use the materials in part on the *rocca*, in part to build a new church within the *castello*.[23] Elsewhere much of the loss of revenue and many of the interminable lawsuits were the product of nothing more untoward than the annual floodings of the Serchio, a problem high on the agenda of fifteenth-century secular legislators.[24] Traditional calamities included the ravages of fire[25] and the vulnerability to time and decay of the walls—and especially the roofs—of ambitious medieval ecclesiastical structures.[26]

Secondly, the destructive effects whether of time or of war could be remedied by both public and private munificence. The petitions of the Franciscan friary of S. Cerbone to the General Council began with a request for a small bell, and soon became pleas for the subsidizing of repairs.[27] The example of the Observant Franciscans was rapidly followed by the friars of S. Domenico, more especially since the damage to their refectory was caused by stipendiaries in the pay of Lucca.[28] The same tactic proved successful for the prior of S. Michele in foro on behalf of S. Michele's subject church of S. Quirico in Monticello.[29] The *operai* of S. Giovanni maggiore merely pointed out that their cupola had been repaired at the expense of the commune, that its present ruinous condition was a great danger to anyone unfortunate enough to be under it, and that 100 ducats spent now would preserve work already completed at great cost to the commune.[30] All petitioners stressed that such work was both for the praise of God and the honour of the commune. And the prior of S. Frediano was able to appeal to a considerable body of precedent when he

[23] ASG MS 5, fos. 16^r–17^r; L. Angelini, 'Una visita pastorale quattrocentesca alla pievania di Gallicano', in *Miscellanea di Studi: Carfaniana Antiqua*, i (Lucca, 1980), 35–7.

[24] ASL Raccolte Speciali: S. Frediano, 20, no. 5; AN 700(3) (ser Benedetto Franciotti), 13 Aug. 1457; 702, pp. 223–4.

[25] NAC, N 115 (ser Nicolao di Coluccio di Pellegrino da Pietrasanta, 1432–4), fo. 52^{r-v}; N 116 (1428–32), fo. 90^{r-v}.

[26] NAC, N 115 (1432–4), fos. 2^r–3^r.

[27] Rif. 16, pp. 105, 693–4, 802; 17, p. 55. The latter petitions were handled by the Council of Thirty-Six.

[28] Rif. 17, p. 44. The friars asked for 80 florins; they were given 40.

[29] Ibid., p. 80.

[30] Ibid., p. 119.

in turn looked to the commune for the repair of roofs that had already fallen or were about to do so.[31] Precisely this same need was addressed in numerous patrician wills. Most comprehensively, the testament of Lorenzo di M. Federigo di Ciomeo Trenta not only made extensive provisions for repairs to the roofs of S. Frediano, the site—in the chapel of S. Caterina—of the family tombs; he showed considerable (if lesser) concern for the roofs of S. Frediano's subject church of S. Giovanni capo di borgo, for those of houses belonging to the bishopric, and for the roofs of a list of other Lucchese churches and religious houses including S. Romano, S. Francesco, S. Salvatore in muro, S. Pier Cigoli, S. Maria Servorum, S. Giustina, S. Cerbone, S. Clara, and S. Nicolao Novello.[32]

Despite such acts of public policy and private piety, all the indications—certainly until the 1460s—suggest a Church that had sustained lasting damage in the early years of the fifteenth century as a result of wars and natural disasters. In a treaty made between Lucca and its bishop in June 1443, the bishop spoke of his declining income as an accepted fact of some permanence.[33] Landed transactions in the middle decades of the century clearly identify the Church as a net seller of property, though such transactions fail to note testamentary bequests for the endowment of altars.[34] Some of the best evidence for continuing crisis relates to S. Frediano. In 1439 Lorenzo Buonvisi had written to Cosimo de' Medici to arrange for the most effective channelling of a legacy made to S. Frediano by the Cardinal of S. Marcello, of whom Cosimo was executor. In that letter Lorenzo told how Lucca's monastery of S. Frediano 'had so far suffered a deterioration in its circumstances that only with great difficulty was it possible to provide for daily necessities'.[35] In the 1470s, and probably earlier, ser Benedetto di ser Giovanni Franciotti was chancellor of the prior of S. Frediano.[36] Franciotti's protocolli are a rich source for the history of S. Frediano, and they show how little things had changed by the 1450s. There are continuing references to the hard times

[31] Ibid., pp. 130–1. The prior of S. Frediano had the added advantage that if subvention was given to S. Cerbone and S. Quirico in Monticello, a church of the importance of S. Frediano could hardly be denied.

[32] AN 576(2) (ser Benedetto Guarguaglia, 1439–47), fos. 37^{v}–40^{r}.

[33] Rif. 16, p. 315. ASL Archivio Diplomatico: Pergamene (Fregionaia), 22 May 1444.

[34] See above, pp. 182–3. Regional studies of other parts of Tuscany have shown a steady increase in church lands from the early 15th to the mid-16th cent.: R. Bizzocchi, *Chiesa e potere nella Toscana del Quattrocento* (Bologna, 1987), 16.

[35] MAP, xi. 280: 'ae molto peggiorato sua conditione in tanto che non sensa grande difficoltà puo provedere ala necessità del vivere'.

[36] ASL Raccolte Speciali: S. Frediano, 20, no. 6, fo. 2^{v}.

that had befallen the church and to the need to sell lands to meet urgent obligations which in 1456 included the papal *colletta* and *decima*.[37] Problems were not confined to S. Frediano. As late as 1455/6 the files of the same notary show concern to repair a hospital for the poor and infirm attached to the church of S. Donato extra muros. Noting the need to protect Christ's poor, a bull of Calixtus III granted permission to S. Donato to alienate property for the repair of the hospital devastated by war and general disturbances.[38]

Whatever the material condition of the Lucchese Church, bishop and chapter retained significant independent administrative and judicial powers. The lands of Decimo, Aquilea, Sesto di Moriano, S. Stefano di Moriano, S. Cassiano, S. Lorenzo, S. Michele, and S. Quirico di Moriano were commonly called the Iura of the bishop of Lucca, and fell under his temporal jurisdiction. To the north he exercised temporal authority over the *contea* of Piazza and Sala in Garfagnana, though here spiritual authority belonged to the bishop of Luni. To the west the area around Massarosa was under the jurisdiction of the canons of the cathedral of S. Martino. In the city of Lucca and in the lands under Lucchese jurisdiction crimes such as blasphemy, gambling, and sodomy were handled by the complex nexus of secular courts; indeed, the *Capitano del contado* was required regularly to issue a proclamation against a range of offences including the above.[39] But a layman like the *farsettaio* Iacopo del Voglia, who was accused of numerous usurious transactions in the city and *contado* of Lucca, might find himself hauled before the bishop's court.[40] It is true that at first Iacopo denied the bishop's jurisdiction, but only because he claimed that the case rightly belonged to the prior of S. Frediano.[41] When the men of Oneta threatened with arms the rector of the church of Rocca a Mozzano, demanding that he renounce the benefice of Terzono, they were summoned to appear before the court of the bishop's vicar under pain of

37 AN 700(2) (ser Benedetto Franciotti), 24 Sept. 1454, Feb. 1455; 700(4), 8 Jan. 1456.

38 AN 700(4), 15 Oct. 1456; 700(5), 15 Oct. 1456; 706, pp. 186–92.

39 See, e.g., ASL Capitano del Contado, 51, 1st foliation, fos. 1ʳ–2ᵛ.

40 LA 99A, fos. 33ʳ–41ʳ. One witness attributed to Iacopo the words 'Io intendo che li miei denari guadagnino qualcosa et non stiano in perdita'. Usury cases do seem to have been the prerogative of the episcopal court; see, e.g., Angelini, 'Una visita pastorale quattrocentesca', 39. Bigamy cases, on the other hand, despite frequent reference to the canons of Holy Church, might well be handled by the court of the *Podestà*: SB 192, fos. 2ʳ⁻ᵛ, 21ʳ; ASL Podestà di Lucca, Inquisizioni, 5329, fos. 160ʳ–162ʳ.

41 The church and monastery of S. Frediano received a series of privileges from Rome, dating from the eleventh century onwards, exempting the parish from episcopal jurisdiction: BSL MS 415, Notizie antiche del monastero e chiesa di S. Frediano, fos. 64ʳ–66ʳ.

excommunication.[42] Most criminal cases of assault against clerics and many civil actions brought to the bishop's court by religious institutions for unpaid rent seem to concern defendants who were residents of the Iura.[43] Churchmen often preferred to pursue such actions before the regular secular courts. More jealously guarded was the privilege of men in holy orders to be tried by ecclesiastical courts.

Benefit of clergy could be claimed in fifteenth-century Lucca not only by men in or progressing towards the sacramental priesthood, but also by merchants and professional men who had no intention of advancing beyond minor orders. Within the Guinigi family, both Azzo di Dino and Michele di Giovanni could claim benefit of clergy.[44] Michele's half-brother Girolamo records his own entry into minor orders without hint of vocation;[45] he arranged minor orders for a succession of young sons and nephews, not because he intended them to pursue clerical careers but because of the convenience and advantages that clerical status would bring in later life.[46] The Libri Antichi record the taking of minor orders by young men of leading Lucchese families whose subsequent lives were to be profoundly worldly: notably the merchants Raffaele di Piero Tegrimi and Cipriano di Raineri Mansi.[47] Clerical status was likely to be recollected by men detained by the state and anticipating the rigours of torture.[48] More generally, an appeal to benefit of clergy was a useful delaying or obstructionist tactic when the ponderous machinery of secular justice seemed to be grinding towards unfavourable conclusions. Thus the claim against Tommaso di Giovanni Moriconi by the company of Lorenzo Buonvisi and Cello Martini for mercantile debts of 300 florins was at least impeded when Tommaso claimed the privileges of a *clericus in minoribus*.[49]

[42] LA 99A, fo. 1^{r}. It is less clear why the assault by Pietro Tegrimi and companions on Iacopo di Antonio Ruffini at the instigation of Giovanni Mariani should also appear in the records of the vicar's court: ibid., fo. 8^{r}.

[43] Ibid., fos. 4^{r}–5^{r}; AAL Cause civili della Curia (ser Ciomeo Pieri, 1453), *passim*. My general impression from the records of the bishop's court is that in the 15th cent. episcopal civil and spiritual jurisdiction was operating reasonably effectively, but that criminal jurisdiction was always more problematic.

[44] Rif. 18, p. 213; AN 591 (ser Giovanni Nocchi), fos. 198^{r}–203^{v}.

[45] ASL Archivio Guinigi, MS 29, Girolamo Guinigi, Libro di ricordi, fo. 3^{r}.

[46] Ibid., fos. 19^{v}, 38^{v}, 42^{r}.

[47] LA 87, fo. 65^{r}; 88, fo. 51^{v}.

[48] Rif. 14, p. 431.

[49] ASL Podestà di Lucca, Curia Civile, 1176, fos. 26^{r}–29^{r}; 1180, fos. 29^{r}–30^{v}, 32^{r}, 60^{r}–62^{r}; Curia del Fondaco, 694, fos. 51^{r}–54^{v}. Later in the century Giovanni Morovelli appealed to benefit of clergy, at least twice, in cases brought before the court of merchants: Corte de' mercanti, Cause civili, 164, fo. 71^{v}.

Ser Benedetto di ser Bartolomeo del Guarguaglia openly admitted that he had defended himself *per chierico* when unable to repay public money which he had retained as *officiale al macello*;[50] Bartolomeo di Piero Nicolini was equally frank in admitting that he had used benefit of clergy as a device to free himself from prison, where he lay for debts owing to Baldassare Benettoni.[51]

Exemption from secular jurisdiction applied to places as well as individuals. Many of the criminal cases appearing before the bishop's court involved allegations that secular officials had offended against the liberties of the Church by taking the accused whilst he was on holy ground: within or on the steps of churches or in the cemetery. The bishop of Lucca might also intervene in lawsuits as the protector and administrator of Christ's poor. Often, though not always, he appears in this capacity in inheritance disputes between poor women and religious foundations.[52] For the protection of the poor of the city and diocese the bishop appointed a procurator and syndic,[53] just as the republic of Lucca itself appointed an *advocatus pauperum et viduarum et miserabilium personarum*—an office combined with that of *Iudex vicariarum*.[54] There was nothing unusual about this overlap of functions and jurisdictions. The independent powers, exemptions, and privileges of the Church were nevertheless a source of potential conflict.

The frustration of individual litigants is well articulated in the case between Lorenzo Buonvisi and Tommaso Moriconi. Not unreasonably, Buonvisi protested against Tommaso's assumption of clerical immunity when his opponent was married, untonsured, and was daily engaged with mercantile affairs.[55] The state tried to discourage its citizens from invoking clerical privilege by declaring ineligible for all offices of honour or profit those who claimed exemption from secular jurisdiction.[56] The real target of this legislation is clarified in proposals of 1482 which, whilst denying any intention of infringing the liberties of the Church, sought to distinguish priests and those who were actually engaged in the service of churches from others whose offences less legitimately remained unpun-

[50] Rif. 15, pp. 361–2.

[51] Rif. 16, p. 353.

[52] e.g., NAC, N 115 (ser Nicolao di Coluccio di Pellegrino da Pietrasanta, 1409–68), fo. 99^{v}. But see also AAL Cause civili della Curia (ser Ciomeo Pieri, 1453), fos. 70^{r}–72^{r}, 105^{r} ff. Most cases of episcopal intervention seem to have taken place outside the city of Lucca itself.

[53] LA 87, fos. 76^{r}, 78^{r}.

[54] ASL Statuti del comune di Lucca, 13, xlvii.

[55] ASL Podestà di Lucca, Curia Civile, 1180, fo. 29^{v}.

[56] ASL Statuti del comune di Lucca, 13, lviiii.

ished because of resort to clerical privilege.[57] The scale of the problem is probably indicated in a decree of 1489 which specifically mentioned *clerici* among those who went about armed in the city at night.[58] More generally, a mid-seventeenth-century dispute—which drew largely on fifteenth-century evidence and rekindled fifteenth-century conflicts—shows the kind of contest for jurisdiction that might arise on and beyond the coast to the west of Massarosa between the republic and the canons of S. Martino.[59]

In reality, the opportunities for serious or prolonged conflict remained largely theoretical. The bishop of Lucca was seldom inclined to press too vigorously for clerical protection of political offenders, whether these were priests like Antonio di Giovanni Bertini[60] or merely claimed the privileges due to minor orders.[61] The Pope himself intervened to remit a man to secular jurisdiction in the case of Girolamo di Andrea del Portico who had taken minor orders only after finding himself accused of murder and with the specific intention—so the Anziani claimed—of evading penalty by means of this deception. On this occasion, at least, the Church agreed with the commune of Lucca that such obvious abuses could only end in setting a bad example to others.[62] Similarly, despite all the legislation, the republic in practice preferred to deal gently with citizens who had temporarily removed themselves from its jurisdiction. Men like the Guinigi were periodically readmitted to civic honours with a remarkable casualness.[63] Even when ser Benedetto di ser Bartolomeo del Guarguaglia offended a second time, both cases effectively involving the defrauding not of individuals but of the commune, his readmission to honours was smoothly effected on payment of a fine.[64] It is necessary to seek explanations less for

[57] Rif. 21, pp. 392–3.

[58] Rif. 22, pp. 305–6, 308–12.

[59] BSL MS 1824, Scritture varie sulle controversie dei canonici di S. Martino di Lucca colla Rep. di Lucca.

[60] Antonio Bertini was a canon of the cathedral and prior of Tassignano. His involvement in the Guerrucci affair was negotiated quietly between the bishop and the *secretarii* of Lucca; by Dec. 1460 the bishop had deprived him of his canonry 'per alcuni suoi enormi delitti': ASL Colloqui, 1, p. 71; BSL MS 2953, Giuseppe Vinc. Baroni, Notizie sulla chiesa di S. Martino, fo. 69^r.

[61] An exception would seem to be maestro Giovanni di Iacopo da Firenze, to whose examination the bishop was unwilling to consent: Rif. 16, p. 760. The protest seems to have gone unheeded. When in 1459 some of the rebels of Gallicano were apprehended in the church of S. Frediano, it was considered expedient to explain things to the bishop. The affair seems to have been settled amicably enough: ASL Colloqui, 1, p. 26.

[62] ASL Archivio Diplomatico: Pergamene (Tarpea), 10 June 1473.

[63] Rif. 18, pp. 213–14.

[64] In discussing his readmission to honours, members of the General Council spoke tolerantly of the time that he had stood deprived: Rif. 17, p. 517.

the occasional and inevitable protests and tensions than for the underlying harmony that characterized Church–State relations in the post-Guinigi period.

First, practical constraints made it very difficult for the Church in Lucca to press its theoretical independence too far. The point is well illustrated in an agreement reached in June 1443 between the commune and bishop of Lucca regarding the men of Decimo, S. Leonardo di Aquilea, pieve Sesto Moriano, villa di S. Michele a Castelvecchio, and S. Quirico di Licciano, that area of the Lucchese countryside that was under episcopal jurisdiction. Duane Osheim has shown, through to the fourteenth century, a harmonious relationship between the bishopric, its Iura, and the commune of Lucca, and the effective control exercised by the commune within the episcopal jurisdiction.[65] The composition of 1443 shows a continuing co-operation, and also offers some explanations.[66] At the beginning of the agreement it was conceded that the bishop's jurisdiction consisted of unwalled and scattered settlements which it was impossible to defend in isolation. As shown again in the recent wars, these territories were as much dependent on the commune of Lucca for their protection as were the subjects of Lucca themselves. Because of declining income, the bishop was no longer able even to deploy his own *satelliti* and *armigeri*. By the pact of 1443, the commune was granted full powers to impose and collect *gabelle*, *proventi*, and the salt tax. Essentially (with some local concessions, particularly relating to the butchering of animals for their own consumption and to transactions taking place within the Iura) the men of the Iura were subject to precisely the same exactions as those of the Sei Miglia. Obligation to punish fraud was shared by the bishop, his vicar-general, and the officials of the *Gabella Maggiore*. In return, the bishop received half the fines occasioned by customs fraud, prior notification of the detention of his subjects for offences against the *dovana salis*, and concessionary rates and exemptions regarding the supply of his own household with salt and provisions. Above all, the bishop could look to the commune for defence. The agents of the *Podestà* were placed at his service (their bread and wine to be provided by the bishop and by the men of the Iura); he could freely imprison offenders in the communal prison; and there was a reciprocal agreement for the apprehension of *banniti*. The

[65] Osheim, *An Italian Lordship*, 70–85.

[66] Rif. 16, pp. 311–18. An earlier agreement of 27 Dec. 1442 was confirmed by a bull of Eugenius IV on 9 Jan. 1443: ASL Archivio Diplomatico: Pergamene (Tarpea), 9 Jan., 26 Jan. 1443. For the despatch by the Anziani of a messenger to obtain papal approval for the revised agreement of 27 June, see ibid., 29 June 1443.

composition was by no means unfavourable to the bishop or his subjects, but left little doubt concerning the locus of power. The General Council carefully repudiated the offering of wax by the commune—symbol of subordination—in return for the customs revenues. A very similar agreement was reached three years later with the canons and chapter of the cathedral of S. Martino concerning their lands of Massarosa, Fibbialla, Gualdo, and Ricetro.[67] Again, there was the acknowledgement that the commune of Lucca had always protected these lands and their inhabitants as their own subjects. For the canons too, as reaffirmed in a pact with the commune of 1492,[68] the obedience of their temporal subjects presupposed the full co-operation of the officials of the state.

The bishop had his own prisons; sometimes it might be convenient for the custodian of the Sasso prison to insist that he was answerable only to the lay and not to the ecclesiastical authorities.[69] In practice, such neat distinctions could hardly be maintained. Secular facilities proved irresistible, as shown, for example, on 17 March 1453, when a letter under the small seal of the bishop's court was sent to Pietro Guinigi, vicar of Camaiore, asking him expeditiously to administer justice against the iniquitous sons of Mommio and Camaiore, who were withholding payments due to the *opera* of S. Andrea of Mommio.[70] Even more telling, in 1483 when Sixtus IV ordered the bishop of Lucca to apprehend and detain the *pievano* of Marlia, Giovanni di Iacopo, the bishop—clearly conscious of his own limitations—immediately commissioned the agents of the *Podestà* of Lucca to undertake the act of arrest on his behalf.[71]

Beyond such practical constraints, many of the obvious points of tension familiar to students of northern Europe were absent from Lucca (and indeed from Church–State relations in Italy as a whole). There were, for example, none of the professional rivalries between common and canon lawyers that were to bedevil relations in England from Becket to the Reformation. In a Roman-law society, notaries and doctors *in utroque iure* served promiscuously both Church and State. A man like ser Benedetto Franciotti, chancellor to the prior of the church and monastery of S. Frediano, was among the rulers of Lucca in the college of Anziani in both 1489 and 1491. Lawyers appointed by the bishop to examine candidates for doctorates or to act as procurators of the poor were likely to be men

[67] Rif. 16, pp. 609, 628–30.

[68] Rif. 23, pp. 190–1.

[69] ASL Podestà di Lucca, Curia Civile, 1176, fo. 28^{r}.

[70] AAL Cause civili della Curia (ser Ciomeo Pieri, 1453), fo. 53^{v}.

[71] AAL Cause civili della Curia (ser Acconcio del fu ser Antonii, 1483), fo. 22^{r-v}.

prominent in the political affairs of the republic, and were often drawn from the most distinguished Lucchese families.

Of course the Church had its own judicial and administrative structures. At the centre the bishop was represented by his vicar(s)-general; in parts of the diocese by a *vicario foraneo*. On 11 December 1433 (until his powers were revoked in April of the following year) the rector of the hospital of S. Pellegrino nell'Alpi was appointed by Bishop Nicolao Guinigi as *vicario foraneo* for the Garfagnana, with powers to hear civil cases involving sums of less than £25 and criminal suits involving less than £40.[72] Here, too, the distinctions in practice tended to become blurred, not least under Bishop Nicolao Guinigi himself. During the last years of the Guinigi episcopate, official acts, including the conferring of first tonsure and the minor orders of door-keeper and lector (*prima tonsura*, the *ostiariato*, and *lettorato*), were as likely to be performed in the palace of the heirs of Dino Guinigi as in the bishop's palace.[73] Having full faith in Dino's son and wishing to provide for his see's temporal jurisdiction in the Iura, it was to Azzo di Dino Guinigi that Bishop Nicolao turned in October 1433, appointing him *visconte* of the Iura with 'imperium merum et mixtum'.[74] Azzo may have been in minor orders; neither he nor successors like Chello di Antonio di Poggio or ser Francesco di Gabriello degli Antelminelli were churchmen in that more limited sense that contemporary Lucchese legislators were striving to define.

The corollary is that some churchmen lived very close to the frontiers of the secular world. By the mid-fourteenth century, the chapter of the cathedral of S. Martino had ceased to live the communal life, and Nanni has shown, for a slightly later period, how far the canons before Trent were likely to have received only minor orders.[75] Stefano di Giovanni, canon and archdeacon, son of a *speziale*, was inevitably drawn into mercantile disputes relating to the spice shop of his late father. But throughout the 1450s, from the house in which he lived above the spice shop in the *contrada* of S. Maria in palatio, Stefano was peculiarly active in the private buying and selling of land, in the leasing of both rural and urban property, in the advancing of small loans, and in the affairs of the spice shop. It was his brother Mariano who was usually described as exercising the art of *speziale* in Stefano's shop in *contrada* S. Maria in palatio. Nevertheless,

72 LA 87, fo. 75^{r-v}.

73 Ibid., fos. 65^{r}, 67^{r}.

74 Ibid., fos. 71^{r}, 75^{v}. Bishop Stefano Trenta also turned to a kinsman—Silvestro del fu Gregorio—in a later attempt to restore order in the lands of the bishop's temporal jurisdiction: AAL Collazioni, A (1448), fo. 10^{r-v}.

75 Nanni, 'Clero della cattedrale di Lucca', 259, 271–2.

when the archdeacon was not summoning convocations of the canons or attending to his affairs as rector of S. Lucia of Veghiatoia, he too might be called '*speziale*'. There are periodic references to Stefano di Giovanni under the somewhat incongruous title of *speziale* and *arcidiacono* of Lucca.[76]

Recent work on the fifteenth-century Church throughout the wider Florentine state suggests that a co-operative relationship stemmed not merely from close contacts and exchanges, but from the active penetration and control of Church structures by local patrician families. At the level of personnel, Roberto Bizzocchi has written of the institutionalization of aristocratic control of cathedral chapters with the founding of new canonical prebends under the patronage of individual families, of the control of the monasteries and the infiltration of Dominican and Augustinian convents by the same families that ruled the communes, and of an even more marked aristocratic intrusion into the nunneries.[77] With respect to the secular benefices of local churches, Bizzocchi has argued that the fifteenth century saw a general 'aristocratizzazione dei giuspatronati ecclesiastici'. The *giuspatronato* of churches by dominant local families, both in the city and in the *contado*, was well entrenched from the time of the Gregorian reforms; it came to provide one of the defining qualities of nobility and an index to the rise and fall of families. But Bizzocchi has shown the extension of noble patronage over new churches from the mid-fifteenth century, particularly over churches where the *giuspatronato* had previously belonged to the body of parishioners.[78] These findings are useful in explaining Church–State relations in contemporary Lucca, though the Lucchese experience would seem to differ in important respects.

Political weakness ensured that places in the cathedral chapter of fourteenth-century Lucca did not become the prerogative of the local patriciate to the extent that has been traced elsewhere. In the decade 1350–60 fewer than half the canons of the cathedral were even of local birth. The balance had shifted in favour of Lucchese by the end of the century, though few came from families of the first rank.[79] Benedetto has

[76] ASL Corte de' mercanti, Cause civili, 151, fos. 21^{r}, 102^{r}, 180^{r-v}, 181^{v}–182^{v}; AN 700(3) (ser Benedetto Franciotti), 31 Mar. 1457; 700(4), 28 and 29 July, 15 and 22 Sept., 13 Dec. 1455, 23 June, 17 July, 3 and 18 Sept., 14 Dec. 1456; 700(5), 5 and 11 Jan., 19 and 20 June, 19 Aug. 1456; 702, pp. 11, 23–4, 25–7, 149, 217–18; 703, pp. 189–94; 704, pp. 45–6, 63, 83, 98–100, 141, 166.

[77] Bizzocchi, *Chiesa e potere*, 17–33.

[78] Ibid. 36–53.

[79] Benedetto, 'Potere dei chierici e potere dei laici', 8, 17–19.

argued that a combination of papal difficulties at the time of the Schism and of Guinigi policy towards the Church resulted in a dramatic change in the composition of the chapter: at least eleven of the sixteen appointments to prebends for the period 16 June 1401 to 24 September 1418 being 'inequivocabilmente fedelissimi' of Paolo Guinigi.[80] One might add that, excluding Lazzaro di Giovanni Guinigi, the new *prebendari* may have been politically reliable, but were hardly drawn from Lucca's leading families, or even from families that had been established in Lucca before the time of Guinigi himself.

The cathedral chapter of the post-Guinigi period offers a rewarding area of research. In the absence of such a study, there remain the eighteenth-century manuscript volumes of Giuseppe Vincenzo Baroni, Notizie sulla chiesa di S. Martino, the third volume of which deals with the canons of the cathedral for the period 1400 to 1789.[81] The Baroni manuscript shows that at the time of Paolo Guinigi's deposition thirteen of the sixteen canons were Lucchese, a fourteenth coming from Aramo in the diocese of Lucca.[82] Despite the impressive Guinigi presence, that of Gerardo di Arrigho Bandelli, and the election on 7 July 1430 of Paolo Sandei (son of Nicolao and of Giovanna, *nipote* of Paolo Guinigi), the cathedral chapter of 1430 was still less than representative of Lucca's greater families.

The last member of the Guinigi chapter had disappeared by March 1467. The Baroni manuscript provides the names of seventy-seven new canons (perhaps as many as eighty-two)[83] elected over the period 1430–1500. Some were the product of free election by the chapter; some were named under pressure from the bishop of Lucca; throughout the period the greater part appear to have been appointed 'alla collazione' of a succession of Popes. Papal intervention might result in tension, as in 1495, when the canons elected Giovanni Vannelli to the *arcipretato* only to be confronted by the procurator of Giovanni Gigli, ambassador of Alexander

[80] Ibid. 27–32.

[81] BSL MSS 2951–3.

[82] Nutus Cecchi de Aramo, Arrigus Iohannis de Tadiccionibus de Luca, Taddeus Simi de Luca, Benedictus Iacobi de Luca, Paulus Nicolai de Sandeis, Dinus ser Pacis Dini de Luca (sive de Montecatino), Nicolaus Francisci Arrigi, Lazarius Iohannis de Guinigiis, Angelus Bertini, Philippus Iohannis Iacobi de Guinigiis, Andreas Petri de Luca, Franciscus Iohannis Michaelis de Guinigiis, Michael Ranuccii Marsucchi de Luca, Gerardus Arrigi de Bandellis. The two outsiders were Iacobus Franchi de Sareçana and Lucas Laurentii de Florentia. The former—a priest for fifty years, *cappellano* for about twenty years, canon of S. Martino for about thirty years—received Lucchese citizenship in 1433.

[83] The manuscript presents some ambiguities, and it is unclear whether some of the men promised prebends ever actually received them.

VI to the king of England, bearing *lettere apostoliche* and demanding that his principal be given possession of the vacant office. On this occasion the chapter accepted the papal appointment, 'out of obedience, but with protest, and reserved the rights of the said Sig^{e} Giovanni Vannelli'.[84] The prevalence of papal collation was not prejudicial to the election of native Lucchese, including those members of Lucca's leading families in high papal service. Generally, through to the mid-1470s, the chapter's composition seems to differ little from that described by Benedetto for the Guinigi period. Thereafter the chapter becomes a more faithful reflection of Lucca's secular councils. By the late 1490s the ranks of the canons of S. Martino included Lorenzo di Cristoforo Trenta, Giorgio di Galeotto Franciotti, Domenico Sinibaldi, Ruberto Guinigi, Bartolomeo di Francesco Balbani, Guglielmo di Francesco di Poggio, Riccardo Cenami, Nicolao di Silvestro di Gregorio Trenta, Silvestro Gigli, and Michele di Piero da Sandonnino. The last decades of the century also seem to provide more examples of the 'resignatio in favorem'. In 1483 Timoteo Balbani, *scrittore apostolico*, by *lettere apostoliche* resigned his canonry in favour of Bartolomeo di Francesco Balbani; in 1495 Silvestro Gigli similarly succeeded to the canonry resigned by Marco di Antonio Gigli.[85]

With regard to the bishopric itself, the usual negotiations and compromises resulted in the election between 1394 and 1499 of six bishops, all of whom were acceptable to the political authorities in Lucca, even if—as in the case of Iacopo di Cristoforo Ammannati—they were not the candidate for whom the Anziani pressed. Ammannati, who held Lucca whilst also bishop of Pavia and Cardinal bishop of Tuscolo, though born in Lucca, came from a prominent family of Pescia. The others were all of Lucchese families: two of them—Nicolao di Lazzaro Guinigi and Stefano Trenta—from Lucchese families of great power and prestige.[86]

Writing primarily of the Florentine Church, Bizzocchi has argued that by the fifteenth century Augustinian and Dominican foundations had come to resemble the cathedral chapters as centres of aristocratic control.[87] Again, the process seems to be taking place rather later in Lucca, and was

[84] BSL MS 2953, Baroni, Notizie sulla chiesa di S. Martino, fo. 102^{r}. Giovanni Vannelli, citizen of Lucca, *famigliare* and *auditore di Rota* in Rome, was elected by the chapter *in canonicato* on 1 Aug. 1497: ibid., fo. 103^{r}.

[85] Ibid., fos. 93^{v}, 102^{r}.

[86] Bongi, *Inventario*, iv. 105–6. The bishops were Nicolao di Lazzaro Guinigi (1394–1435), Lodovico Maulini (1435–40), Baldassare Manni (1441–8), Stefano Trenta (1448–77), Iacopo di Cristoforo Ammannati (1477–9), and Nicolao di Bartolomeo Sandonnini (1479–99).

[87] Bizzocchi, *Chiesa e potere*, 28–9.

far from complete by 1494. The priors of the great Dominican convent of S. Romano included Ugolino Guidi (1439), Giovanni Gigli (1475), Sebastiano de' Lambardi da Montecatino (1480), and Sebastiano Taissi (1486);[88] but before the reform of 1498 they were not for the most part native Lucchese, nor yet the body of friars over whom they ruled. Indeed, the most chronicled event in the fifteenth-century history of S. Romano was an incident in 1453 when Benedetto Santini, loath to lose his only son ('mal volentieri si privava di quest'unico figlio'), opposed his son's wish to become a friar of S. Romano. The friars agreed to receive Santini's son anyway, resulting in an affray at the altar when Benedetto, with his *parenti* and adherents, entered armed into S. Romano to recover the boy as he was being invested.[89] To the north of the city, the church and monastery of the Augustinian canons regular of S. Frediano was certainly ruled by priors born of Lucca's most ancient and distinguished families: Dino di Poggio (1414–30), Guglielmo Cenami (1464–1502), and Pasquino Cenami (1502–10).[90] But, as noted above, the period and aftermath of the Florentine wars were a difficult time for S. Frediano. The small number of surviving canons under prior Giovanni di Antonio da Massa di Luna (1430–64) were of very mixed provenance; by 1511 half the canons of S. Frediano were Lucchese, though very few were of distinguished parentage.[91]

A more marked difference relates to the nunneries. Bizzocchi writes of a Tuscan Church in which the nunneries had already become an essential ingredient of family politics and in the preservation of aristocratic

[88] BSL MS 2572, Cronica del Convento di S. Romano di Lucca scritta dal P^e^ Ignazio Manandro Ferrarese dimorante nello stesso convento, fo. 12^r–v^; MS 2623, Liber chronicorum Conventus S. Romani, fos. 7^r^–8^v^, 87^v^; MS 2636, Annales Conventus S. Romani praedicatorum ordinis Luc: Civitatis, fos. 4^v^, 6^r^. Unfortunately, all the chroniclers of S. Romano were reluctant to write of the bad old days before the 'padri della riforma of fra Girolamo Savonarola'. See also I. Taurisano, *I Domenicani in Lucca* (Lucca, 1914), 210–12.

[89] The story is recounted with characteristic vigour by the Dalli: BSL MS 710, fo. 149^r^; MS 939, p. 236.

[90] BSL MS 415, Notizie antiche del monastero e chiesa di S. Frediano, fos. 49^r–v^, 53^v^–54^v^; Coturri, 'La canonica di S. Frediano', 71–3.

[91] D. Gerardus de Cagniolis de Luca prior, D. Jo: Antonius Palanzanus vicarius, D. Johannes de Riciis de Ferraria, D. Leonardus mag^i^ Petri de Luca, D. Fridianus Pasquini de Luca, D. Laurentius Corsi de Carraria, D. Augustinus Johannis Boni de Luca, D. Innocentius Johannis de Papia, D. Baptista Antonii Turini de Luca, D. Martinus Antonii de Castiglono, D. Blasius magri Antonii de Mutina, D. Matheus Franchi de Santo Terentio, D. Benedictus Rustici de Luca, D. Filippus magri Blasii de Luca, D. Deodatus Luchesini de Luca, D. Franciscus Tome de Vergoletta, D. Nicolaus Bernardi de Luca: ASL Raccolte Speciali: S. Frediano, 72, Diversorum 1128–1725, no. 13. With the reforms of 1517 it was provided that twenty-eight canons regular should reside continuously in S. Frediano: eighteen priests and ten *clerici*.

wealth.[92] In analysing the structure of Lucchese politics, it was noted that Lucchese patricians seemed willing to endure the marriage of almost endless supplies of daughters.[93] Dowries offered to daughters and sisters entering convents in fifteenth-century Lucca do not necessarily support the image of the convent as a cheap alternative to marriage.[94] The aristocratic composition of urban nunneries was certainly as marked in Lucca as elsewhere. Iacopa Guerci was succeeded as *superiora*, or *badessa*, of the nuns of the monastery of S. Giustina by Giustina di Giovanni Bandini and later by Giustina's sister Margharita.[95] In 1489 Elena del fu Cristoforo Trenta, after many years of childless marriage to Gerardo di Gregorio Arrighi, now wishing to devote her life entirely to God and learning that the nuns of S. Nicolao Novello lived honestly under the rule of S. Augustine, received the permission of Innocent VIII—and of her husband—to leave the married state and enter the same.[96] Lists of nuns appended to notarial documents attest to the aristocratic composition of urban and suburban houses; they also reveal the very small size of these foundations.

S. Giustina was able to muster nine nuns, including the abbess, for a chapter meeting in 1456.[97] The Gesuate fled Lucca during the troubles, leaving behind them a sister of advanced years ('una sorella di matura età') who was clearly at the point of death; they were to return only after 1485. The Cistercian nuns of S. Cerbone were so far impoverished by war and plague that their monastery was given in 1441/2 to the Observant Franciscans; it is true that the surviving nuns, from a house in *strada* SS. Giovanni e Reparata, continued vigorously to resist their suppression for some years to come.[98] None of these cases provide much evidence for that massive aristocratic intrusion into the nunneries for which historians of

[92] Bizzocchi, *Chiesa e potere*, 30–3.

[93] See above, pp. 107–11.

[94] Maddalena del fu Raffaele Tegrimi, on entering the Dominican house of S. Nicolao Novello, was given a dowry by her brothers of 600 florins in land around Sorbano which rendered 30 *staia* of grain per annum: ASL Archivio Diplomatico: Pergamene (S. Nicolao), 3 Aug. 1481.

[95] ASL Archivio Diplomatico: Pergamene (S. Giustina), 23 Mar. 1451, 10 Apr. 1462, 11 Feb. 1479, 27 Mar. 1480.

[96] ASL Archivio Diplomatico: Pergamene (S. Nicolao), 3 Sept. 1489.

[97] ASL Archivio Diplomatico: Pergamene (S. Giustina), 29 July 1456.

[98] P. Antonio di Brandeglio (teologo e guardiano di S. Cerbone di Lucca), *Vita di S. Cerbone vescovo di Popolonia, e confessore raccolta fedelmente dall'Opere di S. Gregorio Papa, e di altri gravi autori: con alcune notizie del medesimo Convento, e degli altri della Riforma nel Dominio Lucchese* (Lucca, 1706), 4–5, 216–30, 307–29; ASL Archivio Diplomatico: Pergamene (S. Ponsiano), 19 July 1452; Pergamene (Fregionaia), 24 Mar. 1453; Pergamene (Miscellanee), 2 Nov. 1453.

the Florentine Church have argued. Nor have I found indications for the fifteenth century that the Lucchese houses were a 'scandalum populorum'.[99] In 1435 (for reasons that remain unclear) the abbess of S. Giustina, supported by the rest of the community, expelled suor Lena del fu Nicoletto Ciomei of Lucca.[100] But the only instance that I have found among the criminal cases before the court of the bishop of Lucca of nuns arranging for nocturnal male visitors involves Florentine nuns in a Florentine convent.[101]

The final ingredient in Bizzocchi's aristocratization of the Church in fifteenth-century Tuscany centres on the extension of aristocratic patronage. Within the walls of Lucca the formal possession of *giuspatronato* over churches (as opposed to altars and chapels) by a single family seems to have been quite rare. The di Poggio, dominating their quarter of Lucca with less ambiguity than any other family, certainly controlled their church of S. Lorenzo in Poggio. Indeed, S. Lorenzo was the regular meeting-place of that *consorteria* when summoned together by their consul.[102] By the end of the fifteenth century the newly arrived Minutoli controlled the election of the rector of S. Michele dei Guinithinghi.[103] But elsewhere even the Guinigi, however decisive their informal influence must have been, participated together with their fellow parishioners in the election of rectors to their church of SS. Simone e Giuda.[104] The most heated conflict over *giuspatronato* in fifteenth-century Lucca was not occasioned by the ambitions of an individual family to extend its rights over benefices, but rather by the infringements of the

[99] Sant'Antonino, quoted in Bizzocchi, *Chiesa e potere*, 31–2.

[100] AN 406 (ser Matteo di Giovanni de' Nobili), fo. 99r. Suor Lena was described as absent from a convocation summoned by the senior nun Iacopa del fu ser Piero Guerci and attended by the remaining eight nuns in Oct. 1441: AN 542(6) (ser Nicolao di Ranieri Mansi), fo. 160r–v.

[101] LA 100, unfoliated and undated, but placed between June and Sept. 1484. The priest involved was Agostino da Firenze, rector of SS. Vito e Iusto of Collegalli in the diocese of Lucca.

[102] BSL MS 62, Memorie diverse di Lucca, pp. 378–9.

[103] LA 119, fo. 132r–v. The church of S. Michele dei Guinithinghi of Lucca is among those listed as already destroyed by 21 Dec. 1555: BSL MS 38, Martino Bernardini, Ricordi Storici, fo. 422v.

[104] ASL Archivio Guinigi, 29, Girolamo Guinigi, Libro di ricordi, fo. 8v; AN 541 (ser Nicolao di Ranieri Mansi), fo. 8r–v. The parishioners of SS. Simone e Giuda also elected the chaplain of an altar in that church dedicated to the BVM and founded by the Pettinati: ASL Archivio Guinigi, 29, fo. 37v. The altar of S. Maria in SS. Simone and Giuda was under the patronage of the heirs of Lazzaro di Francesco di Lazzaro Guinigi: ASL Archivio Guinigi, 151, Michele Guinigi, Memorie e note, fo. 46r–v. The grant of patronage required the consent of bishop, rector, and parishioners. This altar provides a good example of how quickly, through inheritance, the right of election could be dispersed beyond the founding family.

closely guarded rights of the canons of S. Frediano by the parishioners of S. Salvatore in Mustiolo.[105] The late fourteenth and fifteenth centuries provide many examples of families (including the whole *agnazione*) obtaining the patronage in urban churches of altars and chapels endowed by them—though in S. Frediano the choice of rector was likely to be limited to one of the canons, and was always subject to approval and confirmation.[106] There was certainly no large-scale appropriation of the *giuspatronato* of city churches in Lucca by the end of the fifteenth century.

The situation in the wider Lucchese diocese is more complicated. The processes by which individual families in the localities acquired the *giuspatronato* of country churches are clear enough. Francesco di Brunetto Malizardi, having rebuilt and endowed the church of S. Concordio di Arsina (di Moriano), received the *giuspatronato* of a church of which his family had in fact long been patrons. Malizardi's rights became an issue only in 1482, when he was in danger of losing them for an unambiguous act of simony. He had sold the rectorship of S. Concordio to *presbitero* Urbano Domaschi in return for 20 ducats and for half the fruits of the benefice for the year 1482; the use of a Genoese banker failed to disguise the transaction from interested parties.[107] The Bernardini repaired the church of S. Vito in Vignale di Vicopelago, and this, together with the offer of 6 *staia* of grain per annum and an annual *censo* of 4 oz. of wax to the bishop on the feast of S. Martino, emboldened Bartolomeo di Paolino Bernardini to petition for confirmation as patron.[108] Through the repair and reconstruction of churches and in return for the assignment of lands and rents, powerful local families did hope for rights of *giuspatronato*. The offensive was hardly new in the fifteenth century, and there is little evidence that it was particularly successful. The Bernardini, after electing a new rector to S. Vito in Vignale di Vicopelago in March 1491, and after receiving confirmation in the *giuspatronato* in July 1493, saw the bishop restore S. Vito 'in suo pristino stato' in October 1493—presumably because of local objections.[109] The claim in 1487 by Colo and Antonio di

[105] ASL Raccolte Speciali: S. Frediano, 20, no. 6; 76, no. 1; BSL MS 415, Notizie antiche del monastero e chiesa di S. Frediano, fo. 80^{r-v}. For background, see BSL MS 415, fo. 20^{r}; NAC, N 116 (ser Nicolao di Coluccio di Pellegrino da Pietrasanta, 1435–9), 10 Feb. 1435; AN 704 (ser Benedetto Franciotti), pp. 75, 85.

[106] For the chapels and altars of S. Frediano, a convenient source remains: BSL MS 415, Notizie antiche del monastero e chiesa di S. Frediano, fos. 6^{r}, 9^{v}, 16^{v}, 20^{v}, 23^{r}. For an attempt to regulate the patronage of chapels and altars in the Lucchese diocese, see LA 88, fo. 19^{v}.

[107] ASL Archivio Diplomatico: Pergamene (Corte dei mercanti), 17 Nov. 1482; Biblioteca (Manoscritti), 126, B. Baroni, Famiglie Lucchesi, fos. 10^{v}–11^{v}.

[108] LA 120, fo. 55^{v}.

[109] LA 119, fo. 133^{v}; 120, fos. 55^{v}, 57^{v}, 88^{r}.

Baldassare Coli and by Giuliano di Lazzaro Nanni Pietri to be co-patrons of the church of S. Bartolommeo di Collegoli (apparently against the body of parishioners) was certainly not received with easy acquiescence by the bishop's vicar-general.[110]

The evidence for a formal, institutionalized aristocratizing of the Church in fifteenth-century Lucca would appear less compelling than for other parts of Tuscany. Harmonious relations in Lucca rested rather on a less structured interpenetration of secular and clerical society, on the absence of major occasions for conflict, and on the essential fragility of the independent power structures of the local church. Perhaps most important of all, no matter how irritating specific clerical claims and exemptions might prove, the Church remained for Lucca's rulers a useful arbiter and protector, the font of legitimacy, and the channel of divine favour in defence of Lucca's precarious political liberty.

The Church's contribution to the internal and external stability of the Lucchese state was in part highly practical. In this sense the independent judicial and administrative powers of the Roman Church, far from being a challenge to some anachronistic concept of statehood, were useful and welcome. In February 1458 the General Council of Lucca received with some gratitude the offer from Rome of the cardinal-priests of S. Lorenzo in Lucina (Filippo Calandrini) and of S. Prisca to intervene in a dangerous dispute which was developing in Lucca between the Arnolfini and the Guidiccioni. Both parties enjoyed powerful support in Lucca; a settlement in Rome by the cardinals, or by those commissioned by them, offered the Lucchese authorities an easy escape from their difficulties. In consequence, on 23 February Piero Guidiccioni and Bartolomeo Arnolfini were ordered to depart for Rome within twenty days, under pain of banishment and a fine of 1,000 florins each.[111]

Throughout the fifteenth century, whether in disputes of major international significance or in those of trivial local interest, appeals flowed to Rome and to local churchmen for arbitration and settlement. In the 1440s the Anziani of Lucca hoped in vain to settle the difficult dispute with Pippa di Paolo Guinigi, wife of Tommaso Ravaschieri of Genoa, by

[110] LA 118, fos. 107^{v}, 110^{v}. It may be significant in the light of Bizzocchi's findings that many of the claims for *giuspatronato* within the Lucchese diocese relate to areas deep in Florentine territory. See esp. LA 119, fos. 130^{r}–131^{r}.

[111] Rif. 18, pp. 104–6. Bartolomeo Arnolfini had already cited the Guidiccioni to appear before the court of Rome early in the previous year, though the parties then decided to try to reach a private agreement and to delay pursuing the case before the courts either in Rome or in Lucca until the end of Sept. 1457: AN 597 (ser Luviso di Antonio Buonaccorsi), fos. 263^{r-v}, 299^{r-v}, 314^{r-v}.

placing the case before the *tribunale della Chiesa romana*.[112] The sympathetic Nicholas V was a valued counsellor in the jungle of fifteenth-century inter-state relations;[113] the same Pope was no doubt, for Lucca, a most agreeable choice of arbitrator in the dispute with the Este over the territories of Gallicano.[114] Lucca was always in search of powerful friends, and the Riformagioni Pubbliche of the General Council are littered with grants of property and citizenship issued to the relatives and familiars of popes and cardinals. For similar reasons Lucca watched with pride and self-interest the advancement in papal service of her own citizens. Bishop Stefano Trenta was granted 400 ducats in 1460, so that he might reside honourably for two years at the court of Rome.[115] At a more local level the bishop of Lucca might appear as a convenient companion when reviewing judicial sentences, particularly following some of the more sensitive political trials.[116] And the elevated fifteenth-century reputation of the Franciscan *Minori Osservanti* could be put to good use in the settlement of local border disputes on the periphery of the Lucchese state.[117]

No less important than the concern to win material support from the Church was the preoccupation of Lucca's rulers with retaining divine favour and protection. At both levels the rhetoric focused on the defence of liberty, on the preservation of order, and on the honour and prestige of the city. Perhaps the most concrete expression of civic intercession centred on the altar of Liberty in the cathedral of S. Martino, originally established by the republic to celebrate the end of Pisan rule in 1369. Antonio di Giovanni Bertini, later of ill repute, was appointed chaplain and rector in 1436, with a salary of 30 florins a year. In December 1443 it was decided that the Anziani holding office every November/December should annually appoint a chaplain to celebrate a daily mass at the altar of Liberty, continually interceding for the physical and spiritual well-being of the city and people of Lucca and their subjects.[118] Running throughout the fifteenth-century sources is the theme that holy relics, and particularly the bodies of the saints, preserved in Lucchese churches within and beyond

[112] ASL Archivio Diplomatico: Pergamene (S. M. Fiorentini), 4 Sept. 1447.

[113] ASL Archivio Diplomatico: Pergamene (Tarpea), 22 Oct. 1449.

[114] Ibid., 28 Mar. 1451.

[115] ASL Biblioteca (Manoscritti), 65, Pietro Carelli, Sommario delle Cronache, fo. 106^v.

[116] See, e.g., Rif. 15, p. 355.

[117] AS Massa, Archivio dei Malaspina di Fosdinovo Marchesi di Massa, 1, no. 40.

[118] Rif. 15, p. 78; 16, p. 364. In Dec. 1446 it was decided that henceforth for the next five years the Anziani in office in Nov./Dec. were to appoint a chaplain, taken each year in turn from one of the five orders of regulars, daily to celebrate a plain mass at the hour of Terce in the church of S. Paolino: Rif. 16, p. 645.

the walls constituted the surest defence of Lucca's liberty. Fearful that neglect was displeasing both to God and to the saints themselves, provision was made in 1446 for the Anziani (the due number remaining always in the palace) to go on the saint's day to the church where the body of the saint lay and make an appropriate offering of wax.[119] In the late summer of 1458 only the most pressing fears regarding the spread of plague impelled the Lucchese authorities not to hold the feast of Santa Croce and to suspend the games. The following year, whatever the risks, Lucca's honour determined that the celebrations should proceed.[120]

The public expressions of civic religion were accompanied by a parallel, related determination on the part of the authorities to free Lucca from practices that might occasion divine displeasure. In 1436 the General Council, conscious of God's chastisement as evidenced by Lucca's immediate past misfortunes, decided in future to forgo the revenues of the public gaming-houses, decreeing that the *provento della baratteria* was not to be sold again after its next expiry.[121] The same preoccupation (together with the need to avert the more immediate threat posed by local rivalries and factions) prefaced nearly every piece of legislation concerned with moral purification and with the restraint of gaming and conspicuous display. Inevitably—and, it appears, with rather less ambiguity than was the case with the greater and more secure regional power of Florence[122]—Lucca's rulers were interested that intercessions for peace and liberty should be channelled through a purified Church. Certainly, some acts of state intervention were occasioned primarily by a concern for public order: the decision in 1442, for example, that to prevent future scandals, the celebrations of the confraternities henceforth required special licence from the Anziani.[123] Equally clearly, some interventions were suggested by a determination to protect lay patronage rights: probably the determined resistance by the General Council to the bishop's plans to convert the abbey of S. Salvatore at Sesto into a school for clergy.[124] But elsewhere there is evidence of a plain supervisory intent. In 1452 the Anziani wrote to Pope Nicholas V asking him to provide a remedy for the precarious situation of various churches, chapels, and religious

[119] Rif. 16, pp. 581–2, 604, 608. The days of all the saints whose bodies were in Lucca or beyond the walls were declared holy days, and the courts and shops were to remain closed.

[120] ASL Colloqui, 1, pp. 16, 32. In 1476 the *palio* had to be suspended (together with some of the other festivities of Santa Croce) because of financial constraints on the commune.

[121] Rif. 15, p. 48.

[122] Bizzocchi, *Chiesa e potere*, *passim*.

[123] Rif. 16, p. 159.

[124] Ibid., p. 352.

houses in the diocese of Lucca, which was caused (according to the Anziani) by the 'incuria' of those charged with their care.[125] In 1460, a *Colloquio*, knowing that the Pope 'vehemently desires that all convents should be of the best and most religious', provided for the appointment of two Lucchese citizens for each of the religious houses of Lucca and its district with unspecified duties to oversee reform in both material and spiritual matters.[126]

It is difficult to assess how far the periodic attentions of the secular councils were merited. The condition of the fifteenth-century Lucchese Church remains largely unexplored, as do the faith, beliefs, and observances of the mass of the laity. With regard to the latter, the court records suggest the prevalence of various superstitious practices largely concerned with foretelling future events through the medium of religious texts and images.[127] The woman who casts spells ('La donna che fa l'incantatrice') joins the usurer among the lay sinners regularly recorded in the pastoral visitations. But there is no sign of identifiable heretical movements—at least, not after the early fifteenth-century attempt by Florentine *fraticelli* to evangelize the Lucchese countryside.[128] Accusations of blasphemy are common enough, particularly against the Blessed Virgin Mary. But these expletives seem to represent no more than the oaths of the desperate or the indiscreet expression of anger, as when in April 1437 Piero Menichi, originally from Pisan territory but then living in the suburbs of Lucca, hungry for bread and refused by a succession of neighbours, said—to the grave danger of his soul and against God and his saints—'Che maladetto fuisse dio con tutti Sancti'.[129] From the pilferings of habitual criminals no special sanctity seems to have protected the precious objects of the altar or the adornments of the Virgin or even the pockets of individual worshippers; indeed, when the village was at lunch, the local church offered tempting pickings.[130] Almost without exception, those arraigned for blasphemy and sacrilege were drawn from the poor, from the outsiders, from the migrants on the margins of society. For

125 ASL Archivio Diplomatico: Pergamene (Tarpea), 3 Oct. 1452.

126 ASL Colloqui, 1, pp. 53–4.

127 e.g., ASL Cause Delegate, 3, pp. 20–1, 26.

128 G. Lami, *Lezioni di antichità toscane e spezialmente della città di Firenze*, 2 vols. (Florence, 1766), ii. 595; F. Tocco, 'I fraticelli', *Archivio storico italiano*, 5th ser., xxxv (1905), 359–60.

129 SB 161, fo. 115^{r-v}. Piero was fined £90 15*s*. (58*s*. per florin), and subsequently produced an instrument of peace with the rector of S. Leonardo 'in capite Burgi', in which parish the offence was committed.

130 SB 159, fos. 260^{r-v}, 267^{r}, 346^{r-v}, 375^{r-v}; 162, fos. 58^{v}–59^{r}; Capitano del Popolo e della città, 33, unfoliated, 1st case; 35, fos. 47^{r}–49^{v}; 36, fo. 34^{r}.

Lucchese citizens of all grades it is difficult to penetrate beyond the expressions of faith and the pious bequests of the testaments. The expectations of patrician society were most clearly expressed in the *ricordi* of Girolamo Guinigi: the satisfied noting of the deaths of relatives well confessed; the hopes for salvation of his wife Pippa, daughter of Lorenzo Buonvisi, who died very devoutly, always with the name of Jesus upon her lips.[131]

An overview of the parish clergy and of the Orders of regulars is even more elusive. The pastoral visits—certainly later in the century with a return to relative peace and stability—frequently adjudged the local rector sufficiently good and suitable ('satis bonus et idoneus'), a verdict often not incompatible with the injunction to study and learn. These reviews are difficult to use without a clearer sense of contemporary standards. There is no difficulty in compiling a list of crimes and misdemeanours to which priests, monks, and friars were particularly prone. Gambling would appear high on any such list, treated more seriously if indulged in with laymen or in the presence of laymen.[132] Some priests were natty dressers to the point of public scandal; and there are many references to the carrying of prohibited arms for self-defence, sometimes for reasons more discreditable than the carrying of arms itself. The *cause criminali*, as might be expected, include many enquiries into the presence in the priest's household of suspect women, the keeping of mistresses, and activities with married women. Sometimes the details are sordid; sometimes, as in the case of *presbitero* Gabrielle of Lucca and Caterina, slave of messer Alessandro Rapondi, the court records hint at tender and tragic relationships.[133] In some instances the priest may have been as much victim as instigator: in Corsagna, for example, where the brother and husband of Francesca di Baldassare began to extract, with threats of violence, significant sums of money from gentlemen (including the local priest) whom they surprised with Francesca.[134] Illicit relationships and efforts to terminate the pregnancies that resulted caused individual priests to dabble in medicine, to bring about abortions.[135] In other cases it is impossible to decide whether the medical attentions of the clergy were denounced because of the professional jealousy of doctors of medicine or because of the genuine incompetence of these amateur practitioners.[136]

131 ASL Archivio Guinigi, 29, Girolamo Guinigi, Libro di ricordi, fos. 22^{v}–23^{r}, 30^{v}.

132 LA 100, 9 Jan., 28 May 1483, 24 Jan. 1486.

133 LA 99A, fos. 16^{v}–17^{v}.

134 SB 192, fos. 340^{r}–341^{r}.

135 LA 99A, fos. 10^{r}–11^{v}.

136 LA 100, undated, 1486.

Some offences relating to going abroad wearing masks, the keeping of concubines, simony, and the revealing of confessions are peculiarly clerical. In other respects churchmen merely participated, to an unmeasurable degree, in the misdoings of the society in which they lived. Before the *Tribunale ecclesiastico* individuals faced charges of petty theft (and sometimes more than petty theft of the sacred objects of the altar),[137] of throwing stones, of injurious words, of coining false money, of sodomy, even of being notorious usurers.[138] Certain figures—the friar drunk with wine whose clumsiness and insults allegedly provoked laymen into the acts for which they were arraigned—occur so frequently in the sources that they must relate to contemporary perceptions, and probably to realities. For the rest, the fact that for serious offences the names of the same accused tend to reappear again and again must caution against the drawing of general conclusions. Two points would appear to emerge irresistibly from those sources to which I have had access.[139]

The first is that in a quarrelsome and litigious age the clergy were among the most active in quarrels and litigation. At an institutional level the surviving records are dominated by disputes over precedence, rights, privileges, and exemptions. The prior of the church and monastery of S. Frediano was at one moment preoccupied with the never ending battle to retain control of distant churches in Carrara, Castelfranco, and Bologna; at another the conflict was nearer home with the parishioners of subject churches within the walls of Lucca itself.[140] The conflict between S. Frediano and Bishop Nicolao Guinigi was carried over into the post-Guinigi years. It came to involve the precise meaning of the prior's exemption from the jurisdiction 'dell'ordinarii' and also the prior's own powers of jurisdiction over the parish of S. Frediano, and over the priests and laity of churches which he claimed to control.[141] To the usual disputes with lay and ecclesiastical opponents over land rights, we may add the quarrels over purity of descent that the Augustinian canons regular of the Lateran Congregation at S. Frediano were likely to have with the Hermits

[137] AAL Collazioni, A (1448), fo. 15^{r}. More common are cases of religious pilfering provisions from their houses: LA 100, 3 Dec. 1481.

[138] A distinction achieved by p. Guglielmo, chaplain of Massa Cozzile: LA 100, 5 Mar. 1484.

[139] I have not seen the series AAL Tribunale ecclesiastico: Cause criminali.

[140] BSL MS 415, Notizie antiche del monastero e chiesa di S. Frediano, fos. 38^{r}, 80^{v}, 97^{r}–98^{r}; ASL Archivio Diplomatico: Pergamene (S. Frediano), 20 July 1474.

[141] BSL MS 415, Notizie antiche del monastero e chiesa di S. Frediano, fos. 6^{r}, 64^{r}–65^{v}, 126^{r}–131^{r}, 140^{v}–141^{v}; ASL Archivio Diplomatico: Pergamene (S. Frediano), 18 Apr. 1458; Pergamene (Archivio di Stato), 12 Jan. 1467.

of S. Augustine.[142] Ancient and wide-ranging privileges ensured that S. Frediano was well represented in a jostling for position which was characteristic of the Church as a whole. Arbitrators (whose judgment was not accepted by the losing party) were appointed to settle a dispute between the monasteries of Fregionaia and S. Ponziano over right of precedence in processions.[143] The prior of S. Pietro maggiore (exempt from the jurisdiction of the bishop) pointedly chose to fight a lawsuit relating to land in Moriano (under the jurisdiction of the bishop of Lucca) before the secular court of the *Podestà*.[144] And the efforts by the *barbieri* of Lucca to transfer a mass celebrated in honour of S. Appollonia to the church of S. Sensio were successfully resisted in 1483 by S. Michele in foro, which claimed the right on the grounds of established custom.[145]

The rival claims of institutions were contested at law. The quarrels of individuals not infrequently were conducted through less formal channels. Thus two priests playing cards in a house in the cloisters of S. Martino came to words, before one of them took up arms.[146] A squabble on the piazza of S. Michele in foro between *pievano* Nicolao Lommori and the German organist maestro Giorgio over vague hints of past or anticipated criticism by the organist of the 'maestro del canto' led to a lively exchange of insults before the priest struck the organist, who self-righteously refused to respond out of respect for the clergy and the bishop's authority. The priest's offence was compounded, it appears, by a subsequent attempt to suborn witnesses.[147] The same Nicolao Lommori was accused of issuing threatening and injurious words to *presbitero* Iacopo Luporini (occasioned, as so often, by concern for position) in the choir of S. Martino during the celebration of mass. That event was the more memorable since it happened in the presence of bishop and Anziani as Church and State came together in the cathedral church to honour the feast of SS. Vincenzio and Benigno.[148]

The second point to emerge clearly from the judicial and administrative

[142] ASL Archivio Diplomatico: Pergamene (S. Frediano), 11 May 1484.

[143] The arbitrators, appointed by the parties themselves and by the Anziani, found in favour of Fregionaia: ibid., 13 Sept. 1485.

[144] ASL Podestà di Lucca, Inquisizioni, 5284, fos. 159r–162v.

[145] LA 117, fo. 5v. In 1494 the corporation of barbers met in the church of S. Sensio to revise their statutes: ASL Archivio Diplomatico: Pergamene (Archivio di Stato), 19 Mar. 1494.

[146] LA 100, 6 Sept. 1481.

[147] Ibid., no date, May/June 1484.

[148] Ibid., no date, June/July 1485. For a more serious disturbance by secular priests in the church of S. Frediano, also in the presence of the Anziani, see ASL Raccolte Speciali: S. Frediano, 7, fos. 165r, 166r.

records of the Church is that, at least periodically, bishops of Lucca throughout the later fifteenth century were concerned to restore ecclesiastical discipline and to reform the lives of both clergy and laity. In 1487, during the episcopate of Nicolao Sandonnini, a number of priests (and two parishioners) were interrogated under oath regarding the reputation of priests and clerics of the city and diocese of Lucca.[149] The enquiry was concerned particularly with the keeping of concubines, but received evidence of the unlicensed practice of medicine and of simony (involving the prior of S. Giovanni and canons of the cathedral) and of a carnival atmosphere in Pescia which allegedly saw priests dancing, wearing masks and fancy dress, hearing confessions, and singing secular ditties. Federigo ser Federighi's denunciation of *presbitero* Bartolomeo di Michele da Casabasciana of S. Maria Filicorbi was particularly severe; other witnesses were anxious to insist that they spoke only of rumours of which they possessed no direct knowledge. Nicolao Lommori, *pievano* of S. Stefano, dutifully produced the rumours, but was inclined to dismiss most of them as ill-founded. The list of offenders is not particularly long, and the same names were continually repeated by those interrogated. The affair shows an awareness of imperfections, but also a determination by the bishop of Lucca to review and remedy.

The same doubled-edged evidence of reform, and of the failings that provided the impetus for reform, can be drawn from any number of episcopal orders and decrees. This evidence is perhaps particularly rich for the Sandonnini episcopate. Thus in 1484 priests were yet again forbidden to go about masked, and support was given to the determination of the secular authorities to act against this and related abuses.[150] In 1489 there was a general edict from the bishop against priests and clerics who went about untonsured and without clerical dress, who carried arms, who moved around at night without lamps, who wore masks, who kept concubines, and who played at dice or cards.[151] In 1492 the bishop granted licence to the *Capitano del contado* to take away weapons from priests and clerics, the ecclesiastical authorities promptly to be advised of such offences.[152] Lay conduct was taken care of through such prohibitions as that issued to the men and women of Corsanico against playing any ball game in the cemetery or other holy place of the local church of S.

[149] LA 100, no date, but clearly 1487.
[150] LA 117, fo. 73^{r}.
[151] LA 119, fo. 41^{r-v}.
[152] LA 120, fo. 9^{r}.

Michele.[153] At the level of more narrowly ecclesiastical discipline, efforts were made from time to time to restore the ancient system of *pievi*.[154] And the ecclesiastical records are full of injunctions to rectors to attend to or to provide for the care of souls, and to chaplains—particularly the chaplains of the cathedral—to participate in divine service as and when obligated to do so, under pain of deprivation. More positive was the convocation by the bishop's vicar in 1486 of the rectors of city churches to appoint and pay a priest as chaplain to have care of the souls of the sick during time of plague.[155]

Evidence of pastoral concern and of internal supervision and renewal failed to satisfy Lucca's ruling oligarchy, or indeed Lucchese society at large. In the councils of the republic, the link was continually drawn between the Church as intercessor and the efficacy of that intercession in the sight of God. For the embattled republic, the purity of the Church became an instrument of public policy. No doubt this was not new. Neither were the unrealistic expectations placed on a priesthood whose qualities might palliate, vicariously, the manifest imperfections of secular society. Nor yet was there novelty in the preoccupation of that society with decency and honour: no priest's concubine was hounded as those with numerous and powerful 'affines' to protest the disgrace and dishonour. But old prejudices and perceptions, combined with the precariousness of the restored republic and with dimensions of late medieval spirituality, came together to forge very special bonds between the Lucchese state and the growing Observant movements within the Church, particularly with the Franciscan *Minori Osservanti*.

There is a political myth, deeply entrenched in Lucchese chronicle traditions, that has tended to attribute the introduction of the Observants—and their later triumphs—entirely to the faith and initiative of the Lucchese patriciate. The Observant Franciscans in fact came to Lucca during the pontificate of Eugenius IV, most vigorous proponent of all the Observant movements. The Blessed Bernardino Tomitano da Feltre was first invited to Lucca by the bishop, Nicolao Sandonnini, in 1488.[156] But such details do not alter the fact that the Observants were welcomed and fostered by the secular authorities; in Lucca, apparently, with rather less ambiguity than in contemporary Florence.[157] S. Bernardino da Siena had

153 LA 118, fo. 85ʳ.

154 AAL Cause civili della Curia (ser Ciomeo Pieri, 1453), fos. 58ʳ–59ᵛ, 78ʳ–80ᵛ.

155 LA 118, fos. 82ᵛ–83ʳ.

156 E. Lazzareschi, 'Il beato Bernardino da Feltre, gli Ebrei e il Monte di Pietà in Lucca', *Bolletino Storico Lucchese*, a. xiii, XIX (1941), 18.

157 Bizzocchi, *Chiesa e potere*, 74–81.

made a deep impression during the Lenten sermons of 1428; the preaching of the Blessed Ercolano da Piegaro helped to sustain a people under siege during the first Florentine war. The latter's accurate prophecy of an imminent Florentine withdrawal added further to the prestige of the Franciscan Observants, and fra Ercolano himself was given in reward the convent at Pozzuolo. The establishment of an Observant community at S. Cerbone after May 1442 resulted from a combination of Lucchese pressure, the influence of S. Bernardino of Siena, and the underlying sympathy of Eugenius IV. Thereafter S. Cerbone was to receive significant subvention from the state. It was at the petition of the Lucchese government that the great monastery in Lucca of S. Francesco was taken away from the Conventuals, in 1458, and given to the *Minori Osservanti*. In 1477, following the death of Stefano Trenta, the Anziani wrote many times to the Pope requesting the appointment of the Observant fra Paolo Iova as bishop of Lucca. And at the end of the century, following his Lenten sermons of 1489, the Anziani pressured (eventually successfully) for the return to Lucca of the Blessed Bernardino da Feltre.[158] Similarly, in the community of Pietrasanta—no longer, by 1449, under Lucchese rule—the General Council gave authority to the local Anziani to respond favourably to the request of the Francisans for a house, on condition that they were 'dell'Osservanza'.[159]

Michele Luzzati has argued that the Observant Franciscans provided a new dynamic in the political history of Lucca, sometimes pushing Lucca's rulers in directions about which they were less than enthusiastic. Specifically, he has contrasted the traditional prudence and tolerance of Lucca towards Jews with the radical solutions pressed upon Lucca's rulers by Bernardino da Feltre and fra Timoteo da Lucca.[160] Certainly the Lucchese patriciate might justly fear the power of emotional sermons to arouse the *popolo minuto*; on occasions they might resent the appearance that public policy was being determined by friars. On specific actions like

[158] P. Antonio di Brandeglio, *Vita di S. Cerbone*, esp. 4–5, 224–35; *Bibliotheca Sanctorum* (Rome, 1964), iv. 1308; *Acta Sanctorum: Maii*, vi (Antwerp, 1688), 862–4; Bongi, *Inventario*, iv. 106; Lazzareschi, 'Il beato Bernardino da Feltre', 19–21.

[159] ASCP Libro di Consigli (1449), fo. 14^{r}.

[160] M. Luzzati, 'Fra Timoteo da Lucca (1456–1513): appunti di ricerca', in *Miscellanea Augusto Campana (Medioevo e Umanesimo, 45)* (Padua, 1981), esp. 378–9, 383–5; *idem*, 'Lucca e gli Ebrei fra Quattro e Cinquecento', in *Città italiane del '500 tra riforma e controriforma: Atti del Convegno Internazionale di Studi, Lucca, 13–15 ottobre 1983* (Lucca, 1988), esp. 207, 211. Elsewhere in the above articles Luzzati is more inclined to argue that hostility to Jews came rather from society than from the Church, that 15th-cent. Lucca (among Italian cities) demonstrated a peculiar terror of contamination, and that there were powerful opponents of Jewish money-lenders within the ruling councils.

the expulsion of Jewish money-lenders, fears for social and economic consequences might engender genuine and heated differences of opinion within the patriciate. But generally the religious programme of the Observants sanctioned and encouraged the vision of the magistrates for a godly, ordered, and pacific community. And before the 1490s, apart from visiting preachers and papal emissaries, the Observant movement in Lucca was primarily represented by the Franciscans.[161]

Throughout the post-Guinigi years concern for public order resulted in periodic legislation to control festivities, dress, display, and morals. From at least the 1450s the Observant Francisans were at hand to give reasons and provide encouragement. Measures of the late 1450s to curb pomp and excessive display were explicitly attributed to the preachings and teachings of the Observant Minorite fra Angelo da Siena; the renewed campaign against sodomy undoubtedly received encouragement from the same quarters.[162] During the same period the great processions of the innocents—children between the ages of 4 and 15, all dressed in white—were orchestrated in Lucca by the Dominican Observant friar Giovanni da Napoli, papal commissioner and preacher against the Turks.[163] The link between Lucca and the reform movement was sealed by the attraction of the Observant orders for the sons of the Lucchese patriciate. Girolamo, son of Pietro di Nicolao Guinigi, entered the reformed house of S. Francesco in 1469.[164] The Blessed Giovanni Buonvisi, brother of that Lorenzo who was a leading conspirator in 1430 and thereafter a major political figure until his death in office as Gonfaloniere di Giustizia in 1460, took the religious habit in a Conventual Franciscan house in the kingdom of Aragon. In the years that followed, Giovanni Buonvisi travelled in search of an ever purer and stricter discipline, ending his days as Guardiano del Monte di Perugia.[165] Fra Timoteo da Lucca was the son of Benedetto di Nicolao dei Medici da Moncigoli and of Beatrice di Stefano di Poggio.[166] From such a conjunction, personal and political,

[161] The Observant Carmelites at S. Pier Cigoli received a subvention of 40 florins in 1458 for building and repairs: Rif. 18, p. 156.

[162] ASL Biblioteca (Manoscritti), 65, Pietro Carelli, Sommario delle Cronache, fo. 105^{r}.

[163] BSL MS 62, Memorie diverse di Lucca, pp. 95–6.

[164] ASL Archivio Guinigi, 29, Girolamo Guinigi, Libro di ricordi, fo. 17^{v}.

[165] *Acta Sanctorum: Maii*, v (Antwerp, 1685), 100–24; BSL MS 99, Nicolao Tucci, Elogia, fo. 25^{r}; U. Nicolini, 'Giovanni Buonvisi', in *Dizionario biografico degli italiani*, xv (Rome, 1972), 325–7.

[166] Luzzati, 'Fra Timoteo da Lucca', 381–2. In 1457, fra Timoteo's father Benedetto cited the Jew Gaietto for 11 ducats, part of a larger sum of 30 ducats owing by virtue of a public instrument: ASL Podestà di Lucca, Curia Civile, 1307, fo. 94^{r}.

stemmed the expulsion of the Jewish money-lenders from Lucca with which the present study ends.

The history of Jewish money-lenders in Lucca dates back no further than the time of Paolo Guinigi. From 1432 agreements were made between the commune and Jewish money-lenders—initially with the bank of Angelo di Gaio and Isaac Manuele and partners—granting them for a set term the monopoly of lending money at interest. The compositors were warned that nothing should be agreed that was contrary to the Christian religion or to the ordinances of the Church.[167] The agreements nevertheless offered the local Jewish community considerable protection and freedom. They were given security of life and property (including pledges), freedom of worship, a place to bury their dead, and exemption (for a time) from wearing any sign.[168] These agreements were concluded 'for the subvention of the poor and for the public good'.[169] With the Christian ban on usury, the Jews offered necessary subsistence loans to the indigent, though at a high rate of interest, which came to be fixed for private loans at 30 per cent per annum. The life of the state and of institutions were no less likely to be punctuated by financial crises than were the lives of the indigent. It was to the Jews that Lucca turned in 1436 for money for the recovery of Motrone.[170] It was with the Jews that the prior of S. Frediano pledged his habit in the 1450s, generally a difficult time for the great Augustinian foundation.[171]

The notarial and court records in part confirm this image of a tolerated and protected Jewish community. Jews appear regularly before the courts as litigants, and also in numerous notarialized commercial transactions which only sometimes seem to involve unredeemed pledges. Giuliano di Iacopo da Brancoli, replaced as guardian of the heirs of Silvestro di Battista di ser Castruccio da Pietrasanta by orders of the General Council of Lucca, became personally responsible for interest owing to the Jews of Lucca for a loan obtained on behalf of the inheritance.[172] The court of merchants in 1457, having ordered the sequestration of pledges held by

[167] e.g., Rif. 17, p. 75.

[168] The material from Riformagioni Pubbliche is conveniently summarized in Lazzareschi, 'Il beato Bernardino da Feltre', 14–17; Luzzati, 'Lucca e gli Ebrei', 215. For a comparable agreement with Pietrasanta and for its operation in practice, see ASCP Libro Partiti (1452–3), fo. 63^{v}; NAC, N 115 (ser Nicolao di Coluccio di Pellegrino da Pietrasanta, 1409–68), fo. 282^{r}.

[169] Rif. 16, p. 332.

[170] Rif. 15, p. 92.

[171] ASL Raccolte Speciali: S. Frediano, 14, fos. 12^{v}, 153^{r}, 13^{r}, 78^{v}.

[172] AN 705 (ser Benedetto Franciotti), p. 133.

the Jew Isaac, ordered the successful plaintiff to pay the interest due, and also granted Isaac permission to appear before the court to obtain justice if the award proved harmful to him.[173] Gaio Sabbatini, party to a lengthy dispute between the former partners of a Jewish company established for public money-lending, invoked the aid of the state in appealing for a safe conduct and freedom from arrest during a visit to his son in Florence.[174] The murder in 1442 by a German Jew of a co-religionist in Gaio's house adjoining the piazza of S. Matteo was handled by the Lucchese courts in the usual way; the culprit confessed, and was summarily executed.[175] As late as 1487 the bishop of Lucca was granting licence to three Jews, including Perle, wife of Abram da Bologna, to go to the baths of Corsena and Villa at the due and customary hours together with Christians.[176]

Impressionistically, the routine civil and criminal cases involving Jews in the earlier records appear from mid-century increasingly supplemented by accusations of offences by Jews against the Christian religion and against Christians. In 1449 four Jews were fined for openly parading in the streets during Holy Week and for various acts of contempt against Our Lady and in derision of Christians.[177] In 1457, when the Jewish money-lender Bonaventura stood accused of concealing usury through a fictitious sale of corn, the *lanaro* Nicolao Genti argued that the Jew should not be heard by the court as it was well known that he was a public usurer and thus of ill fame. At the same time, Genti denied the right of Bonaventura's procurator, as a Christian, to swear on behalf of a Jew.[178] In 1467 the visit of the Bolognese Jew Consilio alias Baseo, son of Musetto, to a public (Christian) prostitute—a Ferrarese girl named La Margarita—resulted in complex legal arguments over whether the statutes referred to prostitutes; it also seems to indicate (contrary to Luzzati) that Jews having sexual relations with Christians were punishable by burning.[179] In 1487 the Jew Davide di Dattilo da Tivoli, having failed to turn up to purge himself under torture, was fined £450 in the court of the *Podestà* for

173 ASL Corte de' mercanti, Cause civili, 152, fos. 10^{r}, 29^{r}.

174 ASL Archivio Diplomatico: Pergamene (Archivio di Stato), 14 June 1453; AN 700(4) (ser Benedetto Franciotti), 2 July 1456.

175 SB 162, unfoliated pergamena.

176 LA 118, fo. 159^{v}.

177 SB 165, fos. 121^{r}–122^{r}.

178 ASL Podestà di Lucca, Curia Civile, 1309, fos. 97^{r-v}, 113^{v}–114^{v}, 129^{r}–134^{r}. The civil records of these years are full of references to the sequestration or release of goods held by Jewish money-lenders; the criminal records indicate how stolen property was likely to end up as pledges in the hands of the Jews.

179 ASL Capitano del Popolo e della città, 33, no foliation, 2nd case. Cf. Luzzati, 'Lucca e gli Ebrei', 215.

offences against the images of Saints Antonio, Matteo, and Sebastiano. On other charges, including the celebration of the Jewish religion in the presence of Christians and blasphemy, Davide was absolved.[180]

Following the overthrow of Paolo Guinigi, the Jews continued to be tolerated in Lucca as useful. The toleration was limited. In the later fifteenth century suggestions of a hardening of attitudes appear not only in mounting accusations of the kind illustrated above, but also in the slightly less favourable terms obtained in the agreements with the commune after 1462. Radical change came only with the founding of the first Monte di Pietà in 1489 and the expulsion of the Jewish money-lenders in 1493–4. These changes were partly the work of the Observant Franciscans: of men like the Blessed Francesco dalla pieve S. Stefano. Fra Francesco at S. Cerbone had a vision of God seated above the city of Lucca who, turning His gaze upon him, entrusted to the Franciscan the mission of driving the Jews from Lucca and erecting there a Monte di Pietà. At least according to canon Gio: Lunardo Dalli, the lords of Lucca built according to the divine specifications revealed to fra Francesco.[181] But the founding of the Monti di Pietà and the legislation against the Jewish money-lenders remain the work of a native political élite. Not without dissenters, that élite had moved from its earlier ambivalence of conscience to a principled stand. This change entailed the implementation of new policies which would not be without their practical difficulties and which were to require sacrifices. For Lucca, as for Italy as a whole, the legislation against the Jews offers as clear an indication of changing preoccupations in a perilous world as does the coincidental arrival of the armies of the great powers.

[180] SB 202, fos. 183^r–185^v.

[181] BSL MS 939, Gio: Lunardo Dalli, Cronache, pp. 375–6.

9
CONCLUSION

Lucca after the fall of Paolo Guinigi was open to the same influences, and confronted many of the same challenges faced by contemporary and more comprehensively studied Italian societies. The most obvious comparison is with Florence. Whilst the parallels are self-evident, it is equally clear that Lucca was a very different political community from its more powerful Tuscan neighbour. In part, it was a question of chronology: trends well entrenched on the Arno were still only dimly perceivable in the restored republic. But Lucca's situation was manifestly different from Florence's, and so too were her policies and solutions. The great danger has long been for historians to take Florence as the measure; to view Florence as synonymous with Tuscany, and even with Italy as a whole. Lucca was no more typical, at least in the fifteenth century, when she retained meaningful control over her own destiny.

In part, Lucca's distinctiveness was a product of weakness. Nowhere is this more apparent than in the political arena. The leading families of late fifteenth-century Lucca achieved practical, if élitist, fulfilment of the civic rhetoric of the past. This oligarchy, despite the conspiracies of the 1430s and the continuing plots of later years, was much more successful than its Florentine counterpart in avoiding the endemic factionalism which became—finally even in Florence—the theoretical justification of princely rule. In the cautious treatment of powerful families and in the vigilant guard against the ambitions of individuals, Lucca's ruling councils were continually and explicitly mindful that internal strife was a luxury that Lucca could no longer afford. To some extent, the lesson was drawn from the misfortunes of the previous century. But it was kept alive by the periodic Florentine threat: the wars against Lucca of the 1430s, the appeal by Cosimo de' Medici to Francesco Sforza for Milanese aid to help Florence conquer Lucca in 1463–4, and the renewed Florentine plotting against Lucca of the 1490s.

The underlying fragility of Lucca's position is no less central to any understanding of the relationship between the restored republic and its subject territories. It is true, of course, that recent work on communities that fell under Florentine control has stressed less the rigours of Florentine domination than the gradual economic and political penetration from the centre and the protection of local interests by the metropolitan power.[1] But the limited intervention that, in Florence, can be explained by limited resources and contemporary mentalities, in Lucca was dictated also by the fact that co-operation and appeasement were often the very preconditions of political control. *Contadini* might protest about the ravages of 'citizen wolves'; the countryside might offer the most promising support for a Guinigi restoration. In reality, many regions, particularly those most distant from Lucca, were able to negotiate very attractive terms as the price of loyalty. Even more than in other regions of northern and central Italy, the relations between hegemonic city and subject communities rapidly become a history of local interests and local factions.

The same restraints that operated in relations between centre and periphery are apparent in relations between Church and State. Writing of the Church elsewhere in fifteenth-century Tuscany, Roberto Bizzocchi has described how the powerful voice of the lay power in episcopal appointments had come to limit the capacity of bishops to act independently, how the state now enjoyed decisive influence in the appointment of episcopal vicars, and how far churchmen—even those in major orders—had lost their exemption from secular jurisdiction when guilty of serious crimes.[2] The independent judicial and administrative powers of the Church were clearly much more firmly entrenched within the diocese of Lucca, at least in those parts of the diocese that remained under Lucchese political control. That benefit of clergy remained a difficult and sensitive issue for the restored republic is amply attested by both the political and court records. Ultimately in Lucca, as in Florence, harmony prevailed in Church–State relations. But in Lucca the harmony was a product of mutual self-interested caution, not least on the part of the State. It was not determined, as in Florence, by power politics, nor by the kind of identification of interests then developing between the Roman curia and the growing territorial state of the Medici.

In such respects the distinctiveness of Lucca reflects Lucca's

[1] G. Chittolini, 'Ricerche sull'ordinamento territoriale del dominio fiorentino agli inizi del secolo XV', in *La formazione dello stato regionale e le istituzioni del contado: Secoli xiv e xv* (Turin, 1979), 292–352; J. Brown, *In the Shadow of Florence: Provincial Society in Renaissance Pescia* (Oxford, 1982); L. Gai, 'Centro e periferia: Pistoia nell'orbita fiorentina durante il '500', in *Pistoia, una città nello Stato Mediceo* (Pistoia, 1980), 9–153.

[2] Bizzocchi, *Chiesa e potere*, 240–1, 254–7, 270–5.

vulnerability in relations with her neighbours, with her dominions, and indeed with Rome. But weakness was only one ingredient. The culture, political development, and society of quattrocento Florence were products of discrete influences which are only very partially relevant to the Lucchese experience. The dynamics were different, and consequently the society and its political structures. Most obviously, there is the Medici ascendancy itself, which has provided the central problem and central challenge to historians of Florence. The Lucchese patriciate—at least domestically—was not constrained to live '"sotto la ... umbra" di Lorenzo de' Medici'.[3] No less important was the painful memory, deeply ingrained in the collective memory of Florence's great 'popular' families, of the events of 1378. Without the Ciompi (and with the revolt of the Straccioni far in the future), there is no hint in Lucca of the kind of redefining of social relationships that some historians have sought and found on the Arno. The point is made without prejudice to concepts of right order and appropriate status which were as characteristic of Lucca as of any other late medieval community.

Beyond the specific and obvious comparison with Florence, the political and administrative development of all the leading centres of fifteenth-century Italy was determined, at least in part, by the fact and demands of territorial expansionism. By and during the quattrocento the political map of Italy had become greatly simplified. Much of the fiscal and institutional history of the period has been written in terms of the transition from the old-style city-state, enclosed within its walls and supplied and serviced by its traditional *contado*, to the small number of larger territorial states with which the future was to lie. No such transition was demanded of fifteenth-century Lucca. The present study has noted the growth of specialist administrative councils, and has examined significant changes that were clearly taking place during the fifteenth century in the way in which Lucca collected revenue and ruled over its dependent territories. Thus far Lucca reflected wider Italian trends. It remains true that one of the major dynamics in the history of contemporary Florence, Milan, and Venice, was absent from a city like Lucca that was to remain so unambiguously within its walls.

The flavour of the respective societies probably owes as much to imperatives of less spectacular but more pervasive character. Already by the late fourteenth and early fifteenth centuries dowries of 900–1,100

[3] F. W. Kent, 'La famiglia patrizia fiorentina nel Quattrocento. Nuovi orientamenti nella storiografia recente', in *Palazzo Strozzi metà millennio, 1489–1989, atti del Convegno di studi, Firenze, 3–6 luglio 1989* (Rome, 1991), 84.

florins were being required for the marriage of the daughters of prominent Florentine families.[4] Equivalent figures for Lucca are not available; but there remains no doubt that Lucchese dowries lagged far behind Florentine ones in the period after 1430. Whether for this or for other reasons, there is very little sign in Lucca of the restrictions on marriage for which Florentine studies have prepared us. Lucchese fathers too might suffer the financial burden of a surfeit of daughters; but the burden does not seem to have discouraged them from marrying off as many daughters as possible. Certainly in Lucca before 1494 there is no evidence of the overflowing nunneries that were becoming a feature of the Florentine Church. Impressionistically, the sons of socially prominent Lucchese families appear to have been marrying much earlier than has been found from the Florentine data—though this did not preclude in Lucca the range of social problems that have traditionally been ascribed to late, regulated marriages. The chapters on political structures have indicated that family history and marriage politics in fifteenth-century Lucca complement parallel studies undertaken in this field elsewhere in Italy; here it is appropriate to underline the significant disjunctures.

Beyond the conditioning of the external threat, and beyond the basic truism of Italian diversity, much of the character of fifteenth-century Lucca is captured in the imagery of restoration. The political ambition in Lucca from 1430 was to restore the republic. Exercises in historical nostalgia are seldom entirely successful: political power came to rest in a General Council that was smaller than its fourteenth-century counterpart, and whose composition became more obviously aristocratic as the century progressed. Yet the theme of continuity remains more convincing for Lucca than for Florence. In Florence, despite the tenacity of the myth of a civic society,[5] political structures and social relationships were substantively transformed by the emergence of one family as the centre of power and patronage. Attitudes and values were modified in Florence with the growth of a *de facto* court. Fifteenth-century Lucca saw no more radical change than the gradual consolidation of oligarchical rule: the monopoly of power, even more markedly than in the fourteenth century, by a relatively broadly based group of 'wealthy merchants, bankers, and entrepreneurs, usually belonging to old-established families'.[6]

[4] J. Kirshner, *Pursuing Honor while Avoiding Sin: The Monte delle Doti of Florence* (Milan, 1978), 2.

[5] R. Bizzocchi, 'La crisi del "vivere civile" a Firenze nel primo Cinquecento', in S. Bertelli (ed.), *Forme e tecniche del potere nella città (secoli xiv–xvii)* (Università di Perugia, Annali della Facoltà di Scienze Politiche—a.a. 1979–80, 16), 87–103.

[6] Meek, *Lucca 1369–1400*, 346.

The political restoration was accompanied by an economic recovery, itself achieved through the reviving fortunes of Lucca's traditional manufacture. The old norms were reimposed; traditional techniques survived; industrial processes remained within the framework of traditional guild structures. Attempts at innovation—the encouragement, for example, of a luxury woollen industry—attracted periodic attention, but produced few practical results. These practical experiences, the assumptions of those families restored to power in 1430, and the pressing external dangers combined to produce a society that was profoundly conservative, even in the context of fifteenth-century Italy. The constitutional settlement of 1430 was to become permanent. The pattern of a patrician-dominated, technologically stagnant silk industry was fully entrenched by the time of the restoration. The introduction of capitalist agriculture (not just in Lucca) was probably rendered impossible by socio-political priorities. And the physical transformations of the Renaissance are less obvious in Lucca than in other major urban centres.

In some senses the distinctive character of Lucca was to survive, and even become accentuated in later centuries. This was assured by Lucca's survival as a small, oligarchic republic in a world where small states and republican governments had become a rarity. With the passage of time, Lucca's distinctiveness became not untainted with an element of quaintness. In the fifteenth century Lucca continued to combine individuality with significance: the restoration of political forms, the recovery of traditional industries, and the external threat all proved compatible with a dynamic economic life and with an independent political identity. Nowhere does this appear more clearly than in the role of Lucchese merchants and bankers outside Italy, particularly in northern Europe. Lucchese merchants were prominent amongst those Italians taking advantage of the new opportunities in Lyons, Bruges/Antwerp, and London. From the mid-fifteenth century, for a century and more, Lucchese companies were in the forefront of those servicing the newly revitalized economies and monarchies of the north.

In other respects, Lucca from the end of the fifteenth century was to become part of that more homogenous Italy arising in the wake of renewed foreign invasions, and eventually moulded into shape by pervasive Spanish and Counter-Reformation influences. Most obviously there was the declining potential for independent initiatives, particularly in areas of foreign policy; there was the growing formal aristocratization of government; there was the economic decline and commercial with-drawal—frequently pre-dated and exaggerated, but real enough, nevertheless. The year 1494 was no doubt less portentous for Lucca than for neighbouring Florence, at least at the level of domestic politics. The first French invasion remains both symbol and precursor of changes that were to transform the Lucca of the sixteenth and later centuries into a very different society—I believe one less dynamically active, less richly diverse, and essentially more conventional than the restored republic of the post-Guinigi years.

APPENDIX

The parlamento of 16 August 1430 (Rif. 14, pp. 21–2)

d. Bonaiuncta de Fundo
d. Nicolaus d. Manfredi
d. Urbanus Pauli Ghuccii
mag. Nicolaus mag. Michaelis de Corellia
mag. Antonius Turignani de Silico
Laurentius mag. Federigi Trenta
Stefanus qd. Nicolai Cecchorini de Podio
Nicolaus qd. Gerardi Burlamachi
Charolus qd. Bartholomei de Buzolinis
Forteguerra qd. Johannis Totti
Tegrimus qd. Pieri de Tegrimis
Paulus qd. Bartholomei de Balbanis
Brunectus qd. Johannis de Malizardis
Landuccius qd. Stefani Bernardi
Johannes qd. Jacobi Bandini
Nicolaus de Dardagninis
ser Dominicus Arrigi
Therius qd. Manfredi Gentilis
Bartholomeus qd. Jannini de Fatinellis
ser Johannes Therii
Laurentius qd. ser Nicolai Parpaglionis
Nannes qd. Francisci Berindelli
ser Francischus Ghabriellis de Interminellis
Gerardus qd. Bartholomei Angiorelli
ser Antonius Morrouelli
Guilielmus qd. Johannis Sbarre
Bectus qd. Guasparis Schiatte
Tomasius qd. Johannis Teste
Christoferus qd. Tomasii Ricciardi
Filippus qd. Bartholomei de Podio
Jacobus qd. Nicolai de Anorfinis
Paulinus qd. Bartholomei Bernardini
Nicolaus Dini de Aduocatis
Dinus Ciuchini de Aduocatis

Dinus qd. Iusfredi de Cenamis
Banduccius Nesis Banduccii Trenta
Johannes Landuccii Bernardi
Dinus qd. Macthei de Fondora
Michael qd. Jacobi Gratta
ser Johannes qd. Nicolai Nesis
ser Pierus qd. ser Simonis Alberti
ser Siluester Johannis
ser Janninus Nocchi Jannini
Francischus Nicolai Saluini
Meus Blasii
Filippus ser Justi, speciarius
Nicolaus Mei Bon Johannis
Bartholomeus Nocchi Jannini
Nicolaus Rodulfi
Johannes Pieri de Ghiuizano
d. Dinus mag. Dauini +
Nicolaus qd. Laurentii Nerii
Nicolaus qd. ser Nicolai Streghi
Johannes qd. Foresis Malpigli
ser Jacobus Ruggerii
ser Dominicus Totti
ser Leonardus ser Francisci de Massa
ser Laurentius Nucciorini
Tomasius Laurentii Neri
Bartholomeus qd. Johannis Testa
Ghaluanus qd. Macthei Trenta
Pierus qd. Blasii Nucchelli
Laurentius et Stefanus Spada
Mactheus qd. Nicolai Ioue
Mactheus qd. Bartholomei de Bernardinis
Jacobus qd. Filippi Mugia
Bartholomeus Puccini
Andreas Jannini, tintor
Arrighus qd. Petri de Balbanis
Julianus Blasii, planularius
Laurentius Juncte, prozoneta
Geppus Francisci, coriarius
Pierus Dominici, merciadrus
Andreas Stefani, merciadrus
Nicolaus Antonii de Giglis
ser Gerardus Prosperi
Michael Johannuoli de Mordecastellii

Laurentius Francisci de Marianis
Nannes Boni, textor
ser Nicolaus Antonii Lupori
ser Bartholomeus Buoni
ser Antonius Luporini
Guaspar Johannis, macellator
Paulus et Dominicus Johannis, speciarii
Johannes Ciuoli, speciarius
Andreas Petri Miliani
ser Bartholomeus Nicolai Martini
Laurentius ser Bianconis
Urbanus Bonifatii
Pierus Jacobi Luporini
Bartholomeus Michaelis Junctini
Andreas Dominici, pannarius
Michael mag. Nicolai Liene
Nicolaus Campori Parpaglonis
Bertinus Andree, coriarius

BIBLIOGRAPHY

ARCHIVE AND OTHER UNPRINTED SOURCES

Archivio di Stato, Lucca

Archivio Diplomatico.
Statuti del comune di Lucca, 10, 13.
Statuti di comunità soggette, 20.
Capitoli, 7, 35.
Consiglio Generale, Riformagioni Pubbliche, 14–23.
Colloqui, 1.
Anziani al tempo della libertà: Minute di Riformagioni, 5–6.
Anziani al tempo della libertà: Deliberazioni, 134.
Anziani al tempo della libertà: Lettere originali, 442.
Anziani al tempo della libertà: Lettere, 531–2.
Anziani al tempo della libertà: Appelli agli Anziani, 674.
Cause Delegate, 2–4.
Gabelle del contado e delle vicarie: Gabella di Pietrasanta, 80–1.
Estimo, 126, 131.
Esattore Maggiore, 54.
Imprestiti, 21.
Corte de' mercanti, Libri de' mercanti, 82–6.
Corte de' mercanti, Libri de' sensali, 94–9.
Corte de' mercanti, Cause civili, 150–2, 159, 164, 186, 187.
Arte della Seta, 33.
Amministrazione delle comunità soggette e delle vicarie, 38–9.
Podestà di Lucca, Curia Civile, 1176–80, 1251, 1306–9.
Podestà di Lucca, Bastardelli, 2131–2.
Podestà di Lucca, Inquisizioni, 5224–5, 5229–30, 5232, 5237, 5253, 5257, 5268–70, 5283–4, 5329–30, 5362.
Capitano del Popolo e della città, 31–45.
Vicario di Massa Lunese, Atti Criminali, 260–7.
Vicario di Pietrasanta, Atti Criminali, 233, 236–7.
Vicario poi Commissario di Castiglione, Atti Criminali, 722.
Podestà di Casoli oltre Giogo, Atti Civili, 30–1.
Podestà di Casoli oltre Giogo, Atti Criminali, 72.
Capitano (o Bargello) del Contado, 51–2, 55, 79, 97.
Curia del Fondaco, 534–5, 693–4.

Sentenze e bandi, 150–1, 159–62, 165, 171, 192, 202, 544.

Archivio de' Notari, parte 1, 255, 259 (ser Simone Alberti); 289–90 (ser Domenico Lupardi); 327 (ser Antonio Morovelli da Castelnuovo); 366, 370–1, 374–5 (ser Paolo Michele Federighi Bianchi da Massa); 385 (ser Massino di Bartolomeo da Pietrasanta); 401, 405–6 (ser Matteo di Giovanni de' Nobili); 429, 431 (ser Domenico Arrighi); 446–7 (ser Pietro di Simone Alberti); 459 (ser Giovanni da Gallicano); 462–3, 466 (ser Michele Giovanni Pieri); 504 (ser Antonio Nuccorini); 514 (ser Francesco ser Vito Pini); 538, 540–2 (ser Nicolao di Ranieri Mansi); 548, 552–3, 555 (ser Ciomeo Pieri); 561 (ser Pietro Arrighi); 576 (ser Benedetto Guarguaglia, ser Girolamo Nesi, ser Nicolao di Pietro da Camaiore); 580 (ser Francesco di ser Bartolomeo da Massa); 591 (ser Giovanni Nocchi); 597 (ser Luviso di Antonio Buonaccorsi); 620 (ser Ambrogio Narducci); 700–6, 731–2 (ser Benedetto Franciotti); 770–1 (ser Giovanni Roffia); 1519 (ser Michele di Giovanni da Mommio); 1789 (ser Lazzaro Franchi); 1929 (ser Giuseppe Piscilla).

Archivio de' Notari, Originali Testamenti rilegati in volumi, 11 (ser Domenico Ciomucchi); 15–16 (ser Benedetto Franciotti).

Archivio Arnolfini, 2, 15, 18, 25, 138.

Archivio Guinigi, 29, Libro di ricordi e note di contratti di Girolamo quondam Giovanni quondam Michele Guinigi, fatto e cominciato nel 1468, segnato AA—anzi in sua origine era segnato B—dell'archivio di nostra casa Guinigi.

Archivio Guinigi, 151, Memorie e note di Michele q. di Giovanni q. Michele q. di Lazari Guinigi, principiate l'anno 1447.

Archivio Mansi, 493, Carte Nieri.

Raccolte Speciali: G. B. Orsucci, 28–30, Note di Casati e Famiglie Lucchesi.

Raccolte Speciali: S. Frediano, 4, 7, 14, 19, 20–1, 72, 76.

Raccolte Speciali: S. Romano, 2.

Biblioteca (Manoscritti), 20–2, B. Baroni, Alberi di Famiglie.

Biblioteca (Manoscritti), 26, Historie della terra di Camaiore e suoi contorni e altre guerre descritto da M. Bianco Bianchi da Camaiore, Dottore in medicina l'anno 1528.

Biblioteca (Manoscritti), 30, Pellegrino di Bartolomeo Pellegrini da Camaiore, Libro di Memorie.

Biblioteca (Manoscritti), 38, Giuseppe Civitali, Storia di Lucca scritta da Giuseppe Civitali e riordinata da Daniello De' Nobili, dall'origine di essa città sino al 1572.

Biblioteca (Manoscritti), 57, Carteggio di Monsignore Telesforo Bini lucchese.

Biblioteca (Manoscritti), 65, Libro del Sommario delle Cronache della città di Lucca del Sig. Pietro Carelli Dottore, dal 1369 al 1499 inclusive. Con giunte posteriori.

Biblioteca (Manoscritti), 116, Memorie domestiche e varie di Pellegrino di Bartolomeo Pellegrini da Camaiore.

Biblioteca (Manoscritti), 124–8, B. Baroni, Famiglie Lucchesi.

Biblioteca Statale, Lucca

MS 26, Alessandro Spada, Storia di Lucca.
MS 38, Ricordi Storici di Martino Bernardini.
MS 46, Miscellanea Storica.
MS 47, Antichità di Lucca e sue famiglie con repertorio delle famiglie e notizie annuali dal 1368.
MS 50, Libro ove sono notati li nomi di tutti quelli che sono stati eletti consiglieri della Rep. di Lucca dal 1369 fino al 1719.
MS 62, Memorie diverse di Lucca.
MS 71, Compendio delli successi più notabili della città e Rep. di Lucca di Paulo Minutoli.
MS 91, Storie di Lucca.
MS 97, Memorie antiche della città di Lucca estratte da più autori manoscritti e stampati e parte dall'Archivio dei canonaci della Cattedrale, come ancora di materie spettanti alla Repub. chiesa di S. Martino suo vescovo e canonaci.
MS 98, Croniche della città di Lucca composte per messer Bastiano Puccini e Sommario de' successi di Lucca di Gherardo Sergiusti.
MS 99, Elogia insignium virorum lucensium Nicolao Tuccio autore.
MS 102, Compendio delle storie scritte da Alessandro Boccella ricavate da vari frammenti compendiate da Giuseppe Civitali.
MS 103, Memorie di uomini illustri lucchesi e cronaca della guerra dei fiorentini fatta a' lucchesi nel sec. xv di Lorenzo Trenta.
MS 108, Historie di Lucca descritte da Nicolao Tucci e Cronache di Giovanni Saminiati.
MS 116, Notizie di Lucca.
MS 121, Compendio istorico delle memorie di Lucca più degne di osservazione circa le mutazioni e alterazioni di stato o governo accadute in detta città dalla sua edificazione fino all'anno 1660 di Martino Manfredi.
MS 142, Racconto del principio e del progresso della famiglia Lucchesini.
MS 324, Notizie intorno alle chiese e benefizi dello Stato di Lucca, autore don Frediano Pera.
MS 415, Notizie antiche del monastero e chiesa di S. Frediano.
MS 710, Salvator Dalli, Croniche della inclita città di Lucca e di altre città cavate da molti autori brevemente per me Salvator Dalli dell'anno 1583, 84 e 85.
MS 885, Memorie intorno a Pietrasanta di Giuseppe Altogradi (seniore) con varie scritture per la lite coi fiorentini a causa del detto castello e di quelli di Montignoso, Rotario, Monteggiori e Vegghiatoja.
MS 896, Memorie ecclesiastiche riguardanti le chiese e monasteri di Lucca.
MSS 936–41, Can: Gio: Lunardo Dalli, Cronache della città di Lucca.
MSS 1101–39, G. Vincenzo Baroni, Notizie genealogiche delle famiglie lucchesi.
MS 1824, Scritture varie sulle controversie dei canonici di S. Martino di Lucca colla Rep. di Lucca.

MS 2572, Cronica del Convento di S. Romano di Lucca scritta dal P^e Ignazio Manandro Ferrarese dimorante nello stesso convento.
MSS 2598–9, Antonio Iova, Annali Historici della città di Lucca.
MS 2623, Liber chronicorum Conventus S. Romani.
MS 2636, Annales Conventus S. Romani praedicatorum ordinis Luc: Civitatis.
MSS 2951–3, Giuseppe Vinc. Baroni, Notizie sulla chiesa di S. Martino.
MS 3380, Terrilogio ove sono notati li beni stabili che possedeva Benedetto Buonvisi.
MS 3381, Libro di contratti antichi della nobile famiglia de' Buonvisi di Lucca cominciato addì xi settembre MCCCCXXXVI finito il 1514.

Archivio Arcivescovile, Lucca

Libri Antichi, 87–8, 99A, 100, 116–20.
Collazioni, A (1448), D (1477–82).
Cause civili della Curia (ser Ciomeo Pieri, 1451–2); (ser Ciomeo Pieri, 1453); (ser Acconcio del fu ser Antonii, 1483).

Archivio di Stato, Firenze

Le carte strozziane—serie prima, CCXCIV, CCCV, CCCXXV, CCCLII, CCCLVII.
Archivio Mediceo avanti il principato.
Consulte e pratiche, 56.
Pergamene Medicee, 14 June 1449, 90.
Signori—Legazioni e Commissarie, 19.
Archivio Notarile AnteCosimiano, G 163 (ser Gherardo da Pietrasanta); M 646 (Francesco di Piero di Neri Molletti da Firenze); N 115–16 (ser Nicolao di Coluccio di Pellegrino da Pietrasanta); T 573–4 (ser Paolino di Tomuccio Tomucci).

Archivio Storico, Gallicano

MS 5, Libro delle Compositioni et Gratie concesse dall'Eccellentissima Repubblica di Lucca al Castello et Huomini di Gallicano et sua Vicaria fino nell'anno 1450.
MS 6, Primo Libbro delli Statuti del MCCCCLXI.
MS 13, no title (Council proceedings 14 July 1482–12 June 1496).

Archivio Storico Comunale, Pietrasanta

Civile—Frammenti filze giusdicenti 1378–1493 (A 3, A 6).
Atti dei Genovesi 1433–1482 (I 2).

Consigli 1395–1429 (E 3):
Consiglio (1429), (1479–84).
Libro di Consigli (1395).
Soluzioni di denari e condanne di danno dato 1398.
Liber Reformationum (1418).
Libro partiti (1423).
Libro di Riformagioni e Consigli (1428).
Consigli 1431–1453:
Libro di Consigli (1431).
Libro di Consigli (1435).
Libro di Consigli (1440).
Libro di Consigli (1442).
Libro di Consigli (1446).
Libro di Consigli (1447).
Libro di Consigli (1448).
Libro di Consigli (1449).
Libro Partiti (1452–3).
Contratti di ser Gio: di ser Iacopo da Castiglione 1404–5 (E 1 229).
Memorie della Versilia di V. Santini (MSS I 159–61).

Archivio di Stato, Massa

Archivio dei Malaspina di Fosdinovo Marchesi di Massa, 1–2.
Archivio Notarile: Notai Forestieri 1340–1517.
Pergamene, 349/374.

Archivio di Stato, Pisa

Archivio del Comune di Pisa, Divisione C, 90/1, Gabella Maggiore o Dogana.

Archivio di Stato, Napoli

MS Inventario: Sommario partium, 'Pandetta del repertorio, 1468–1580'.

Archivio di Stato, Catanzaro

Fondo Diplomatico (Pergamene), 8 May 1406.

Public Record Office, London

Exchequer K. R. Customs Accounts, E122/73/40, E122/194/19, E122/194/20, E122/194/22, E122/194/24, E122/194/26.
Exchequer K. R. Lay Subsidies, E179/144/67–8.

PRINTED SOURCES

BONGI, S. (ed.), *Inventario del Regio Archivio di Stato in Lucca*, 4 vols. (Lucca, 1872–88).

CIVITALI, G., *Historie di Lucca*, ii, ed. Mario F. Leonardi, RIS Recentiores, 4 (Rome, 1988).

'Croniche Milanese scritte da Giovan Pietro Cagnola, Giovanni Andrea Prato e Giovan Marco Burigozzo', *Archivio storico italiano*, 1st ser., iii (1842).

EDLER, F., *Glossary of Medieval Terms of Business: Italian Series 1200–1600* (Cambridge, Mass., 1934).

FUMI, L. (ed.), *R. Archivio di Stato in Lucca: Regesti*, iv, *Carteggio degli Anziani (dall'anno MCCCCXXX all'anno MCCCCLXXII)* (Lucca, 1907).

LAZZARESCHI, E. (ed.), *L'Archivio dei notari della repubblica lucchese* (Siena, 1916).

—— (ed.), *R. Archivio di Stato in Lucca: Regesti*, v, *Carteggio degli Anziani MCCCCLXXIII–MCCCCLXXXXII* (Pescia, 1943).

—— (ed.), *Libro della comunità dei mercanti lucchesi in Bruges* (Milan, 1947).

Lo Statuto della corte dei mercanti in Lucca del MCCCLXXVI, ed. A. Mancini, U. Dorini, and E. Lazzareschi (Florence, 1927).

MACHIAVELLI, NICCOLÒ, *Istorie fiorentine*, ed. Plinio Carli, 2 vols. (Florence, 1927). Trans. as *Florentine History* by W. K. Marriott (London, n.d.).

MORELLI, GIOVANNI DI PAGOLO, *Ricordi*, ed. Vittore Branca (Florence, 1956).

Ordini che devono osservare li gonfalonieri delle contrade, Approuati dall'Eccellentissimo Consiglio Generale A 20. Luglio 1635 (Lucca, 1635).

PELÙ, P. (ed.), *I libri dei mercanti lucchesi degli anni 1371, 1372, 1381, 1407, 1488* (Lucca, 1975).

ROMITI, A. (ed.), *Riformagioni della Repubblica di Lucca (1369–1400): Volume primo (Marzo 1369–Agosto 1370 e aggiunte)* (Rome, 1980).

—— and TORI, G. (eds.), *Statuti e matricole del collegio dei giudici e notai della città di Lucca 1434, 1483, 1541* (Rome, 1978).

SERCAMBI, G., *Le Chroniche Lucchesi*, ed. S. Bongi, 3 vols., *Fonti per la Storia d'Italia* (Rome, 1892).

TEGRIMI, N., *La vita di Castruccio Castracani de gl'Antelminelli Principe de Lucca, tradotta da Giusto Compagni da Volterra* (Lucca, 1556).

SECONDARY WORKS

ABBONDANZA, R. (ed.), *Il notariato a Perugia* (Rome, 1973).

ACTON, F., *La morte di Pietro Cenami e la congiura di ser Tommaso Lupardi raccontate sui documenti dell'Archivio di Lucca* (Lucca, 1882).

AMMIRATO, S., *Dell'istorie fiorentine* (Florence, 1600).

ANDERSON, P., *Passages from Antiquity to Feudalism*, Verso edn. (London, 1978).

ANDREOLLI, B., 'Considerazioni sulle campagne lucchesi nella prima metà del secolo xiv: paesaggio, economia, contratti agrari', in *Castruccio Castracani e il suo tempo: Convegno Internazionale, Lucca 5–10 ottobre 1981*, published as anni xiii–xiv, nos. 1–2, of *Actum Luce* (1984–5), 277–301.

Angelini, L., 'Una visita pastorale quattrocentesca alla pievania di Gallicano', in *Miscellanea di Studi: Carfaniana Antiqua*, i (Lucca, 1980), 33–50.

—— *Un Francescano nella Garfagnana del Quattrocento (Il Beato Ercolano da Piegaro)* (Lucca, 1990).

Aymard, M., 'From Feudalism to Capitalism in Italy: The Case that Doesn't Fit', *Review: A Journal of the Fernand Braudel Center for the Study of Economies, Historical Systems, and Civilizations*, vi (1982–3), 131–208.

Baker, G. R., 'Nobilità in declino: il caso di Siena sotto i Medici e gli Asburgo-Lorena', *Rivista storica italiana*, lxxxiv (1972), 584–616.

Banchi, L., 'La guerra de' Senesi col conte di Pitigliano 1454–1455', *Archivio storico italiano*, 4th ser., iii (1879), 184–97.

—— 'Il Piccinino nello stato di Siena e la lega italiana (1455–1456)', *Archivio storico italiano*, 4th ser., iv (1879), 44–58, 225–45.

Bartelletti, A., 'Boschi ed incolti nel paesaggio, nell'economia e nella cultura del medioevo. I. Il caso della pianura Pisano-Versiliese', *Studi Versiliesi*, ii (1984), 13–36.

Becker, M. B., *Medieval Italy: Constraints and Creativity* (Bloomington, Ind., 1981).

Belli Barsali, I., *Lucca: Guida alla città* (Lucca, 1988).

Benedetto, G., 'I rapporti fra Castruccio Castracani e la chiesa di Lucca', *Annuario della Biblioteca Civica di Massa* (1980–1), 73–97.

—— 'Potere dei chierici e potere dei laici nella Lucca del Quattrocento al tempo della signoria di Paolo Guinigi (1400–1430): Una simbiosi', *Annuario della Biblioteca Civica di Massa* (1984), 1–54.

Berengo, M., *Nobili e mercanti nella Lucca del Cinquecento* (Turin, 1965).

Beverini, B., *Annalium ab origine lucensis urbis*, 4 vols. (Lucca, 1829–32).

Bini, T., *I lucchesi a Venezia: Alcuni studi sopra i secoli xiii e xiv*, 2 vols. (Lucca, 1854–6).

Bizzocchi, R., 'La crisi del "vivere civile" a Firenze nel primo Cinquecento', in S. Bertelli (ed.), *Forme e tecniche del potere nella città (secoli xiv–xvii)* (Università di Perugia, Annali della Facoltà di Scienze Politiche—a.a. 1979–80, 16), 87–103.

—— 'Chiesa e aristocrazia nella Firenze del Quattrocento', *Archivio storico italiano*, cxlii (1984), 191–282.

—— *Chiesa e potere nella Toscana del Quattrocento* (Bologna, 1987).

Blomquist, T. W., 'Commercial Association in Thirteenth-Century Lucca', *Business History Review*, xlv (1971), 157–78.

—— 'The Castracani Family of Thirteenth-Century Lucca', *Speculum*, xlvi (1971), 459–76.

—— 'The Dawn of Banking in an Italian Commune: Thirteenth-Century Lucca', in *The Dawn of Modern Banking*, Center for Medieval and Renaissance Studies, University of California, Los Angeles (New Haven, Conn., 1979), 53–75.

—— 'Lineage, Land and Business in the Thirteenth Century: The Guidiccioni Family of Lucca', *Actum Luce*, ix (1980), 7–29.

—— 'La famiglia e gli affari: le compagnie internazionali lucchesi al tempo di Castruccio Castracani', in *Castruccio Castracani e il suo tempo: Convegno Internazionale, Lucca 5–10 ottobre 1981*, published as anni xiii–xiv, nos. 1–2, of *Actum Luce* (1984–5), 145–55.

BOLTON, J. L., *The Medieval English Economy 1150–1500* (London, 1980).

BONGI, S., *Di Paolo Guinigi e delle sue ricchezze* (Lucca, 1871).

BRANCHI, E., *Storia della Lunigiana feudale*, 3 vols. (Bologna, 1971), repr. of the Pistoia edn. of 1897–8.

BRANDEGLIO, P. ANTONIO DI (teologo, e guardiano di S. Cerbone di Lucca), *Vita di S. Cerbone vescovo di Popolonia, e confessore raccolta fedelmente dall'Opere di S. Gregorio Papa, e di altri gravi autori: con alcune notizie del medesimo Convento, e degli altri della Riforma nel Dominio Lucchese* (Lucca, 1706).

BRATCHEL, M. E., 'Italian Merchant Organization and Business Relationships in Early Tudor London', *Journal of European Economic History*, vii (1978), 5–32.

—— 'Regulation and Group-Consciousness in the Later History of London's Italian Merchant Colonies', *Journal of European Economic History*, ix (1980), 585–610.

—— 'The *Consorteria* in 15th-Century Tuscany: In Pursuit of a Historical Definition', *Unisa Medieval Studies*, i (1983), 13–33.

—— 'Patrician Life in Fifteenth-Century Lucca: Lorenzo di Neri Buonvisi and his Peers', in *Conference Papers: Seventh Biennial Conference of the Medieval Society of Southern Africa* (1984), 33–56.

—— 'The Return to the Land: Investment Opportunities and Commercial Decline in Late Medieval Italy', *Middeleeuse Studies* (1984), 22–47.

—— 'The Silk Industry of Lucca in the Fifteenth Century', in *Tecnica e società nell'Italia dei secoli XII–XVI: Centro italiano di studi di storia e d'arte Pistoia, Atti dell'undicesimo Convegno di studio tenuto a Pistoia nei giorni 28–31 ottobre 1984* (Pistoia, 1987), 173–90.

BRENNER, R., 'The Origins of Capitalist Development: A Critique of Neo-Smithian Marxism', *New Left Review*, civ (1977), 54–71.

BROWN, J., *In the Shadow of Florence: Provincial Society in Renaissance Pescia* (Oxford, 1982).

BULE, S., 'Matteo Civitali's Statues for the Cathedral of Genoa', in S. Bule, A. P. Darr, and F. Gioffredi (eds.), *Verrocchio and Late Quattrocento Italian Sculpture* (Florence, 1992), 205–15.

—— 'A Unique Partnership: Matteo Civitali and Domenico Orsolini', in S. Bule, A. P. Darr, and F. Gioffredi (eds.), *Verrocchio and Late Quattrocento Italian Sculpture* (Florence, 1992), 363–4.

BULLARD, M. M., 'Marriage Politics and the Family in Florence: The

Strozzi–Medici Alliance of 1508', *American Historical Review*, lxxxiv (1979), 668–87.

CALLMANN, E., *Beyond Nobility: Art for the Private Citizen in the Early Renaissance* (Allentown, Pa., 1980–1).

CAMAIANI, P. G., 'Le magistrature di Barga dal xv secolo alle riforme leopoldine', in Carla Sodini (ed.), *Barga medicea e le 'enclaves' fiorentine della Versilia e della Lunigiana* (Florence, 1983), 13–32.

CANNING, J., *The Political Thought of Baldus de Ubaldis* (Cambridge, 1987).

CARMICHAEL, A., *Plague and the Poor in Renaissance Florence* (Cambridge, 1986).

CASALI, A., 'L'amministrazione del Contado Lucchese nel '400: il Capitano del Contado', *Actum Luce*, vii (1978), 127–37.

—— 'Aspetti della criminalità nel contado lucchese intorno alla metà del 1400, secondo i registri del "Capitaneus Comitatus" ', *Annuario della Biblioteca Civica di Massa* (1981), 1–21.

CASSANDRO, M., 'Strategia degli affari dei mercanti-banchieri italiani alle fiere internazionali d'oltralpe (secoli xiv–xvi)', in *Aspetti della vita economica medievale: Atti del Convegno di Studi nel X Anniversario della morte di Federigo Melis, Firenze–Pisa–Prato, 10–14 marzo 1984* (Florence, 1985), 140–50.

CERVIETTI, O., 'Pietrasanta dalla fondazione al Lodo di Leone X', *Rivista di archeologia, storia, economica, costume*, v, no. 2 (1977), 31–42.

CHITTOLINI, G., 'Ricerche sull'ordinamento territoriale del dominio fiorentino agli inizi del secolo XV', in *La formazione dello stato regionale e le istituzioni del contado: Secoli xiv e xv* (Turin, 1979), 292–352.

—— 'Progetti di riordinamento ecclesiastico della Toscana agli inizi del Quattrocento', in S. Bertelli (ed.), *Forme e tecniche del potere nella città (secoli xiv–xvii)* (Università di Perugia, Annali della Facoltà di Scienze Politiche—a.a. 1979–80, 16), 273–96.

CIANELLI, A. N., *Dissertazioni sopra la storia lucchese*, in *Memorie e documenti per servire all'istoria della città e stato di Lucca*, ii (Lucca, 1814).

COHN, S. K., *The Laboring Classes in Renaissance Florence* (New York, 1980).

CONCIONI, G., 'La Zecca della repubblica lucchese nel xv secolo', *Rivista di archeologia, storia e costume*, xviii, nos. 3–4 (1990), 141–246.

COOPER, J. P., 'In Search of Agrarian Capitalism', *Past & Present*, lxxx (1978), 20–65.

COTURRI, E., 'La canonica di S. Frediano di Lucca dalla prima istituzione (metà del sec. xi) alla unione alla congregazione riformata di Fregionaia (1517)', *Actum Luce*, iii, nos. 1–2 (1974), 47–80.

—— 'La chiesa lucchese al tempo di Castruccio', in *Castruccio Castracani e il suo tempo: Convegno Internazionale, Lucca 5–10 ottobre 1981*, published as anni xiii–xiv, nos. 1–2 of *Actum Luce* (1984–5), 113–24.

COZZI, G., 'Authority and the Law in Renaissance Venice', in J. R. Hale (ed.), *Renaissance Venice* (London, 1973), 293–345.

DAVIS, J. C., *A Venetian Family and its Fortune (1500–1900)* (Philadelphia, 1975).

De Roover, F. Edler, 'Lucchese Silks', *Ciba Review*, lxxx (1950), 2902–30.

De Roover, R., *Money, Banking and Credit in Medieval Bruges: Italian Merchant-Bankers Lombards and Money-Changers, A Study in the Origins of Banking* (Cambridge, Mass., 1948).

—— *The Rise and Decline of the Medici Bank 1397–1494* (Cambridge, Mass., 1963).

De Simoni, C. (ed.), *Documenti ed estratti di documenti per la storia di Gavi* (Alessandria, 1896).

De Stefani, C., *Storia dei comuni di Garfagnana* (Modena, 1923; repr. Pisa, 1978).

Di Poggio, F. V., *Saggio di storia ecclesiastica del vescovato e chiesa di Lucca* (Lucca, 1787).

Dizionario biografico degli italiani (Rome, 1960–).

Dobb, M., *Capitalist Enterprise and Social Progress*, 2nd edn. (London, 1926).

—— *Studies in the Development of Capitalism* (London, 1946).

Fallico, G., 'La presenza dei lucchesi in Sicilia in epoca castrucciana', in *Castruccio Castracani e il suo tempo: Convegno Internazionale, Lucca 5–10 ottobre 1981*, published as anni xiii–xiv, nos. 1–2 of *Actum Luce* (1984–5), 173–85.

Foster, P. E., *A Study of Lorenzo de' Medici's Villa at Poggio a Caiano*, 2 vols. (New York, 1978).

Fox-Genovese, E., and Genovese, E., *Fruits of Merchant Capital: Slavery and Bourgeois Property in the Rise and Expansion of Capitalism* (Oxford, 1983).

Franciotti, C., *Historie delle miracolose imagini, e delle vite de' Santi, i corpi de' quali sono nella città di Lucca* (Lucca, 1613).

Fryde, E., 'The English Cloth Industry and the Trade with the Mediterranean *c.*1370–*c.*1480', in M. Spallanzani (ed.), *Produzione commercio e consumo dei panni di lana (nei secoli xii–xviii), Istituto internazionale di storia economica 'F. Datini' Prato: Atti della 'seconda settimana di studio' (10–16 aprile 1970)*, ii (Florence, 1976), 343–67.

—— 'Italian Merchants in Medieval England, *c.*1270–*c.*1500', in *Aspetti della vita economica medievale: Atti del Convegno di Studi nel X Anniversario della morte di Federigo Melis, Firenze–Pisa–Prato, 10–14 marzo 1984* (Florence, 1985), 215–31.

Fubini, R., 'From Social to Political Representation in Renaissance Florence', in A. Molho, K. Raaflaub, and J. Emlen (eds.), *Athens and Rome, Florence and Venice: City States in Classical Antiquity and Medieval Italy* (Stuttgart, 1991), 223–39.

Gai, L., 'Centro e periferia: Pistoia nell'orbita fiorentina durante il '500', in *Pistoia, una città nello Stato Mediceo* (Pistoia, 1980), 9–153.

Gascon, R., *Grand commerce et vie urbaine au XVI*[e] *siècle: Lyon et ses marchands*, 2 vols. (Paris, 1971).

Ginatempo, M., *Crisi di un territorio: il popolamento della Toscana senese alla fine del medioevo* (Florence, 1988).

Gioffrè, D., *Il mercato degli schiavi a Genova nel secolo xv* (Genoa, 1971).

GIORGETTI, G., 'Contratti agrari e rapporti sociali nelle campagne', in *Storia d'Italia*, v, pt. 1 (Turin, 1973), 699–758.

GOLDTHWAITE, R. A., 'The Renaissance Economy: The Preconditions for Luxury Consumption', in *Aspetti della vita economica medievale: Atti del Convegno di Studi nel X Anniversario della morte di Federigo Melis, Firenze–Pisa–Prato, 10–14 marzo 1984* (Florence, 1985), 659–75.

GREEN, L., 'Il Capitolo della Cathedrale di Lucca all'epoca di Castruccio Castracani', in *Castruccio Castracani e il suo tempo: Convegno Internazionale, Lucca 5–10 ottobre 1981*, published as anni xiii–xiv, nos. 1–2 of *Actum Luce* (1984–5), 125–41.

—— *Castruccio Castracani: A Study on the Origins and Character of a Fourteenth-Century Italian Despotism* (Oxford, 1986).

GUENÉE, B., *States and Rulers in Later Medieval Europe* (London, 1985).

GUIDI, G., *Il governo della città-repubblica di Firenze del primo Quattrocento*, 3 vols. (Florence, 1981).

HAY, D., and LAW, J., *Italy in the Age of the Renaissance 1380-1530* (London, 1989).

HEERS, J., *Family Clans in the Middle Ages* (Amsterdam, 1977).

HERLIHY, D., 'The Tuscan Town in the Quattrocento: A Demographic Profile', in *Cities and Society in Medieval Italy* (London, 1980) (no continuous pagination).

—— 'Vieillir à Florence au Quattrocento', in *Cities and Society in Medieval Italy* (London, 1980) (no continuous pagination).

—— 'The Problem of the "Return to the Land" in Tuscan Economic History of the Fourteenth and Fifteenth Centuries', in *Civiltà ed economia agricola in Toscana nei secc. xiii–xv: problemi della vita delle campagne nel tardo medioevo: Centro italiano di studi di storia e d'arte Pistoia, Ottavo Convegno Internazionale, Pistoia 21–24 aprile 1977* (Pistoia, 1981), 401–16.

—— 'The Rulers of Florence, 1282–1530', in A. Molho, K. Raaflaub, and J. Emlen (eds.), *Athens and Rome, Florence and Venice: City States in Classical Antiquity and Medieval Italy* (Stuttgart, 1991), 197–221.

HOSHINO, H., *L'arte della lana in Firenze nel basso Medioevo* (Florence, 1980).

—— 'La seta in Valdinievole nel basso medioevo', in *Atti del Convegno su artigianato e industrie in Valdinievole dal Medioevo ad Oggi: Buggiano Castello, giugno 1986* (Buggiano, 1987), 47–59.

HUDSON, P., *The Genesis of Industrial Capital: A Study of the West Riding Wool Textile Industry c.1750–1850* (Cambridge, 1986).

ILARDI, V., 'The Assassination of Galeazzo Maria Sforza and the Reaction of Italian Diplomacy', in L. Martines (ed.), *Violence and Civil Disorder in Italian Cities 1200–1500* (Berkeley, Calif., 1972), 72–103.

—— 'The Italian League, Francesco Sforza, and Charles VII (1454–1461)', in *Studies in Italian Renaissance Diplomatic History*, Variorum Reprints (London, 1986) (no continuous pagination).

—— 'The Banker-Statesman and the Condottiere-Prince: Cosimo de' Medici and

Francesco Sforza, 1450–1464', in *Studies in Italian Renaissance Diplomatic History*, Variorum Reprints (London, 1986) (no continuous pagination).

JONES, P. J., 'An Italian Estate, 900–1200', *Economic History Review*, 2nd ser., vii (1954), 18–32.

—— 'From Manor to Mezzadria: A Tuscan Case-study in the Medieval Origins of Modern Agrarian Society', in N. Rubinstein (ed.), *Florentine Studies: Politics and Society in Renaissance Florence* (London, 1968), 193–241.

—— 'Economia e società nell'Italia medievale: il mito della borghesia', in *Economia e società nell'Italia medievale* (Turin, 1980), 3–189.

KENDALL, P. M., *Louis XI: '. . . the universal spider . . .'* (London, 1974).

KENT, D. V., and KENT, F. W., *Neighbours and Neighbourhood in Renaissance Florence: The District of the Red Lion in the Fifteenth Century* (New York, 1982).

KENT, F. W., *Household and Lineage in Renaissance Florence: The Family Life of the Capponi, Ginori, and Rucellai* (Princeton, NJ, 1977).

—— 'La famiglia patrizia fiorentina nel Quattrocento. Nuovi orientamenti nella storiografia recente', in *Palazzo Strozzi metà millennio, 1489–1989, atti del Convegno di studi, Firenze, 3–6 luglio 1989* (Rome, 1991), 70–91.

KIRSHNER, J., 'Some Problems in the Interpretation of Legal Texts re: the Italian City-states', *Archiv für Begriffsgeschichte begründet von Erich Rothacker*, xix (1975), 16–27.

—— *Pursuing Honor while Avoiding Sin: The Monte delle Doti of Florence* (Milan, 1978).

KOTELNIKOVA, L. A., 'Condizione economica dei mezzadri toscani nel secolo xv (consumo, livello di vita)', in *Domanda e consumi, livelli e strutture (nei secoli xiii–xviii): Atti della sesta settimana di studio dell'Istituto internazionale di storia economica 'F. Datini'* (Florence, 1978), 93–9.

—— 'Il ruolo dello sviluppo delle città e delle relazioni mercantili-monetarie nei mutamenti delle condizioni economiche e sociali dei contadini toscani nei secoli xii–xv', in *Studi in Memoria di Federigo Melis*, 5 vols. (Florence, 1978), i. 409–31.

LAMI, G., *Lezioni di antichità toscane e spezialmente della città di Firenze*, 2 vols. (Florence, 1766).

LAZZARESCHI, E., 'Francesco Sforza e Paolo Guinigi: Contributo di documenti inediti', in *Miscellanea di studi storici in onore di Giovanni Sforza* (Turin, 1923), 403–23.

—— 'Il beato Bernardino da Feltre, gli Ebrei e il Monte di Pietà in Lucca', *Bolletino Storico Lucchese*, a. xiii, XIX (1941), 12–43.

LEVEROTTI, F., 'Ricerche sull'amministrazione della vicaria di Massa alla fine del xiv secolo', *Annuario della Biblioteca Civica di Massa* (1980), 99–173.

—— *Massa di lunigiana alla fine del trecento* (Pisa, 1982).

LITCHFIELD, R. B., 'Demographic Characteristics of Florentine Patrician Families, Sixteenth to Nineteenth Centuries', *Journal of Economic History*, xxix (1969), 191–205.

Livi, G., 'I mercanti di seta lucchesi in Bologna nei secoli xiii e xiv', *Archivio storico italiano*, 4th ser., vii (1881), 29–55.

Lucchesini, C., *Della storia letteraria del ducato lucchese*, in *Memorie e documenti per servire all'istoria del ducato di Lucca*, ix–x (Lucca, 1825–31).

Luzzati, M., 'Politica di salvaguardia dell'autonomia lucchese nella seconda metà del secolo xv', in *Egemonia fiorentina ed autonomie locali nella Toscana nord-occidentale del primo rinascimento: Vita, arte, cultura. Settimo convegno internazionale del Centro Italiano di Studi di storia e d'arte, Pistoia, 18–25 settembre 1975* (Pistoia, 1978), 543–82.

—— 'Fra Timoteo da Lucca (1456–1513): appunti di ricerca', in *Miscellanea Augusto Campana (Medioevo e Umanesimo, 45)* (Padua, 1981), 377–401.

—— 'Lucca e gli Ebrei fra Quattro e Cinquecento', in *Città italiane del '500 tra riforma e controriforma: Atti del Convegno Internazionale di Studi, Lucca 13–15 ottobre 1983* (Lucca, 1988), 205–23.

McArdle, F., *Altopascio: A Study in Tuscan Rural Society, 1587–1784* (Cambridge, 1978).

Mackenney, R., *Tradesmen and Traders: The World of the Guilds in Venice and Europe c.1250–c.1650* (London, 1987).

Maiocchi, R., 'La macchina come strumento di produzione: il filatoio alla bolognese', in G. Micheli (ed.), *Storia d'Italia*, Annali 3 (Turin, 1980), 5–27.

Mallett, M., 'Pisa and Florence in the Fifteenth Century', in N. Rubinstein (ed.), *Florentine Studies: Politics and Society in Renaissance Florence* (London, 1968), 403–41.

Martines, L., *Power and Imagination: City-States in Renaissance Italy* (New York, 1979).

Marx, K., *Capital*, 3 vols., Penguin edn. (Harmondsworth, 1976–81).

—— *Pre-Capitalist Economic Formations*, ed. E. J. Hobsbawm (London, 1964).

Massa, P., *Un'impresa serica genovese della prima metà del cinquecento* (Milan, 1974).

Matraia, G., *Lucca nel '200* (Lucca, 1843).

Mazzaoui, M. F., *The Italian Cotton Industry in the Later Middle Ages 1100–1600* (Cambridge, 1981).

Mazzarosa, A., *Storia di Lucca dalla sua origine fino al 1814*, 2 vols. (Lucca, 1833).

Mazzei, R., *La società lucchese del seicento* (Lucca, 1977).

Meek, C. E., *Lucca 1369–1400: Politics and Society in an Early Renaissance City-State* (Oxford, 1978).

—— *The Commune of Lucca under Pisan Rule, 1342–1369* (Cambridge, Mass., 1980).

Melis, F., *Tracce di una storia economica di Firenze e della Toscana in generale dal 1252 al 1550* (Florence, 1966–7).

Mirot, L., *Études Lucquoises* (Paris, 1930).

Miskimin, H. A., *The Economy of Early Renaissance Europe, 1300–1460* (Englewood Cliffs, NJ, 1969).

MUIR, E., *Civic Ritual in Renaissance Venice* (Princeton, NJ, 1981).

NAJEMY, J. M., 'The Dialogue of Power in Florentine Politics', in A. Molho, K. Raaflaub, and J. Emlen (eds.), *Athens and Rome, Florence and Venice: City States in Classical Antiquity and Medieval Italy* (Stuttgart, 1991), 269–88.

NANNI, L., 'Il clero della cattedrale di Lucca nei secoli xv e xvi', in Lamberto Donati (ed.), *Studi e ricerche nella biblioteca e negli archivi vaticani in memoria del Cardinale Giovanni Mercati (1866–1957)* (Florence, 1959), 258–84.

ONORI, A. M., *Abbazia di San Salvatore a Sesto e il Lago di Bientina: Una signoria ecclesiastica (1250–1300)* (Florence, 1984).

ORIGO, I., *The Merchant of Prato: Francesco di Marco Datini* (London, 1957).

OSHEIM, D., *An Italian Lordship: The Bishopric of Lucca in the Late Middle Ages* (Berkeley, Calif., 1977).

—— 'I sentimenti religiosi dei lucchesi al tempo di Castruccio', in *Castruccio Castracani e il suo tempo: Convegno Internazionale, Lucca 5–10 ottobre 1981*, published as anni xiii–xiv, nos. 1–2 of *Actum Luce* (1984–5), 99–111.

—— 'Countrymen and the Law in Late-Medieval Tuscany', *Speculum*, lxiv (1989), 317–37.

OTSUKA, H., *The Spirit of Capitalism: The Max Weber Thesis in an Economic Historical Perspective* (Tokyo, 1982).

PAOLI PUCCETTI, S., *Di Messer Domenico Bertini da Gallicano (1417–1506)* (Pescia, 1936).

PELÙ, P., *Priorità della mercatura lucchese in alcune forme collective di investimento aziendale nel xiv e xv secolo* (Lucca, 1974).

—— 'Dalla Compagnia tradizionale al sistema d'azienda: conquiste della mercatura lucchese nei sec. xiv e xv', *La Provincia di Lucca*, xvi, no. 1 (Jan.–Mar. 1976), 30–5.

—— 'Figure della vita economica medievale lucchese: Michele di Lazzari Guinigi', *La Provincia di Lucca*, xvi, no. 3 (July–Sept. 1976), 13–19.

PILONI, M., *Pietrasanta e i Medici (1255–1513): ipotesi di ricerca* (Pietrasanta, 1983).

PINTO, G., *La Toscana nel tardo medio evo: Ambiente, economia rurale, società* (Florence, 1982).

POLICA, S., 'An Attempted "Reconversion" of Wealth in XVth-Century Lucca: The Lands of Michele di Giovanni Guinigi', *Journal of European Economic History*, ix (1980), 655–707.

—— 'Le famiglie del ceto dirigente lucchese dalla caduta di Paolo Guinigi alla fine del Quattrocento', in *I ceti dirigenti nella Toscana del Quattrocento: Comitato di studi sulla storia dei ceti dirigenti in Toscana: Atti del V e VI Convegno: Firenze 10–11 dicembre 1982; 2–3 dicembre 1983* (Florence, 1987), 353–84.

PONI, C., 'All'origine del sistema di fabbrica: tecnologia e organizzazione produttiva dei mulini da seta nell'Italia settentrionale (sec. XVII–XVIII)', *Rivista storica italiana*, lxxxviii (1976), 444–97.

—— 'Norms and Disputes: The Shoemakers' Guild in Eighteenth-Century Bologna', *Past & Present*, cxxiii (1989), 80–108.

Rapp, R. T., 'Real Estate and Rational Investment in Early Modern Venice', *Journal of European Economic History*, viii (1979), 269–90.

Reynolds, S., *Kingdoms and Communities in Western Europe, 900-1300* (Oxford, 1984).

Rubinstein, N., *The Government of Florence under the Medici (1434 to 1494)* (Oxford, 1966).

Sabbatini, R., 'La cartiera Buonvisi di Villa Basilica XVI–XIX secolo', *Archivio storico italiano*, cxl (1982), 263–307.

Sambito Piombo, S., 'Una famiglia lucchese a Palermo nei primi decenni del secolo xiv', *Rivista di archeologia, storia e costume: Istituto storico lucchese*, ix, no. 3 (1981), 37–44.

Santini, V., *Commentarii Storici sulla Versilia centrale*, 6 vols. (Pisa, 1858–63).

Sardi, C., *Dei mecanti lucchesi nel secolo xvi* (Lucca, 1882).

Seghieri, M., 'La contea vescovile di Piazza e Sala in Garfagnana: Origini e primi sviluppi', *Rivista di archeologia, storia e costume*, viii, no. 1 (1980), 3–18.

Sforza, G., *Memorie storiche di Montignoso* (Lucca, 1867).

Starn, R., *Contrary Commonwealth: The Theme of Exile in Medieval and Renaissance Italy* (Berkeley, Calif., 1982).

Strauss, G., 'Protestant Dogma and City Government: The Case of Nuremberg', *Past & Present*, xxxvi (1967), 38–58.

Taurisano, I., *I Domenicani in Lucca* (Lucca, 1914).

Tazartes, M., 'Osservazioni sulle arti e corporazioni a Lucca nel xiv secolo', *Actum Luce*, xi (1982), 35–51.

Tettoni, L., and Saladini, F., *Teatro Araldico ovvero Raccolta Generale delle Armi ed Insegne Gentilizie delle più illustri e nobili casate che esisterono un tempo e che tuttora fioriscono in tutta l'Italia*, 8 vols. (Milan, 1841–8).

Thrupp, S. L., *The Merchant Class of Medieval London (1300-1500)* (Chicago, 1948).

Tirelli, V., 'I "libri di ricordanze" a Lucca', in *La Famiglia e la vita quotidiana in Europa dal '400 al '600: Fonti e problemi: Atti del convegno internazionale Milano 1–4 dicembre 1983* (Rome, 1986), 123–65.

Tocco, F., 'I fraticelli', *Archivio storico italiano*, 5th ser., xxxv (1905), 331–68.

Tommasi, G., 'Sommario della storia di Lucca dal MIV al MDCC', *Archivio storico italiano*, 1st ser., x (1847).

Trexler, R. C., *Public Life in Renaissance Florence* (New York, 1980).

Vale, M. G. A., *Charles VII* (London, 1974).

Vaughan, R., *Valois Burgundy* (London, 1975).

Weissman, R. F. E., *Ritual Brotherhood in Renaissance Florence* (New York, 1982).

Wickham, C., *Early Medieval Italy: Central Power and Local Society 400–1000* (London, 1981).

—— 'The Other Transition: From the Ancient World to Feudalism', *Past & Present*, ciii (1984), 3–36.
—— *The Mountains and the City: The Tuscan Appennines in the Early Middle Ages* (Oxford, 1988).
WRIGHTSON, K., 'The Social Order of Early Modern England', in L. Bonfield, R. Smith, and K. Wrightson (eds.), *The World We Have Gained: Histories of Population and Social Structure* (Oxford, 1986), 177–202.

UNPUBLISHED DISSERTATIONS

BLOMQUIST, T. W., 'Trade and Commerce in Thirteenth-Century Lucca' (Univ. of Minnesota Ph.D. thesis, 1965).
BOLTON, J. L., 'Alien Merchants in England in the Reign of Henry VI, 1422–61' (Univ. of Oxford B. Litt. thesis, 1971).
BRATCHEL, M. E., 'Alien Merchant Communities in London, 1500–1550' (Univ. of Cambridge Ph.D. thesis, 1975).

INDEX

Italic numbers denote reference to illustrations.

To the memory of
Albert Bratchel

Oxford University Press, Walton Street, Oxford OX2 6DP
Oxford New York
Athens Auckland Bangkok Bombay
Calcutta Cape Town Dar es Salaam Delhi
Florence Hong Kong Istanbul Karachi
Kuala Lumpur Madras Madrid Melbourne
Mexico City Nairobi Paris Singapore
Taipei Tokyo Toronto
and associated companies in
Berlin Ibadan

Oxford is a trade mark of Oxford University Press

Published in the United States
by Oxford University Press Inc., New York

First Published 1995

British Library Cataloguing in Publication Data
Data available

Library of Congress Cataloging in Publication Data
Bratchel, M. E.
Lucca, 1430–1494: the reconstruction of an Italian city-republic/
M. E. Bratchel.
p. cm.
Includes bibliographical references and index.
1. Lucca (Italy)—History. I. Title.
DG975.L82B73 1995
945'.5305—dc20 94-28693
ISBN 0-19-820484-1

1 3 5 7 9 10 8 6 4 2

Typeset by Cotswold Typesetting Ltd., Gloucester
Printed in Great Britain
on acid-free paper by
Bookcraft Ltd., Midsomer Norton, Bath

Lucca 1430–1494

THE RECONSTRUCTION
OF AN ITALIAN CITY-REPUBLIC

M. E. Bratchel

CLARENDON PRESS · OXFORD
1995

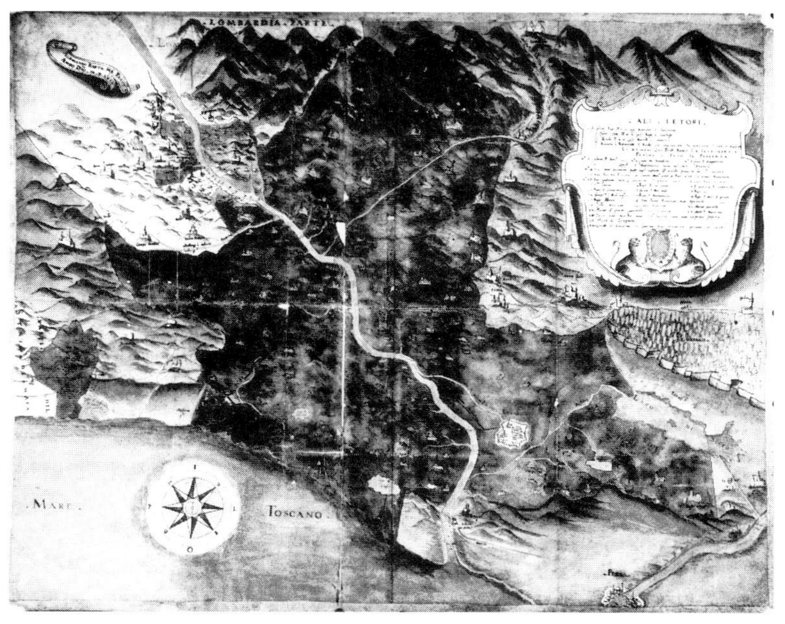

Map of Lucca painted in 1569 by Alessandro Resta

LUCCA 1430–1494

£45-00